AF651652

STATE, NATION AND DEMOCRACY

ABOUT THE EDITORS

- **Dr. Partha Pratim Basu** is a Reader in the Department of *International Relations*, Jadavpur University. His research interests include Media and Politics, Religion and Politics, and Politics of Foreign Trade.
- **Dr. Purusottam Bhattacharya** is a Professor in the Department of *International Relations*, and the Director, School of International Relations and Strategic Studies, Jadavpur University who specializes in the Politics of European Integration as well as India's Foreign Relations.
- **Mr. Rochana Das** is a Selection Grade Lecturer in the Department of International Relations, Jadavpur University and specializes in South Asian Politics with reference to North-east India.
- **Dr. Anjali Ghosh** is a Professor in the Department of *International Relations*, Jadavpur University. Her areas of research interests cover South and South Asian Politics and Gender and Politics.
- **Mr. Kanak Chandra Sarkar** is a Senior Lecturer in the Department of *International Relations*, Jadavpur University who specializes in South Asian Politics.

STATE, NATION AND DEMOCRACY

Alternative Global Futures

Edited by
Partha Pratim Basu
Purusottam Bhattacharya
Rochana Das
Anjali Ghosh
Kanak Chandra Sarkar

CONCEPT PUBLISHING COMPANY, NEW DELHI-110059

Cataloging in Publication Data—DK
Courtesy: D.K. Agencies (P) Ltd. <docinfo@dkagencies.com>

Seminar: Alternative Global Futures (2003 : Kolkata, India)
State, nation and democracy : alternative global futures / edited by Partha Pratim Basu ... [et al.].
p. cm.
Papers presented at the Seminar: Alternative Global Futures, held at Kolkata during 5-6 March 2003 and the Seminar: State, Nation and Democracy : Global Politics in the 21st Century, held at Kolkata during 9-10 March 2004.
Includes bibliographical references.
Includes index.
ISBN 8180694208

1. Democracy—Congresses. 2. National state—Congresses. 3. State, The—Congresses. 4. World politics—Congresses. I. Basu, Partha Pratim, 1961- II. Seminar: State, Nation and Democracy : Global Politics in the 21st Century (2004 : Kolkata, India) III. Title.

DDC321.8 22

All rights reserved. No part of this work may be reproduced, stored in a retrieval system, or transmitted in any form or through electronic, mechanical, photocopying, micro-filming recording or otherwise, without prior written permission of the copyright owner and the publisher.

ISBN 81-8069-420-8

First Published 2007

© Editors

Published and Printed by
Ashok Kumar Mittal
Concept Publishing Company,
A/15-16, Commercial Block, Mohan Garden,
New Delhi-110059 (INDIA)

Phones : 25351460, 25351794
Fax : 091-11-25357103
Email : publishing@conceptpub.com

Contents

PART II
Democracy and the System of States

PART III
Foreign Policy: The Diplomat's Perspective

Introduction

The essays in this volume pivot around the array of challenges the state encounters in the era of post-coloniality and globalization, and the way it seeks to grapple with them. Some of these challenges emanate from domestic sources, while others pertain to the realm of the international/global system, and accordingly the contributions have been assorted in two parts although no watertight demarcation is implied. And as the state responds to these challenges, it renegotiates its relationship with the principles of nationalism and democracy, and new directions in global politics are opened up. What is intended here is to present a brief overview of the themes covered in this compilation.

One of the major tasks facing especially the state-nations of the post-colonial world relates to "democratizing ethnicity", i.e. incorporating the multifarious ethnic communities into their ambit and forging a cohesive national identity which can accommodate the socio-political aspirations of these categories. Closely aligned to this is the problem of "ethnicizing democracies", i.e. a process whereby certain groups and communities are systematically denied the right to become part of the democratic contract as signatories and as full-fledged rights-bearing bodies of citizens which precipitates insurgencies and secessionism. Ethnic resurgence may also result from long suppression of ethnic expressions e.g. in Central Asia under Soviet rule and what appears as "ethnic" outburst may in fact be linked to political mobilization. Either way, however, it leads to the question of new experiments with the existing framework of the rules, institutions and practices of democracy and evolving one capable of facilitating integration as well as identification.

The state-nation-democracy triad is further complicated when the religious dimension is introduced as revealed by the treatment of state, democracy and Islam. While nationalism in the European sense requires national and territorial units to coincide, Islam is basically transnational and the primary allegiance is not to any territory but to the *ummah*, the community made of Muslims all over the world. Nonetheless, this Brotherhood is more spiritual than temporal as territorial boundaries have always been there. Modern Muslim nationalism has shifted from a transnational religious ideology to the acceptance of a modern Muslim national state, though religious ideology and law play a major role in the sustenance of the state. Even when the Arab or Turkish empires existed, these were temporal powers and the polity was that of the state but the law was largely based on *sharia*. Similarly, though Islam believes in the sovereignty of God and as such is incompatible with popular rule, Islamist groups, in countries like Pakistan, for example, developed a preference for democracy since it provided them an avenue of power; democracy in turn survived on the legitimacy furnished by its association with the Islamist categories.

Another striking feature of global politics in recent decades has been the wave of democratic transitions between the 1970s and 1990s. The phenomenon was witnessed in the Southern parts of Europe in the 1970s which strongly influenced the transitions in Latin America in the 1980s. The process was replicated in East Asia in the mid-1980s when the "people power" democratization of Philippines was followed by the democratic transformation of many countries of Eastern and Central Europe. South Africa followed suit in the early 1990s when the formal structure of apartheid was dismantled and a settlement enfranchising the African majority was reached. However, the two notable countries of Asia where the worldwide wave of democracy failed to reach have been the People's Republic of China whose leaders feel confident that a non-competitive one-party rule can convert their country into a modern democratic state, and Myanmar which has been one of the most outstanding examples of majoritarianism, cultural authoritarianism and a garrison-state where human rights violations have become a regular feature of its political culture.

Some of the essays have turned to the external facets of the encounter to take into account how the forces of globalization and regionalism impinge on the nation-state. Thus the evolution of the European Union underscored the interplay of the forces of nationalism and the imperatives of supra-national integration. The exercise in building an "ever closer union" captured the story of increasing encroachments and limitations imposed on national power and the sovereign state in Europe. Yet it remained far from a linear process: debate over the widening and deepening of the Community refused to subside and nationalism in Europe continued to remain a formidable force as has been recently demonstrated in the rejection of the European Constitution by several EU member states.

Again, the authority of the nation-state is eroded and its ability to deliver welfare to its people undermined in several ways. The forces of neo-liberal globalization have brought into being an irreversible post-territorial world dominated by the functioning of the Multinational Corporations, cross-border flows of foreign investment, technology and patterns of consumption. These together with the increasing intrusions by international financial institutions propagating mercantile ideology have contributed towards the prioritization of the economy over social values and steadily undercut the capacity of the state apparatus to plan and execute its desired programmes of action. The problem has been further exacerbated in some regions where following significant demographic changes the number of people in the job market has been outnumbered by those retiring which in turn has led to reduction in contributory revenues and increase in social expenditures.

As the state carries out the globalization agenda and sheds its welfarist thrust while continuing to use its repressive machinery to deal with anti-globalization protests, its reactive effects have let loose the forces of cultural nationalism and particularity independent of the state. They have also produced an alternative understanding of democracy which assumes a progressively anti-statist connotation and focuses more on the ideas of pluralism, multiplicity, localism etc. and opening up the space for civil society, community rights, identity politics and so forth. However, the 'democratic' character of these particularist stirrings couched in the language of ethno-nationalism, community identity and localism remains open to question while the possible devices for the democratization of the state is left curiously unattended.

Turning to the international systemic dimension, one finds that concerns relating to a deficit of democracy in the domain of international relations and a plea for combating it in the intellectual realm in addition to the realm of political practice run through all the essays contained in this section. At one level, the highly oligarchic nature of the international system(s), further aggravated by the collapse of the Soviet Union and processes of economic, military and ideological globalization (as already mentioned), have been noted and future – and more democratic – alternative world orders have been contemplated in terms of a stateless international system, a quasi-anarchical pluralistic order and a democratic world government. In this connection the importance of sustained struggle led by third world states in the face of predictable resistance by the oligarchic forces determined to thwart any attempt to democratize the world order has also been stressed.

In this backdrop, the liberal faith in the capacity of liberal democracy and market capitalism to usher in an unprecedented epoch of material prosperity as well as peace is bound to appear suspect. The champions of the thesis of "democratic peace", who plead for exporting democracy to create conditions of peace and stability, it has been argued, need to clarify the *kind* of democracy they support and also address at least three sets of inter-relationships: between (i) democracy and multiculturalism; (ii) development and democracy and (iii) democratization within states and democratizing the world order.

To take up the question of subverting the prevalent inequitable and discriminatory global order, communication, it has been suggested, remains a potent instrument in the "struggle from within". The anti-globalization struggle which is disparate and plurilateral in character need to be carried out simultaneously in physical and virtual spaces. The struggle for alternatives remains a struggle not only *through* communication but *in* communication, and the path towards a more equitable global order lies through creating and nurturing diffused communication channels which question global issues in their own way and within their own spaces.

Responses to the globalization process have been sought to be captured in regional contexts as well. The South-east Asian region – often portrayed as the archetype of neoliberal development strategy – experienced in the late 1990s the downside of globalization through the contagion effect of the financial crisis. The adverse impact on its economic, political and security environment led to efforts to develop the alternative model of a New Global Order which laid stress on a community building mindset and prescribed a human agenda for building a South-east Asian Community for the 21st century. The agenda included peace and material well-being, promotion of family institutions, social equity, cultural synergy and the spirit of a just, tolerant and caring local community – in short, the democratic values of human society.

Again, one of the starkest reminders of power asymmetry within the post-colonial global scenario has been the phenomenon of neocolonialism, especially in Africa. On the one hand, it created weak and corrupt dictatorships, murderous civil wars and hapless dependence on foreign resources. On the other hand, it not only denied the African people any platform to independently participate in, manage or theorize about international relations but also enabled the neocolonial hegemons to project Africa as a disintegrating continent beset with poverty, crises and hopelessness, while the infinite capacity of its people to survive in a hostile environment found no mention in this one-sided portrayal.

Thus, combating neo-colonialism calls for a proactive approach on the part of third world statesmen and intelligentsia to regain mastery over the conduct of international relations as well as the process of producing knowledge about it. And this brings us to a consideration of the possibilities – as well as the pitfalls – of applying the insights drawn from the post-colonial theory to the study of International Relations. True, the amenability of the spatially-inclined discipline of IR to analytic and discursive approaches remains open to question. Still "niches of applicability" could be identified, especially in *decolonizing* the notion of the "international" which strongly smacks of a "structural Eurocentrism".

The papers incorporated in this volume were originally presented in two seminars held in the Jadavpur University: the first, titled "Alternative Global Futures", was organized under the auspices of the UGC-sponsored DSA Programme (Phase III) of the Department of International Relations on 5-6 March, 2003, and the second, bearing the theme "State, Nation and Democracy: Global Politics in the 21st Century" was a collaborative venture of the DSA Programme (Phase III) of the Department of International Relations, the School of International Relations and Strategic Studies, Jadavpur University and the West Bengal Political Science Association, Kolkata, held on 9-10 March, 2004. We take this opportunity to thank the sponsors of the seminars as well as the contributors who have enriched us with the written versions of their presentations or taken the pains of revising their papers and submitting them afresh. Also, our very special thanks go to Shri Nitin Mittal of the Concept Publishing Company, New Delhi who has all along evinced a keen interest in the work.

Further, we had been honoured to have two distinguished diplomats, Mr. Erherd Zander, the then Hon'ble Consul General of the Federal Republic of Germany, and Mr Andrew Hall, former Hon'ble Deputy High Commissioner, United Kingdom, at Kolkata in our panel of speakers in the seminars and we publish the original versions of their addresses in the third and final section of this collection.

Finally, we note with a heavy heart that Dr. Prasanta Sengupta who had made his presentation in the second seminar expired while in the process of completing his paper. The draft he presented before the seminar is published here as a mark of respect to our departed friend.

Department of International Relations
School of International Relations
and Strategic Studies,
Jadavpur University, Kolkata

Partha Pratim Basu
Purusottam Bhattacharya
Rochana Das
Anjali Ghosh
Kanak Chandra Sarkar

List of Contributors

Bandyopadhyaya, Jayantanuja, Professor Emeritus, Jadavpur University, Kolkata.

Basu, Partha Pratim, Reader, Department of International Relations, Jadavpur University, Kolkata.

Bhattacharya, Purusottam, Professor, Department of International Relations, and Director, School of International Relations and Strategic Studies, Jadavpur University, Kolkata.

Bhattacharya, Sanjukta Banerji, Professor, Department of International Relations, Jadavpur University, Kolkata.

Chakraborti, Tridib, Professor, Department of International Relations, Jadavpur University, Kolkata.

Chatterjee, Shibashis, Senior Lecturer, Department of International Relations, Jadavpur University, Kolkata.

Das, Rochana, Senior Lecturer, Department of International Relations, Jadavpur University, Kolkata.

Das, Samir Kumar, Reader, Department of Political Science, Calcutta University.

Dattagupta, Sobhanlal, Professor, Department of Political Science, Calcutta University.

Ghosh, Anjali, Professor, Department of International Relations, Jadavpur University, Kolkata.

Hall, Andrew, (Former) Hon'ble Deputy High Commissioner of United Kingdom in Kolkata.

Mukhopadhyay, Amartya, Professor, Department of Political Science, Calcutta University.

Rutanga, Murindwa, Head, Department of Political Science & Public Administration, Makerere University, and Senior Research Fellow, Centre for Basic Research, Kampala - Uganda.

Sengupta, Anita, Fellow, Maulana Abul Kalam Azad Institute for Asian Studies, Kolkata.

Sengupta, (Late) **Prasanta,** (Former) Reader, Department of Political Science, Kalyani University, Nadia, West Bengal.

Sinha, Dipankar, Reader, Department of Political Science, Calcutta University and Hony Adjunct Fellow, Institute of Development Studies, Kolkata.

Sundarraman, Sankari, Associate Professor, Centre for South and Southeast Asian Studies, School of International Studies, Jawaharlal Nehru University, New Delhi.

Vivekanandan, B., Professor and Chairman (retd), Centre for American and European Studies, School of International Studies, Jawaharlal Nehru University, New Delhi.

Zander, Erherd, (Former) Hon'ble Consul General of Federal Republic of Germany in Kolkata

PART I

State, Nation and Democracy: Shifting Alignments

1

Some Reflections on Nation, State and Democracy in the 21st Century

—SOBHANLAL DATTA GUPTA

I

The theme of the proposed seminar, intellectually speaking, is quite challenging as well as stimulating, since the advent of the 21st century has, indeed, generated certain very major questions concerning such leading concepts as nation, state and democracy in a world that has changed beyond recognition over the last one decade. The emergent scenario may broadly be defined as one that is pervaded by two distinctly related yet sharply contradictory moods, namely, rejection of anything that is universalist in nature, universalism being considered as something pejorative, antithetical to democracy and aut-onomy. Simultaneously, anything that valorizes identity, that which is particularistic, is necessarily given the label of democracy and freedom. The critiques of Enlightenment, radical scepticism about the universalist claims of western modernity, the rise of post-modern and post-colonial theories have set the parameters of this new understanding and have come to affect global politics in a decisive manner. I will try to argue that in this changed context as the state is being increasingly considered as a threat

---

[Based on the Keynote address delivered in the seminar on "State, Nation and Democracy" in the Department of International Relations, Jadavpur University, Kolkata on March 9, 2004].

to democracy, a rather nuanced understanding of the relation between democracy and nationalism is taking place, opening up in its trail a number of contentious issues.

Let me start off briefly with the hypothesis that of the two representative models of nationalism, namely, the French and the Germanic, the claim of the first one, which is state centric, is now seriously questioned, is considered anti-democratic and is on the wane; the second one, which is culture-centric, is considered to be anti-statist and conducive to the promotion of democracy and is vociferous about its claims. As the French principle has its focus on the territorial dimension of the state, this may be considered as the strategy of vertical mobilisation of nationalism, which has given birth to what has come to be known as the typical nation-state in the West. This, in its turn, has generated an inclusivist, integrationist understanding of nationalism, which makes nationalism safe, by keeping the nationalist urges and aspirations on leash, the nation being coterminous with the state. This understanding, steeped in eurocentrism, for a long time considered as standard, was virtually universalised (Kedourie, Gellner) and anchored in the West's notion of modernity. The Germanic notion, rooted as it is in the idea of a cohesive culture, community, language etc. anchored in the realm of subjectivity and consciousness, in this understanding there is a delinking of the nation and the state, and nationalism acquires an exclusivist orientation with focus on horizontal mobilisation.

Understandably, it is the Germanic notion which becomes highly effective for legitimation of nationalist struggles in non-Western societies. Thus, in India, for instance, the strategy of the colonial rulers to forge an integrated nation-state was directly challenged by an Indian nation, the nation standing opposed to the colonial state. In the eyes of the West, this becomes unsafe nationalism, since, delinked from the state, it stirs up the aspirations of the community, articulates the consciousness of the masses and thereby acquires a radical democratic temper. Thus, in the French notion, the state appropriates the nation, while in the Germanic version it is the nation which appropriates the state and becomes subversive in its outlook.

II

This contrast between the two models becomes deeply relevant in the age of globlisation in the 21st century on two levels. On one level, it relates to globalisation's strategy of universalising certain values and goals by repositioning and altering the welfarist agenda of the state. On another level it refers to the assertion of nationalist identities, particularities, localisms, which constitute the backlash effects of globalisation. Globalisation standardises and universalises modernity along a distinct trajectory in which the national, the local, the particular gets lost and elided. While this, indeed, has been the experience of globalisation so far, it has become urgently necessary to explode two common myths surrounding it. First, the myth that globalisation promotes globalism. Globalisation valorizes and thereby universalises certain values and goals which have nothing to do with promotion of any global culture in the true spirit of cosmopolitanism or internationalism, because the phenomenon of globalisation universalises per se a technocratic culture, a typical mind set, that is essentially anchored in the neo-liberal market society of the West. Globalisation is basically a mobilisational strategy, worked out vertically to ensure hegemonisation along a distinct axis which is completely and irreversably inclined towards the West. The other myth refers to the so-called idea of withdrawal of state and restoring the freedom of the individual in the name of reforms. The agenda of globalisation certainly advances such a cause but it actually purports to eclipse the welfarist and not the repressive dimension of state power. The neo-liberal state unabashedly sheds its social responsibilities but actively intervenes to protect the market forces if they are threatened even by peaceful marches, slogans and demonstrations, as has been evident from recent experiences all over the world. In other words, globalisation unpacks a programme that essentialises, homogenises and universalises the agenda of neo-liberal modernity and while this is being laid down as a policy by the WTO, World Bank and such other basically corporate agencies, for the states which have by and large accepted this agenda it is an imperative to use the repressive machinery of the state against the protestors who challenge this programme that ostensibly is geared to promote reforms and development. The state thus assumes a crucial position in the smooth execution of the agenda of globalisation by warding off the threats to market that is dominated by speculative capital and by actively engaging in a tie-up with the market forces through an elaborate programme of privatisation. Globalisation, therefore, is very much statist sans welfarism. Viewed in this perspective, the French model of the nation-state, together with its inclusivist, integrationist character assumes relevance.

The backlash effects of globalisation are expressed in the delinking of the state and the nation in the sense that the state that executes the agenda of globalistaion is challenged by the forces which feel threatened and insecure by the latter's integrationist and homogenizing juggernaut. Strongly reminiscent of the German model, the reactive effects of globalisation have thus set free the forces of cultural nationalism and particularity independent of the state and they call for an alternative framing of the understanding of democracy and freedom. As against the vertical strategy of homogenous mobilisation engendered by globalisation, its opponents adopt a horizontal strategy, and the focus now is on autonomy, identity, pluralism, absence of boundaries, fluidity and hybridity, voiced by groups and communities. This becomes the nation's (not in a homogenous, modernist sense) critique of the integral state, leading to a situation where the state looses grip over the nation and the nation, in turn, in an assertive mode releases the multiple forces of diversity and heterogeneity against the state that acts as the agent of globalisation.

Consequently, we are increasingly confronted with a situation where the acts of the state are pitted against the acts of the nation and the understanding of democracy acquires an altogether new meaning in this changed context. Thus, the proactive role of the state in promoting the cause of globalization, that is, the programme of neo-liberal modernity, is considered with deep suspicion, violative as it is of the cultural autonomy of the concerned nation. This, for instance, was strikingly manifest in the recent negative votes registered in the French and Dutch referendum against the proposed Constitution of the European Union. This was a classic illustration of how the French and Dutch nation were pitted against the French and the Dutch state in a show of democratic temper. To be more precise, it is a restatement of the state *vs.* society debate, reframed as authoritarianism *vs.* democracy. The debate has particularly sharpened for another reason, which has come up after 9/11. This refers to the growing surveillance and control of the state over the lives of its citizens in the name of providing security and combating terrorism. The globalised state thus, in effect, is becoming a closed state, giving rise to the contradiction between its strategy of opening up of the economy and that of closing in increasingly on the lives of its citizens. The state is thus getting not only isolated and alienated from the life of the individual but is becoming irrelevant too for the reason that the state has virtually withdrawn its welfarist agenda, as public investment in the social sectors is registering decline at an alarming rate over the years. Accordingly, democracy's meaning is now at the crossroads, caught as it is in the crossfire between the state and the nation.

Thus, interestingly, anything that is statist is considered as antithetical to democracy by the defenders as well as the critiques of the globalised state. For the advocates of globalisation the idea of an interventionist state in the name of welfarism is simply anachronistic, as it creates obstacles to the free play of market forces and allegedly constrains the unfolding of freedom and autonomy of the individual. For the critiques the modern state in the age of globalisation is an agent of corporate capital and an inveterate enemy of the rights and freedoms of its citizens. Democracy, accordingly, has come to be associated negatively with anything that is anti-statist, anti-integrationist and anti-universalist/essentialist. Positively, it connotes the idea of pluralism, multiplicity, localism etc., opening up the space for civil society, community rights, identity politics etc. Democracy thus is acquiring a new meaning, as it is becoming associated with this shift from macro to micro, from global to local, from universalism to relativism.

It is no longer a statist project, framed in the language of Western modernity. Delinked from the state, couched in the language of post-modernism/post-colonialism, the urge for democracy has, as a consequence, become inseparable from the assertion of these local, regional, community rights, the drive for freedom, the search for identity, the craving for autonomous space, motivated by a deep sense of subjectivity at the level of consciousness. All these underscore the relevance of the Germanic notion of nationalism which carries the baggage of anti-statism and nationalism thus gets linked up with the question of democracy in an altogether new perspective in the 21st century. It becomes an alternative strategy of horizontal counter mobilisation of all anti-statist forces, assuming different forms and claiming justification on different grounds. These may now be briefly considered.

First, nationalist stirrings sometimes imply a return to history by conjuring up past memories through valorization of a mythical past and this may have quite unsavoury consequences ,for the society at large. The votaries of Hindu nationalism in India precisely bank on this strategy to carry through their agenda and this has also been the practice of the Right in Eastern and Central Europe after 1991, a strategy against which Hobsbawm has cautioned us in uncompromising terms. Second, nationalism is expressed as a critique of the agenda of modernization undertaken by the states in the regime of globalisation. This, too, may assume conservative as well as radical stances, as manifest, for instance, in the distinctly different programmes of Swadeshi Jagaran Mancha, controlled by the RSS in India, and the World Social Forum. Third, nationalist feelings tend to sweep societies which have been the victims of the failure of institutionalisation of state power, as evident, for instance, in Russia, Eastern Europe and Central Asia. The virtual non-existence of civil society, together with the appropriation of the civil space by the state in these societies for decades, has led to replacement of revolutionary ideology by liberalism and reformism, the local variants of which are often being traced to the pre-revolutionary era of these societies. Fourth, the vacuum created by the collapse of authoritarian regimes in a number of states (i.e. in Africa, Iraq) has led to the appropriation of the vacant space by the forces of religious and ethnic nationalism. Fifth, religious, cultural and ethnic intolerance exhibited by a regime (i.e., Israel) is being challenged by a counter assertion of militant nationalism of the repressed which draws its strength to a large extent from the kind of religion and culture in which it is nourished. In all these cases it is an indisputable fact that nationalism acquires a fairly radical orientation, as it gets identified with protest against and critique of repression; it becomes particularly appealing because it becomes an exercise in the recovery of a collective self, in the assertion of its identity, in the valorization of its particularity.

III

While recognising the validity of these claims, by way of concluding remarks a number of questions, however, follow. First, are particularist stirrings, couched in the language of rights, ethno-nationalism, community identity and localism necessarily democratic? How really democratic are tribal societies, various ethnic groups and communities in accommodating dissent and the notion of difference? Second, is universalism per se a pejorative outlook ? While it is certainly true that universalism in its eurocentric connotation has wreaked havoc on non-Western societies and thanks to Edward Said, nobody can today accept uncritically the totalizing claims of European Enlightenment. But does it mean that one has to discard the Enlightenment altogether? Habermas's critique of Lyotard and the distinction that he made between the possibilities and the practice of Enlightenment perhaps was not that irrelevant, while warning against the sweeping criticism of universalism. What one can perhaps think of in this age of critical reasoning is that universalism has got to be anchored off its eurocentric baggage and assume a different meaning by becoming negotiated universalism. Amartya Sen's warning that the binary opposition between the downplaying of reason and modernity in the name of critique of universality and the valorization of identity under the slogan of autonomy and freedom may have disastrous consequences for our civilization is a pointer in this regard. Third, while statism is certainly pejorative, what is missing in the current attacks against the state is that nobody talks of the perspective whereby the possible devices for democratisation of the state can be discussed. After all, if the common man is to be made the beneficiary of the resources of society, then is it possible to think of any agency other than the state which can shoulder this responsibility? In fact, experiments in democratisation of the state by reaching out to the masses are already under way in a number of countries in Latin America (i.e., Venezueala, Brazil), where the state and the nation are getting engaged in negotiation and not necessarily confrontation, thus reframing the relation between state and democracy. The linkages between democracy, state and nation require to be understood in a spirit of negotiation and flexibility and it would be undesirable, if not unsafe, to effect any kind of closure in the exceedingly complex and uncertain age in which we have landed with the arrival of the 21st century.

2

The Ethnic Core

On Some Limits of Parliamentary Democracy in Contemporary India

—SAMIR KUMAR DAS

> ... We believe in that form of government, which permits the rule, not of the majority, but of the people as whole (sic). We govern ourselves by a government which do not govern at all—T. Shakhire—the Naga rebel leader ruminating on the traditional system of Government of the Nagas.[1]

This paper proposes to re-examine the complex inter-relationship between ethnicity and democracy in contemporary India. While the main objective of democracy has been to incorporate the diverse segments of individuals and groups including of course the multifarious ethnic communities into its ambit, little attempt has been made so far to assess and take into account the ability of the *established framework* of democratic institutions and practices to incorporate them. Indeed, the strongest plea for democratising ethnicity in India comes from some of the early writings of Kothari. Way back in 1976 he for example, observed: "The task now was to construct a stable political framework and to integrate the enormous diversity of a segmented society into this framework" (Kothari 1976: 204). Democratic institutions and practices for him do not have any intrinsic value: they are valuable to the extent they perform their integrative function and help diverse social segments in identifying themselves with the established democratic framework.

Any plea for democratizing ethnicity is thus critically dependent on the capacity of the established democratic framework to actively facilitate and promote the twin processes of integration and identification. The two processes are expected to widen our democratic horizon and make the hitherto unrepresented groups and ethnicities an integral part of our democratic framework. If some of these forces simply refuse to come under the democratic framework and voice their opposition through democratic means, the democratic framework per se cannot be blamed for having left them out of its ambit. These forces may have to be tackled through coercive and undemocratic means. Democracy applies only to those forces that are ready to play within the rules of the game set by it. Even as late in 1989 Hewitt for example, argues:

> Where (ethnicities) have used the language of secessionism they have been persuaded to change their tactics, or crushed. The Assamese and the Gurkha agitations are, pace Punjab, evidences that there are still strong incentives to bring back ethnic demands from the brink of ethnicity and secession (Hewitt 1989:18).

Thus, democratic rules of the game implicitly bring into existence a yawning gap between the forces that consent to abide its rules and therefore have the potential of being incorporated into the framework and those that do not.

But the project of democratizing ethnicity, as we will argue, has its limits in the sense that it brings in its wake what we call, a certain *ethnicization* of democracy. Insofar as the democratic institutions and practices get ethnicized, newer ethnic groups and communities hitherto remaining outside the democratic framework find it difficult—if not impossible—to be incorporated into its ambit and become its integral parts. We will try to draw our attention to some of the limits and deficits of these institutions and practices and make a plea for being flexible in its rules and experimenting with newer institutional alternatives. Only democracy holds out the promise of being an alternative to democracy and making good the democratic deficit highlighted above.

As we argue in this manner, it becomes necessary on our part to begin with a brief working definition of the concept of ethnicization and its connection to democratic theory. To begin with, some idea of social contract remains at the heart of democratic theory. Social contract theorists define democracy primarily as a contract between the people organizing them into a collective body—often defined as "civil society" in classical liberal theory and their political dispensation—a contract according to which the people as a body are under the abiding obligation of acquiescing to the political dispensation on condition that it helps them secure and guarantee in return their own "right to life, liberty and pursuit of happiness". While the idea of contract is central to the functioning of any form of democracy, the history of *actually existing* democratic countries all over the world has been one of almost endless experimentations with varieties of institutions and practices that would serve the purpose. Democratic theory by definition has always been open to the idea of experimentations. A democracy that ceases to be self-critical and is held captive to any given framework of democratic rules and institutions is only a contradiction in terms. The term "ethnicization" is thus reflective of the underlying contradictions of our actually functioning democracy. It refers to a process whereby certain groups and communities are systemically denied the right to be part of the democratic contract as signatories and as full-fledged rights-bearing bodies of citizens. They are forced as it were to acquiesce to the established political dispensation without correspondingly enjoying "the right to life, liberty and pursuit of happiness". The rule by the established political dispensation for them therefore exceeds the ambit of democratic contract. We describe it as the underside of democracy. Formation of this underside ironically is not incidental to but constitutive of the given framework of democratic institutions and practices. This paper as we will see proposes to explore democracy's underside and examine the mechanics of its operation.

Our concept of ethnicization may at first sight appear to be the same as the otherwise widely used concept of exclusion. Yet, it will be difficult to lose sight of at least two very significant points of difference between them. One, exclusion as a concept is much wider in scope in that it takes into account groups and communities as only one and not necessarily the only segment being excluded from the democratic ambit. The term ethnicization is of course reserved to refer to the exclusion of groups and communities as only one segment of an otherwise "vast number of lower and invisible segments" of population (Sinha 1999). For us on the other hand, if "vast number of lower and invisible segments" is excluded from the country's democratic ambit, it is so not because it is "lower and invisible" per se, but because it belongs to certain groups and communities. Their being "lower and invisible" is only secondary to their ethnic marginality. Two, exclusion is always looked upon as the inevitable erosion of democracy (Kothari 1988; also Sinha 1999). It by all accounts, marks the failure of democracy in India. Had democratic institutions and practices struck their roots more deep and wide into the body politic, they would not have excluded the "vast number of lower and invisible segments" of India's population. Proponents of democracy usually dismiss it as a problem of its deepening and penetration. Exclusion as we argue in this paper, is the constitutive underside of and therefore indispensable to the existing framework of democratic institutions and practices. It is rather the success of the existing framework of India's democracy—and not its failure, that creates its vast underside and is responsible for exclusion of certain groups and communities from its ambit. Viewed in this light, ethnicization is not only distinct from, but the reverse of exclusion. Democracy cannot strike its roots amongst these groups and communities, unless it becomes critical of itself and transcends its existing framework of rules, institutions and practices.

Ethnicization in other words, spells out a systemic crisis of democracy. As we have already pointed out, it refers to a process whereby certain ethnic groups and communities are systematically kept out of the ambit of contract. The insurgent organizations that locate the respective communities they claim to represent, outside the democratic framework established in India critique it not because it is undemocratic per se for it is not undemocratic vis-à-vis the communities that are incorporated into and represented in it. It is only undemocratic vis-à-vis those that do not consider them as a part of it and refuse to play the game within the rules that are set by it.

Accordingly, the paper is divided into two very closely inter-related sections: While the first section dwells on some aspects of the process of ethnic articulation in contemporary north-eastern India, the second seeks to warn us against the commonplace tendency of regarding the experience of the north-east as only marginal or peripheral to the democratic experience of contemporary India. This section in other words focuses on the limits and deficits of parliamentary institutions and practices in addressing the question of ethnic articulation in contemporary north-eastern India.

Viewed thus, this paper has some limitations, four of which may be mentioned at this point: One, it restricts itself to an analysis of only the ethnic challenges to the existing democratic institutions and practices. The existing framework is vulnerable not only to ethnic challenges but to many other challenges. Nor is it to say that these non-ethnic challenges are any less significant or inconsequential for our democratic prospects. Although the north-east as a region is often cast in ethnic stereotypes, ethnic challenges are not unique to the region. Two, the paper draws our attention to the limits, rather than the limitations of parliamentary democracy in India. Since the limits are built in the parliamentary democracy itself, it is impossible to overcome them from within its existing institutions and practices. In simple terms, it is not the failure, but the success of parliamentary democracy that accounts for its ethnicization. Three, although the paper underlines the necessity of exploring deep into the new democratic alternatives and emancipating democracy from the given framework of parliamentary institutions and practices, it has a tendency of rolling all our democratic institutions and practices into the same parliamentary framework and then blaming it. There is always a danger involved in such an exercise for India as we know, hardly offers the exemplar of classical parliamentary democracy. India at best can only provide one of its very imperfect examples. Democracy in India contains at least some features that do not go well with the institutions and practices characteristic of classical parliamentary democracy. While we are aware of them, we ignore these imperfections for purposes of convenience. Four, it is true that the paper makes a plea for reviewing our democratic institutions and practices. But it carefully refrains from offering any particular democratic model for our consideration. The idea is to initiate a debate rather than putting an end to it.

ETHNIC ARTICULATION

Ethnic articulation may be defined, as a process whereby an ethnic community makes certain claims to the right to some form of autonomy before the political system. These rights claims have at least three properties: one, they are made by or on behalf of the community as a collectivity, most importantly, as an undivided and albeit indivisible whole. While making a comparative study of fifteen "extreme" cases of secessionist movements across the world, Martin J. Dent for example observes: "The lesson is clear: it is as though the rock of the separate national identity of the minority must be incorporated into the structure of the larger country as a whole, rather than making an attempt to break it up into small pieces, in order to incorporate as smaller stones in a cement mixture" (Dent 2004:15). The communities making such claims first of all want the state to recognize them as full-fledged, rights-bearing collectivities.

Two, a community's claim to autonomy is usually expressed through some form of exclusive control over the non-replenish able and life-bearing resources (like, timber, oil, coal, water and agricultural land etc.) that are located within a particular territorial space that it considers as its "homeland".

At one level, it is expressed through a community's desire of immediately ending the extraction of these resources by the outside forces. Insurgent groups of the region term it, as "colonial" and look upon the Indian state as "an outside agency". Even such students' organizations as All-Assam Students' Union (AAASU) and Khasi Students' Union (KSU) have been vehemently opposing the flow of oil from Assam's oilfields and felling of trees in the rainforests of Meghalaya respectively. While insurgent groups of the region criticize extraction by the outside forces including the Indian state, which to many of them, is only an outside agency, they are not opposed to the process of extraction and depletion of resources per se. Viewed in this light, theirs is not an ecological critique. Many of these organizations themselves have been accused of indulging in counter-extraction. Their critique of extraction is a patently anti-colonial critique that is seldom guided by any kind of pure ecological concerns. A community's right to resources in this context is only an adjunct to its right to self-determination. Elsewhere we defined ethno-ecologism as a syndrome that subordinates ecological concerns to an ethnic community's abiding quest for self-determination (Das 1997: 21-35).

Shrinking employment opportunities especially in the government sector—thanks to globalization, have been one of the most contentious issues in the region that has often triggered off wide schism between the "locals" and the "outsiders". The recent protests organized by AASU against the recruitment of the *khalasis* (porters), gangmen, trackmen and pointmen in North-east Frontier Railway in 2003 are a case in point. In Assam there are about 15 lakh (1.5 million) uneducated youths. The North-east Frontier Railway has the longest kilometer coverage of its tracks in Assam (2529.60 kilometers as against 975.71 kilometers in West Bengal and 363.61 kilometers in Bihar). But in matters of employment, West Bengal and Bihar account for 40.52 and 25.02 per cent of the total work force while the percentage share of Assam happens to be only 16.97.[2] Even those who had graduated in engineering had applied for Group D posts in the railways, where the minimum qualification is eighth standard. In the Railway Service Recruitment Board examinations for Group D posts held on November 9 and 16, 2003, 54 per cent of the applicants were from outside the state specially Bihar. Candidates from Bihar alone numbered about 95,000. The trouble ensued when the advertisement for these jobs was published in *The Employment News* as per a Supreme Court of India order. The earlier practice was that the examinations for these posts were conducted at the divisional levels in which the youth sponsored by respective employment exchanges would be called. This infuriated the local youth who tried to prevent the outside candidates from appearing at the examinations. The students' body accused the railways of discriminating against the locals and reportedly harassed Bihari candidates who had come to Guwahati for recruitment test while demanding for cent per cent reservation for the locals in Group D jobs of the railways. This led to retaliatory attacks on the passengers from the North-east passing through Bihar. AASU also organized a bandh in protest on 17 November. There were reports of attacks on the Biharis and the wildfire spread far and wide particularly in upper Assam. While the United Liberation Front of Assam (ULFA) had issued quit orders to all Hindi-speaking people in the state, the Ranvir Sena of Bihar—an outlawed organization had given a counter-ultimatum to the ULFA. The Sena had warned that if the Government of Assam failed to protect the lives and property of the Hindi-speaking people of the state, it would send its armed cadres to take on ULFA militants. By 19 November, 2003, the toll according to official estimates, mounted to 27 as the ULFA continued to mow down the Biharis particularly, the women and children. The carnage had at least awakened the Union Government that is now exploring the possibility of reserving all Group D posts in the Indian Railways for the locals (Anonymous 2004: 10-13).

Three, such claims of right to autonomy obviously are likely to reduce others living within the same territorial space to minorities and hence, are necessarily in conflict with those made by them. Ethnic articulation in short is the process that marks the coincidence of the ethnic community with a determinate territorial space that it considers as its "homeland". The space is considered as determinate only by the ethnic community/ies that make/s the claim over it. Two or more ethnic communities making similarly "determinate" claims over the same tract of land point to the contested nature of the space in question. Such coincidence is usually achieved through a varying combination of at least three relatively distinct means: consolidation of an ethnic community by way of bringing its diverse fragments together within one administrative unit, getting rid of those parts of the already established administrative unit that are inhabited by people who do not belong to the same ethnic community and ethnic cleansing. Let us see how. Ethnic articulation represents a certain coincidence between an ethnic community and the territorial space that the community claims as its "homeland". In their coincidence, they produce what Bernard Cohn describes as "ethnic space" (Cohn 1987:Chap. 6). How does this coincidence come about? Even a cursory glance at political trends in contemporary India points to at least three modalities of such coincidence: One, coincidence may be effected through consolidation of a particular ethnic community by way of bringing together its fragments strewn over a host of states and administrative units of our Union under one political dispensation. The newly resurgent demand for the formation of a greater "Nagalim" comprising the present state of Nagaland and the Naga-inhabited areas of the neighbouring Manipur, Assam and Arunachal Pradesh—although vociferously resented by the communities that are going to be affected by the decision, will have to be understood in this light. Notwithstanding all its diversities, a significant part of the militancy in Kashmir may be attributed to the common aspiration for unification with their cousins living in the Pakistan-held part of the valley. Such irredentist aspirations are very much an integral part of militancy in present-day Kashmir.

Two, coincidence is often achieved by getting rid of those areas where members of another community are concentrated in numbers and thereby making the political unit culturally and ethnically homogeneous. The Sylhet referendum of 1947 may be cited as an illustration. The then leadership of the Assam Pradesh Congress Committee—dominated by the Assamese-speaking Varna-Hindus, is said to have virtually conceded the district to East Pakistan supposedly on the ground that its inclusion as a Bengali-majority area in Assam would have meant a percentage decline of the Assamese-speaking populace in the state. The Assamese therefore had "little stake in Sylhet" (Chakrabarty 2002:346-7). Amalendu Guha has pointed out how division between the pro- and anti-inclusion votes in the referendum roughly matched with the prevailing numerical distribution of the relevant linguistic communities in the district (Guha 1977:320). In this connection it will be interesting to see how the Assamese discourse on an Assamese homeland developed in present-day Assam. Lakshminath Tamuli accuses "the Bengali-speaking public of being 'the first' to raise the demand for dividing Assam and tag Jalpaiguri and Cooch Behar with the district of Cachar and the then Dhubri and Goalpara sub-divisions of Assam thereby making way to the formation of a separate 'Purbanchal' consisting of the predominantly Bengali-speaking population of Assam" (Tamuli n.d.: 13).

Last but not the least, the coincidence is sought more often than not, to be achieved through what today is known as ethnic cleansing. The strategy of "ethnic cleansing" resorted to by a section of militant Bodo leadership was initially characterized by their potent desire of *creating* a majority of their own for laying hold of the villages under the jurisdiction of Bodoland Autonomous Council (BAC) that were denied to them on the ground that they did not form a majority (50 per cent or more) in them. The Bodos' access to state power was strategically dependent on their ability to establish them as the numerically preponderant community in these villages. As the Assam administration maintained that the Bodos were not a majority in more than half the villages that were to fall in the Council area, Bodo militants began targeting non-Bodo communities to spark off an exodus. A series of riots was reportedly organized in an apparently planned manner to achieve the purpose of forming a majority in these villages. While the Bodos have been the victims of an irreversible historical process of being depleted into a minority in what they claim as their homeland, they are accused of further reducing the non-Bodo inhabitants (like, the Santhals and the Bengali-speaking Muslims etc.) of the proposed Bodoland area situated mainly on the northern banks of the Brahmaputra, into a minority. The case is interesting for it turns the democratic logic of numbers on its head.

The Hmar-Dimasa clashes that have been intermittently taking place in North Cachar (NC) Hills since March 2002 also exemplify the point. Dima Halam Daoga's (DHD) policy of cleansing the N.C. Hills of the outsiders initially the Hindi-speaking people dates back to its formation. In May 1999, DHD militants reportedly killed about 5 of them in an encounter in the district. While Hmar Peoples Convention (HPC) claiming to represent the Hmars sprang surprise attacks on the Dimasa-inhabited villages in the neighbouring district of Cachar way back on 31 March, 2002, the Dimasas under the leadership of such organizations as, DHD and All-Dimasa Students' Union (ADSU) have also been responsible for torching tens of Dimasa-inhabited villages, killing and evicting them. According to one estimate, about 3,500 Hmars were forced to leave their homes and some of them even took shelter in neighbouring states including Manipur.[3] Such organizations as Kuki Inpi and Hmar Students' Association (HAS) of Manipur organized the movement of the Kuki and Hmar IDPs respectively. These organizations have been conducting these raids apparently in their bid to cleanse these areas of the "outsiders" and gradually consolidate and establish their claim to *Dimaraji*—a separate Dimasa homeland comprising N.C. Hills, parts of Cachar and Dimapur districts of Assam and Nagaland respectively. Hmar Students' Association even accused the DHD of having attempted at changing the name of N.C. Hills to "Dima Halali" without taking the sentiments of the minorities particularly the Hmars and the Kukis into account. Many of the Dimasas too were displaced as a result of these clashes and some of them fled to neighbouring district of Cachar. The minority tribes submitted in protest a memorandum to the Governor of Assam that led Dimasas to organize their attacks on the minority tribal groups.

Besides, in Karbi Anglong, Karbi National Volunteers (KNV) was formed in March 1995 with the specific objective of combating Citizens Rights Preservation Committee (CRPC) whom it considers as the umbrella organization representing the non-Karbi groups in the district. It accuses the latter of spreading communal feelings among the people "with the active help from the Centre" and vowed to oppose the "imposition" of Hindi as the official language in its memorandum.

DEMOCRATIC DEFICIT

Parliamentary democracy in India comes with a package; it is always coupled with what we call, ethnicization of our nationhood. The institutions and practices in other words contribute to the formation of an ethnic core that either gradually appropriates the margins within it or pushes them into oblivion. The point may be appreciated by way of focusing on at least three major doctrines that are commonly regarded as the three main pillars of parliamentary democracy in India:

The doctrine of rational choice

First, there is the doctrine of "rational choice" to be expressed through the instrumentality of elections. Elections are crucial to the formation and functioning of parliamentary institutions right from national parliament down to the local body of panchayats. While elections make rational choice possible, participation in them is usually regarded as the mark of rational beings. On the one hand, elections offer to the people the right to make their choice from amongst the alternatives. The presence of alternatives in short makes the choice possible. On the other hand, these also give them the opportunity of being a part of state power by way of getting elected by the people. Elections provide the mechanism through which state power is made available to the people at large and they are thereby entitled to hold and exercise it.

It is obvious that the electoral choice will have to be made only from amongst the alternatives available to them. While they can abstain from the act of voting in case they refuse to exercise their franchise from within the alternatives available to them, such abstentions may be caused by a whole host of factors other than their discontentment with all the available candidates. Besides, such abstentions are not normally encouraged in democracy. In other words, choice directly depends on the extent of availability of the alternatives. Alternatives influence and shape people's choices and the people are forced as it were to vote from amongst a set of candidates—none of whom may be found to be suitable by a voter. Some of the civil rights organizations including Association for the Protection of Democratic Rights (APDR), West Bengal have been demanding the right to record people's "no choice" for the last few years although a public interest litigation brought by them to the Supreme Court of India was dismissed by the apex court (APDR 2000).

The ethnic core of our nation is composed of these rational beings, who are entitled to take part in elections and thereby exercise their free and unfettered rational choice. In a country like India, rational choice is not necessarily expressed through the instrumentality of elections. The participation of ethnic forces in parliamentary elections may not necessarily reflect rational choice as much as their abstention and non-participation does not necessarily reflect its absence. The boycott of assembly elections of 1983 in Assam (that most of the Assamese I interviewed continue to describe as "non-elections") and the "plebiscite" held under the auspices of Naga National Council (NNC) in 1951 and the subsequent boycott of the first general elections in 1952 in Naga Hills—then a district of undivided Assam, illustrate the point. 99.9 per cent of the eligible Naga adults voted with their feet up in the air against the inclusion of their territory in India in a "plebiscite" organized against the wishes of the Government of India. It was as a tribute to this verdict that the Nagas abstained from casting their votes in the first general elections and all the ballot boxes returned empty from Naga Hills. Similarly, non-participation in elections does not necessarily imply the absence of rational choice. Even a significant portion of the few who turned out for voting in the state assembly elections of Jammu and Kashmir in 1996 was reportedly compelled to cast their votes against their will (see, Balagopal *et al.*, 1996).

Politics of numbers

Secondly, there is the doctrine of majority rule. For Locke, the parliamentary majority is culturally vacuous—"ideological cypher" as Sheldon Wolin in one of his recently published books paraphrases it. For the majority per se—whether at the federal level or at the state level, does not constitute a culturally defined "nation". Nor does it pose any threat to the survival of the nation of which it is only a part. Liberal political theory operates on the axiomatic presence of a particular nation as a basis of the functioning of parliamentary institutions, without of course duly acknowledging it. The division between the majority and the minority is a division internal to the nation. For Locke, the distinction between them is of ephemeral nature. As he puts it: "... the act of the majority passes for the act of the whole, and of course determines as having, by the law of nature and reason, the power of the whole". The doctrine of majority rule thus presupposes the presence of a nation in which the majority constitutes the ethnic core and the minority is expected to "acculturate" into it. A minority that refuses to "acculturate" is always regarded as an irritant to the liberal democratic framework. Notwithstanding their social and cultural differences, they share the same nationalist consensus. The minority in other words is necessarily a national minority. The differences between the majority and the minority should not be too wide to tear the national body apart. The states of the Indian Union according to the States Reorganization Commission (1955) were reorganized (and are being reorganized) not because the process was expected to accommodate ethnic interests and concerns—particularly, the language-based demands but because it was supposed to bring the institutions of government closer to the people and enhance the representativeness of our democratic set up. In other words, the democratic argument of popular participation in parliamentary institutions was sought to be disentangled—albeit with little success, from the otherwise strong plea for ethnicity.

It is for this reason that a minority's refusal to "acculturate" into the ethnic core of the nation necessarily takes on an ethnic character. Its refusal has necessarily to harp on the ethnic and cultural difference that separates them. Ethnicity therefore is the unavoidable rhetoric of minority politics in contemporary India. While majoritarian democracy necessarily produces ethnicity, ethnicity in its turn makes our nationhood perpetually uneasy and ambivalent. While involving themselves in various social and political movements, ethnic communities look upon the territorial space as their "homeland" enjoying varying degree of autonomy from the so-called "nation".

Let us now concentrate on the critique of the prevailing democratic form propounded by the secessionists. It has two elements. First of all, the secessionists harp on a distinction between "interest" and "value" and argue that while interests can be represented, values are not. A community does not seem to recognize any moral value that is superior to what it cherishes and upholds. Its members are supposedly guided by them in course of interacting with others, among themselves and passing moral judgments. Interests on the other hand are likely to bind people together into some form of a contractual association. The implication is that people come together on the basis of some commonality of interests, which once fulfilled are no longer potent enough to cement them together. Viewed in these terms, values serve as relatively inflexible bases of solidarity than interests do (Tonnies 1957). As a sequel to it, secessionists point out that the communities they represent are ensconced in values that the "outsiders" are simply unable to appreciate and represent on an enduring basis. The ostensibly fleeting eagerness of the political representatives to represent the values of these communities is always issued from their insidious interest in "colonizing" them and falling back on their vote banks. Thus community values are subordinated to "colonial" interests. To cite an example, the United Liberation Front of Assam (ULFA) in its letter to the UN Secretary General in 1990 contests the claim of the Indian National Congress (INC) to represent the "Indian nation" in its struggle against the British Raj: "... efforts at nation-building during the nationalist struggle left unresolved many national and sub-national question" (*Budhbar* 1990:8,9,12). It also questions the authority of "New Delhi" to represent the ethnic communities languishing in the periphery. What is interesting to note is that in support of its contention, it highlights the "ethnic" distinctiveness of the Assamese and how the Assamese as a "nation" are more close to the pan-Mongoloid fraternity of groups than to the Indo-Aryan people of Northern India.

If democracy is over and above a game of numbers, then obviously the marginal communities are fated to be its perpetual losers. They perceive themselves as the ultimate victims of an imperceptible "tyranny of the majority". The victimhood of the marginal communities in North-eastern India has already pushed them to take on an anti-majoritarian character. The secessionist discourse is first of all, characterized by a certain element of desperation. If one tracks the evolution of the Assamese mood on the question of identity and culture right from the days of the Assam movement (1979-85), one is surprised to note how the desperation has shot up by leaps and bounds. A joint statement issued at the heyday of the movement by Shri Prafulla Kumar Mahanta and Shri Bhrigu Kumar Phukon, President and General Secretary respectively of the All-Assam Students' Union (AASU) pointed out that the Central Government could afford to insult the "Assamese people" because "they are the Assamese people". Had it been the case of any other community, the Government could not have inflicted this kind of "insult". The point is simple. Since the Assamese are the solitary victims of the otherwise unlimited influx of immigrants from across the borders, they have to fight the battle single-handed though of course they expect that they would be joined by others and they have no problems with the Central Government allowing the immigrants to pour in, provided they are settled outside Assam.

Secondly, if democracy is a perpetually losing game for these communities in which they are facing the threat of being reduced to a minority in no time, then they cannot pull the political strings of the state any more (Hazarika 2000). For example, it is being noticed that the immigrant votes of the isolated pockets of Brahmaputra Valley exercise a decisive influence on the outcome of all elections held in Assam since 1991 including the most recent one. Insofar as the lever of political power slips out of the hands of autochthonous ethnic communities, they cannot beat their adversaries in the same democratic game. They prefer to opt out of it and seek a change in the rules of the game. They envisage an altogether new and sovereign dispensation in which they would no longer be elbowed out and outnumbered by others. Secessionism is generated out of a maddening fear of being ruled by *the ethnic other* and works for the creation of a political space in which they will feel secure and hope to establish themselves as empowered subjects. The arguments put forward by ULFA in justification of its decision to follow a violent, secessionist path is noteworthy in this connection. Ajit Kumar Bhuyan for example wrote:

> The Indian state has already let us understand that the Assamese nation (sic.) is unable to survive in the way it wants. It will never be given the right to survive in the way it likes under any condition. That is to say, the Assamese native has to live like, slaves, or in the way the Hindi-speaking politicians and bureaucrats who are increasingly dominating on the responsibility of conducting the state (Bhuyan 1993:23, trans. mine).

ULFA's persistent rejection of the "talks" offer extended to it by the Government of India is attributed to its realization that it will not be able to achieve the objective of establishing "a Sovereign and Independent Assam" without "revolutionary means". ULFA does not object to the idea of holding "scientific dialogues"—that is to say, dialogues that will exclusively focus on the question of "sovereignty and independence" of Assam. Since the Constitution of India does not guarantee the right to secede, ULFA's objective cannot be achieved through Parliamentary and Constitutional means. It actually sets forth the precondition of amending the Constitution in order to lay down and safeguard this right before sitting on the negotiating table. Commenting on how ULFA's *Swadhin Asom* holds out the promise of establishing a secure political space for the "Assamese", Udayon Misra writes:

> All the contradictions within the Assamese nationality notwithstanding, the idea of a *Swadhin Asom* seems quite often to be a sort of rallying point for a people who are faced today with a grave crisis of identity. It could be seen as part of a strategy to continue to ensure the hegemonic role of the Assamese in the region (Misra 2000:178).

This point may be illustrated with reference to Bodo demand for secession. The post-Accord political developments are noteworthy in this context. The Accord of February, 1993 sought to provide the Bodos with some measure of "autonomy"—however little and insignificant that be, in areas, which are "contiguous" and in which they constitute a numerical majority consisting of 50 per cent or more of the total population. For the sake of preserving contiguity, areas where Bodos constitute even less than 50 per cent would be the constituent parts of the Council. Defining its jurisdiction, the Memorandum of Settlement, popularly known as the Bodo Accord signed on 23 February, 1993 points out:

> ...There shall be, by an Act of Assam Legislative Assembly, a Bodoland Autonomous Council (BAC) within the State of Assam comprising the contiguous geographical areas between river Sankosh and Mazbat/river Pansoi. The land records authority of the State will scrutinize the list of villages furnished by the ABSU-BPAC having 50 per cent and more of tribal population which shall be included in the BAC. For the purpose of providing a contiguous area,

> even the villages having less than 50 per cent tribal population shall be included. BAC also include Reserve Forests as per the guidelines laid by Ministry of Defence and Ministry of Environment and Forests, Government of India, not otherwise required by government (of Assam) for manning the international border and tea gardens located completely within the BAC contiguous area.[4]

Even a cursory look into the population figures of the autochthonous Bodos living in the villages claimed by ABSU-BPAC combine points out, their percentage has been rapidly on decline right from the middle of the 19th century. Such factors as massive influx of outsiders, rapid environmental degradation and huge land alienation of the indigenous people are primarily responsible for this remarkable decline.[5] The figures have now hit the rock bottom so much so that contrary to the expectations of Bodo leadership, in over 500 villages they have reportedly been reduced to a minority. Never before in their history has the Bodo leadership been caught in such a quandary.

Unless they can convincingly prove their majority in a space that they prefer to define as their homeland, they cannot get themselves entitled to whatever political autonomy is granted to them. In its 28th Annual Conference held at Langhin Tinali, Karbi Anglong on 3-5 March, 1996, the ABSU disowned the Bodo Accord and revived its demand for separate Bodoland. Their self-representation is possible only in a compact political space freed from the threatening presence of the outsiders. A section of Bodo leadership sought to resolve the circularity by way of taking to arms and resorted to the path of secessionist militancy. The roots of secessionism are thus embedded in the prevailing democratic form that insists on the twin criteria of number and compactness in order to be entitled to it. But NDFB's (National Democratic Front of Bodoland) or for that matter ULFA's assertion of the right to exit inevitably meets with resistance. The government after all is too unwilling to accede to it. We know that democracy is a system of government in which there is what Lefort calls, "a fundamental indeterminacy about the basis of power". If democratic form allows for constant changes of rulers, one group replacing another and replaced in turn by still another, then very unlike any other form of government, it "undermines the representation of organic totality" that T. Sakhire was perhaps alluding to, in the epigraph of this paper. None of the groups coming to power represents or is supposed to represent the society as a whole. It implies what Lefort calls, "the disembodiment of the society". Hence, a society that does not hold itself together independently of political support is unlikely to play host to the democratic form. As he writes:

> There is always a possibility that the logic of democracy will be disrupted in a society in which the foundations of the political order and the social order vanish, in which *that which has been established never* bears the seal of full legitimacy, in which differences of rank no longer go unchallenged, in which right proves to depend upon the discourse which articulates it, and in which the exercise of power depends upon conflict. When individuals are increasingly insecure as a result of an economic crisis or of the ravages of war, when conflict between classes and groups is exacerbated and can no longer be symbolically resolved within the political sphere, when power appears to have sunk to the level of reality and to be no more than an instrument for the promotion of the interests and appetites of vulgar ambition and when, in a word, it appears *in* society, and when at the same time society appears to be fragmented, then we see the development of the fantasy of the People-as-One, the beginnings of the quest for a substantial identity, for a social body which is welded to its head, for an embodying power, for a state free from division (Lefort 1988:19-20, emphasis mine).

In simple terms, a political system that cashes in on the "fantasy" of creating "the People-as-One" is anathema to democracy while an extremely multi-cultural and fragmented society is too fragile to survive it. It is true that democracy is the only form of government that offers to the ethnic communities the right to enact their respective subject positions within the polity. But without some amount of value consensus already existing in the society it is unable to hold itself together. A society shorn of minimum value consensus frequently calls upon the government to swing into action and integrate the society from outside through whatever means it has under its disposal.

As the democratic form feeds on secessionism, secessionism per se cannot be the guarantor of the democratic form. It always compels the government to cast aside its democratic form and militarize itself. Secessionism sows the seeds of anti-democracy within the given democratic form.

We have seen in the above section how democracy feeds on secessionism. But how is democracy fed by it? What is the form of democracy that the secessionists envisage while establishing their sovereign state? Does it mark a paradigmatic discontinuity with the prevailing one that feeds on secessionism? I would like to argue that the democratic form that most of the secessionists envisage is not paradigmatically different from the prevailing one. In order to illustrate the point, we may refer to the case of Bodo secessionism. The Bodos' access to the democratic form is strategically dependent on either of the two options: depending on the benevolence and democratic wisdom of the outsiders who have already come to settle there and secondly, to move to those villages and decisively "cleanse" them of the ethnic adversaries so that they can obtain a majority. Bodos seemed to have opted for the second. Referring to the Bodo movement, Sanjib Baruah observes:

> At least to some Bodo activists, ethnically targeted violence seemed to hold the promise of changing the demographic facts on the ground, which they have been told repeatedly stand in the way of a separate Bodoland (Baruah 2000:196).

While National Democratic Front of Bodoland (NDFB) under the leadership of Ranjan Daimary demands complete secession from the Indian Union, such moderate organizations as All-Bodo Students' Union (ABSU) and Bodo Liberation Tigers (BLT) insisted on the formation of a separate state within it. In simple terms, whether within India or without, both considered demarcation of space that the Bodos can claim as their own, as crucial for the establishment of the Bodos as a majority. The problem was addressed by way of signing the Bodo Accord with the BLT leaders on 10 February, 2003 that led to the institution of the Bodoland Territorial Council (BTC). The BTC was formed with the objective of "providing Constitutional protection under the Sixth Schedule to fulfill economic, educational and linguistic aspirations and the preservation of land rights, socio-cultural and ethnic identity of the Bodos and speeding up the infrastructure of develop-ment in BTC area". Article 4 that consists of 8 clauses of the Memorandum of Settlement (MOS) aims to "safeguard" the interests and concerns of the "non-tribals in the BTC area" by way of ensuring their special representation in the BTC (clause 2) and promising suitable modification in the Sixth Schedule while securing their settlement rights and transfer and inheritance of property. The promised amendment is based on the general principle laid down in the MOS:

> The amendments to the Sixth Schedule shall include provisions in such a manner that non-tribals are not disadvantaged in relation to the rights enjoyed by them at the commencement of the BTC and their rights and privileges including land rights are fully protected.

But there is always a problem with these experimentations. This is likely to infuriate the ethnic majority whose dominance is threatened as soon as the ethnic minorities are allowed to have their say. Hiranya Kumar Bhattacharya for one believes that the establishment of BTC amounts to a blatant violation of at least three key principles of democracy: One, since the Bodos are not in a majority, the majoritarian principle is violated. Two, in the name of granting political autonomy to the ethnic Bodos, the non-Bodos (about 12 hundred thousand) living in these areas will lose their right to self-representation. We may note that the discontent amongst some non-Bodo tribal groups living in these areas has already started simmering and has acquired a militant turn. Three, the establishment of the Council will mean that the numerical minority of about 6 hundred thousand Bodos will have no accountability to about 12 hundred thousand Indian citizens (Bhattacharya 1995:2). The circularity in the argument should not escape our notice: the Bodos are not entitled to democratic rule because they are a minority and they are a minority because they can never be a majority.

A community that opts for the second obviously turns the democratic logic on its head. It creates a majority wherever there is not any. It thus subscribes to the same democratic form that thrives on the constitutive exclusion of some other communities. The irony is that while the Bodos have been the victims of the otherwise irreversible historical process of being depleted into a minority in a space that they claim to be their homeland, they may be accused of ethnicizing the space in a manner that feeds on secessionism. Their attempts at establishing them as the invincible majority—whether by forcing others to migrate and thereby reducing them into a minority or by completely eliminating them through ethnic cleansing, drive others, especially the Santals or the Bengali-speaking Muslims of the area to organize and fight back, while asserting their rights to exit. Exactly the same democratic form seems to be reproduced in the secessionist practice of the Bodo militants.

Unless the search for alternative democratic institutions begins in right earnest, ethnic minorities are likely to be pushed towards insurgencies and rebellions. The search by all accounts seems have already begun. We may refer to at least four broad strands of this debate over institutionalisation. These are not necessarily mutually exclusive: First of all, reform-minded scholars and activists like, B.K. Roy Burman for example, recommend a Scandinavian SAMI-like multi-layered parliamentary system in which ethnic communities will have the right to represent themselves instead of being bound by the majoritarian commands of our existing parliamentary system (quoted in Routray 2001). Secondly, we may refer to the argument of those who point out that the "first-come-first-served" electoral system in which the minorities dispersed over a large space are constantly under the subjection of the numerical and therefore political majority is incompatible with the pluralistic nature of our society. As Jayaprakash Narayan observes: "Large, but scattered social groups are always under represented. The consequent marginalization of large segments of public opinion in a plural society has evidently led to ghettoization of numerically important groups like minorities and dalits" (Narayan 2003:38). Even reservation of seats for them will not according to him help the situation. He makes an advocacy for introducing proportional representation as a means of protecting these groups from majority rule and retaining their autonomy. Thirdly, there has also been a case for widening the consociational base of our democratic system. Lijphart for example shows how the basic preconditions of a consociational (power sharing) democracy were met during the first few decades of our Independence and how the base has been weakened as a combined result of "centralization of the Congress Party and the federal system" in the 1980s and growing "attack on minority rights" in different parts of India. He in fact pleads for resuscitating the institutions and practices of consociational democracy that protected India reasonably well in the first few decades against inter-group violence and communal riots (Lijphart 1996). Fourthly, the present series of "Indo-Naga" dialogues has brought the issue of institutional experimentation to the forefront of political agenda. It seems that the NSCN (I-M) with whom the Government of India has been conducting a series of dialogue since 1997 is veering towards a notion of what we may for want of a better term call, shared sovereignty. While the organization is reportedly settling for "a special federal relationship with India" that is likely to culminate in the creation of a "federation of India and Nagalim", the Government of India is believed to be yet unreconciled to the proposition.[6] A "federation of India and Nagalim" is according to its chief—Tuengaling Muivah, not the same as the existing Indian Union of States.

The doctrine of democratic opposition

Thirdly and as a corollary to the second, there is the doctrine of what Rawls calls, "civility". While voicing rights claims necessarily puts one into some kind of opposition to those from whom they are claimed, parliamentary institutions are considered as sites where such claims are made, oppositions are met and most importantly, rights are guaranteed and safeguarded. The ethnic forces are called upon to voice their opposition and dissent only through the very institutions of parliamentary democracy. "Civility" as we see, is responsible for creating a new ethnicity—indeed a new ethnic core that makes it impossible for others outside it, to voice their rights claims. Rawls interprets this as "hardship"; but for him, "accepting these hardships is simply recognizing and being willing to work within the limits imposed by the circumstances of human life". What he does not seem to be aware of is how the "acceptance of these limits" entails a transformation in the very agenda of rights and thereby restricts the scope and agenda of democracy for rights are the life-blood of democracy. Many of the insurgent groups for example, insist on the inclusion of the right to self-determination in the Indian Constitution. Do the institutions of parliamentary democracy exist for rights or they exist for themselves? The doctrine of civility keeps us from any serious questioning of the parliamentary institutions and searching for new democratic alternatives. As one observes in a seminar paper: "... I even share the sentiments of some of my fellow Assamese who are waging a war with the Indian state as a result of ... grievance. But grievances need not mean war, there could be a debate quite like this one where we gather to debate on the 'issue of treatment from New Delhi' and how we should demand what is rightfully ours. Moreover debate is less troublesome than war" (Saikia 2005:171).

North-east is usually dismissed as an exception to what the rest of India demonstrates to us. It is what the rest of the country is not as much as the rest of the country is what the north-east is not. The region in short, is the *other*—both literally and figuratively. One should not be unduly alarmed about our democratic prospects, if the doctrines of parliamentary democracy are evidently violated and eroded almost on an everyday basis. We on the other hand have argued that the North-east represents the other in the very opposite sense of the term. It is the other not because it shows how the democratic doctrines are secretly violated and eroded, but because how the very institutions and practices of parliamentary democracy create their vast underside and produce and reproduce the margins. Margins in our argument are constitutive of and therefore central to the architecture of parliamentary institutions and practices.

We seem to have reached a stage when ironically the very imperative of democracy has turned the logic of parliamentary democracy on its head. Unless the search for new democratic institutions and practices begins in right earnest, the future of democracy in this country is going to be very bleak.

NOTES

1. See, (Sakhire quoted in Elwin, 1961).
2. The figures are taken from Hiren Gohain's interview (Phukon 2004:16).
3. See, "500 Hmars to take refuge in Manipur" (*Times of India* 2003).
4. See, Paragraph 3(a) of the Accord.
5. For an appraisal of these figures, see, (Das Gupta, 1989: 15-7, 23; Also, Bhattacharjee, 1996).
6. T. Muivah interviewed by Karan Thapar in BBC Hardtalk India on 29 April, 2005 at 22 Hrs. IST.

REFERENCES

APDR (2000): *Apachhander Adhikar* (in Bengali) [Right of no-choice]. Kolkata: Tapas Chakraborty, APDR.

"Assam: Bleed and burn" (2003) in *Eastern Panorama,* December.

Balagopal, K. *et al.,* (1996): *Voting at the Point of a Gun: Counter-Insurgency and the Farce of Elections in Kashmir*. Mumbai: Lokshahi Hakk Sangathana.

Baruah, Sanjib (2000): *India Against Itself: Assam and the Politics of Nationality*. Delhi: OUP, 2000.

Bhattacharjee, Chandana (1996): *Ethnicity and Autonomy Movement: Case of Bodo-Kacharis of Assam*. New Delhi: Vikas.

Bhattacharya, Hiranya Kumar (1995): *Nirab Asomar Sarab Yantrana* (in Assamese) [The voice of pain of silent Assam]. Guwahati: Granthapeeth.

Bhuyan, Ajit Kumar (1993): "ULFA: Eya Netritwar Atmaraksha Ne Jatir Atmaraksha" (in Assamese) [ULFA: Is this the self-defence of the leadership or the nation?] in Ajit Kumar Bhuyan & Parag Kumar Das, *Aami Ji Katha Koisilo*. Guwahati: Purbanchal Prakash.

Budhbar (Guwahati), 26 December, 1990.

Chakrabarty, Bidyut (2002); "The 'hut' and the 'axe': The 1947 Sylhet referendum", *The Indian Economic and Social History Review*, 39 (4), October.

Cohn, Bernard (1987): *An Anthropologist among Historians and Other Essays*. Delhi: Oxford University Press.

Das, Samir Kumar (1994): *ULFA: A Political Analysis*. Delhi: Ajanta.

Das, Samir Kumar (1997): "Ethno-Ecologism: A Reconsideration of the Assam Movement (1979-1985)", *Journal of Politics*, Vol. IV, December 1997.

Das Gupta, Barun (1989): "Bodo Agitation: Background Prospects" in *Mainstream*, 24 June.

Dent, Martin J (2004): *Identity Politics: Filling the Gap between Federalism and Independence*. Aldershot: Ashgate.

Elwin, Verrier (1961): *Nagaland*. Shillong: Tribal Adviser's Secretariat.

"Fighting for survival" (1999): *Grassroots Options*, March-April.

Hewitt, Vernon (1989): "Ethnicity, Sub-Nationalism and Federalism in South Asia", Hull Papers in Indian Politics. Middlesex: Shakti Communications Ltd.

Guha, Amalendu (1977): *From Planter Raj to Swaraj: Freedom Struggle and Electoral Politics in Assam*. New Delhi: PPH.

Hazarika, Sanjoy (2000): *Rites of Passage: Border Crossings, Imagined Homelands, India's East and Bangladesh*. New Delhi: Penguin India.

Kothari, Rajni (1976): "Integration and performance: Two pivots of India's model of nation-building" in Rajni Kothari (ed.), *State and Nation-Building: A Third World Perspective*. Bombay: Allied.

Kothari, Rajni (1988): "Integration and exclusion in Indian politics", Hull papers in Indian politics. Middlesex: Shakti Communications.

Lefort, Claude (1988): *Democracy and Political Theory*, trans. by David Macey, Cambridge: Polity.

Lijphart, Arend (1996): "The puzzle of Indian Democracy: A consociational interpretation", *American Political Science Review*, 90 (2), June.

Misra, Udayon (2000): *The Periphery Strikes Back: Challenges to the Nation-State in Assam and Nagaland*. Shimla: Indian Institute of Advanced Study.

Narayan, Jayaprakash (2003): "Early barriers in politics: Time for change", *Liberal Times*, XI (4), 2003.

Parekh, Bhikhu (1993): "The cultural particularity of liberal democracy" in David Held (ed.), *Prospects for Democracy: North South East West*. Stanford, Calif.: Stanford University Press.

Phukon, Adip Kumar (2004): "Niwnuwa samasya aru Asomar goshthi-bibad" (in Assamese) [The unemployment problem and Assam's group conflicts], an interview with Hiren Gohain in *Prantashree*, January.

Routray, Bibhu Prasad (2001): "Analysing insurgency on the trail of Nagalim" in *Bharat Rakshak Monitor*, 49(2), September-October.

Saikia, Jaideep (2005): "Word as war: Resort to reason" in Imdad Hussain (ed.), *The Guwahati Declaration and the Road to Peace in Assam*. New Delhi: Akansha.

Sinha, Dipankar (1999): "Indian democracy: Exclusion and communication", *Economic and Political Weekly*, 7 August.

Tamuli, Lakshminath (n.d.): *Bastawar Bidambana* (in Assamese) [Travails of the reality]. Panbazar: Lawyer's.

Times of India (2003): "500 Hmars to take refuge in Manipur", 11 April.

Tonnies, Ferdinand (1957): *Community and Society*, trans. & ed. by Charles P Loomis. New York: Harper & Row.

3

Democracy and Marginalization

The North-east Indian Context

—ROCHANA DAS

I

The principle of democracy begins with some basic ideals. That it would ensure equality and freedom for all and, would also ensure participatory governance.

Democracy is said to be the system which ensures government for the people, of the people and by the people. But as it is practiced, it is essentially a rule by the majority which supposedly takes care of the rights and aspirations of the minorities too. It is well known that the institutions of representative democracy based on the principle of majority rule and one person-one vote generate dilemmas in multi-cultural societies, where minorities based on race or religion may be systematically deprived/ disprivileged on account of their small numbers and therefore unlikely to have their will prevail. The net result of these is marginalization of a significant section of population - political, economic and cultural often leading to internal security problems like separatism, secessionism and terrorism.

In the context of north-east India, the paper will try to examine the following issues:

(a) Whether democracy as it is practiced now represents the interests of the majority and/or the elite. As it is said 'an elite dominated democracy has also structured the pattern of political mobilization'.[1] Leaders have mobilized socio-economic groups using "multi-symbol congruence" or the manipulation of a single cultural marker. They were mere pawns in intra elite struggles than independent movements to satisfy group aspi-rations.

(b) This also brings up the question whether in a given situation "marginalization" of a specific community is real or artificial. Very often the feeling of marginalization may be created or manufactured by propagating the idea of relative deprivation, economic or otherwise. And this "manufactured marginalization" may serve as a symbol or a tool for political mobilization.

(c) Another important issue is how much is marginalisation related to bad governance. Is it a result of misgovemance irrespective of any system, democratic or otherwise? One tends to agree with Atul Kohli when he argues that unprincipled mobilization and over-politicization has led to ever increasing demands on the state seen as the controller of scarce resources.[2] The weakening of state institutions unable to accommodate and manage these conflicting demands has led to a crisis of governability.

(d) Related to these is the problem of distributive justice. Low levels of economic development and cultural diversity have reinforced existing inequalities along regional, ethnic, rural *vs.* urban and class lines. It is said that in the broader South Asian perspective, more so in the context of post-colonial societies, the assumption that democracy slows down and even hinders development resulted in a debate as to whether democracy and development are compatible.[3]

(e) Finally, globalization has also thrown up some challenges. One of the negative effects of globalization is that today the "marginalized are more marginalized" in every sense of the term as they do not have either the resources or the capability of taking up the challenges of globalization. They are more on the receiving end rather than being a partner in the whole process.

II

Democracy in India may be termed as a multifaceted and multilayered experience. On the one hand it has taken root "amidst a low income economy, widespread poverty and illiteracy and immense immense ethnic diversity".[4] On the other hand, it has failed to bring about an equal and free society even not to the extent of guaranteeing equal rights and privileges. Liberal democracy, till today, is an elite exercise. On the whole representative democracy practised in India ensures only formal-legal and not socio-economic equality.

As we have earlier noted, the end-result of all these is marginalization—pushing a particular category and/or categories of people to the periphery. An elite-centric "mainstream" is constructed. Besides, this mainstream is constituted with politically dominant and culturally homogenous categories of population. As far as South Asia is concerned the mainstream may also embrace economically weak but politically and ethnically dominant population.

Significantly, while economic marginalization may be categorised or quantified there is no foolproof yardstick to measure political or cultural marginalization. It is more a "feeling", a sort of sense of "neglect" on the part of the marginalized.

It is a fact that long-lasting democracies of the developing world failed to eliminate poverty. In a way, it seems to justify the case for incompatibility between democracy and development. One may agree with Ashutosh Varshney by saying that there is no point to argue about the relative economic merits of direct and indirect methods of poverty alleviation.[5] Part of the reason that no democracy in the developing world has successfully eliminated poverty is simply that direct methods of poverty alleviation have greater political salience in democracies, but indirect, market-based methods of poverty alleviation are both sustainable and effective.[6]

One is tempted to examine questions such as how much does democracy create marginalization? Is it such a political system which only serves the interest of the elite and the educated and the rich? Is there a basic conflict between political liberty and the fulfillment of economic needs? Are human rights and civil rights of no use to a starving people?

According to Amartya Sen, the "helpful" economic policies and circumstances that led to the success of South-east Asian countries are well understood. These include openness to competition, the issue of international markets, or high level of literacy and school education, successful land reforms and public provision of incentives for investment, exporting and industrialization.[7] He says that none of these policies is inconsistent with democracy or requires the authoritarianism that prevails in South Korea, Singapore or China.

Besides, the poor in the third world are not indifferent to political and democratic rights. The poor want both rights and better living. One tends to agree with Larry Diamond that political freedoms and liberties are permissive advantages and their effectiveness would depend on how they are exercised. He further argues that the fault lies not in democracy but in its partial implementation or hijacking by elites.[8]

Coming to India one finds that the "direct method to tackle poverty have failed to uplift the condition of the poor. These policies have always been poorly managed. Besides investments in infrastructure, primary education and basic health are subject to massive leakage, waste and inefficiencies".[9]

All these have led to natural backlashes. Real or imaginary, a substantial segment of the population particularly residing in the fringe areas were made to feel economically deprived, politically sidelined and socio-culturally suppressed. As the regional and/or caste religious leaders began to give leadership to these sort of dissatisfaction and grievances it quickly assumed a reactionary colour. Thus "in India the poor have begun organizing themselves along lines other than economic class. Identities based on caste, religion, language and so on have become rallying calls".[10]

III

The north-east region of India covering a total area of about 2,55,000 sq. km. is surrounded by Bangladesh, Bhutan, China and Myanmar. Less than one per cent of boundaries of the region are contiguous with the rest of India while remaining ninety-nine per cent are international boundaries. There is not only geographical isolation of this region but also problems of cultural and psychological integration with the mainstream. Many ethnic groups especially in the areas bordering the international boundaries have more in common regarding population living across the boundary than with the rest of India.

Francis Mading Deng, remarked, "Liberal Democracy presupposes a framework characterized by a broad consensus on the fundamental principles of nationhood, the structure of government and the shaping and sharing of power, wealth and other national resources. Where consensus on these fundamentals is lacking, and people lack even a shared sense of belonging to the nation ... parliamentary democracy under those circumstances becomes the rule of a numerical majority imposed on an alienated minority, whether numerically determined or otherwise marginalized. Such a structure cannot enjoy legitimacy or stability. This means that we must address the pending fundamental issues of nationhood before we can legitimately invoke majority votes as justification for imposing any decisions on the minority."[11]

Democracy did not really get off the ground in the north-eastern states barring Assam. Even there too the image of "democratic" India is only through the Indian electoral process. Needless to say that though the electoral system and the process of voting is a part and parcel of democratic system, the attempt to impose legitimacy through electoral process has not been successful.

As earlier mentioned, one may start with Deng's observation that "liberal democracy presupposed a framework characterized by a broad consensus on the fundamental principles of nationhood". As far as nation-building in India is concerned the north-eastern states had a very traumatic experience.

According to Bipan Chandra, "the process of nation formation depends on concrete historical development. For a nation to be formed, its economy and polity and (to some extent its) culture have to be increasingly integrated".[12] The hill people of the north-east share a racial, historical, anthropological and linguistic kinship and have long felt and continue to feel alienated from the non-Mongolian communities that generally constitute the Indian mainstream. The British policy of divide-and-rule (manifested through the imposition of inner-line permit and the Excluded Areas Act) had accentuated this alienation.

While the colonization of Indian economy, society and polity strengthened the process of Indian unification, on the other hand, "both anti-colonialism and the Indian nation" were "in part the result of the political and ideological struggle by the national movement". It was during this movement that the Indian people acquired the necessary collective self-consciousness and identity of being one nation.[13]

Most of the north-eastern states were not participant to this process of unification. Assam, however responded to the national liberation movement to some extent. But here too regional-national consciousness and pan-Indian consciousness went on simultaneously in the Assamese psyche and the former often dominated the latter.

This also brings us to an important issue: the idea and concept of the Indian nation. India can best be described as a multi-national state. The idea of a "mainstream" is absolutely absurd in this context. At the cultural level too, the idea of a great Indian tradition which essentially means a Brahmanic, Aryan and Sanskrit dominated tradition faces great challenges from the so-called little traditions. In the north-east too people have increasingly begun to align themselves with the Indo-Burman and Mongolian cultures and heritage. It is evident that in countries with ethnically mixed population, attempts by any state to compel all its members to identify with the norms of the dominant elite can lead to war, violation of human rights, genocide and mass migration. Assimilationist and/or discriminatory policies of the dominant/national elite have frequently provoked ethnic unrest and interstate conflicts in north-east India as well, where most states have ethnically interspersed populations.

It is said that in some of the north-eastern states "through Christianisation of the native tribes" they are not only cut off from the mainland of India, "but also debarred to integrate in the socio-cultural national stream. This is regarded as a major obstacle against their constitutional integration in post-independence India".[14]

It is true that Christianity had given some north-eastern communities a distinct identity and a dominant political elite. There is perhaps a sort of cultural exclusivism among the tribal communities in the hill areas, where the urban educated elite generally follow a western style of living. The general impression it creates is that the north-eastern hill people are more pro-West than pro-India. Nevertheless it is worthwhile to recall here that the north-eastern tribal leadership almost to a man repudiated the idea of a markedly Christian Tribal Crown Colony covering the north-east, Myanmar and the Chittagong Hill Tracts (CHT) with Chittagong as an outlet to the sea. Furthermore, the Meiteis, Tripuri and the Assamese insurgents are not Christians, but elements among these communities have turned to militancy and separatism as have the Naga and Mizo insurgents who are/were Christians. The roots of insurgency, whether for autonomy within India or secession from it, lie elsewhere.

As earlier mentioned, while the British policy of divide-and-rule led to the alienation of peripheral ethnic groups at different points of time, the post-independence period is generally characterized by the centralization of political and economic powers by the ruling classes. This has resulted in political and economic discontent and despair in almost all the peripheral areas.

The quasi-federal framework of the Indian polity also came as a rude shock to the north-east. Already pushed to the wall as a result of uneven economic development the regional bourgeoisie felt that they had no future in the existing federal arrangement which was heavily biased in favour of the centre. Besides almost all the north-eastern states were/are witnessing immigration on a large scale to the extent of altering or threatening to alter the demographic balance and taking over the control of the economy and politics of the constituent units. It was indeed a very "conducive" situation for the regional leadership. Among many other issues, they successfully manipulated the symbol of migration to their advantage by creating an apprehension that in no time the "indigeneous" population will be swamped by the outsiders. The fear of being marginalized in their own homeland, the threat of 'power sharing' loomed large. As a result the axe fell on the immigrants. While Assam saw the rise of the famous "Assam Agitation" against the foreigners in the late seventies, other states spearheading separatist/secessionist movements also added hatred for the outsiders to their agenda. Shunned by the "mainstream democratic" India which was indifferent to its aspirations and grievances, ethnic upsurges in the north-east have been manifested in the form of cultural revivalism in most of the north-eastern states of India.

It is said that the political participation of the electorate is crucial in a democratic society because it is only through participation that the public can choose and decide their options and interests. However it is difficult for democratic mechanisms to function under conditions where state agencies either coerce or bribe the electorate to cast their vote. Thus there is an inherent difference in the definition of "political participation" between the Indian state and the Naga people. Electoral politics defined "polities" and significantly redefined the language of political participation.[15] Politics thus became a state patronage politics.

As Sanjib Baruah observes, "political violence, murders, kidnappings, extortion by militants and militants by security forces in actual or staged encounters has become a regular news from the North East. True there is also news of elections, cease-fires and the prospects of talks with insurgents. Nevertheless no one finds the image of democratic elections being conducted by massive military presence anomalous. Nor does anyone expect talks with insurgents to bring about sustained peace. Indeed in some ways insurgencies themselves have been incorporated into the democratic process. Good political reporters of the region know the precise role that insurgent factions play in elections on the ties that they have with particular mainstream politicians".[16]

This is the paradox of insurgencies that while on one hand, "it must draw on the elected establishment",[17] on the other it must protect itself from being branded as pro-establishment. There is also a dilemma of the state response to the insurgencies in north-east India. Generally speaking it has been two fold:

(a) An increasing dependence on military and para-military forces which has sometimes led to violation of some basic human rights.
(b) Granting lavish funds to accelerate development which eventually gave rise to a sort of "dole culture".

This policy was founded on the principle that the measures to contain insurgency must proceed on two fronts. These are:

(i) To bring military pressure to bear on the militants and force them to enter into negotiations with the state in a spirit of realism and compromise; and
(ii) To create a constituency within the ethnic group with a vested interest in cooperating with the state.

As a result of all these, in the insurgency-hardened North-east, democratic India has developed a de-facto system somewhat autonomous of the formal democratically elected governance.[18] This parallel system is intricate, consisting of the army, and other military, police and intelligence units controlled by the central government with participation of the political functionaries of insurgency affected states. No doubt this parallel administration is authoritarian in nature with scant or no regard for democratic values and human rights.

There is a perception that the tacit participation of elected governments of the states to counter-insurgency operations gives at least partial legitimacy to it. Besides what is true for many regional parties in the north-east is true for the national parties as well. In the May 2001 elections former Chief Minister of Assam Sri P.K. Mahanta repeatedly accused the Congress party of having a nexus with the ULFA. Whether this is to be considered as a bankruptcy of the ideology of the insurgencies or a paradox of democracy defies an easy answer. Nevertheless all these in no way strengthen democratic institutions nor do these brighten the prospect of democratic governance.

The success of any political system democratic or otherwise is measured by the effectiveness of governance. However the whole issue of human rights assumes a peculiar meaning in the context of the north east. First of all, in the perspective of north-east the whole idea of human rights becomes relative. It is relative to the respective communities, conception of their role in Indian federal systems—political, economic and cultural. As earlier said, also important is the impact of the continuous flow of migrants on the region's demographic profile, political-economic power equation and cultural life. It is true that custodial death, "encounter" death and denial of every type of civil rights have become rampant in most of the north eastern states. It is even accused by extremist organizations particularly by the ULFA that the government has engaged "secret agents" for killing the extremists. One recent addition is the protest against the Armed Forces Special Powers Act which according to Ravi Nair violates the Indian constitution's right to life and almost all relevant international human rights.[19]

Nevertheless the violation of human rights in the north-east is seen as the necessary cost of keeping the nation safe from internal and external enemies. Thus in 1991, when the United Nations Human Rights Committee asked the Attorney General of India to explain the AFSPA (Armed Forces Special Powers Act) in terms of international human rights law, he defended it on the sole ground that it was necessary in order to prevent the secession of the north-eastern states. The government, he argued, had a duty to protect the states from internal disturbances and there was no duty under international law to allow secession.[20]

Though, keeping in mind the ground situation in the north-east, it is difficult to classify what activities of armed opposition groups should be tolerated as legitimate protests, one cannot help saying that violence is no answer to violence. In a democratic system of governance basic human rights should be available to all, terrorist or no terrorist. Resort to counter-insurgency measures solely based on violence only exposes the hollowness of our democratic values and institutions and questions the very legitimacy of an elected government.

Samir Das makes a point when he argues that "while terrorism today is universally stigmatized as democracy - enemy number one...the recent outbreaks point to the limits of our democracy"...and "since the limits are built in the basic structure itself, it may not be possible for us to meaningfully respond to the so-called terrorist phenomenon from within the same structure". He further contends that "while democracy finds it impossible to tackle the terrorist menace without ceasing to remain democratic, the challenge before democracy is how to cope with this without being undemocratic and authoritarian". The problem is that democracy in India runs the risk of slowly slipping into authoritarianism as much as insurgency, according to some commentators, has degenerated into terrorism but the state's success in handling the so-called terrorism does not always count as democracy's success.[21] As earlier mentioned, the effectiveness of any political system is measured by the qualitative level of its governance. To that extent India's problems of governability are more located in the country's political structure than socio-economic in nature. According to Atul Kohli, a highly interventionist state dealing with a poor economy has become an object of intense political competition. The spread of egalitarian political values and the opportunities provided by democracy have, in turn helped to transform what was once a heterogeneous social structure into many groups of mobilized activists. Failure of leaders to make timely concessions has only intensified political demands and activity and finally the growing weakness of fragmented political parties, which both reflects and exacerbates this process of over-politicization has made it difficult for leaders to rule effectively.[22] Together with economic under-development, bad governance or the failure of the strategies of democratic management have led the wounds of north-east to fester. This has intensified the feeling of "marginalization", ultimately leading to separatists, and secessionist activities of varied kinds.

As it is known that one of the effects of globalization, economic reforms, have emerged from above - through policy initiatives taken by governments and encouraged by international financial institutions.[23] As Ashutosh Varshney has argued, "it has to be more clearly demonstrated in the political not economic realm that reforms are not only about economic efficiency but also about enhancing mass welfare especially that of the poor".[24]

As of now particularly in India, including the north-east the masses are "precipitously" worse off. The benefits of economic growth, however small, have not been distributed evenly. Ethnic minorities rural and tribal populations, women and other disadvantaged groups lag behind - economically politically and socially. As earlier said in the context of north-east India the issue of accentuated disparity has serious fall outs in the nature of wide spread frustrations, narco-terrorism and AIDS. The delicate social fabric of north-east has become vulnerable to disruptions of a large scale.

The overbearing attitude of the USA to promote political democracy in South Asia and Asia-Pacific regions could considerably increase political instability and thus possibly retard democratic institutions taking hold in the area. Recognition is needed that the state system will be better able to cope with and manage both ethnic diasporas and ethnic separatism if more emphasis is given to strengthening of individual states rather than to the inevitable deterioration of state power in the face of globalization.

Democracy and development is compatible because the ultimate goal of development is to build human capabilities, to create a safe and secure environment where citizens can live in freedom and with dignity and equality. This is one of the major goals of democracy too. Nevertheless, raising a country's GNP is one of the essential means towards achieving overall development. Holistic and participatory development which requires use of democratic strategies of mobilization needs much broader policy interventions.

The main reason for human deprivation is not just economic. These problems go hand-in-hand with socio-political factors rooted in poor governance. Governance is a continuous process through which conflicting or diverse interests may be accommodated and co-operative action may be taken.[25] It is here that the Indian democratic system has failed. There is not only a failure of strategies of unification; even fifty plus years of independence have failed to develop true democratic values and behaviour. The gradual turn of events since independence shows that local issues including caste and ethnicity have come to centre stage at the cost of national issues. Contemporary India of over half-a-century is indeed a grown-up democracy and perhaps needs a radical transformation in its federal structure for constitutional integration of its entire population.

NOTES AND REFERENCES

1. This argument is developed by Atul Kohli in his edited work, *The Success of India's Democracy*, Cambridge University Press, 2001.
2. Cited from Niraja Gopal Jayal (ed.). *Democracy in India*, Oxford University Press, New Delhi, 2001, p. 25.
3. *Ibid.*, p. 5.
4. Atul Kohli (ed.). *The Success of India's Democracy*, Cambridge University Press, 2001, p. 1.
5. Ashutosh Varshney, "Why Have Poor Democracies Not Eliminated Poverty?", A Suggestion', *Asian Survey*, Vol. XI, No.5, Sept-Oct, 2000, p. 723.
6. *Ibid.*, pp. 723-24.
7. Cited from, S.L. Rao, 'Is Democracy Good for the Poor? Power *versus* Poverty', *The Telegraph*, 23 May, 2005, p. 18.
8. *Ibid., The Telegraph.*
9. This is the opinion of Ashutosh Varshney. Cited from The Telegraph, 23 May, 2005, p. 18.
10. *Ibid.*
11. Francis Deng (1967-69). Cited from Dolly Kikon, 'Carnival of Nationalism from the North-eastern Frontiers of India: Interpreting Naga Nationalism: Questioning Indian autonomy and Three Suggestions for the Indo-Naga Peace Talk'. http://www.nscnonline.org/webpage/Article/Carnival_of_nationalism.htm
12. Bipan Chandra, 'Will the Indian Nation Hold', Miscellany, *The Statesman*, June 7, 1992.

13. *Ibid.*
14. R. Upadhyay, Manipur - In a Strange whirlpool of Cross-Current Insurgency, 13/paper 1210.html
15. n.11.
16. Sanjib Baruah, Generals as Governors: The Parallel Political Systems of North East India. http://www.himalmag.com/june 2001/essay.html
17. *Ibid.*
18. *Ibid.*
19. Ravi Nair, South Asian Human Rights Documentation Centre, New Delhi. Cited from Sanjib Baruah, 'Generals as Governors: The Parallel Political Systems of North East India'. http://www.himalmag.com/june2001/essay.html.
20. Sanjib Baruah, 'Generals as Governors: The Parellel Political Systems of North East India'. http://www.himalmag.com/june2001/essay.html
21. Samir Das, Terrorism and the Limits of Democracy: The Case of Contemporary Assam', in Omprakash Mishra and Sucheta Ghosh (ed.), *Terrorism and Law Intensity Conflict in South Asian Region*, Manak Publications, New Delhi: 2003, pp. 474, 484-85.
22. Atul Kohli, '*Democracy and Discontent: India's Growing Crisis of Governability*', Orient Longman, New Delhi, 1987.
23. n.5, p. 735.
24. n.5, p. 736.
25. Deepak K. Mishra and Vandana Upadhyay, 'Governance and Development in Arunachal Pradesh: The Emerging Challenges. *Dialogue*, April-June 2004, Vol. 5, No. 4, http://www.asthabharati.org/Dia_Apr04/deepak.htm.

4

The Emergence of "Ethnic" Conflicts in Central Asia

—ANITA SENGUPTA

There is today an increasing focus on the emergence of "ethnic" conflicts in Central Asia. This is inevitably linked to the political role that Islam plays in the region and stresses on the fact that the "ethnic" and the "religious" will play an important part in social collisions in the future.[1] A group of scholars thus point to the distinct possibility of an Islamic *Jihad,* particularly in Tajikistan. This is because, in Tajikistan, since independence a pro-Communist government has been seen as being faced with what is identified as an "Islamic" opposition.[2] And therefore the focus on the "religious" and the "ethnic" as the root cause of conflicts affecting the security of the states in the region.

The most widely held conception about "religious" and "ethnic" conflicts in the states of the former Soviet Union is that the current unrest is the direct result of the disintegration of the former Soviet Union where there has been a "national revival" of cultures that had long been suppressed by the Soviet system. This, however, is a rather simplistic position that requires critical examination. From early Tsarist times, the expanding Muscovite state incorporated numerous distinct groups. The early Bolshevik policy of declared support for the national aspirations of these groups was tempered by a policy where delimitation into distinct territories became significant. On the other hand, social and economic policy over the years fostered the emergence of local elites, who though strictly tied to the party apparatus, became crucial in the local structures of power. When the Soviet Union disintegrated, power structures were based on these local structures, which had been the traditional relays of political and economic control. What appeared as the "reemergence" of the "ethnic" factor could well be the result of this political mobilization.

In any case the first question that requires attention is the extent to which the conflicts can be defined as "ethnic". Here, the possibility that ethnicity may have become a useful though simplifying catch all for different kinds of conflicts remains. In fact the only potential conflict that could be defined as "ethnic" would be an Uzbek-Tajik conflict. However, it has been noted that an emphasis on this divide, even in the case of the Tajik conflict, would be to ignore the reality of the fact that alliances often cut across ethnic lines. The Uzbeks in Leninabad behaved no differently from the Tajiks in the regions. On the other hand the Pamiris joined the Islamic Opposition though as Ismailis they are the most secular group. Similarly, the Uzbek support for the pro-Nabiev Popular Front, during the Tajik conflict, was less a reflection of support for the ethnic Uzbeks within the Tajik state than of the recognition that an anti-government challenge, by a coalition of secular and Islamic forces across the borders, could have significant impact for the Uzbek Government itself.

This paper is an attempt at critically examining the reemergence of "ethnic" factors in Central Asian conflicts. It shows how local traditions and social heritages as also linkages need to be reexamined in order to make a correct assessment of the situation. It begins with a general examination of "ethnic" linkages and then goes on to show that, what is seen as an extension of "religious" and "ethnic" conflict in Tajikistan actually has its roots in secular causes. An examination of the nature of affiliation and a chronology of events leading to the Tajik conflict provides a context of analysis of the problem. In the course of this examination, it becomes evident that it was the mobilization of "ethnic" identities and the creation of new identities, in many cases as a result of relocation of groups that became crucial in the course of the conflict.

A study of the Tajik Civil War allows alternative interpretations of issues like "ethnic identity" and "religious revival". The Tajik conflict is also interesting since it is posited as a typical example of a post-colonial conflict where a "weak state" with non-existent "national identity" erupted into conflict. What remains unrecognized is the process of reconciliation through peace talks that brought an end to the conflict by recognizing that while the construction of a "national identity" remains important, amorphous local linkages are also significant as constituting the basis of identity. It was this recognition that ensured the success of the peace process and in the course of looking into global alternatives these local initiates and alternatives could prove useful.

Ethnies and the Nation-State

The emergence of new states in Eurasia has meant that once again reconfiguration of states on the basis of ethnicity has come into focus in the process of the formation of states. Of course "ethnicity" and particularly "majority ethnicities" had always defined nation-states. However, the formation of the "nation-state" had somehow signaled that problems of ethnicity within states had been resolved. The underlying assumption behind this was the fact that once the "nation" had been formed the need to take recourse to "reconstructed" ethnic pasts would no longer be significant. Yet, it is noted that recent events seem to point out that modern nations and nationalism have only deepened the meanings and scope of older ethnic concepts and structures.

While the existence of numerous groups within the territorial limits of the states is a reality, from the perspective of the modern nation-state the existence of ethnically distinct "sub-national" groups, particularly when they are politically organized, is always seen to represent a potential threat and as a destabilizing force. This is specially the case when power in the state rests principally with a dominant or majority ethnic group, or when the national society itself constitutes an ethnically stratified system. Indeed, it is noted, that it is within the idea of a nation-state itself that the possibility of ethnic conflict remains inherent since within a world territorially divided into a number of political units there exist, numerous groups who do not identify with the dominant model of the nation-state or who are not accepted as full members of this state or the nation which it purports to be or represent, or who are actually excluded from it.

In fact, today it is a truism that few states are "nation-states" in the sense of their territories being congruent with their ethnic populations. Not only are ethnic populations of most states mixed, as most states today have significant ethnic minorities, but they are also deeply divided. Boundaries of states do not coincide with the extent of any single ethnic population. And within each "nation state" are fully-fledged nations, *ethnie* and ethnic groups. However, the nationalist political demand remains that groups with historical myths of common origin, culture and destiny should rule themselves and that political boundaries should be coterminous with cultural boundaries. This is because while nationalism is a political identification, at its core lies a cultural claim that national movements are motivated by a desire to assume the existence and flourishing of a particular community, culture, tradition and language identified with a particular "ethnic" group.

Ethnic groups are formed and acquire their identities as a result of different historical processes. Thus, some ethnies have ancient origins and are able to trace their ancestry continuously from earlier times to the present. Others have been constituted more recently. While most nations argue that they consist of ancient ethnies, in most situations, modern ethnies develop as a result of structural changes in their countries. This is true of the Central Asian states today, all of which claim continuous descent from ancient times and note that the ancient homelands coincide with the limits of the modern state.

One of the most significant problems that any examination of the ethnic question involves, is a determination of the clarity in the concepts of ethnie, ethnic groups, people, nation, nationality, community, clan and tribe. Here, a significant difficulty lies in the fact that the terminology used by scholars frequently reflects regional or national intellectual traditions or ideologies. For example, the connotation of the word tribe, used principally to denote groups in Africa and Asia, reflects the nineteenth century imperial ideas about these groups as lacking any organization or structures of governance. A correct understanding of the terms is therefore crucial in any analysis. In the Tajik case a correct understanding of the word clan assumes significance since scholars like Ahmad Rashid have noted that the "civil war was a battle of clans". Clans generally denote a unit of social action whose solidarity is based on kinship or a kinship like form of solidarity. Among the Uzbeks and the Tajiks clans in the strict sense of the term does not exist. What are present are lineages of various sorts known as *qawm, taifa* or *avlod*. As Shahram Akbarzadeh notes, what have been identified as "clans", in the Central Asian region are a collection of separate extended families living in the same area though subsequent intermarriage could lead familial bonds.[3] Patron/client relationships and local alliances that are today dubbed as "clans" actually represent geographically based factions among the elite.

Kamolouddin Abdoullaev, a professor of history at the Tajikistan State University, points out that in all the post-Soviet states today the paradigm of class-consciousness has been replaced by ethnicity and ethnic nationalism has emerged as the dominant ideology. Replacing the proletariat and his ally the peasant, the "ethnic person" is gradually becoming a central and dynamic figure in events throughout the former Soviet Union.[4] He goes on to say:

> Ethnicity may be said to represent an inheritable group solidarity based on common origin, culture and historic destiny. In other words ethnicity emerges as a social instinct of a collective way of life. A positive feature of ethnicity is that it is an important means of group adaptation to the surrounding world, helping it to survive under difficult political and economic conditions. Hence the instinct of group identity appears as an instinct for national self-preservation.[5]

The significance of the relationship between the ethnies and the nation-state lies in the fact that it has been traditionally assumed that it is either with the transformation of an ethnic group in a multi-ethnic state into a self-conscious political entity or by the amalgamation of diverse groups and the formation of an inter ethnic, composite or homogeneous national culture through the agency of the modern state that a nation is formed. The latter which is also identified as a "state to nation" model gives a strong role to the state in the construction of the new civic nations and political communities. Although the "state to nation" route was historically territorial it has always included within it cultural elements. The political nation therefore always incorporated both civic and ethnic factors based usually upon the ethnic core that created the state.

Another factor that has to be kept in mind is that objective ethnic attributes and collective identities are never permanent unchanging feature of groups. Culturally transmitted identities often become politicized and in fact an understanding of this transition is crucial since in a number of situations failure to identify this transition or a lack of understanding of these changes lead to conflicts. The next section will show how a transformation of Tajik "ethnic" identity becomes crucial in the course of the conflict and how a reordering of identities induced by the Soviet system, through population displacements and the reformation of groups around the *kolkhozes,* becomes significant. Here, a *kolkhoz* became either the expression of a solidarity group old or new, or the object of a power struggle between rival groups who are thus inclined to identify themselves with ethnic or political opposition conceptualized elsewhere. The "clans" that went to war in Tajikistan were solidarity groups or parallel power networks organized around the administrative and economic assets of the Soviet state.

However, it must also be kept in mind that ethnic and cultural diversity by itself does not lead to conflict between groups. [6] In most cases ethnic conflicts pit specific groups against an ethnocratic state, that is a nation state controlled by a dominant ethnie. In any case it has to be kept in mind that there are different kinds of ethnic groups and different kinds of conflict. In numerous cases ethnic minorities who are marginalized or discriminated against may organize or mobilize in order to achieve parity. Such civic and political movements do not necessarily lead to conflict but they may evolve into conflict if the legitimate demands of the groups are not met. A different kind of situation obtains when a subordinate ethnic minority demands recognition of its group rights by the state, relating to a recognition of the distinctiveness of the group. Other kinds of conflicts occur between politicized ethnic groups that compete for state power within the framework of the modern electoral process or by extra legal means.

The Reemergence of "Ethnic" Conflicts

Irina Zviagelskaya points to a number of conflict generating factors that helped to trigger the Tajik conflict and kept it alive for a long time:

1. Contradictions between clans inside Tajikistan.
2. Interethnic tensions.
3. Ideological confrontation (the conservatives including the adherents of communist ideology *versus* democrats and Islamists).[7]

She notes that, in actual fact, all these dimensions were present in the course of the conflict. The Tajik conflict presented a model of a complicated mix of traditional and modern factors. She goes on to note that it would also be wrong to see the conflict in terms of a rebellion of a traditional society against modernization, helped by Islamist propaganda. Zviagelskaya writes:

> In Tajikistan the conflict assumed a clear-cut regional tenor because the country has a fragmented society with minimum of countrywide identification. The Tajiks prefer to identify themselves according to the region, locality, village or city of their origin. They would rather say that "I am a Kulyabi or a Penjekenti" than "I am a Tajik". The latter

identification is used only for outsiders. For the Tajik population it lacks informative substance, whereas local identification can say more about the person than official biodata.[8]

A brief examination of what is identified as "ethnic conflict" in Tajikistan would be an useful pointer to the complexities inherent in the situation. Since the existence of local affinities or regionalism is noted as the most crucial factor in the emergence of the conflict, this section begins with a brief look at the four regions that are said to exist within Tajikistan. However, it would not be entirely correct to assign affinities in "regional" terms alone. For one, there are cleavages within the regions themselves. Gorno Badakshan, for instance, itself divides into various linguistic and religious groups.[9] In the western Pamirs various eastern and western Iranian languages are spoken. In Darvaz and Vanj, Tajik is widely spoken while in other districts the so called Pamiri dialects, sometimes defined as mountain Tajik are used like Shugnan, Ishkashimi, Bartangi. In the eastern Pamirs, Kyrgyz is the language most widely heard since the overwhelming majority of the population is Kyrgyz. The religion of the majority of the people is Ismaili, a moderate form of Shiaism. Only in the districts of Darvaz and Vanj as well as in the Kyrgyz settlement areas most people are Sunni.

The nature of the four main opposition groups that emerged in the post-independence period, is also reflective of this. Though generally implied to represent regional factions and interests and concentrated in certain regions, they actually represented a combination of tendencies. The Islamic Renaissance Party was established in 1991 and its leader Muhammedsharif Khimmatzoda is from the Garm region. The Democratic Party of Tajikistan, which was established with the purpose of establishing a democratic electoral system and protection of basic human rights, is headed by Shodmun Usupov also from the Garm region. Both of these parties derive most of their support from the Garm region. The *Rastokhez,* or Rebirth Party, was created as a nationalist party calling for a cultural revival within the country and also derives its support from the Garm region. *Lali Badakshan* (Ruby of Badakshan), the only party with a regional agenda, advances the rights of the Pamiris (natives of Gorno Badakshan) of the Autonomous Republic and demands greater autonomy for the region. These parties formed a coalition for the Presidential election of November 1991 and were known as the Islamic Democratic Opposition.[10]

This, however, does not reduce the significance of regional politics and the fact that geography has played a significant role in determining the nature of alliances. The Leninabad oblast is situated in the north-west of the state bordering Uzbekistan and the Ferghana Valley. This region dominated Tajik politics since the creation of the Republic in 1929. The Kulyab faction is from the oblast of that name centered in Southern Tajikistan. Both of these regions are of a pro - communist orientation historically and have been over represented in the former Soviet Government. The two other regions are where the opposition is centered. The Kurgan Tyube oblast has been a stronghold of Islamic piety and is the Islamic Renaissance Party's stronghold. The region contains many of the Garmis (a term that includes the natives of the areas of Qarategin, Wakhiha and Darwaz) who were relocated in the 1940's and 1950's to provide labour for the cotton fields in the Southern Vakhsh Valley. In the course of the transfer of populations, mountain Tajiks were moved en mass from their resource poor homelands to newly irrigated areas in the plains. Most of these people came from the Garm region, Gorno Badakshan and Maschah sub-division of the upper Zarafshan valley. Many were also moved from Kulyab. They were mostly moved to Kurgan Tyube, a barren arid area mainly populated by nomads, many of whom had fled to Afghanistan during the suppression of the *basmachi* revolt. The lack of assimilation of these peoples with other groups within the region has meant that a separate Garmi identity is still present here.[11] The importance of Islamic religion to this separate identity divides them even further from the rest of the population. The Pamiri people of Gorno Badakshan feel that they are a different group of people from the ethnic Tajiks and the demands of the *Lali Badakshan* Party has been for greater autonomy. Although the two latter regions form the centre of the opposition they should not be confused. Kurgan Tyube and the Garm region are Sunni Muslim. The Pamiris who live in the east are Ismailis and speak Eastern Iranian languages and not Farsi. What they have in common is the common grievance of a history of discrimination.

In fact in the Tajik case, geography has been identified as a crucial factor in the lack of contact among the people and the resultant low level of integration. Over 90 per cent of the Republic is mountainous. The Autonomous Oblast of Badakshan, for instance, is situated in the Pamir highlands. The northern oblast of Leninabad is located at the entrance of the Ferghana Valley and separated by mountain ranges from the rest of Tajikistan, with the only pass connecting the region being closed throughout winter. This has meant that traditionally there has been a lack of central control at the margins of the state. It has been noted that just as central newspapers from Dushanbe do not reach Khojent, Dushanbe's rule does not extend over the Zarafshan range into Leninabad.[12] The conspicuous absence of central newspapers outside Dushanbe is significant if one accepts that the emergence of print capitalism is assumed to be a principal requirement for the emergence of a "imagined community."[13]

Geographical disparities, in Tajikistan, are similarly bolstered by lack of economic development at the margins. It has been pointed out that unemployment is highest in the southern oblasts of Kurgan Tyube, Kulyab and the Autonomous Oblast of Badakshan.[14] Tajikistan, had in many respects a typical colonial economy. Two principal areas of the country, the Ferghana Valley in the north (the Leninabad oblast) and the Vaksh-Panj Valleys in the south (mainly Kurgan Tyube oblast) became part of the Central Asian cotton bowl. The Ferghana Valley received the bulk of the republic's industrial investment, largely in their production of cotton textiles, but there was also significant industry in the Hissar valley near Dushanbe. In the rural areas, the population was subject to different incentives and control. A substantial part of the rural population's income came from private plots or other forms of petty commodity production or private exchange.[15] This in its turn produced overpopulation, disguised rural unemployment and hence pressure on the land. This increased competition for resources led to conflicts among different groups, mainly between different *kolkhozes* and their sub-divisions, the *qishlaks,* which tended to have uniform ethnic population. Hence these took on the appearance of "ethnic" conflicts.

The competition for influence in the state, however, is not only based on regional ties but also on linkages to the former Communist Party and therefore the extent of share in political power and resources. The antagonism between the Pamiris from Badakshan and the Kulyabis is a case in point. In order to ensure Badakshani loyalty during the Afghan war, the Badakshan regional elite were given important positions within the Ministry of Interior at the expense of the Kulyab faction. This shift of traditional privileges appears to have become one of the exacerbating factors that furthered the enmity between the two groups. During the Tajik Civil War, the Kulyabis represented the main fighting force of the government viewing it as an opportunity not only to regain political influence but as a chance to enhance it.[16]

Commenting on this V.I. Bushkov and D.V. Mikalsky, Russian specialists in ethnology,

> In Tajikistan regionalism is also manifested in the fact that people originating from different localities, or even villages, have special social niches assigned to them. Those from Leninabad have had a monopoly on party and government posts and often became managers of various enterprises including those situated in the south. People from Karategin used to control the consumers unions and the entire trading system. Until recently (i.e, 1991) the rank and field sergeants of the internal security forces were recruited mostly from the Kulyabis. When M Navjuvanov, a Pamiri, became Minister of Interior, his compatriots began to drive the Kulyabis out of this sphere. [17]

It is obvious that a system like the one cited above may be challenged on many accounts, the most common ones being the growing strength of one of the partners or attempts to divide the sphere of influence. After the dissolution of the Soviet Union and the declaration of independence, these possibilities became more apparent. A brief description of events leading up to the conflict clearly illustrates this.

Shortly after independence the new President of the Republic, Kadriddin Aslonov, who had replaced the former First Secretary of the Tajik Communist Party (CPT), banned the CPT and allowed the registration of opposition parties. However, this flourishing of democracy was short lived and brought to an abrupt end by Aslonov's dismissal and his replacement by Rakhman Nabiev in November 1991. Nabiev defeated the Opposition candidate Davlat Khudonazarov, a Badakshani. The fact that Khudonazarov was from Badakshan and an Ismaili was extensively used in the propaganda against him. Safarali Kenjaev was elected Chairman of the Supreme Soviet of Tajikistan. His appointment led to a fresh crisis as in the March of 1992 he attacked the Minister of Interior Affairs, Mamadaez Navjuanov, a Pamiri and questioned his Tajik identity and relieved him of his duties.

The Badakshani youth took to the streets demanding the reinstallation of Navjuanov. In the course of this *Lali Badakshan* a socio cultural club, joined the Badakshan youth and was transformed into a political movement. Opposition to the government became more entrenched when Kazikalon Akbar Turajanzade's (the highest Islamic authority in the Republic and a deputy to the legislature and who had been nominated as a candidate for the first Presidential elections) suggestions, in March 1991, for incorporating a number of symbolic changes to accommodate Tajikistan's Islamic character, was rejected by the Parliament. This refusal incited Turajanzade to forbid *imams* from performing *janaza* for the communists. This unprecedented action led to an uproar following which he withdrew his *fatwa*. The next year there was crisis once again as Turajanzade's attempts to ban the Communist Party of Tajikistan led to further crisis.

Pro-and anti-government forces took to the streets with the pro-government forces demanding the removal of Turajazade. A Government of National Reconciliation was eventually formed in May 1992 to get over the crisis. However, neither Leninabad nor Kulyab accepted the compromise. Armed activism began in Kulyab with the creation of the Popular Front. Since the government was in disarray, the only forces capable providing a brake to the Popular Front were the self-defence units in Kurgan Teppe, Garm and Badakshan. The most effective led by Abdullah Nuri was able to push the Front out of Vaksh. This transformed the conflict into one that posed the Kulyabi's against the Pamiris and Garmis. President Nabiyev was forced to resign and this led to the loss of credibility of the Government of National Reconciliation. Akbarsho Iskandarov, a Badakshani, took over as acting President. The coalition government that was formed tried to reconcile Leninabadis by bringing a leading Leninabad figure, Abdulmalik Abduljanov as Prime Minister and Chairman of the Council of the Council of Ministers.

Unable to defeat the Kulyabi Popular Front, that was being reinforced by Russian military hardware, the coalition of opposition parties resigned at the 26th Convention of the Parliament in Khojent. The assembly reaffirmed Abduljanov as Chairman of the Council of Ministers and voted for Imamali Rakhmanov to chair the legislature and head the state. The new government was however, staffed exclusively by ministers from Kulyab and Leninabad and could enter Dushanbe only after bloody clashes between the opposition and the Popular Forces. The Front's military campaign carried out reprisal attacks for those who sympathized with the opposition, particularly Garmis and Badakshanis. After the fall of Dushanbe in December 1991, most opposition sympathizers left the capital. The civil war that followed led to massive deaths, displacement and loss of property.

It would probably not be incorrect to note that the key to the Tajik conflict lay not in "ethnic" affinities but in localism, that is factions defined by geographical origin reshaped and restructured by population displacements.[18] Almost all the officials of the IRP are Garmis and almost all the current leaders of the country are Kulyabis or come from Leninabad province. Similarly the two main solidarity groups involved in the current conflict are primarily defined by geographical origin, the Kulyab Valley and the Garm Valley. This phenomenon of regional identity occurs throughout Central Asian society. Further, social restructuring, brought about by the Soviet regime through collectivization and the role of *kolkhozes* in the formation of community identity, reduced the significance of the older clan affiliations. Nevertheless, relations between older segmentations and newer identities remained significant.

The violence was thus less a clash of traditional "ethnic" groups than of groups formed by restructuring within the framework of the Soviet system.[19] This system, through collectivization and *kolkhozes* "territorialized" solidarities and made them depend on a single source and collective framework for the distribution of goods and access to wealth. In the Soviet system social existence and economic survival were dependent on belonging to a collective. These collectives eventually transformed themselves into clans. The Soviet state itself was a powerful factor in turning society into networks. This territorialization in its turn was supported by developmental policies that could only be implemented by moving people from mountainous areas, where the birth rate was high but opportunities for development was weak, to regions where opportunities for cultivation were higher. These displaced groups however, failed to merge with the local populations but instead solidified their identities according to their region of origin. The Kulyabi identity, for instance was forged in the 1930's when people were brought down from the foothills to develop dried up marshes. The province of Kurgan Tyube was latter settled by people from Garm and Kulyab. The valleys where they were resettled were not uninhabited and the groups who populated them were already sedentarised in relatively homogeneous *kolkhozes*. When the two new groups were resettled in the *kolkhoz*, instead of blurring differences, each group formed its own *mahallah* where there were very few intermarriages.

The resultant development of patron client networks in regional administration has also been considered to be significant. However, once again it should be noted that similar networks were extensive all over Central Asia. It was the Soviet experience, of rule from Moscow, that created a need for the creation of informal relations at various levels and very particularly at the level of regional officials. Regional offices were staffed by people loyal to regional leaders as the most effective means of countering Moscow's unceasing demands for higher production rates. The exposure of "clan" based groupings during the "cotton affair" brought this common practice to light. This tended to be a self perpetuating circle, in which regional cadres promoted members of their clique for top positions, and they in their turn depended on the support of the cadres to stay on top and negotiate with republican authorities.

Another reason for the weakness in the development of a common "Tajik" identity is said to lie in a lack of social cohesion, which, in turn, meant that common perceptions of a Tajik nation failed to develop. It is generally assumed that cohesive tendencies within the civil society are crucial for the development of social cohesion. The term civil society is used to describe the social relations and structures that lie between the state and the market. Civil society delineates a sphere that is formally distinct from the body politic and state authority on the one hand and from the immediate pursuit of self-interest and the imperatives of the market on the other. Its voluntary associations, interest groups and social movements always strive to maintain a measure of autonomy from the public affairs of politics and the private concerns of economics.[20] It has been noted, that it is possibly in the existence or lack of a civil society that explanations for conflicts lie. In the Central Asian context, it would mean that the existence of civil society institutions in Uzbekistan and the lack of viability of such institutions in Tajikistan would explain the differences in the levels of cohesion.

However, prior to an examination of such a proposition, the concept of civil society in the Central Asian context requires attention. In the specifically Central Asian context civil society developed in the form of *mahallahs*. Most visitors to the region would notice that houses are built close to one other and that common walls shared by adjoining houses often have small doors through which the intercourse of daily life continues. The importance of this social bondage, in the *mahallah* was recognized as crucial by the Soviets and continues to be important even today. As an extended household that shares its daily joys and sorrows it plays an important role in the maintenance of social conformity. This social conformity that the members of the *mahallah* enforced was considered important by the Soviet power for the maintenance of social order. And it was the development of social cohesiveness through the institution of the *mahallah* that the Uzbek state was able to appropriate in the course of nation building. Recent research on the Uzbek economy has stressed that the informal groupings among groups in the *mahallah* also plays an economic role by providing support in times of financial stress or festivals and ceremonies.[21]

However, civil society is subject to the same contradictory imperatives of autonomy and determination that characterize all intermediate spheres. And in the Tajik situation *mahallahs* actually represented and exacerbated the cleavages that had developed as a result of a variety of factors. Resettled groups formed their own *mahallahs* that remained segregated from those of the local population. Whether this was primarily the cause of the reorganization of identities in the course of population movements requires attention. In any case a multiplicity of factors should be taken into account in any examination of the nature of societal cohesiveness and assimilation of groups within states.

Conclusions

It is undeniable that the Central Asian states like Tajikistan, did not inherit a modern "national" identity that was uniform throughout its population. Here, attachments to region, for instance, persisted. While these attachments and the resultant multiple identities remain problematic, there is now recognition of their salience in Tajikistan, for instance, through partial regional representation in the Lower House (*Majlisi Namoyondagon*) of the Supreme Legislature *(Majlisi Oli)*. This is indicative of the fact that while efforts at the construction of a new civic loyalty will continue, it is not necessary that in the course of this construction, the amorphous linkages that actually constitute the basis of identity will be completely transformed. Recognition of these local specificities provides better understanding of the nuances of broader questions of identity and also alternative ways of dealing with issues that are today of global concern.

NOTES AND REFERENCES

1. See for instance, Peter King and Olga Orkunova (eds.) *Ethnicity and Conflict in a Post-Communist World: The Soviet Union, Eastern Europe and China*, New York: St Martin's Press, 1992.
2. See for instance, Allen Hetmanek, "Islamic Revolution and Jihad Come to the Former Soviet Central Asia: The case of Tajikistan," *Central Asian Survey*, Vol. 12, No. 3, 1993; Dilip Hiro, "Islamic Strengths and Weaknesses in Central Asia," *Middle East International*, No. 443, 5 February, 1993.
3. Shahram Akbarzadeh,"Why did Nationalism Fail in Tajikistan?" *Europe Asia Studies*, Vol. 48, No. 7, 1996.
4. Kamoulouddin Abdoullaev, "The Civil War in Tajikistan", *Journal of the TODA Institute for Global Peace and Policy Research*, Vol. 3, No. 1, Spring 1998.
5. Abdoullaev, "The Civil War in Tajikistan".
6. For details see, Rodolfo Stavenhagen, *Ethnic Conflicts and the Nation State*, London: Macmillian, 1996.
7. Irina Zviagelskaya, *The Tajik Conflict*, Scientific Publication of the Russian Centre for Strategic Research and International Studies, Joint Edition with Ithaca Press, Reading, UK, Moscow, 1997.
8. Zviagelskaya, *The Tajik Conflict*.
9. For details and a map see Hiltrud Herbers,"Transformation in the Tajik Pamirs: Gornyi Badakshan — An Example of Successful Restructuring?," *Central Asian Survey*, Vol. 20, No. 3, 2001.
10. John Glenn, *The Soviet Legacy in Central Asia*, Basingstoke: Macmillan, 1999.

11. Barnett R. Rubin,"Russian Hegemony and State Breakdown in the Periphery: Causes and Consequences of the Civil War in Tajikistan", in Barnett R. Rubin and Jack Snyder (eds.) *Post-Soviet Political Order: Conflict and State Building*, London and New York: Routledge, 1998.
12. Shahram Akbarzadeh, "Why did Nationalism Fail In Tajikistan?" *Europe Asia Studies*, Vol. 48, No. 7, 1996.
13. Benedict Anderson, *Imagined Communities — Reflections on the Origin and Spread of Nationalism*, London: New Left Books, 1983.
14. "Za Dva Shaga do Bezrabotitsy", *Narodnaya Gazeta*, 24 December, 1991, cited in Akbarzadeh, *op cit.*
15. Rubin, "Russian Hegemony and State Breakdown in the Periphery: Causes and Consequences of the Civil War in Tajikistan". (See note 11).
16. Refer to Shahrbanou Tadjbakhsh,"National Reconciliation: The Imperfect Whim", *Central Asian Survey*, Vol. 15, No. 3/4, 1996.
17. Cited in Zviagelskaya, *The Tajik Conflict.*
18. Olivier Roy, "Is the Conflict in Tajikistan a Model for Conflicts Throughout Central Asia?" in Mohammad Reza Djalili, Frederic Grare and Shirin Akiner (eds.) *Tajikistan, The Trails of Independence*, Surrey: Curzon, 1998. (See note 18)
19. Roy, "Is the Conflict in Tajikistan a Model for Conflicts Throughout Central Asia?".
20. John Ehrenberg, *Civil Society: The Critical History of an Idea*, New York and London: New York University Press, 1999.
21. Deniz Kandiyoti,"Rural Livelihoods and Social Networks in Uzbekistan: Perspectives from Andijan", *Central Asian Survey*, Vol. 17, No. 4, December 1998.

5

Islam, Nationalism and Democracy

—SANJUKTA BANERJI BHATTACHARYA

Nationalism and democracy are terms coined in the West and relates to the social and political formations of Western states. However, there is a certain universality to these terms, specially in the context of the twentieth and twenty-first centuries, with the democratization venture following the collapse of the Soviet Union and the attempt to create national unity in the post-colonial world in the second half of the previous century. It must be noted at the outset that although the concepts of nationalism and democracy have an universal appeal today, there is a wide variance in the forms in which they are adapted in different countries. National feelings in Third World states for instance, are often filtered through several layers of affiliations based on multiple identities. Further, no two democracies are alike, whether in the West or the East. The United Kingdom's (U.K.) governance is marked by a greater degree of social welfare activity than that of the United States (U.S.), while people's participation through the system of primaries is quite unique to the U.S. So far as states with Muslim majorities are concerned, the religion of Islam shaped their polity, and the historical context of the socio-political development of these countries is very different from the countries which coined the terms nationalism and democracy. However, many states with a Muslim majority population now follow some of the basic practices of democracy, and despite the transnationalism of Islam, Islamic and Muslim states have all developed a stake in their own countries. This paper will examine whether Islam is compatible with democratization and the modern concept of a nation-state. But first, an understanding of the basic tenets of Islam in the context of the nation and the state is in order.

The Concepts of Nation and State and the Basic Tenets of Islam

According to some scholars, there was an extraordinary silence in the 1970s and 1980s on the issue of nationalism among political scientists.[1] One reason could be that nationalism was blamed for the onset of the Second World War, and as such statesmen paid no attention to national self-determination when dividing Germany and Korea. Also, there was a strong impact of economics in the field of the social sciences, and topics like nationalism were obscured by economic analyses. In addition, the discipline of International Relations (IR), which developed in the post-war period, concentrated on state centric forces, ignoring the role of non-state actors and individuals in relations among states.

However, the relevance of nationalism, especially nationalist conflict, can be seen in international relations, particularly from the time of the French Revolution. In recent times, there has been a large amount of nationalist activity in all parts of the world, especially from the 1990s. And nationalism has special importance for Third World countries, which went through long nationalist struggles for independence. It should be noted that studying nationalism from the IR point of view will give only a one dimensional perspective. History, historical sociology, cultural anthropology, social psychology and social theory are all relevant to the study of nationalism.

Max Weber described the state as being a territorial organization exercising legitimate control over its bounded territory, unchallenged by internal power competition or external intervention. Against this, he placed the "nation"—"a community of sentiment which would adequately manifest itself in a state of its own", and hence "tends to produce a state of its own".[2] A nation need not correspond to its ethnic "cultural" community, which may exist at its core, since most modern states are multicultural. However, Ernest Gellner holds that "nationalism is primarily a political doctrine, which holds that the political and national units should be congruent". [3]

What happens then if the unification pressures are transnational? When the "cultural community" looks beyond the territorial space and seeks the "sacred space" of the nation, to borrow the term from Benedict Anderson,[4] beyond territorial borders in the community of people who believe in the tenets of a religion? While nationalism in the European sense requires national and territorial units to coincide, European models do not fit all moulds, because religion is the state in Islam and the community is made of Muslims all over the world—the Muslim ummah.

To comprehend the concept of the state in Islam, one must understand some of the basic tenets of the faith. The fundamental ideology of Islam is embodied in the words "La ilaha il illah, Muhammad rasul Illah"—there is no God but God, and Muhammad is His Prophet, something that all Muslims are required to accept without questioning. The *Koran* is the word of God, and thus differs from the Gospels or other works written by men, and as such, must be followed. About one-third of the *Koran* is devoted to a discussion of the attributes of Allah, about one-third extols the virtues of reason, thinking, reflection, study, knowledge and wisdom and approximately one-third is on issues of law, legislation, public policy and family life.

The words "Allahu Akbar"—God is Great—summarizes the centrality of God, and in a way, the wedding of personal religious conviction and political life in Islam. Man's vocation is to surrender—"islam"—to God's will and to be God's instrument in establishing and spreading God's rule on Earth, the Islamic order. The Muslim community, the "*ummah*", is the principal vehicle for the realization of God's will. Tribal solidarity in pre-Islamic Arab society had represented the basic social law, which was obviously arbitrary. Islam replaced this with a community whose membership was based on common faith rather than male blood ties. Religion rather than tribal affiliation became the binding factor, and all members of the *ummah* were considered equal before God. It is interesting that among the five pillars of Islam—faith, prayer, concern for the needy, self-purification and pilgrimage to Mecca—compassion for one's fellow being ranks high. Muslims believe that all things belong to God and man is a kind of trustee. He can enjoy His beneficence in this world, but nothing is man's property. *Zakat* is a kind of setting aside for the needy. It means both purification and growth. Goods which we possess on Earth are purified by setting aside a portion for those in need, something akin to the pruning of plants which encourages new growth. Each Muslim calculates his or her own *Zakat* individually and for the most part, this involves the payment each year of 2.5 per cent of one's income for the less fortunate. A pious person may give "*sadaqa*", voluntary charity, which involves more money.

According to the Prophet, "He who eats his fill while his neighbour goes hungry is not a believer". He also said that even "meeting your brother with a cheerful face is charity". According to the *hadis,* the life of the Prophet, if a person has nothing to give, he "should check himself from doing evil. That is also charity". Muslims are also required to fast during the month of Ramadan. What is notable is that if he is physically totally incapable of fasting, he has to feed a needy person for every day that he has missed. There appears to be a kind of socialistic feeling involved here in that while property does not belong to the state, because Islam does not speak of any territorial state, there being only the state of God—Dar-ul-Islam—which has no boundaries of the kind that political science speaks of, all property belongs to God and not individual persons. Further, while it is inevitable that some are more fortunate than others, it is a duty of the better endowed to look after the less fortunate, because they are actually all partaking of God's bounty and all are equal before God. Equality is also fundamental to Islam. When Muslims go to Mecca for the *hajj* to join in prayers for God's forgiveness, they are all dressed in the same white pieces of cloth, with no rank or riches to distinguish them before God.

Moreover, both individual and collective life should be shaped according to some basic tenets of Islam. *Tawheed,* which lies at the core, literally means "unity of God", but its implication is the unity and equality of all humanity. *Khalifa* defines man's position as "trustees" of God. As trustees, man is responsible for God's creation and will be accountable for its abuse both in this world and the Hereafter. *Ilm* means knowledge, the pursuit of which is a duty for all Muslims. *Adl* is to do justice, which is a primary obligation. The next three concepts, *shura* or consultation, *ijma* or consensus and *ijtihad* or interpretation have been used in public life and show that despite the non-democratic character of many Islamic states, Islam is based on the democratic principles of consultation, consensus and interpretation (of the *Koran,* the *hadis* and Islamic law). To these, one can connect another concept, *istilah,* which means public interest. This is a fundamental source of Islamic law. It is the responsibility of individuals and communities to consider the good and welfare of society as well as the planet as a whole. To this is added *ihsan,* which means kindness and the implication is that human behaviour should be guided by this principle. And what is needed for all this is *hikma* or wisdom to discern the difference between what is good or better and that which is bad or worse.[5]

The concept which has created the most misunderstanding over the centuries is *jihad.*[6] It literally means "righteous struggle", and the greatest *jihad* is against one's own self, that is, against one's own inadequacies in the path to God. But it can also mean fighting injustice and oppression, spreading and defending Islam and creating a just society, if necessary, armed struggle, depending on the circumstances in which one lives. Muhammad himself had to engage in armed conflict to defend and spread the fledgling faith. There is a Prophetic tradition which notes that when Muhammad returned from battle, he told his followers, "We return from a lesser *jihad* to a greater *jihad*", the greater *jihad* being the more difficult struggle against one's ego, selfishness, greed and evil.

At the same time, Muhammad also said, "Fight in the cause of God against those who fight you". This saying has been used by Muslim extremists to justify "holy" war and even terrorist acts. What is not quoted by these same people is the line following the previous statement, "but do not transgress limits, God loves not transgressors". The Prophet also said, "God has no mercy on one who has no mercy for others".

To understand the concept of "holy" war, one has to place it in the historical context. Islam emerged in 7th century Arabian peninsula where tribal and clan warfare were a natural state. Muhammad's reformist message was an unwelcome challenge to the existing political and religious establishment, steeped in materialism. Mecca was already a pilgrimage site as well as a center of trade. Muhammad's message denounced the selfish avarice, called for social justice for the poor and most vulnerable, and the replacement of clan ties by a community of faith, cutting across tribe, race and territory. He condemned polytheism and Mecca's corruption, which he called *jahalliyah*, a state of ignorance and unbelief, and he called on his followers to strive and struggle—*jihad*—to reform the community and live a good life based on the belief in one God and God's law, the *shariah*. His message that people were not accountable to tribal law but God's law shook the very foundations of Arabian society. He also claimed to be God's messenger and this was a challenge to the political and social elite of the times. There was obvious resistance including threats on his life, and he was forced not only to emigrate to Medina and form cross-tribal alliances based on the Islamic ideal, but also fight. The first references to "defensive" *jihad* in the *Koran* appear in the revelations after his emigration to Mecca—"Leave is given to those who fight because they were wronged—surely God is able to help them who were expelled wrongfully from their homes for saying 'Our Lord is God'".

Such statements have been taken out of context over the centuries to justify wars which are merely political, sometimes seeking territorial gain or even revenge, as *jihad*. However, in its fundamentals, Islam as a religion is based on the equality of all believers and a society at the core of which is the concept of justice for all. There are elements of consultation, consensus and public interest interwoven into Islamic law, which perhaps were revolutionary for the times.

Islam, Nationalism and Islamic Law

The *Koran* is the source of law in Islam, tempered by the traditions of the Prophet and the early followers, the *hadis* and the *sunnah*. Islamic jurisprudence developed later based on all three of the sources. There are four main schools of Islamic law, the *sharia*, drawing on the interpretations of leading scholars, but there are other interpretations as well, since Islam passed through different historical conditions. The *Koran* provides for no state in Islam. All it says is that there is no God but God and Muhammad is His Prophet. There is no mention about who will rule in God's name, although there had to be someone or group to mete out justice following the *Koranic* precepts, after Muhammad.

However, there is no real concept of statehood as we know it, in Islam. Neither is there any church in Islam. No government or religious establishment is supposed to regulate or enforce the prayers of Islam. Islam, fundamentally, is truly transnational and one can speak of an Islamic brotherhood in a transnational sense. The institutions which have developed are because of historical circumstances, and they are there to serve the religion and not to be served by it. This they are supposed to do through ensuring God's rule on earth by observing the *sharia*, since all are subject to the *sharia*. There is, of course, the idea of Dar-ul-islam—the land of Islam—and Dar-ul-Harb, the land of the infidels or non-believers, which had to be Islamicized. But beyond these, the idea of statehood, either modern or medieval, did not exist. In the new community formed by Muhammad, the Prophet was the political as well as the religious leader, and Islam in Medina was both a faith and a socio-political system as the Arab tribes gradually united under a single polity, centralized authority and law.

Historically, however, the Arabs developed a huge empire within a few decades of Muhammad's death, stretching from Spain to Sindh. Interestingly, this is never called the Islamic empire, although the Arabs spread the religion wherever they went. Islam was, in fact, the motivating factor that led the Arab hordes to establish such a huge territorial empire. Muhammad's followers had decided by consultation and consensus, *ijma* and *shura*, to appoint a caliph to guide the new sect, and although there were many splits along the way, and the caliphate became hereditary to a large extent, the Sunni caliphate continued for over six centuries. The caliph was the head of the Islamic *ummah, Khilafat Allah* (vicegerent of God), *amir-al-muminin* (Commander of the Faithful), and as he held the authority of Allah, he had to be obeyed. These titles gave the caliphate a two-fold duty—political and religious. As the commander of the faithful, he was the political head of the community, and as the custodian of the authority of God, he had religious responsibilities. The caliphate was necessary at that point of time to the maintenance of the *sharia*. And the *sharia* was important to maintain the new faith. The precepts of Islam could be followed by a binding commitment to the Islamic law, which was considered to be God's law. The *sharia* preceded the caliphate or any other form of government in the Islamic world, and the *ummah*, that is, the totality of Muslims, were held together by adherence to the *sharia*. In this kind of reckoning, the *ummah* is the nation and Islamic law is what binds it together.[7]

The reality, however, proved to be quite different. The power of the caliphate declined with the expansion of the empire and the establishment of various sultanates. This was a problem because there is no concept of kingship in Islam. Therefore, an after the fact justification came about and rulers ruled in the name of the caliph, at least initially. The title "sultan" originally pertained to temporal power, specially military power, but later the rulers attempted to assume religious titles like "guardian of the true faith" and even caliph, the functionalist view being that religion is an indispensable ally of government. In the context of the conquest by different ethnic groups of disparate regions inhabited by people of different races and religions, Islam proved to be a unifying factor. As such, Islam is ultimately understood by Muslims to be both *din* and *dawla*—religion and government.

By the sixteenth century there were several major empires in the Muslim world—Sunni Ottoman, Shia Safivid and Sunni

Mughal to mention a few. The wars which had preceded the setting up of these empires, however, went against the tenets of Islam, because they were against other Muslim powers and not against "infidels". So, although Islam was a transnational brotherhood in theory, without reference to race or ethnicity, Muslim rulers were engaged in wars whose motivations were purely political. Although the idea of a temporal state was absent in Islam, these were nothing but temporal states. However, to get legal validity under Islam all such states had to adhere to the Islamic law and it was Islam which provided the legitimacy, the political ideology and the law. The unique feature of the Islamic state was that the minimum requirement for Islamic government was not the moral character of the head of state but rule according to the *sharia*.

The message of equality was able to build the disparate empires under Islamic rule. At a time when nation-states were developing in Europe, the concept of nation as the people from the same race, region or ethnic background did not take root among the Muslims. One reason was the Arabization of large areas under Arab rule—and the fact that the *Koran* was written in Arabic helped to further facilitate matters. Arab civilization also adapted to and adopted from local cultures. Apart from literature, music, architecture and science, local customs, language and even a bit of the existing civil laws were modified and taken over. In India or in Hungary, there was a lot of intermarriage and local people, by virtue of their work output, were able to rise to the highest levels of governance. Suleyman I elected Ibrahim Pasha, the son of a Greek to the Grand Wazirate in1524, and his second successor, Muhammad Sokolli, was a Slav. Muhammad Ali, who ruled Egypt more absolutely than any other pasha although acknowledging the titular leadership of the Ottoman sultan, was an Albanian. As such, the Western idea of "nation" was alien to Muslim kingdoms and empires. The religious identity was more important than the ethnic or regional identity. No leading Muslim, for instance, advocated separation from the Ottoman empire, which was also the seat of the caliphate till the beginning of the twentieth century, though there were calls for autonomy and decentralization.

The impact of colonialism, however, led to the emergence of modern nationalism, but here too, Islam played an important role. Firstly, it provided the rallying call for anti-colonial independence movements and secondly, modern Muslim nationalism was the *via media* for the transition from a transnational religious ideology to a modern Muslim national state. In Egyptian as well as Arab nationalism, one finds the basic tenets of Islam being invoked. Jamal al Din Afghani (1838-1897), who has been called the Father of Muslim nationalism, appealed to faith and pride in the divine mandate and mission, and emphasized on the return to Islam for Muslim unity and political autonomy. He supported both Muslim nationalism and pan-Islamism because he felt that both national and transnational unity and solidarity were prerequisites for the reassertion of Muslim political and cultural independence.[8] His disciples, Muhammad Abduh (1849-1905) and Rashid Rida (1865-1935) also spoke of resistance to European expansionism through Muslim solidarity and the revival of dormant Islam through reinterpretation and reform.[9]

The political reality, however, was very different. New states were emerging or being carved out from the remains of erstwhile empires. How did pan-Islamism reconcile itself with the emergence of nation-states? A ruling of Rashid Rida in the 1930s is interesting in this context. In response to a query from an Indonesian Muslim as to whether patriotism and nationalism were un-Islamic, he said that Holy War was incumbent when enemies aggressed against Muslims and occupied their land, but when it came to the contemporary notion of patriotism, which implied the unity of different religions for the defense of a specific homeland, Muslim youth should cooperate with others irrespective of religion in every legitimate action for independence. However, "in his service of his homeland and his people he must not...neglect Islam which has honoured him and raised him up by making him a brother to hundreds of millions of Muslims in the world. He is a member of a body greater than his people and his personal homeland is part of the homeland of his religious community. He must be intent on making progress of the part a means for progress of the whole". In an earlier book, *The Caliphate or Imamate* (1923), Rida had noted that their religion did not exist unless an independent and strong Islamic state had been established and it could apply the laws of Islam and defend it against any foreign domination.

In all the struggles for independence in North Africa, for instance, the Islamic heritage and past provided a natural and indigenous starting point and it was Islam which provided a common history, belief, symbols and language. As such, Islam became the most effective means of mass mobilization in the nationalist struggles. For instance, Islam was the basic impulse behind Algerian nationalism. The slogan of the revolution was "Algerie Musulmane" and the leaders were called mujahidun or "holy warriors", thus making the nationalist movement seem like a *jihad*. In Tunisia, French attempts to offer citizenship were resisted on Islamic grounds—to accept would be apostasy, because citizenship meant transfer from Islamic jurisdiction to a French one. In fact, in 1932, a Tunisian *mufti* passed a legal ruling prohibiting French "naturalized" Tunisians from being buried in Muslim cemeteries. What one sees here is that national aspirations are being given a religious overtone, because there is no separation of politics from religion in Islam. However, when these states did become independent and new states were carved out from the holdings of the erstwhile Ottoman empire in the Arab heartland following the end of World War I, they developed all the attributes of nationhood and a sovereign state. Although the idea of a large Arab state comprising of Jordan, Iraq, Palestine, Syria, Lebanon, Saudi Arabia and even perhaps Egypt was mooted and considered as an ideal which failed to materialize as a result of British and French machinations, subsequent efforts at partial unity like the formation of the United Arab Republic (UAR) were found to be non-sustainable. The Arab League, too, which could have been a strong and centralized organization, remained fractious, the only point of unity being the issue of Palestine and that too, until the Camp David Accord of 1979.

One cannot ignore history and the emergence of caliphates, empires and states in the Muslim world, but theoretically, the

Islamic community—the *ummah*—is one, and the primary allegiance is not to any territory, but to Islam, because it is all God's world and all men who believe in the basic tenets of Islam are brothers. Islam is therefore, basically transnational. When the struggle for independence was going on in India, Mawdudi, an Islamic revivalist thinker, opposed Muhammad Ali Jinnah, the protagonist of Pakistan, who demanded a separate nation-state in the Indian sub-continent for Muslims, on the ground that Jinnah spoke of Islam as an ethno-cultural identity and a source of national identity rather than a living all-comprehensive ideal. Mawdudi considered nationalism, and thereby, the nation-state, as an un-Islamic idea, and that democracy, if construed as sovereignty of the people, was unacceptable, because sovereignty belonged to God alone, and he was sovereign over all without regard to territorial boundaries.[10]

However, there is a definite concept of Islamic nationalism and the creation of an ideal Islamic state based on the *sharia*, lies at the heart of Islam. According to Muhammad Abduh, Afghani's disciple, faith and pride in the divine mandate and mission are important for the setting up of an Islamic state, which implied a return to Islam for Muslim unity and autonomy. He believed that Islam supplied the *raison d'etre* for Muslims as individuals and as a socio-political community. As such, keeping in view the fact that many states have emerged in the so-called Muslim world, all leaders of such states from President Nasser of Egypt to President Saddam Hussein of Iraq, who promoted Arab nationalism and state interests rather than pan-Islamism, had to seek, at some point in their career, legitimacy from Islam by espousing Islamic causes and acting in the name of Islam. Modern Muslim nationalism has shifted from a transnational religious ideology to the acceptance of a modern Muslim national state, but religious ideology and law play a very important role in the sustenance of the state.

Democracy and Islam

If democracy is a form of government in which the people have a say in who should hold power and how it should be used, as the Oxford dictionary explains it to be, Islam has a fundamental problem with such governments, because the concept of Islamic sovereignty is central to Islamic political theory, and therefore a barrier to any form of democracy. The *Koranic* concept of sovereignty is that it is universal (non-territorial), transcendental (beyond human agency), indivisible, inalienable and truly absolute. God, the primary law giver, is the sovereign, while agents such as the Islamic state or the *khalifa,* enjoy the marginal autonomy required to implement God's law. At the theoretical level, therefore, the difference between the modern and Islamic concepts of sovereignty is clear. In a democracy, it is the people who run the government, although indirectly, and it is they who formulate the laws according to which the state is run. Islamists see this as subject to human whim, whereas Islamic principles are eternal and transcendental, and cannot be undermined by popular whim. Islamic law is not the product of judicial decisions, but is as much a system of ethics as law. Therefore, man's law may change, God's do not.

However, when Islam was first propagated, it advocated ideals, which had a "socialistic" nature unheard of in the various socio-political circles of the time. It was perhaps the kind of society that Prophet Muhammad preached about as desirable that led to threats on his life and his subsequent expulsion from Mecca. Pristine Islam speaks of the unity and equality of all humanity, because all are equal before God, which implies that no man is superior over another and therefore, by extension, slavery is forbidden. All property belongs to God, and we are here as trustees (*khalifa*) of God, not as the possessors of property, which can be handed down from father to son as though it belonged to us. In India, during the reign of the Mughals, the *mansabdari* and *jagirdari* systems were not meant to be hereditary. Each person earned his own rank according to his own abilities, and his sons did not inherit the benefits that he had earned. The early Muslims even believed in sharing the booty collected during a war or conquest with the lowliest of soldiers. The *Koran* stipulates that one-fifth of a person's income has to be given to persons who are less fortunate. There is also no usury in Islam, and the taking of interest on a loan is forbidden. When we speak of a "democratic" society, we are implicitly implying an egalitarian society. Early Islamic society, which good Muslims try to emulate, was a kind of "classless" society, wherein God was sovereign and Muhammad was his Prophet.

The early Muslims also believed in a kind of democratic process for the selection of the Caliph. As mentioned earlier, there were no rulers or ruled in God's world, and Prophet Muhammad had not left any selected heir to inherit his position. The practical problem of keeping the fledgling faith alive against a hostile environment led to the creation of the Caliphate through the democratic process of consultation—*shura*—and consensus or agreement—*ijma*. There is a *Koranic* verse which notes "and consult with them on the matter". This has been interpreted to mean that if there is nothing in the *Quran* to guide the *ummah* on any specific matter, the *ummah* can consult among themselves and come up with a verdict based on consensus (*ijma*), and this is acceptable because Muhammad also said that "My community will never agree upon an error". Later, justifications were provided for the institution of the caliphate, on the grounds that the caliph was to serve as the vicegerent of God. He was to be elected/ nominated by a group of influential community leaders or may even be designated by his predecessor, but this had to be followed by community acceptance—*ba'ya*. This *ba'ya* is very important in governance of Islamic states even today, even though it may be a kind of forced or fictitious community acceptance. In a theoretical way, therefore, Muslim states were more democratic than others in medieval times because there was no hereditary rule, and community acceptance, which was a kind of pledge of office, was required for ascension to a governing position.

Moreover, Muhammad created what is widely seen to be the first Islamic state on the basis of an agreement. When he left Mecca for what came to be known as Madinat ul Nabi, he consulted with the residents of the city, who agreed to a *Dastur-al-Madina*, the Constitution of Medina. This was a tripartite compact signed by the Muslim immigrants from Mecca, the indigenous Muslims of Medina and significantly, the Jews of Medina. This demonstrated a democratic spirit, because although the *Dastur* was a historically specific constitution based on eternal and transcendent principles revealed to the Prophet by God, it also required the consent of all those who would be affected by it. So, in one sense, the first Islamic state was a pluralistic state and the principles of equality, consensual governance and pluralism were central to the compact.

It must also be noted that despite the overarching importance of the *sharia,* which in Islamic theory is the only recognized law, a parallel system of laws and courts began to develop from the time of the Ummayad caliphate itself. The *sharia*'s idealism sometimes proved to be impractical especially in criminal law, which required the evidence of two adult Muslim witnesses, lacking which the rules of evidence required the court to accept an oath sworn in the name of God. The *sharia* rules of procedure also excluded circumstantial evidence and the cross-examination of witnesses. Moreover, as the Arab/ Islamic empire expanded, many issues and problems came up which had not existed in the time of Muhammad, and therefore, not covered by the *Koran,* the *hadis* or the *sunnah*. The Caliph's desire to govern personally also must have grown with time, but since God was the only law giver, a legal fiction was used to create a parallel system of courts—the *mazalim* courts, which initially enabled the caliphs to hear cases against judges themselves, but whose scope was later expanded to functions defined by the temporal ruler. As such, over time, the *sharia* courts got increasingly restricted to personal law (marriage, divorce, inheritance, religious endowments, etc.), while the *mazalim* (complaint) courts dealt with public law—criminal law, taxation, commercial regulations, etc.

As massive empires began to develop in the Islamic world, the rulers became more and more autocratic and arbitrary, and although a class of religious scholars (*ulama*) also developed, whose primary function was to interpret the laws, a powerful ruler could bend the rules with impunity, keeping a façade of Islamic governance. In more modern times, governments are permitted to issue regulations and ordinances for administrative purposes, as long as these are not contrary to the *sharia*. *Fatwas*, too, can be issued by religious scholars, based on their interpretation of the religious texts, to accommodate issues for which it is difficult to find answers in regular rulings. In fact, the right of the head of state to issue ordinances, not laws, is justified in all Muslim states today. In Saudi Arabia, for instance, the Mining Code (1963) and the Civil Service Law (1971) are examples of such supplementation of the *sharia* law, since such requirements did not exist in the 7th century. The accommodation of non-Muslim employees like Christians and Hindus in Muslim Middle Eastern countries, or the deployment of "infidel" foreign troops in Saudi Arabia, where Islam's holiest pilgrimages are located, also require such governmental ordinances and religious *fatwas*. Operationally, therefore, Islamic laws have been interpreted to accommodate the needs of the times. Apart from *ijtihad* (interpretation), historically speaking, the bulk of customary laws in any region conquered by Muslims, were incorporated into law books as long as they were not contrary to Islam, and sometimes, like in medieval Persia, customs like kissing the feet of the monarch, which go against the dictum for equality, also became regular practice.

It should be noted that there was no scope for a ruler in the pristine Islam preached by Muhammad. But the truth is that not only caliphates but also sultanates developed under Islam, and over the centuries these became more and more arbitrary and authoritarian faced with the onerous task of ruling vast regions. The title "sultan" originally pertained to temporal power, but later rulers attempted to assume religious titles, including that of the caliph, and presented themselves as guardians of the faith. The view that kingship and religion went hand in hand began to mature. It was maintained that kingly rule guards against anarchy, while religious authority leads the struggle against evil. This was a functionalist view of religion, that is, religion was an indispensable ally of temporal power. However, in actual terms, this was an after-the-fact justification of kingship to align it to the accepted notions of Islam. There was always the problem of the bad ruler: should Muslims revolt against usurpers? Muslim scholars like al

Ghazzali (d. 1111) and Ibn Khaldun (14th century) provided justifications for harsh realities—as long as the sultan acknowledged the caliph as the spiritual and temporal head, continued to mention the caliph's name in Friday prayers and pledged to uphold *sharia* rule, Islamic government continued to exist and therefore, the sultan was acceptable. Another Islamic jurist-theologian, Al Mawardi (d. 1058), wrote that if an amirate was seized and the new incumbent could not be dislodged, then it was best to put up with him. This went against the theory of *ba'ya,* but Mawardi did add that obedience should be rendered to an "amirate by seizure", only if enough power was delegated to the *ulama* to enforce the *sharia.* These were justifications for a political reality often at odds with normative Islam and legal accommodations to maintain the symbols of Muslim unity and identity.

After the fall of the Abbasid caliphate, all idealism was swept away, and the sultan was accepted as the supreme "Islamic" leader. The Sunni jurist, Ibn Jama'a, put forward the extreme view that if an unqualified person imposed himself on a state by military might alone, his *ba'ya* was automatic and therefore, legal. He did not even mention the *sharia* as the central important authority. Ibn Jama'a was taken to task for his views by Ibn Taymiyah (d. 1328). In a book entitled *Al Siyasa al Shariya* (Administration According to the *Sharia*), he held that the caliphate was not a necessary institution, and neither did its historical existence have any particular virtues. According to him, the caliphate was not required by the *Koran,* the *sunnah* or the consensus of the early companions, although he claims that the first four caliphs were valid caliphs.[11] What is important from the point of view of modern governance is that he said that government is a political matter and should be carried out as far as possible for the welfare of the people. The ruler should, however, enable the *ulama* to function properly. There are two original ideas here, (1) that the Muslim community associates with its fellow members under the *sharia,* and (2) that specific Muslim communities/ nations make a pact of government (enter into a contract) to obey a ruler on condition that he cooperates with and facilitates the work of the *ulama*, thereby upholding and enforcing the *sharia*. It is up to the Muslim community to establish governments in the best way they can and to get rid of bad rulers if the people's consensus is that the *sharia* is not being served. He also insisted that without *ijtihad*—interpretation—the *ummah* could make an ideal of its own past traditions, which was itself the prisoner of *taqlid* ('blind imitation'). The *Koran*, the *sunnah* and the pious *salaf* (the ancestors or early companions of Muhammad) were the only indisputable voices from the past. The unstated corollary to this statement was that even perhaps these could be interpreted afresh, because he laid emphasis on interpretation. Although he was not very influential during his times, his views provided the theoretical and theological underpinning for the rule of the Wahabbis in Saudi Arabia four centuries later. It is also a practical interpretation of governance in the Muslim world. Although the role of the *ulama* is significant in his thinking and by extension, *sharia* rule, what is important is that government has to be for the good of the people and that the people can throw out a bad ruler by consensus (even though the root cause should be that he is not ruling in the light of the *sharia*). Although Islamic extremists draw on his views today to justify their attempts at violence to overthrow governments they consider to be un-Islamic or not sufficiently Islamic, elements of people's choice, though bound by the *sharia*, are evident here.

Today one sees a large number of states which have a Muslim majority population. Some of these are Islamic in the sense that they follow the *sharia*, others are not so Islamic although they profess to be so, and yet others are secular like Turkey. In the Middle East, apart from Israel, which is a paradoxical Jewish state in an Arab-Muslim world and is democratic so far as the Jews are concerned, but not so democratic when it comes to its Arab-Muslim citizens and the rights of the Palestinians in the Palestinian Authority, which derives its right to exist from Israel, there is Turkey which is democratic and secular. So far as the rest of the states are concerned, the system of governance varies from facades of parliamentary democracy to theocratic states like Iran and

Saudi Arabia. Parliaments exist in many of these states and elections take place more or less regularly, but whether these are transparent is a debatable issue. Referendums to select the presidents have taken the place of *ba'ya*, but the level of manipulation is evident in the results, which show approval rates of 98-99 per cent. In any case, in many of these so-called referendums, there is no second candidate, and the citizen has to vote with a simple "yes" or "no" for the incumbent. This was the tradition in Saddam Hussein's Iraq and till recently, in Hosni Mubarak's Egypt. In fact, Egypt provides a good example of 'electoral' practice in the Middle East. There is a parliament, but the political process has been manipulated by the ruling National Democratic Party (NDP) from 1979, through corruption, constant changes in electoral law, supervision of activities of dissenters of the regime, monopolization of the TV and media, etc.[12] The president is nominated by the parliament, so it serves the president's purpose to control the parliament. Only one name is placed before the electorate, and it is not surprising that Mubarak was returned to office in 1999 with 99.96 per cent approval. Recently, under pressure from the West, some electoral changes have been brought in, but what is interesting is that the main challenger to Mubarak's presidency, Nour, was put behind bars on various charges. In Syria, Bashir al Assad became the president with the consensus of an assembly of elders, who gave their *ba'ya*. There was no election in the western sense. There are monarchies like in Jordan and Saudi Arabia, and here too, there is a formality for endorsing the next ruler. In Saudi Arabia, there is no hereditary rule and the princes agree on who should be the next ruler on the death of an incumbent. It has been demonstrated that they also have the power to remove a ruler if they consider him to be unfit. However, the people have no say in this selection. In Iran, which is also a theocratic state, the rules of selection of the president are more in tune with the people's choice, but religion plays an important role in the process.

In the Middle East, despite the theoretical underpinning of consensual rule in Islam and compacts with non-Muslims in the past, the basic ingredients of a western type democracy do not exist. For one, modern civil society institutions like a free press have not developed fully, and these are essential for the proper functioning of a democracy. Moreover, women are considered to have equal rights, particularly political rights, in a democracy. In some states, women are just being given the right to vote, but because of religious traditions, may not be allowed to exercise that right by her family. Also, the long tradition of authoritarianism which goes back to the Ottoman sultanate has left little place for democratic oppositions to grow. This does not mean that there is no opposition—there are serious pressures from below in almost every state. Tradi-tionally, opposition to the government has always taken on a religious hue, because Islamic jurists have never condoned a bad ruler who does not rule according to the *sharia*. In the absence of any democratic form of airing their grievances or overturning the government through legitimate electoral means, the people have turned to Islam again and again to seek justice. Their problems may be of an economic or political nature, but it is Islam which has provided the legitimacy for revolt. The opposition to the Shah's rule in Iran took a religious form, the opposition to military rule in Algeria came through the Islamic Salvation Front and against the long and frustrating occupation of Gaza and the West Bank by Israel, the Hamas and the Islamic Jihad developed in the face of the failure of the Palestinian Liberation Organization to work out a settlement for a long time. And it was Hamas which was returned to power in the elections to a new Palestinian legislative assembly held on 25 January, 2006. Interestingly, although the elections were free and fair according to Western observers, it is the West and democratic Israel which does not want it to hold office or severely restrict its powers and maneuverability if it does, and this goes against the norms of democracy since it is an attempt to subvert the people's will.

So far as Muslim majority countries outside the Middle East are concerned, authoritarian or military rule with Islam being invoked was quite the norm in Pakistan or Bangladesh, while in Indonesia, it was just authoritarian rule. There has been significant change, however, in the last 20 years, particularly after the end of the Cold War. While there has been a degree of democratization in Bangladesh, Indonesia, Malaysia and Nigeria, with multiparty electoral politics coming in, the issue of Islam has to be seen in relation to local, regional and international factors, which involves politics, economics and society. Although an analysis of these factors is beyond the scope of this paper, it must be pointed out that there are conservative traditionalists in all these states, and therefore the governments are careful to temper modernization and democratization with Islam. There has been also the emergence of new Muslim majority states in Central Asia, and though there is an authoritarian tendency, this has more to do with the legacies of the immediate Soviet past rather than a historical Islamic heritage.

Conclusion

According to Gudrun Kramer, Professor of Islamic Studies at Bonn University, "it is not possible to talk of Islam and democracy in general but only about Muslims living and theorizing under specific historical circumstances...There are certainly essentials of the faith *(al-aqida)* accepted by all who consider themselves to be Muslims...But Muslims differ considerably over how an Islamic society should be organized."[13] While the concept of universality in Islam is still pertinent, territorial boundaries have always been there and the concept of the Islamic state goes back to very early times. The brotherhood in Islam is more spiritual than temporal. Even when the Arab or the Turkish empires existed, these were temporal powers and the polity was that of the state although the law was largely based on the *sharia*. These empires also were pluralist, not only in ethnic terms but also in religious terms. In India under most of the Mughals or for that matter in the provinces, a person did not have to be a Muslim to rise to high office. Wars were fought not on religious grounds but for imperialistic or other political reasons, although Islamic idioms were used to inspire the soldiers or justify armed interventions. There are numerous instances of one Muslim ruler waging war against another, for instance Humayun and Sher Shah—the issue was power and not religion. In reality, the temporal state with all its trappings has always existed in Islam, and with that, nascent nationalism has also existed. A person did not belong just to Islam, but also to Persia, Hindustan, Egypt, etc. At the turn of the nineteenth century, when anti-imperialist movements were emerging and sprea-ding in many parts of the world, consciousness of belonging to a territorial state also began to develop in predominantly Muslim areas just as it grew in other colonized parts of the world. In the Muslim world, however, the idea of nationalism was debated because of the nature of Islam. But there is no denying the state or nationalism attached to a particular state in the current context.

While there is general agreement that Islam is comprehensive and inclusive of both religion and state (*al-islam din wa-dawla*) or religion and the world (*al-islam din wa-duniya*), there is actually difference, recognized in Islamic legal theory, between a person's duties and relations with God (*ibadat*), and the *mu'amalat*—all other aspects of a person's life, economic, political and family matters. While the *ibadat* are eternal and can not be changed, the *mu'amalat* can be adapted to the circumstances of the time. It is also generally accepted that the application of the *sharia* is the hallmark of a truly Islamic system and not any kind of particular political order. In fact, there can be no particular political order in Islamic states, because no such thing is mentioned in the *Koran* or *hadis*. On the other hand, the *Koran* does mention justice, equality, freedom, consultation, consensus and public interest, which are all required for good governance and form the core of democratic governance. The vital difference is between non-Muslim and un-Islamic—while Muslims can and have (historically) adopted and adapted to non-Muslim modes of organization, given the time and the locality, they cannot adopt un-Islamic values. Thus, democratic form of governance may be acceptable as a method of political organization as long as it does not lead to the neglect or violation of Islamic norms. It has been noted earlier that the basic tenets of Islam are compatible with the principles of democracy. So far as the *sharia* is concerned, this too, has an immutable core, but the human interpretation (*ijtihad*) is flexible. In modern Muslim states, laws have been adopted in the spirit of the *sharia,* which are not actually in the *sharia,* and there is precedence for this in the *mazalim* courts of the past.

It needs to be reiterated, however, that no two democracies are alike. The deprived in the Muslim world seek popular participation and a say in governance just like any other subjugated people.[14] It is lack of political space which often drives them to the more extreme interpretations of their religion as a form of protest which is justifiable to their co-religionists. Democracy or elements of democracy, when it emerges in a Muslim state may not have the same attributes as in the United States, particularly if it emerges from below, because it is specific historical, political, economic, social and cultural factors which shape the polity of each state. External interference to shape the form of government can only have a reverse effect, particularly in states which have a strong link with religion. It must be remembered that the United States did not become the democracy it is today in one night. It has worked out its own problems with democracy, and it has had many including the denial of the right to vote to women and its largest minority till well into the twentieth century, around and over 150 years after it became independent and declared itself a republic. Great Britain too, went through centuries of evolution. It is difficult to expect that Muslim countries can transform themselves into viable democracies overnight. They will have to go through their own experimentations, and given the basic tenets of Islam and the global consciousness regarding popular participation, it may be hoped authoritarian rule will give way to democratic forms of governance in the long run. A quick fix solution, on the other hand, may lead to further resentment and clear the path for the emergence of a more radical version of political Islam.

NOTES AND REFERENCES

1. John A. Hall, "Introduction" in *The State of the Nation: Ernest Gellner and the Theory of Nationalism* (London, Cambridge University Press, 1998).
2. Max Weber, *Essays in Sociology* (1946). Cited in http://en.wikipedia.org/wiki/Max_Weber (retrieved on 11.03.06).
3. Ernest Gellner, *Nations and Nationalism* (Cornell University Press, 1983).
4. Benedict Anderson, *Imagined Communities: Reflections on the Origin and Spread of Nationalism* (New York, Verso, 1983).
5. See Abdulaziz Sachedina, *Islamic Roots of Democratic Pluralism* (Oxford University Press, 2001). There are also several websites from which the beliefs and practices of Islam can be gauged, for example http://www.islamweb.net and www.al-Islam.org.
6. For an academic study of the concept of *jihad*, see Bernard Lewis, *The Political Language of Islam* (Chicago and London, University of Chicago Press, 1988). Also see, Emmanuel Sivan, *Radical Islam: Medieval Theology and Modern Politics* (New Haven, Yale University Press, 1985) and Stephen Schwartz, *The Two Faces of Islam: Saudi Fundamentalism and its Role in Terrorism* (New York, Anchor Books, 2003).
7. Maxime Rodinson, *Mohammad,* translation. A. Carter (Harmondsworth, Penguin Books, 1971), and John L. Esposito, *Islam and Politics* (New York, Syracuse University Press, 1987).
8. See Elie Kedourie, *Afghani and Abduh: An Essay on Religios Unbelief and Political Activism in Modern Islam* (London, Frank Cass, 1966).
9. Malcolm H. Kerr, *Islamic Reform: The Political and Legal Theories of Muhammad Abduh and Rashid Rida* (Berkeley, University of California Press, 1966).
10. Abu al-Ala Al-Mawdudi, "Political Theory of Islam", translation., in John Donahue and John L. Esposito, eds., *Islam in Transition: Muslim Perspectives* (New York, Oxford University Press, 1982).
11. Frederick Mathewson Denny, *An Introduction to Islam*, p. 228 ff. See also Ann K.S. Lambton, *State and Government in Medieval Islam* (Oxford, Oxford University Press, 1981).
12. See James Jankowski, *Egypt: A Short History* (Oxford, Oneworld, 2000) and Nazih Azubi, *The State and Public Policies in Egypt since Sadat* (Reading, Ithaca Press, 1991) for an analysis of Egyptian politics.
13. Gudrun Kramer, "Islamist Notions of Democracy", in Joel Beinin and Joe Stork, eds., *Political Islam: Essays from Middle East Report* (London, I.B. Tauris, 1997), p. 73.
14. See also John L. Esposito and John O. Voll, *Islam and Democracy* (Oxford, Oxford University Press, 1996), p. 193 ff.

6

Democracy and Islam

The Case of Pakistan

—PARTHA PRATIM BASU

I

Post-Cold War, an influential body of opinion has gained currency within Western policy circles as well as academic community regarding the incompatibility of Islam and liberal democracy. For some, the nature and history of Islam and the perceived relationship between Islam and temporal power make them fundamentally antithetical. The Islamic State, they argue, is a "polity ruled by God"— the ruler derives his power from the holy law and not from the people— which rules out the notions of plurality, disagreement and representative government, the hallmarks of democracy[1]. Those who contest this line of reasoning refuse to accept that the shadows of past beliefs and traditions still continue to determine the character of contemporary Muslim polities defying all social, economic and technological changes; indeed they also question the equation of Islam with one system/civilization[2]. But the former school seeks to consolidate their position by drawing attention to the political practices prevalent in present-day Muslim states where, they contend, such fundamental principles of liberal democracy as freedom of speech and association, equality before law or respect for minority rights are observed only in the breach[3].

The punch of the argument seems to be further enhanced in the context of the recent history of Pakistan, the focus of the present paper, where an "Islamization programme" was launched with much fanfare by its former military-chief-turned-president Zia ul Huq in thel980s. For Zia, this was largely a matter of realpolitik: during the late 1970s, he actively courted the opposition Pakistan National Alliance to topple the regime of Zulfikar Ali Bhutto, the first *elected* head of Pakistan. After assuming power, Zia declared Islamization to be his "divine mission" and projected the army as the custodian of Islam in Pakistan. That it was a part of his survival strategy became obvious when he, on the one hand, announced that Islam had no place for political parties, people's mandate or ruler's accountability, and started building, on the other, expedient alliances with right-wing Islamic groups of various hues. Islamization of the economy, legal codes and education system featured prominently on his political agenda and "export of Jihad" formed a major plank of his foreign policy. Thus the military establishment and the religious right in Pakistan appeared to share a set of illiberal attitudes including an aversion to political moderation and an antipathy towards India. The equation between a military regime and resurgence of Islam encouraged scholars to envisage a "Military-Islamist complex"[4], implying that the authoritarian regime and political Islam were elements of the same package, and seemed to corroborate the thesis of the "natural" hiatus between democracy and Islam.

The present piece, however, proposes to approach the issue from the other end, i.e. to focus on the interface of *democracy* and the Islamist forces in Pakistan. It contends that the democratic phases of Pakistan's polity facilitated the political assertion of the Islamist elements, attempts on the part of some of Pakistan's elected leaders to check these forces ended in fiasco and, indeed, some of the Islamist groups have developed a preference for democracy since it provides them an avenue of power.

II

Before the partition of the Indian subcontinent, Muslim clerics or *ulemas* of undivided India did not appear to be favourably disposed to M.A. Jinnah's proposed Muslim nation state which, they feared, would be based on liberal/ secular principles and not on Islamic laws. The orthodox Muslim leadership in the 1920s and 1930s, wedded as they were to Pan-Islamic ideals, questioned the Islamic credentials of the Westernized, liberal-minded stalwarts of die Muslim League - the champions of the Pakistan demand - and regarded them instead as British stooges. Maulana Mawdudi, who founded the Jammat-e-Islami, arguably the most important Islamist organization of South Asia, in 1941 dubbed Jinnah's Pakistan proposal "a fallacious formulation", and suggested two alternatives to the creation of Pakistan - born within the overall framework of a single India. Once Pakistan became a reality, a section of these *ulemas,* who were sympathizers of the Indian National Congress, stayed back in India; but those who migrated to the new state were further exasperated by the speech delivered by Jinnah in the inaugural session of the Pakistan Constituent Assembly on 11 August, 1947 outlining the vision of an essentially secular Pakistan where "in course of time Hindus will cease to be Hindus and Muslims will cease to be Muslims, not in the religious sense... but in the political sense as the citizens of one nation". These orthodox religious elements were in fact plagued by two problems: they had to make up for their loss of credibility resulting from their earlier opposition to the idea of Pakistan; and they also needed to carve out a niche for themselves within the emerging power structure of the fledgling state[5]. With these twin goals in view they entered into a dialogue with the early leaders of Pakistan - struggling to establish a parliamentary democracy in Pakistan - with the foundation of an *Islamic* state based on the Islamic laws or Shariat as their primary bargaining chip.

The civilian politicians of Pakistan - the first generation leadership of the Muslim League - were not reluctant either to engage with the clerics for they too had their own political compulsions. For one thing, Jinnah expired in the first year of Pakistan's birth and elimination of his charismatic presence came as a big blow to the Muslim League since most of its early leaders were *mohajirs* who hailed from the Muslim *minority* provinces of India (where the Pakistan movement had its strongest roots) and therefore lacked popular base in the territory of Pakistan. Moreover, the organization of the party itself remained weak: before the 1940s, it remained a party run by a small coterie and its claim to be the mouthpiece of Indian Muslims was challenged by many Muslim organizations; many of the leaders who occupied important positions within Pakistan's power hierarchy joined it only between 1937 and 1947 and thus lacked any substantial experience of functioning as a cohesive team, and the League was yet to successfully convert itself from a national movement into a national party[6]. On top of it, a sizeable chunk of its important members seemed to welcome—for whatever reasons—the notion of an Islamic state in Pakistan[7].

As a result, that Pakistan's political establishment was accommodative towards the religious right was amply reflected in several early constitutional documents. The Objectives Resolution moved by Prime Minister Liaquat Alt Khan in March, 1949 deviated grossly from the basic position adopted by Jinnah as it stipulated, among other things, that sovereignty *belonged to God,* and the authority He had delegated to the state of Pakistan "through its people" would be exercised "within the limits prescribed by Him"; that the state would fully observe the principles of democracy, freedom, equality, tolerance and social justice *as enunciated by Islam,* and that it would enable Muslims to order their individual and collective lives according to the teachings and requirements of Islam as set forth in the *Quran* and *Sunnah.* Similarly, the report of the Basic Principles Committee of the Constituent Assembly recommended that no laws contravening the *Quran* and *Sunnah* be made and that a *committee of the ulemas* be constituted to determine from time to time, to monitor the same. The vulnerability of the westernized elites of Pakistan was further exposed during the controversy that erupted in Punjab in the same year over the Ahmadiyas who, according to the orthodox Muslims, were heretical and needed to be expelled. This process of accommodation culminated in the declaration of Pakistan as an Islamic state in the first constitution promulgated in 1956.

This, however, never amounted to allowing a free hand to the *ulemas* in running the new state. Thus, Liaquat Ali made it quite plain that acceptance of God's supremacy did not mean that Pakistan would be a theocracy; it simply acknowledged the *moral basis* of the polity. He also iterated that the apprehensions voiced by the Hindu members of the Assembly that non-Muslims could not become head of administration in an Islamic state were absolutely baseless and denounced in no uncertain terms the "so-called *ulema*" responsible for trading such ideas. The Assembly debates clearly revealed that the scope of the ulemas' participation in the government was sought to be restricted to a consultative status alone. There are reasons to believe that Pakistani politicians expected to *interpret* the principles and ideals of Islam to legitimize a modern, progressive and partially democratic state. As I.H. Qureshi, a close associate of Liaquat observed, Islam was a dynamic concept which "required a new interpretation at every stage of our development" and "cannot be content merely with past precedents and usage". Thus, while the ulemas claimed a guiding/controlling role in the polity because of their knowledge of the medieval schools of Islamic law and of the established interpretations of Islamic principles, the assertion on the part of the politicians that all this was far from sacrosanct and open to reconsideration was a thinly disguised attempt to undercut the *ulemas'* claim to authority[8].

The clerics were not fanatics either as they considerably scaled down their original demand for a Ministry of Religious Affairs to the acceptance of what was basically an advisory role or at best that of an overseer vis-a-vis the legislature. They were also found to make compromises on questions such as the form of government - presidential or parliamentary - to be adopted in Pakistan or whether women would be allowed to participate in politics. It appears that they believed in gradualism and welcomed the commitment elicited from the political elites to honour the *sharia* as a reasonable concession to start with[9].

Two significant points emerge from this brief review of the interplay of religion and politics in Pakistan during its early years: first, it was in the context of the quest for the approximation of a liberal and moderate polity marked by an ambience of democratic bargaining and accommodation that the Islamist forces secured a political space in Pakistan. Second, the religious elements on their part not only exhibited an uncanny ability to live with a democratic system; several features of democratic functioning/mind set including bargaining skills, restraint and compromise too were on display as well.

With the seizure of power by General Ayub Khan in 1958, this democratic space was constricted: the new ruler held the civilian politicians and *ulemas* in equal contempt and his decision to immediately drop the words "Islamic Republic" from the state's official nomenclature clearly indicated his ideological disposition. He sought a reformulation of Islam as a modern and progressive ideology which was easily understandable to the people of Pakistan and, bypassing the ulemas, a number of state-sponsored research institutes were set up to advise him on the problem of bringing the laws of the state in consonance with the *Quran* and the *Sunnah.* Though he had to make amends later—the 1962 constitution through which he sought to civilianize his rule restored the "Islamic" character of Pakistan, and while contesting for the highest office of the nation in 1965 Ayub had to fall back on the support of religious orthodoxy—his authoritarian regime produced two noteworthy consequences: the clerics were to play a potent role in the widespread agitation in the late 1960s for the ouster of Ayub Khan presumably because they were convinced that their case for Islamization could be better pressed in a democratic environment. As Stephen Cohen observes, the "rough treatment" meted out by Ayub instilled into the Islamist parties, especially Jama'at, "a new respect for constitutionalism and civil liberties".[10] Secondly, during the Ayub regime, the empathy the civilian leadership harboured towards the Islamic elements—as against the military leader's explicit disdain—stood out in bold relief. It was through their intervention in the National Assembly that many of the "Islamic" features of the 1956 constitution were smuggled into its 1962 counterpart[11]. Moreover, these ties, however expedient they might have appeared to be, were presumably further cemented through the anti-Ayub movement for restoration of democracy in Pakistan. Indeed, it was this campaign that brought Zulfikar Ali Bhutto, a self-proclaimed socialist and former protègè of Ayub Khan, in closer touch with the Islamist forces.

As the army's down-to-earth approach to the question of Islam stood discredited, the Islamist parties, Jama'at-e-Islami (JI), Jamiat-ul-Ulema-e-Islam (JUI), and Jamiat-ul-Ulema-e-Pakistan (JUP) enthusiastically participated in the first general elections of 1970. The election manifesto of the Jama'at was a historic document in so far as it translated the party's own version of Islam into a detailed programme of reform covering a wide spectrum of issues relating to the constitution, fundamental rights and democratic freedom, agriculture and land reforms, commerce and industry, labour relations, education, health, family planning and foreign policy. To combat Jama'at's challenge, Bhutto, who had emerged as the focal point of the democratic aspirations of the masses, coined the phrase "*Islamic* Socialism" to placate his new found Islamist constituency. The electorate, however, seemed to reject Jama'at's version of Islamic state in favour of Bhutto who had called for "Islamic egalitarianism without demanding Islamic chastity"[12].

Nevertheless, Bhutto's five-year rule witnessed a series of concessions to the Islamists. The 1973 constitution inaugurated by him was more Islamic in character than either of its predecessors: it declared Islam to be the state religion (Article 2) and one of the basic purposes of state policy was declared to be enabling the Muslims of Pakistan mould their lives in accordance with the principles of Islam (Article 31). Learning *Islamiyat* and the Holy *Quran* was made compulsory for Muslims. The Council for Islamic Ideology was formed to give advice to the state and provincial governments as to the compatibility of the existing laws with the *Quran* and the *Sunnah*. True to Islamic practices, a ban was imposed on alcohol and gambling, and Friday was made a non-work day. Bhutto also yielded to the combined pressure of JUI, JI and JUP in proclaiming the Ahmadis as non-Muslims through a constitutional amendment. Finally, Pakistan's foreign and strategic policies were also suffused with Islamic rhetoric: a major Organization of Islamic Conference meeting was held in Lahore in 1974; the programme of making the "Islamic bomb" with the backing of Islamic states like Libya was launched; several Islamic groups were supported against the Afghan government which later played a major role during the Soviet intervention in late 1970s and, more generally, Bhutto sought to play down Pakistan's South Asian identity and turn more and more to West Asia for aid, ideological sustenance and strategic cooperation. Yet—rather ironically—with all this Bhutto failed to win the confidence of the Orthodoxy: his sincerity in introducing and implementing Islamic reforms was questioned; his personal lifestyle was held squarely against him, and Pakistan National Alliance (PNA) the coalition of forces which, manipulated by Zia—the army chief handpicked by Bhutto—was responsible for his ouster had a formidable presence of Islamic parties.

III

Politics of Islam in Pakistan underwent momentous and qualitative shifts during the eleven years of Zia ul Huq's rule. With a view to consolidate his military regime he openly embraced the Islamist groups, cynically used Islam/Islamist outfits to strangulate democracy and browbeat opponents, and also sought to recast law, social norms and the economy according to the "basic tenets of Islam". The Islamization programme was carried deeper within the army barracks, and the groundwork for the proliferation of *madari (madrassah* in singular) or Islamic seminaries in the 1980s and 1990s was firmly laid during the Zia era. Finally, the use *of jihad as* an instrument of foreign policy obtained a seal of legitimacy through his Afghan policy. It has been argued that one of the objects of Zia's hobnobbing with the *ulemas* was to control the

Islamists themselves and to attenuate the strength of the lay Islamists by playing different factions against one another. But the status the *ulemas* had been granted within the state structure allowed them a degree of independence and also to develop a more critical view of the state[13].

It was in this backdrop that Pakistan entered its third phase of democratic rule following the unfortunate death of President Zia in an air crash. The general elections of 1988 were dominated by the People's Democratic Alliance (PDA) led by Benazir Bhutto's Pakistan People's Party (PPP) and the Islamic Jamhoori Ittehad (IJI or Islamic Democratic Alliance), which brought together the Pakistan Muslim League (PML) headed by Nawaz Sharif, a Zia protègè, and the Jama'at in addition to a motley combination of right-of-centre and Islamic parties. During the anti-Zia campaign of the mid-1980s, Benazir did come closer to the Jama'at for tactical reasons, but after mounting the seat of power she began, consciously, pursuing a policy of distancing herself from the orthodox forces. She invoked Jinnah's vision for a Pakistan that would grow as a modern state, promised protection for minorities and enhanced rights for women, and even harked hack to the "socialist" rhetoric of her father Z.A. Bhutto[14]. None of this, needless to say, was likely to endear her to the Islamist lobby already harbouring misgivings about the "woman" prime minister educated in the West, and her inclination, before long, towards mending fences with these elements was amply reflected in the way she backtracked from the changes she had initially wrought in Pakistan's policies towards Afghanistan and India.

During her second tenure (1993-96) she appeared far more conciliatory in her approach to the Islamist forces as she developed the habit of wearing cha'adar during public appearances and visiting the holy Islamic shrines within the country and abroad regularly[15]. In the mid-1990s, a storm gathered around the Blasphemy law which had earned notoriety for its rampant abuse against religious minorities. Following protests by national and international human rights organizations, Benazir's government announced in early 1994 that it intended to introduce two procedural changes which would lessen the possibility of abuse of Section 295-C: first, a formal authorization by a Judicial magistrate would be required before a complaint of blasphemy could be registered and any arrests be effected; moreover, false allegation of blasphemy would itself be made a criminal offence to be punished with up to seven years' imprisonment. The Pakistan Law Commission, presided over by the Chief Justice of Pakistan and attended by the Minister of Law, the Chairman of the Council of Islamic Ideology and the chief justices of the four provincial high courts, decided in February 1994 to send a draft of the Blasphemy amendment Bill to the Council of Islamic Ideology for further scrutiny. Maulana Kausur Niazi, Chairman of the Council of Islamic Ideology, also observed during a press conference that "the law needs modification to ensure that it is not abused by unscrupulous elements for their selfish ends.... The procedure for police registration of a case, the judicial level at which it should be considered and the suitable criteria for admission of witnesses have to be looked at thoroughly". But this drew a howl of protest from expected quarters, the Prime Minister and Law Minister were threatened with dire consequences, and finally they had to retract. The Law Minister explained that the government had never intended to amend or repeal the Blasphemy law as it believed that there should be a deterrent to defiling the name of the prophet and also justified its retention by pointing to legal provisions in the United Kingdom, the United States and other countries which he described as "similar". The bill to bring about the envisaged procedural changes never reached the floor of the parliament[16].

After Benazir's first dismissal in 1990, Nawaz Sharif's IJI alliance attained power with a thumping majority. No wonder, with Jama'at as a coalition partner, Sharif had to speak with a cleft tongue to claim the legacies of both Jinnah and Zia[17]. His government achieved passage in May 1991 of the Shariat Bill, which declared the *Quran* and the *Sunnah* to be the law of the land. A working group was set up to monitor and make recommendations for enforcing Islamic laws in the country.

The working group adopted a nineteen-point plan that included calls for the implementation of all Islamic legislation, especially the laws creating Sharia courts; transformation of the education system to reflect Islamic teaching; controls on the print and electronic media designed to ensure Islamic moral values; uniform and enforced prayer schedules; and the establishment of an Islamic banking system and the total abolition of interest[18]. It may further be noted that when in October 1990, the Federal Shariat Court (FSC) of Pakistan ruled that "the penalty for contempt of the Holy Prophet... is death and nothing else" and directed the Government of Pakistan to effect the necessary changes in the Blasphemy law, the Sharif government chose not to file an appeal against the decision[19]. These measures not only sent wrong signals to the liberal and the secular-minded, they often posed thorny problems for the administration as well. Thus the ruling of the FSC in November, 1991 that payment of interest *(riba)* was prohibited by Islam even if the loan involved was for productive purposes clashed head-on with the government's policy of economic liberalization. Paradoxically, the conservatives felt that these "reforms" did not go far enough, and as the divide between the PML and the JI widened, the ruling coalition fell apart in May, 1992[20].

In 1997, Sharif stormed back to power with a decisive mandate for his PML and this time he decided to move the Fifteenth Amendment of the Constitution in October 1998 which was virtually a prescription for maiming the judiciary and imposing his personal rule under the title *of Amir ul Momineen.* The position of the government was unassailable; there was no perceived need to flaunt its Muslim credentials, and the move quite expectedly generated a heated controversy. But curiously enough, the members of the PPP, the major opposition party, appeared to be rather guarded and defensive in censuring this draconian move which could alone be traced to their reluctance to incur the wrath of the Islamist forces[21]. The Bill was passed by the National Assembly but was not placed before the Senate within the mandatory 90 days because there Sharif did not have the required two-thirds majority. The plan was to wait until the Senate Elections of March 2000—when he was sure of gaming a majority—and then rush the bill through the upper house. But before that Sharif himself was deposed by General Musharraf in a bloodless coup.

IV

Our brief survey of the encounter between democracy and Islam through the five decades of Pakistan's existence gives a lie to the incompatibility thesis elaborated at the outset. Mawdudi's Jama'at, arguably served as the forerunner to the series of Islamist political parties to be created later in the Arab world and beyond[22]. Jama'at and its contemporaries took full advantage of the early democratic churning in Pakistan and enthusiastically engaged in hard bargaining with the civilian politicians to integrate their vision of an Islamic state into its first constitution. They also joined the struggles for restoration of democracy first against the Ayub regime in the 1960s and then the Bhutto dispensation in the 1970s[23]. While it is true that the Zia era thoroughly altered the equation between Pakistan's ruling establishment and the Islamist elements, the latter's zeal for political participation within a democratic electoral framework did not in any way diminish over the years[24].

This, of course, brings one to the disturbing question regarding the *nature of democracy* in Pakistan. True, the democratic phases of Pakistan's polity could never really emerge out of the clutches of the army, and this scenario is unlikely to change without a prior change in the country's threat perceptions. On the other hand, there is no denying that the Pakistani political elites *generally*—and not simply the military—sought to accommodate and manipulate Islamists/Islamic causes to make short-term political gain or divert attention away from ethnic, linguistic, regional or sectarian troubles. However, as against this, two points need to be borne in mind. First, the civilian politicians' attempts to exploit the Islamist forces in order to push their own agendas did not necessarily bear the desired fruits: the elder Bhutto could not win over the aggressive Islamist opposition through his policy of "preemptive surrender"[25]; nor could Sharif keep his IJI flock together in the early 1990s despite vigorously pushing the Sharia Bill (which probably propelled him to move the Fifteenth Amendment to complement his already formidable executive powers with the sanction of religion and outflank the parties on his ideological right)[26]. Thus who has been using whom remained rather an open question[27]. Secondly, electoral democracies all over the world tend at one level to be relegated to a 'numbers game' and consequently making appeals to religious and sectarian forces especially in the developing societies marked by multiple ethno-religious identities becomes a popular strategy of garnering votes. Pandering to the Hindu sentiment in India first in the 1980s by the Congress Party and then, in the 1990s, by the Bharatiya Janata Party to revamp electoral fortunes are handy contemporary examples of such 'vote bank politics'. Pakistani politicians cannot certainly be singled out and pilloried for an offence of which their Indian counterparts are equally guilty, more so when India is often portrayed as a shining example of democracy in the developing world.

To conclude, democracy in Pakistan has to cohabit with Islam and the Islamists for it is unimaginable, at least for the foreseeable future, that the country would shed its religious identity and become a formally secular state. Under the circumstances, the best option on the part of Pakistan's civilian politicians seems to be to engage, accommodate and co-opt the Islamist elements within a democratic framework (a hypothetical scenario, though, for the present) to weaken their ideological rigidity and impel them towards pragmatism and moderation. Pakistani leaders instead, beginning with Z.A. Bhutto, either sought to marginalize the Islamists (e.g. Benazir in 1988) or bent over backwards to placate them (elder Bhutto or early Sharif). On the other hand, the strategy of the first generation of leaders in the 1950s—offering the orthodox groups a political space to function without necessarily capitulating to their demands—seemed rather instructive. No doubt, the character of the Islamist elements, post-Zia, has undergone a sea change: they have secured liberal backing of the army and developed a militant and lunatic fringe. Still, Benazir and Sharif could hardly be said to have exhausted all their options in dealing with the Islamists. On the one hand, they could have devoted greater attention to the task of party-building and strengthening the democratic infrastructure of Pakistan. This together with greater empathy towards the human rights groups, non-governmental organizations and social movements would have enormously helped them to retain support of the liberal constituencies. Instead, their personalized style of functioning accompanied by charges of massive corruption and nepotism, their penchant for hurling abuses at each other and also for striking shadowy deals with the army whenever out of power cost them liberal support, domestic as well as international. Secondly, they could have undertaken a sincere attempt to revive Pakistan's school system which deteriorated beyond recognition during Zia's twelve years of neglect. Unable to send their children to Pakistan's disappearing public schools, many families, especially the poor, took advantage of the madaris, many of which offered free board and lodging facilities in addition to Islamic education. The two prime ministers of the 1990s—one educated in Harvard and Oxford universities and the other representing the Pakistani bourgeoisie—did precious little to arrest these developments. Finally, they could have purposely cultivated the saner and moderate elements within the Islamist circles: this could have contributed towards keeping the militants at bay on the one hand and stabilizing their relations with the army—the chief mentor of the Islamist groups since the 1980s—on the other. In sum, once democracy returns to Pakistan, its civilian politicians would do well to take a leaf out of the books of its early leaders in order to negotiate the Islamist challenge.

NOTES AND REFERENCES

1. For an early exposition of this view see Bernard Lewis, "Islam and Liberal Democracy", *Atlantic Monthly,* February, 1993.

2. Abdou Filali-Ansary, "Muslims and Democracy", *Journal of Democracy*, 10(3), July, 1999.
3. Judith Miller, "The Challenge of Radical Islam", *Foreign Affairs*, Spring, 1993; see also Jahangir Amuzegar, "The Truth and Illusion of Islamic Fundamentalism", *SAIS Review*, January, 1994.
4. Aqil Shah, "Pakistan's 'Armoured' Democracy", *Journal of Democracy*, 14(4), October, 2003, 31.
5. See A.H. Syed, *Pakistan: Islam, Polities and National Sovereignty*, New York: Praeger, 1982, ch 4; Veena Kukreja, *Contemporary Pakistan*, New Delhi: Sage, 2003,159-62; Stephen Cohen, *The Idea of Pakistan*, New Delhi: Oxford University Press, 163-65.
6. Kukreja, ch 1.
7. Syed, 68-70.
8. *Ibid.*
9. *Ibid.*
10. Cohen, 169.
11. Syed, 104.
12. Syed, 119-23.
13. Graham E. Fuller, *The Future of Political Islam*, New York: Palgrave Macmillan, 2003, 131.
14. Seyyed Vali Reja Nasr, "Democracy and Crisis of Governability in Pakistan", *Asian Survey*, 32(6), January 1992.
15. Ifttikhar H. Malik, "State and Civil Society in Pakistan", *Asian Survey*, 36(7), July, 1996.
16. www.thepersecution.org/ai/amnst196.html (last accessed on 18.10.2005). See also M.G. Weinbaum, "Civic Culture and Democracy in Pakistan", *Asian Survey*, 36(70), July, 1996.
17. *Ibid.*
18. http://countrystudies.us/pakistan/76.htm (last accessed on 18.10.2005).
19. www.thepersecution.org/ai/amnst196.html
20. http://countrystudies.us/pakistan/76.htm
21. Mushirul Hasan, "The Islamization of Pakistan", *Indian Express*, 17 October, 1998.
22. Seyyed. Vali Reja Nasr, *The Vanguard of Islamic Revolution*, Los Angeles: University of California Press, 1994, 15, quoted in Fuller, 218 (n 1).
23. The opposition of the Islamist groups to the regime of the elder Bhutto could have several other explanations including their disapproval of his personal lifestyle but it could also be interpreted in terms of the growing authoritarian tendencies displayed by him behind a formal democratic facade.
24. As Cohen observes, "...even some of the Islamist parties have come to value democracy after being on the wrong end of an authoritarian

state" (Cohen, 278) Fuller also notes the growing trend towards electoral participation among Islamist groups (Fuller, 137-38).

25. Shah, 33.
26. Cohen, 173.
27. Shah, 33.

7

Nation, State and Democracy

A Case Study of Indonesia

—SANKARI SUNDARRAMAN

INTRODUCTION

The international system has been dominated by the nation-state as the most integral component of interstate relations. Within this context, the emergence of independent states within the Asian region in the post-colonial phase has sharpened the debate relating to the "nation" *vs.* the "state". Emerging in the aftermath of the colonial period the Asian landscape saw the rise of states from the existing colonial structures that had governed them for several years. In fact the anti-colonial movement itself was a period when the force of the nationalist sentiments was so strongly and intensely articulated that the basic demand of independence from colonial rule remained the foremost goal within the minds of those who led the movement. When the nation *vs.* State debate is viewed within this context, it seems as though the notional and conceptual underpinnings of these two had neither been vigourously debated nor understood by the leaders of the independence movement in several countries. However, if one attempts to analyse the actual essence of the "nation-state", this view of the Indonesian leadership comes under critical examination. This analysis can be better understood by an assessment of the concept of the nation-state itself. The nation, as one understands, is a group of individuals with a common history, desires, goals, and a willingness to identify with a certain geographical territory, while the state is a more legal concept.[1] One of the fallouts of the decolonisation process is evident from the fact that in the newly emerged nations, plural societies have become composite states. It is important to recognise that in most cases of decolonisation, the concept of state with its legal ramifications emerged before nationalism, which is the primary requisite for the creation of a nation-state. As such in the aftermath of decolonisation the emergence was more in the nature of state-nations rather than nation-states.[2]

The Indonesian Case: From Revolution to Independence to the New Order

With specific reference to Indonesia too this was a reality—the notion of "*Indonesia merdeka*" or Free Indonesia was the basic goal of the nationalists. The only thought that dominated the minds of the national leaders was liberation from the Dutch rule.[3] One of the well known Indonesian scholars Ruth McVey, in her work describes the concept that freedom meant different things to the groups that were engaged in seeking this freedom. To those who led the nationalist movement it symbolised the quest toward the formation of a modern state, which would lead to a break from foreign rule as well as breaking the chains that bound them to traditional notions of culture and politics. To the masses, it meant the freedom from overlordship. The basic view that democracy would act as the sustainable political arrangement—with individual rights and justice for all, was the dream of the masses in endorsing *Indonesia merdeka*.[4] McVey further states that,

> "the Indonesian task of locating a national self was complicated by the fact that the nation as a territorial entity has been created by colonial rule, that most traditional cultures seemed too local or `feudal', and that the goal of modernity was located in the West. This was by no means an insuperable barrier, however, for the externality of the model was also part of its attraction."[5]

The territorial boundaries that formed the Dutch East Indies automatically assumed the national boundaries of the modern Indonesian state as envisioned by the leaders of the independence movement. The key concepts that were the basis by which the domination of the West was challenged was through *'perjuangan'* and *'semangat'*, that respectively meant struggle and spirit—and these were intrinsically intertwined with the freedom movement.[6] Even within the freedom movement divergent proponents existed—those who believed that the existing state structures of the Dutch must be retained for the benefit of administrative convenience advocated *diplomasi* in the place of *perjuangan* or struggle. While *semangat* remained the basis for the revolutionary zeal, it was the state structure that emerged stronger in the post-revolution period. The new state emerged as unitary and centralised, committed to secular values with an emphasis on the *panchshila* and an anti-communist orientation.[7] The emergence of a unitary state had as its basis a deep suspicion of the Dutch attempt at trying to institute a federal structure in 1949. This was viewed as an attempt by the Dutch to promote rival nationalist movements within the archipelago and also undermine the leadership that emanated both within Sumatra and Java and culminated in the articulation of the freedom struggle itself.

It is interesting to note that it was during the revolutionary period, between 1945 to1950, that the country actually identified itself as a single unit. This period was significant as it made the struggle for freedom the central episode in the nation's conscience and it remains even today a very critical element of what the nation perceives of itself.[8] It is understandable that in the revolutionary phase there was no attempt to identify the elements that would constitute a single common identity for the nation that emerged. The end of the foreign rule did not result in the dawning of a new and harmonious nation but one where both the personality conflict and social discord was very high. It is therefore essential perhaps to ask the question as to what it is the revolution actually achieved. The end of the revolution clearly indicated what Indonesia would not be—even though it did not indicate what it ought to be! The answers that emerged in the post-revolution period were that it would not be a federal state, it would not be Islamic, it would not be communist and above all it would not remain within the Dutch control. But in terms of redefining and weaving together the social, religious, cultural, communal, ethnic and economic dimensions of nationhood together—the revolution provided no answers at all.[9] This inherent weakness of the revolutionary period has re-emerged after almost half a century and today poses a continuing challenge to the notion or the idea of what constitutes present day Indonesia.

Having emerged from the colonial period the country for the first few years followed a system of parliamentary democracy. This period in Indonesian history was possibly one during which the interests of several groups that formed the nation was actually heard because under the multiparty approach several parties resorted to using primordial loyalties of the groups they claimed to represent. Moreover there was a feeling that since state power or authority was still relatively ill-defined there would be a space for these groups to place their interests within the larger ambit of state policy.[10] Unfortunately for the nascent state three factors undermined its evolution to a full-fledged democracy—first, it inherited the legacy of the colonial period under both the Dutch and the Japanese—as a result of which the foundations of the state structure were basically those that constituted a police state. Second, the mass mobilisation that could have challenged the paternalistic and authoritarian rule remained largely absent in light of the fact that the masses remained poor and illiterate. Added to which the geographical nature of the state contributed to this feeling of divide and isolation where the peripheral areas did not have the clout to force its will upon the Jakarta based political elite. Third, the leadership itself was paternalistic and did not show any commitment to developing the democratic foundations at the grassroots level.[11] This period saw consolidation of both class and state structures and also the beginnings of the military's inclusion in the political framework. The military's inclusion must be seen within the context of the political upheavals that occurred in this early phase—the move for more autonomy from the centre began to surface in the outer regions. In 1950 there was a clamour from the Moluccas, particularly within Ambon, towards independence from Indonesia. Following this the Sumatran crisis also erupted with demands for greater rights over economic assets. The response to such claims was the proclamation of a state of emergency and this period witnessed a greater participation of the military in the political affairs of the state. Moreover, the military also started to project a role for itself in the economic spheres because of its linkages with the Chinese entrepreneurs. It is not possible to give a detailed account of the several parties that existed since the scope of the paper is limited to the current theme of the seminar. Suffice to say that different groups claimed to represent diverse interests. Towards the end of democratic phase however, three separate political groups had clearly emerged as the forerunners within the multiplicity of choices that were present. These were—the Islamic groups, the communist-led left and the military.

From 1957 to 65 the period of Guided Democracy followed—but eventually did not succeed in creating the foundations upon which both nation and state could thrive. While the complementary aspects of the nation and state should have gone hand in hand at this time they were actually working in different directions—the period of Guided Democracy bought with it several nuances of the revolutionary period of the freedom struggle. Three factors became the moot point by which there was an attempt to revert to the emotionalism that had sustained the freedom movement. First, the continuing dependence on the West in terms of the Dutch influence on economic issues. There was a clear attempt to rally public support against this. Second, this period saw the polarisation over the issue of West Irian's transfer to Indonesia. The response to this also led to the emergence of support given to anti-colonial movements the world over. Another factor that tried to enhance the nationalistic fervour was the policy of 'konfrontasi' directed against the creation of Malaysia.[12] It is in the face of such changes that the 1965 coup suddenly and abruptly stopped any attempt at defining what constitutes the nation in Indonesia and brought the cycle completely back to the state. In fact, under the New Order, nationalism was merely a state ornamentation and development became the key ideology of the regime. The following section looks at how the New Order actually constructed a perception of what Indonesia should be both for itself and for the international community.

Indonesia Under the New Order: The Political Tragedy of the Nation

One of the methods used in analysing the political order of the Suharto regime or the New Order state as it was known, includes the structural-functional analysis of politics and society. This deals with the creation of power and the integration of the social system within this existing power structure.[13] It highlights the fundamental contradiction that exists in the Indonesian political structure which emerges from the classic debate between modern political structure and traditional political culture.[14] In one of his earlier works Benedict Anderson states that the Javanese concept of power determined the way in which the distribution of power under Sukarno and Suharto were managed. Moreover he states that the sociology of the power structure in Indonesia is also a significant factor in an understanding of the present day problems that ail this nation-state. The crux of this concept is that the structure of patrimonialism and the traditional concept of power work in the same direction. The centrality of this debate is evident from the personalised character of politics in Indonesia, where the structures of the political set up have contributed to sustaining "individual officials, political factions, client-patron groups and different cultural streams", without an attempt to integrate the social and cultural forces that are a necessary part of the nation-building process.[15] An analysis can be seen in the way in which the leadership has justified its role. The justification for Sukarno's authoritarian posture rested in the effective crystallisation of the popular consensus of the masses—that is in critical terms the authoritarian structure was vested in Sukarno with the endorsement of popular support. In contrast the authoritarian structure of the Suharto regime seemed to emanate from the fact that the New Order believed that such a form of government was a necessary ingredient in the progress towards economic development and growth.[16] The understanding of the concept of power within the traditional Javanese system is critical to this—power is seen as that which is accorded to the ruler and not as a process of due merit. The social impact of this view of power, with its emphasis on peace and unity does not question the person in authority. However, today most serious observers are reluctant to put much emphasis on Anderson's Javanese Idea of Power thesis, partly because today Indonesia is clearly recognized as more than just Java, partly because Anderson's own arguments were based on the differences between Javanese and Western cultures and did not take into consideration the differences within the cultures found in Indonesia itself, and partly because Anderson implies that culture forces people to act in particular manner, rather than simply giving importance to the actions of the individuals themselves. The individuals in this case being the leaders of the state.

The period that is most crucial in this current assessment on the nation, state and democratisation is that of the New Order. The centrality of the political structure and the manner in which power was distributed clearly indicates that the filtering of power was from a top-down process and not a bottom-up process. The concentration of executive power in an autocratic manner automatically stunted the development of democratic institutions and limited the role of civil society. With restrictions on political and social activity, civil society was weakened at the cost of strengthening central authority. In fact, the legal sanction for such a process was justified within the framework of the 1945 Constitution where the President was allowed enormous powers over other aspects of the state structure.[17] In the power pyramid, the President, was placed at the top of the structure, with the ruling family and close allies of the family coming second. In place after this was the military, technocrats and businessmen who received patronage from the military—this group among the business community was often dominated by the Chinese. Small in terms of numbers, they dominated a very large portion of the assets of business within the Indonesian economy. Next to this group, at the fourth level was a small middle class which was growing in numbers. Though some analysts had predicted a middle class led revolution, their strength in numbers indicates that they alone could not have brought about any political changes. It is interesting to note that as long as the middle classes were receiving the benefits accruing from the economic growth, there was really no attempt to change the political structure. But with time the larger share of the benefits of economic development to the ruling classes began to increase and this was the beginning of their alienation, as well as the emergence of a more vibrant and politically demanding middle class in Indonesia. At the lowest order of the pyramid, were the urban workers, farmers and the bulk of the population.[18]

The economic policies of the New Order regime did achieve a modicum of success and was guided by objective and scientific technocrats who were expected to remain detached from the political developments of the state. As far as the economic development of the state is concerned the New Order regime clearly considered its place as one "in which the country had moved from a period of chaos to one of more order; and from mere ideology to more objective".[19] In fact in an attempt to distinguish himself from Sukarno who was acknowledged as the Father of the Nation, Suharto became the "Father of Development". It is important to recognize that the New Order did bring enormous material benefits to a large proportion of the population. The real criticism of the New Order is not that the gains remained in the hands of a powerful few, but (a) that a powerful few prospered disproportionately (and this seems to have been a feature especially of the 1990s rather than earlier decades; there are indications that the inequities began to grow only in the 1990s, when they also grew in most other parts of the world), (b) that the New Order was callous in its treatment of the victims of development (e.g. people displaced from their homes for development purposes)' and (c) that growth could have been very much better with different policies.

Also in the Indonesian case the New Order was seen as a "component of an alliance between foreign capital and indigenous politico-bureaucratic forces dominated by the military. Of course there is a conventional view that in the early years of the New Order the military did dominate politics in Indonesia. But with the increasing authority of Suharto this posture later changed somewhat. In fact after 1974, Suharto began to distance himself from the military and tried to control it in much the same way that he controlled other sections of society. In the late 1980s there was a clear power struggle between the military, under Benny Murdani, and Suharto which ended in victory for Suharto and a process referred to as "de-Bennyization" in which Suharto asserted his authority over the military. Of course there is no doubt that the military remained a pillar of the regime, but as an institution the military became highly dependent on Suharto, and this dependence became one of the major causes for its weakness in the face of the student uprising in 1998 which called for the removal of Suharto himself.[20]

This combination of authoritarian power and the military as its basic pillar undermined completely the vision of Indonesia that had been the essence of the revolutionary zeal in the pre-independence phase. Two factors furthered the process even more—first, personal patronage thrived as a result of which the senior level officials of the ABRI (Angkatan Bersenjata Republik Indonesia), which is the Indonesian Armed Forces, were able to make profits. Suharto himself was not willing to clamp down on this. In fact Suharto himself was very much implicated in this misuse of power. Though there is no evidence that supports his personal greed as in the case of leaders such as the Marcos family—he neither lived ostentatiously nor accumulated possessions, but he allowed his family to do so—and he abused his power in all sorts of ways to accumulate resources which in turn bolstered his political power.[21] As a result thereof, the second related issue of corruption within the administrative set up became institutionalised and bribery remained intact till the late nineties. While corruption is prevalent in many societies, the Indonesian case is probably distinct because of the fact that it has become established as a "traditional right", thus implying that selling of favours was very much a part of the autocratic set up.[22]

The most probable turning point was the Asian financial crisis. Indonesia's currency crisis began when there was an overall fall in the currency position in Southeast Asia. It started with the Thai currency depreciating and then moved on to affect the rest of the region. The Thai baht was the first currency that collapsed and the Thai government was forced to float the baht in July 1997. In the same month changes were seen within the Filipino and the Malaysian economies too and it resulted in both these countries depreciating their respective currencies, the peso and the ringgit. In fact, it was the Indonesian currency that tried to resist the changes for the longest period, but to little avail because the market pressures ultimately led to the collapse of the rupiah in August 1997. In Indonesia the ratio of foreign debt to that of the domestic GDP was high. The problem was further compounded by the fact that the country lacked the necessary foreign exchange reserves to meet the payments of the short-term financial loans. As the crisis worsened in September 1997, the Indonesian government "postponed" projects that were worth $17 billion and placed "under review" those that were to the tune of $3 billion.[23] Sikorski states that the actual meaning of these two terms remain unclear because the government had "left the door open for lobbying by companies to keep their projects on track". In November 1997, some of the projects that had been suspended were reversed—$2 billion worth of projects were given the go-ahead, but these were mainly those that were led by large American multi-nationals and a project that was being led by Suharto's daughter.[24] The form of patronage followed by the regime, had led to the emergence of 50 large conglomerates, some of which were controlled by Suharto's children and key functionaries in the armed forces who had close links with the ruling family. Due to the deeply entrenched nepotism, several businesses that tried to compete were rendered insolvent and others were completely marginalised.

In the aftermath of the 1997 crisis, one of the areas most affected was the banking sector, leading to the liquidation of sixteen banks by the monetary authorities. With the continuing fall of the rupiah, investor confidence took a severe beating, added to which the all pervasive corruption in the economic dealings of the government caused a serious lack of faith in the system—the entrepreneurs were willing to sell the fast falling rupiah and investor confidence was so low that at one point investors simply packed up and left. The move of the IMF, to close down those sectors that were considered untenable, was implemented with the hope that it would restore some confidence into the financial sector, but the actual policy backfired rather badly with the result that several banks began to experience severe runs on their deposits.[25]

Thus by early 1998, Indonesia's economic miracle had veered off badly and it had a huge debt burden of US $ 115 billion.[26] This was because many investors and large companies began to gain access to the international capital markets after the early nineties and this led to the increase in debt burden which has even been placed at US $ 137 billion. What really became the crux of the issue was the closure of some monopolies such as wheat, flour, soybeans and garlic and the control and subsidies on fuel and cement were cut. Added to this the government had to implement austerity measures which left very little for the population. These measures led to a food crisis which lies at the heart of the political unrest that engulfed Indonesia. The long-term effect of these policies was evident in the growing resentment within many sectors of society which was to have a bearing upon the political system in the months following the financial crisis.[27] The clamour for change began by January 1998 and by May of that year Suharto was forced to step down from power.

Post-Suharto Period

In the period after the overthrow of Suharto, under Habibie, the demand for political change began in earnest. This period was marked by the cries of *reformasi*. In reality the entire power structure after Suharto's ouster had to be redefined. The attempt at redefining power had to include several changes. First, the role of the military as a pillar of the political structure shifted; second, there was a need to amend the constitution; third, the state had to safeguard the increase in separatist tendencies at the regional levels and finally implement laws that could strengthen the institutional mechanisms that would advance the cause of democratic freedoms and human values. With the pressure for change at its doorstep, the interregnum period under Habibie was witness to a weakening and less composite idea of what constituted the Indonesian state. The personalised power structure and the well entrenched networks of patronage and bureaucracy began to collapse and resulted in widening the power base, both horizontally and vertically.[28] Three groups emerged in the political struggle—those who wanted to maintain status quo and generally identified with the Golkar and the Armed Forces; secondly, the `moderate reformists', which included the leaders of the main political parties who while seeking reform were unwilling to completely undo the existing structure; and finally the radicals, led by student activists, clamouring for *reformasi total*.[29] The choice left for the incumbent President Habibie was very little—it was under these circumstances that the 1999 elections were announced.

With this in view, a group of seven eminent persons were asked to look into the issues of reform in the existing political set up. Three main issues were placed under the purview of the Team of Seven, comprising of legal experts and eminent personalities. First was the issue of proportional representation. The Golkar group lobbied for changing this to a majority district system because its ranks were more well-entrenched at the grassroot levels and under such a set up they stood a better chance in the elections. The other parties in the meantime wanted the representational pattern to continue. The final decision was combination of both these forms. The second issue was the restructuring of the two political bodies—the DPR which is the People's Representative Council or the Parliament and comprises of 500 members. The other body is the MPR, which is the People's Consultative Assembly—this is a supreme sovereign body. This body under Suharto comprised of 500 members of the DPR and included another 500 members who were appointed by the President who were regional and functional group representatives. It was the task of the MPR to elect the President every five years. The domination of the DPR by the Golkar and the representation in the MPR had successfully seen to the victory of Suharto in five consecutive 'elections'. The team changed the composition of the MPR from 500 to 200—135 regional representatives who were to be chosen by the provincial level parliaments and 65 functional group representatives who were to be selected by government. The initial selection was left under the General Election Committee (KPU) which technically came under the Interior Ministry. But it was felt that such a selection pattern would automatically strengthen the hands of the Golkar vis-à-vis the other parties. The other major change was with relation to the representation of the army within the parliament. Anti-military sentiment was high in the aftermath of Suharto's ouster when the military had played a role in the clamping down against the protesters. Demands were that the military should be excluded totally from the legislature. The military had played a crucial role in the Indonesian political set with the consti-tutional endorsement of the *dwifungsi* or the dual function which included both administration and security of the state and its frontal organisation was the Golkar or the golongon karya which was the functional group. In fact the Golkar was willing to reduce its representation from 75 seats to 40 seats in the DPR. In the final analysis the military received 38 seats within the DPR which was 7.6 per cent of the total seats, and 10% in the provincial assemblies.[30] The elections in June 1999 occurred within the context of these dramatic changes and the PDI-P led by Megawati Sukarnoputri emerged in the lead—however the formation of the "*poros tengah*" or the "central axis", a grouping of Islamic parties did not allow for her to become the President. The choice fell on Wahid who remained a weak and ineffective leader.

Wahid's weakness came from his obvious inconsistency, where his public comments and the policies of the government he headed were out of tune with each other. In recent times he had been described as an individual who lived in his own world. It became increasingly evident that he paid little heed to document protocol and the legal accountability for his actions was not taken seriously, either by him or his supporters. There was mounting criticism at his arbitrary behaviour and the fact that he is shrinking closer into a circle of close cohorts, consisting of his family members and bizarre camp followers. In the period after becoming President, Wahid began to acquire a whimsical quality about himself—many a times at important meetings he has fallen asleep, which reflected the physical difficulties of his health and age. And at the same time when the criticism has been strong against him, he has walked out.[31] Another factor that weakened his position was with regard to the issue of corruption. Despite the many public pronouncements on weeding out corruption the government under his leadership had been unable to effectively tackle this problem. Added to this Wahid himself had been implicated in cases of corruption. First, there was fraudulent withdrawal of 35 billion rupiah (US $ 3.7 million) from the State Logistics Agency or the Bulog by Wahid's former masseur. The second case relates to the handling of a donation made by the Sultan of Brunei amounting to US $ 2 million which was given as a humanitarian relief package for Aceh. The responses to accusations against Wahid have been mixed—there is a group that believes these issues are purely fabricated to undermine his leadership; and the other group that believes he is capable of corruption. Added to this the government had been unable to bring to book various charges of corruption levelled against leaders of the former regime. It was widely felt that President Wahid had not used his office to fight rampant corruption within the country and there was growing discontentment with regard to this.[32] Added to this the parliament and President had been unable to agree on the selection of a Chief Justice—for a judiciary that remains one of the weakest and most corrupt institutions in the country.[33] These growing accusations and the widespread disenchantment with Wahid had come to a head—as early as August 2000, Wahid found himself locked in battle with the parliament—the end result was that he was forced to reshuffle his cabinet to avoid the possibility of an impeachment.[34] In February 2001, this move again gained ground even though there is no concrete proof of his involvement in what is popularly being referred to as the Bruneigate and Bulogate scandals.

Abdurrahman Wahid's own response to the impeachment proceedings that took place on July 23, 2001 was one of denial. During the lead up to the censure vote he even toyed with the idea of having the military declare a state of emergency and dissolve the parliament but this did not meet with approval from the Susilo Bambang Yudhoyono, the Political Coordinating Minister. Wahid has also used some factions of the PKB to carry out pro-Wahid protests in East Java where the influence of the PKB backed by the NU is the strongest. His most effective weapon had been the threat of national disintegration. Analysts stated that the threat of violence appeared to be a strategy that he was using against Megawati who is known for her abhorrence against violence, in the hope that she would call off the impeachment proceedings.[35] However, the calm that Megawati exhibited in the run up to the impeachment adequately reveals the confidence that she had in the results that were to follow. President Wahid's fall has been evaluated thus, "he lost the presidency not because he was blind and dogged by conservative forces, but because he was erratic and impossible to work with and, in the end, he alienated supporters by easily going back on his word and allowing an oversized ego to cloud his better judgement".[36]

Megawati Sukaroputri's emergence was this time round backed by the "poros tengah" itself. An editorial in the Jakarta Post had described her as a "president-in-waiting", but her moves were cautious since there was a growing view among the top leaders of the PDI-P, that the process being set in motion against Wahid is also likely to engulf her at some point. The legacy of the problems inherited by Wahid had really not changed and Megawati's success would be as difficult as that of Wahid. Initially after her appointment two or three factors were seen as challenges—first was that Megawati was seen as being close to the Golkar which has been accused in several cases of corruption. Therefore the problems relating to the legacy of corruption had passed on to her shoulders as well. Second with regard to the issue of separatist tendencies within the state Megawati was seen to be a nationalist and more willing to depend on the army to bring recalcitrant regions under the Centre's control, than Wahid who was seen as a moderate in many ways. This will make it difficult for her to act upon these charges which is one of the problems faced by Wahid. In fact after the impeachment and Megawati's appointment as President, there was an initial positive response at the markets where the rupiah strengthened from 11,300 to 9,900 to the US dollar. Two factors will remain very crucial for the survival of President Megawati—the first is that she should be able to bring in the assistance of technocrats such as Laksamana Sukardi, a leading economist and a very close ally of President Megawati. As Minister of State-Owned Enterprises, he has the unenviable task of bringing more order to the economic conditions of the state and also bringing structure to the Indonesian Bank Restructuring Agency (Ibra). But the presence of Sukardi will ensure more support from financial agencies for he is seen to represent 'reform and good governance....his choice symbolises a determination to clean things up and run them according to the rule of law'.[37] The second factor that is likely to be significant is whether President Megawati will be successful in reigning in the forces that divide parliament. The only worry in this context is that President Megawati has been seen to be allying with the more conservative elements in the political fray and whether this harbours well for the process of reform is still uncertain. In an attempt to appease these conservative factions, reform must not be sacrificed. There is also a view that as far as the issue of separatist movements are concerned, she may be willing to take a less liberal stand on autonomy, and can resort to military means to safeguard the territorial integrity of the state.[38]

Challenges to the Idea of Indonesia

Under these circumstances the political challenges that is facing Indonesia today is probably one of the most crucial issues. Political challenges emerge from several issues—the lack of a coherent identity that can be termed as Indonesian; the growing attempts by separatist forces that seems to be weakening the control of the state, are some of the challenges that today plague the Indonesian state. Added to this in the post September 11 phase the concern relating to the issue of terrorism is another dimension that challenges the state. These factors have been briefly discussed below:

The Identity Factor

The first aspect of the political structure that seems to weaken the Indonesian state is with regard to the concept of identity. Several reasons can be attributed to the fact that the Indonesian state in fifty years has been unable to forge together an identity for itself. It is true that under the Dutch colonial period this aspect was difficult to achieve—what had been the Netherlands Indies automatically assumed the shape of Indonesia in the minds of those who carried forth the independence movement. The movement for freedom, led by Sumatra and Central Java, remained totally isolated to the desires and aspirations of the regional players. As such, there was neither a composite dialogue nor a vigorous debate among the groups, as to what actually constituted an Indonesian identity. Even during the period of Japanese occupation this trend continued and is visible in the framing of the 1945 Constitution where the notion of the Republic has been identified by the Java-based conservative secular nationalists who have drawn on the ideas of Dutch trained legal experts. As such the constitution does not foster a coherent identity. In fact, the 1945 Constitution is a brief document of 37 articles and is extremely paternalistic and centralised in its orientation. It vested all authority and power in the hands of the President and conceded very little to the parliament.[39] Added to this was the fact that the concept of

Pancashila or the five principles of state policy (belief in god, unity of nation, humanitarianism, popular sovereignty and social justice and prosperity for all), have placed unity as the primary goal without an attempt to address the issues of diversity that have been an inherent part of the social and political fabric of the state. Under both Sukarno and Suharto, the need to develop an identity for Indonesian was not looked into—in fact that identity was imposed from above.[40] Added to the identity factor, one must also realise that the political landscape of Indonesia has changed in light of the fact that after the economic collapse several regional groups have started to realise that the centralisation of their resources of wealth and the domination by the Javanese, has led to poorer development of these regions while simultaneously contributing toward the factionalism between the groups themselves. [41]

Issues of Separatism

The second issue that plagues the political scene is that of separatist tendencies which are seen in several parts of the country. There is an overpowering urgency to address issues of separatism within the state which has been unleashed after the East Timor independence—regions such as Aceh, Irian Jaya, Riau and parts of the Moluccas, particularly Ambon are in deep crisis. In the last few years, the certitude of President Sukarno post-Indonesian independence, that anyone could see the unity and singleness of the intertwining chain of islands that stretched between Asia and Australia, seems to have come under threat. These recent events instead seem to support the hypothesis of the well-known historian, J.D. Legge, who in his work "Indonesia's Diversity Revisited" (Indonesia, Vol. 49, 1990), states that "it's archipelagic character, ethnic complexity, and economic diversity, hardly made it a candidate for independent nationhood".[42] Opinion apart, even within the regime there have been references to the possibility of Indonesia falling apart if due consideration is not given to the problems that ail the fragile unity of the state. Much of the moves for separatism have become stronger after the East

Timorese independence.[43] The following section looks at some of the cases where the demand for separatism has been on the increase.

Aceh

This province lies at the northern most tip of Sumatra and has had a history of rebellion against both the Dutch and the Central Government. From the mid-seventies, the Free Aceh Movement or the *Gerakan Aceh Merdeka* (GAM), has been active. This muslim dominated region had been an independent sultanate that had resisted the Dutch occupation—in fact even after the conquest of Sumatra by the Dutch following the Anglo-Dutch Agreements of 1870, this small territory held out till about the early 1900's. During the Japanese occupation, they were able to mount pressure on the Dutch and contributed to the independence movement. In 1949, it acceded to the Indonesian state but revolted in 1953, in favour of a more federal set up. At that time Sukarno accorded it a special regional status.[44] Under the Suharto government the rebellion resurfaced in opposition to the central control and state patronage which was concentrated in the hands of the power wielders. With the discovery of potential amounts of hydrocarbons the region contributed to the oil boom and the benefits went to the Jakarta regime and the foreign companies, thus alienating the locals. It has been stated that rich ghettos of migrants had moved to the region further destabilising the social balance. Two social groups emerged—"a high income, capital intensive, urban, non-Muslim, non-Acehnese" group as compared to the impoverished locals.[45] Though the movement grew for sometime, counter-insurgency operations ruthlessly crushed the same and by 1993 it had abated. Sporadic violence continued and began to resurface after 1997 when the military police found large caches of light weapons in the region which had links with Malaysia. When the *reformasi* process was set in motion, the Acehnese initially backed the civilian group but in the aftermath of East Timor, their clamour for independence has become more pronounced. In the recent past Aceh has again been in the news after the problems being faced by the Exxon Mobil in its oil rigs in the region. Of Exxon Mobil's estimated oil output globally, Aceh accounts for about 2.5 per cent, worrth about US $ 250 million.[46] The issues that are critical in this case are those of restructuring, local autonomy and the looting of the offshore facilities by the armed rebel groups in the area. As such the unique selling proposition of Aceh which had earlier been the security of supply has been undermined. This has been one of the fall-outs of the political instability in the state.[47] The demand still continues and it remains to be seen as to what solution lies ahead for Aceh. In fact over the years the demand for separation from Indonesia has been articulated by several different constituencies—such as the economic, the religious, the political and the social. Even the efforts of the Henry Dunant Centre to broker a peace between the GAM and Jakarta have not met with success since the ceasefire has not been observed by both the military and the GAM. Inspite of the introduction of the autonomy law which allows the region to have greater access over its economic assets the conflict has continued.[48] What is of concern is that the Indonesian government has been trying to get the Gerekan Aceh Merdeka (GAM) or the Free Aceh Movement to be officially recognised as a terrorist outfit on par with the Jemaah Islamiah. There is a clear attempt by the Indonesian government to link up the vertical and horizontal conflicts within the country to suit its own advantage—first it would result in an unquestioned role for the government in dealing with issues that are a threat to state stability. Second, it would certainly extend the theatre of conflict and thus create greater instability to this nascent democracy.

Irian Jaya, Riau

The region of Irian Jaya or West Papua, is basically a non-Muslim area and had remained a Dutch territory till 1962. In 1969 it became part of the Indonesian archipelago after a brief UN interregnum and a referendum. The Act of Free Choice as the referendum was called did not take into account the entire population. It is believed that only about 1000 Papuan leaders were allowed to participate and that too under intense pressure from Indonesia. From 1965 the Free Papua Movement (OPM) began its war against the Jakarta regime. Though the region opposed incorporation within Indonesia, much of the resistance was against the transmigration policy encouraged by the centre. The migration essentially took place from Java and Bali – it set off the contention between what is the *pribumi* (which corresponds with the *bhumiputra* concept), and the settlers. Free port rights were provided as early as 1967, and the loss of agricultural lands to the mining companies has impoverished the region and led to wide-scale environmental degradation. The only answer to the growing discontent has been through the use of the army. The tensions in the area have escalated because of the similarity between the population in Irian Jaya and Papua New Guinea, which has given the issue a more complex direction. Although there is a great deal of ethnic diversity between the two, there is however, some general sense of Melanesian identity and this had complicated the issue. The clamour for freedom has been expressed both through the use of violence and through peaceful demonstrations and appeals to the United Nations.[49]

Riau

Riau poses a similar challenge, where the demand for autonomy has been expressed. However when compared to both Aceh and Irian Jaya, Riau does not become comparable in its intensity. Rich in oil and gas reserves, the area has seen greater demands by the local people for mining and logging concessions. The issue is more in terms of demands for a greater share of the regions wealth and this has been asserted by the levy of taxes on goods and commodities from the region by the locals. [50] This is particularly so after the creation of the Growth Triangle that links Riau to Singapore and Johor. There is a view that Riau provides resources for capital rich Singapore and that the benefits from these do not go to the region but to the centre. With the implementation of the autonomy law there has been an attempt to work out some flexible arrangement in this regard.

West Kalimantan

In contrast with Aceh the problems in West Kalimantan relate to communal conflict rather than being seen as vertical conflicts against the state. The tensions in the West Kalimantan region began to surface in a later period when the policies of *transmigrasi* began to affect the ethnic balance within the region. The local population—the Dayaks—is a non-Muslim community. The region has also become home to several members of the Chinese population who had moved to the region as early as the 19th century and have been engaged in mining activities. In fact as early as 1967 there was a violent attack against the Chinese. The recent migration of the Madurese has led to tensions. The Madurese, a predominantly muslim community are intolerant of the Dayaks over issues relating to eating of pork and the breeding of dogs, which they see as anti-Islamic. As an ethnic community the Madurese are willing to use violence for redressal of grievances and the retaliation by the Dayaks has led to some very violent clashes in the region.[51]

Ambon

From around mid-1999 the region of Ambon in the South Moluccas, had witnessed tensions between the Christian and Muslim communities. A very small territory of the Southern Moluccan island, Ambon was integral to the spice trade as it was the only source of clove while the smaller island of Banda was a source of nutmeg. During the colonial period these islands were contested for by the Dutch, the Portuguese and the British. When the Dutch expanded their control in Indonesia the Moluccas also came under their influence. Religious influences in this area were Muslim, Catholic and Protestant. In fact the Ambonese Christians were favoured by the Dutch and were recruited as soldiers to control several regions under Dutch control. By 1949-50, some Ambonese wanted to form an independent state, the Republic of South Moluccas. But by 1950 they were integrated into the Indonesian state. The causes for vulnerability among the group arise from more recent developments such as internal migration by Muslims and loss of territory within their province. The fear that their faith may not survive the challenges of co-existence in a predominantly Muslim state has been a major cause for concern. With these factors already entrenched in the psyche of the minority community the attacks on the Christian community that occurred at the end of 2000, will do little to quell their misgivings. There is a possibility that the recent attacks will further alienate the groups within Ambon and the South Moluccas. [52]

Terrorism

The third challenge that has emerged in the most recent times is the threat of terrorism. With the 9/11 attacks in the United States, Indonesia too has come under scrutiny with regard to this. The presence of groups such as the Jemaah Islamiah, as well as wings of the Lashkar Jehad and the Lashkar Mujahideen, the fear that Indonesia may have linkages with the al Qaida, has been a cause for friction both within the region and in light of the pressure from the United States. The Bali bombings in October 2002, was crucial in these calculations. However, the effectiveness of the measures which the government took has been well appreciated by the international community and the speed with which it had conducted both the investigation and the trial have been commendable. After the recent bombing at the Marriot Hotel in Jakarta there has been a debate on the restoration of the Anti-Subversion law. The law was used under the Suharto regime to imprison and detain political activists and radical Muslim leaders.[53] There is a fear that the terrorism issue will undermine even the little move that has occurred towards democratisation. One of the fears is that it will be used to clamp down on political dissent. This will remain another challenging hurdle in the evolution of clearer norms of political participation. Another factor for concern is that the Indonesian government has been trying to get the Gerekan Aceh Merdeka (GAM) or the Free Aceh Movement to be officially recognised as a terrorist outfit on par with the Jemaah Islamiah. There is a clear attempt by the Indonesian government to link up the vertical and horizontal conflicts within the country to suit its own advantage—first it would result in an unquestioned role for the government in dealing with issues that are a threat to state stability. Second, it would certainly extend the theatre of conflict and thus create greater instability to this nascent democracy.

Conclusion

Today Indonesia once again stands at a crossroads—in the post-revolutionary phase several questions remained unanswered and today again there is a need to address some of these fundamental question. What lies ahead for the Indonesian state? In the upcoming elections there is to be a direct presidential election and already several leaders have entered the political fray and there is continuing uncertainty regarding leadership. Violence in the country needs to be curbed and efforts must be made to foster a sense of national identity and national unity. It is along these lines that the distinction between the civic nation, as understood in the Westphalian system and the ethnic nation, in the cultural sense, have a bearing on the Indonesian example. While there has been an increase from the provinces calling for increased autonomy and a larger share of the economic benefits to the regions, analysts are skeptical about predicting the break up of the state and other alternatives that can provide better central-regional understanding are being advocated. This has led several people to advocate a federal structure for Indonesia. Federalism can be considered as a viable option because of the challenges to national unity, where identity has become a key factor. With the need to safeguard unity, which can also be extended to include territorial integrity as well as sovereignty, federalism offers a solution. While this has not been acceptable in the past there is a clear need to rethink this issue. Federalism needs to be recognised, not as a fixed concept, but as an evolutionary political arrangement that is capable of balancing the tensions in the central-regional matrix. Finally, the institutions that have failed to deliver in the times of crises will continue to remain weak and ineffective as long as concerted efforts are not made to reform them. This concern of the weakness of institutions is compounded by an extremely weak presidency, and weak administrations cannot help build strong institutions or reform weak institutions. Whether this infant democracy can rise to these challenges and whether the leadership in the country can be bold enough to provide alternatives that are different remains to be seen.

NOTES AND REFERENCES

1. Urmila Phadnis, *Ethnicity and Nation-Building in South Asia* (New Delhi: Sage, 1989), p. 21.
2. *Ibid.*
3. Ruth McVey, "Nation *vs.* State in Indonesia", in Damien Kingsbury and Harry Aveling, eds. Autonony and Disintegration in Indonesia, London: Routledge Curzon: 2003, p. 17.
4. *Ibid.*
5. *Ibid.*, p. 18.
6. *Ibid.*, p. 19.
7. *Ibid.*
8. M.C. Ricklefs, A History of Modern Indonesia Since c. 1200, Hampshire: Palgrave, 2001, p. 261.
9. *Ibid.*, p. 286.
10. McVey, n. 2, p. 19.
11. M.C. Rick lefs, n. 7, p. 289.
12. McVey, n. 2, p. 19.
13. Several works are available which have discussed at length some of the findings that have been addressed. For a detailed analysis see, Donald K. Emmerson, *Indonesia's Elite: Political Culture and Cultural Politics* (Ithaca, Cornell University Press, 1976); Karl D. Jackson, "The Political Implications of Structure and Culture in Indonesia", in Karl D. Jackson and Lucien Pye (ed.), *Political Power and Communications in Indonesia* (Berkeley, University of California Press, 1978), cited in Richard Robison, "Class, Capital and State in New Order Indonesia," in R. Higgot and R. Robison, eds. *South-east Asia: Essays in Political*

Economy of Structural Change, London: Routledge and Kegan Paul, 1985, p. 297. See also Benedict Anderson, "The Idea of Power in Javanese Culture", in Claire Holt, Benedict Anderson and James Siegel, eds. Culture and Politics in Indonesia, Ithaca: Cornell University Press, 1972, pp. 1-69.

14. An example of this debate between modern political structures and traditional political cultures is well emphasised in an understanding of the whole idea of leadership. As in the case of the 'divine right of kingship' or the *devaraja* concept, the leadership of both Sukarno and Suharto was considered absolute where the president was above the law.
15. See, Urmila Phadnis, n. 1, p. 21.
16. Richard Robison, n. 12, pp. 306-07.
17. Kathy Robinson and Daniel Fitzpatrick, "Introduction: Civil Society and Legal Institutions", in Chris Manning and Peter Van Dierman (ed.), *Indonesia in Transition: Social Aspects of Reformasi and Crisis*, Singapore: ISEAS, 2000, p. 255.
18. Richard W. Baker *et al.* (ed.), *Indonesia: The Challenge of Change* (Singapore: ISEAS, 1999), pp. 61-80. For an analysis of the power structure also see Damien Kingsbury, *The Politics of Indonesia*, Oxford: Oxford University Press, 1998, pp. 127-46; Scott B. MacDonald and Jonathan Lemco, "Indonesia: Living Dangerously", *Current History*, Vol. 100, no. 645, April 2001, p. 177.
19. Richard Robison, n. 12, p. 297.
20. For a detailed analysis of the shifting power equations between Suharto and the military please see Adam Schwarz, *A Nation in Waiting: Indonesia in the 1990s* (Boulder, Westview Press, 1994).
21. *Ibid.*
22. See the work by Adam Schwarz where the reference to the selling of political favours is made in the context of Indonesia. Of particular interest is the emphasis that Schwarz lays to the fact that corruption in Indonesia is often socially tolerated. For details see, *Ibid.*, p. 135. Dwight Y. King, "Corruption in Indonesia: A Curable Cancer?", *Journal of International Affairs*, Vol. 53, no. 2, Spring 2000 (University of Columbia, New York), p. 610. Also see, Damien Kingsbury, n. 17, p. 199.
23. Douglas Sikorski, "The Financial Crisis in Indonesia: Explanations and Controversies", *The Indonesian Quarterly*, Vol. 26, no. 4, Fourth Quarter, 1998, p. 366.
24. *Ibid.*
25. *Ibid.*, p. 367.
26. Damien Kingsbury, n. 17, p. 95.
27. For details see, Winters, J., *Power in Motion: Capital Mobility and the Indonesian State* (Ithaca NY: Cornell University Press, 1996), cited in *Ibid.*, pp. 83-84.

28. David Bourchier, "Habibie's Interregnum: Reformasi, Elections, Regionalism and the Struggle for Power", in Chris Manning and Peter Van Diermen, n. 16, p.16.
29. *Ibid.*
30. *Ibid.*, pp. 1-57.
31. Far Eastern Economic Review, Feoruary 15, 2001.
32. A recent report from a German NGO has stated that Indonesia is one of the fifth most corrupt countries in the world. While Wahid himself has been implicated in two cases his lack of action on other cases has led to the mounting criticism against him. During the time of Habibie there was the Bank Bali case when the intermediary consultant at the bank is said to have funneled off government money to members of the Golkar. Another issue was the postponement of the prosecution of three major conglomerates that had close links with the Suharto regime have been cited as glaring examples of the governments lack of response on this issue, n. 17.
33. *Ibid.*, p. 179.
34. Far Eastern Economic Review, August 24, 2000.
35. Straits Times, May 30, 2001 (Internet Edition).
36. Far Eastern Economic Review, August 2, 2001.
37. Far Eastern Economic Review, August 30, 2001.
38. Far Eastern Economic Review, August 2, 2001.
39. This point is well stated in an article that was delivered as a lecture and is available on the internet at the website of Griffith University in Australia. The Tragedy of Modern Indonesian History, An Inaugural Professorial Lecture, Prof. Robert Elson, 22 October, 1998, Griffith University. <http://www.gu.au/centre/gapc/html>
40. *Ibid.*
41. An example of this can be seen in the recent clashes that have occurred in the Riau and East Kalimantan regions, which are both rich in oil and gas resources. While the regions contribute significantly to the per capita income, the control has rested with the central authority. As such the benefits of the income have not filtered down to these regions. Recent developments in Kalimantan and the tensions between the Dayaks and the Madurese is a case in point. For details see, Far Eastern Economic Review, December 16, 1999.
42. Cited in, Robert Cribb, "Not the Next Yugoslavia: Prospects for the Disintegration of Indonesia", Australian Journal of International Affairs, Vol. 53, no. 2, 1999, p. 169.
43. For detailed analysis of the East Timor issue see the following: James Cotton, "The Emergence of an Independent East Timor: National and Regional Challenges", *Contemporary South-east Asia*, Vol. 22, no. 1, April 2000, pp. 1-22; Alexander Downer, "East Timor: Looking Back on

1999", *Australian Journal of International Affairs*, Vol. 54, no. 1, 2000, pp. 5-10; G.V.C. Naidu, "The East Timor Crisis", Strategic Analysis, Vol. XXIII, no. 9, pp. 1467- 80; Shankari Sundararaman, "East Timor and Kashmir: Questioning the Parallels on the Issue of Referendum", *Strategic Analysis*, Vol. XXIV, no. 2, May 2000, pp. 283-300.

44. John T. Sidel, "Indonesia Update: Trends Toward Consolidation, Threats of Disintegration," Writenet Papers, No. 18, December 1999, p. 5 at the website http://www.unhcr.ch/refworld/country/writenet/wn19_99.htm
45. Donald K. Emmerson, "Understanding the New Order: Bureaucratic Pluralism in Indonesia", *Asian Survey*, Vol. 21, no. 11, November 1983, p. 1234.
46. Far Eastern Economic Review, August 16, 2001.
47. *Ibid.*
48. Samantha F Raviche, "Eyeing Indonesia Through the Lens of Aceh", *The Washington Quarterly*, Vol. 23, no. 3, Summer 2000, pp. 7-20.
49. Damien Kinsbury, n. 17, pp. 166-69.
50. Far Eastern Economic Review, 16 December, 1999.
51. Damien Kinsbury, n. 17, pp. 163-65.
52. Shankari Sundararaman, "Indonesia: Can It Hold?", Commentary, *Strategic Analysis*, Vol. XXIV, no. 11, pp. 2097-2100.
53. Anthony L. Smith, "A Glass Half-Full: Indonesia-US Relations in the Age of Terror", Contemporary South-east Asia, Vol. 25, no. 3, December 2003, p. 464.

8

Global Democratic Transition and China's Political Authoritarianism

—PRASANTA SENGUPTA

Democracy can claim to have scored a historic victory over alternative forms of governance. Francis Fukuyama advances a "triumphalist" interpretation of the collapse of European communism and its global superpower, the Soviet Union, in the years from 1989 to 1991. His "The End of History" conveys the message that democracy has won and it represents the highest stage of development of human political institutions. Several parts of the world have witnessed the emergence and consolidation of democratic regimes in the 1970s. The Southern European transitions powerfully influenced the Latin American transitions of the 1980s. A broadly democratic political regime has appeared in many Latin American countries. Although institutional fragility and political ineffectiveness mark many of the Latin American democratic regimes, their medium-term prospects of survival are not definitely dark. A succession of democratic transitions in East Asia in the mid-1980s followed the fading of the cold war. The "people-power" democratization of the Philippines in 1986 strengthens the view that popular pressure from the streets could be more effective than maneuverings of political elites. This does not mean that transition from above cannot happen. A good example comes from Taiwan. There Tartial law was revoked and competitive elections were allowed before any pressure from below had surfaced. The disintegration of the Soviet bloc at the end of the 1980s facilitated democratic transitions in many countries of

Eastern and Central Europe. In South Africa the formal structure of the apartheid was dismantled and a settlement was reached that enfranchised the African majority. In the 20th century democracy defeated fascism and communism. Efforts are now being made to establish democratic systems and institutions in countries which have never known them or where they were swept away by authoritarian take-overs.

Although the world is drifting toward democracy and popular elections are viewed as the most stable and acceptable basis for government, misgivings about democracy persist. Some theorists of democracy feel the need to limit the role of the masses within the political system. Walter Lippmann reasons that the electors' duty is to fill the office and not to direct the office holder. To the classical elite theorists (Pareto, Mosca and Michels) democracy, in the strict traditional sense of rule by the people, is impossible. Any government is government by an elite, or at best one among a number of competing elites. Raymond Aron takes the view that there is government to the people, there is no government by the people. Joseph Schumpeter contends that the proper role of the people is to choose their rulers through competitive elections, and then leave them to get on with the business of governing. Seymour Martin Lipset views with approval the passivity of the electorate. He suggests that political apathy might reflect the health of democracy. However, all this does not involve a direct challenge to the principle of democracy and its politically acceptable position in most parts of the world.

It is of interest to note that the worldwide wave of liberal democracy has failed to penetrate the People's Republic of China. Leaders of China feel confident that a non-competitive one party authoritarian rule can transform their country into a modern democratic state. Significantly, they are critical of the pluralist conception of democracy which, they feel, is defined in terms of procedures instead of substance. Their goal is socialist democracy. In this conception, democracy is a matter of the interests rule serves rather than of procedures for selecting rulers. To the Chinese political leadership procedural guarantees of democracy are relatively unimportant. The

Chinese Communist Party holds that a regime is democratic not when it is open to influence by the people but when it serves their highest interests. Mao Zedong had no trust in elections. He once remarked that "I was elected from Peking (to the National People's Congress), but many have never even seen me. If they have not seen me, how can they vote for me? They have just heard my name." The point Mao wanted to make was that he represented the people not because he was elected by them but because he stood for their interests. As a matter of fact liberal democratic ideals and practices are alien to Chinese cultural and constitutional traditions which express no concern to protect individuals by checking state power. A few words about the Chinese attitude towards the individual and individual rights seem useful.

From the Chinese perspective the individual is an element of the collective. Confucianism sees private interests not as individual but as belonging to a group—a family, lineage, or community. The individual depends on the harmony and strength of the group because he cannot prosper alone whereas the Western belief is that progress should result in ever greater scope for individual autonomy. In traditional Chinese thought the individual is not devalued. The individual should cultivate himself but should do it not for himself but in order to contribute to the welfare of family and community. Chinese Marxism accepts the legitimacy of individual interests but only in a limited sense. It argues that this interest is subordinate to the higher interests of the party and state. The Enlightenment Daily wrote in 1981 that "not all individual interests in accord with socialist laws are necessarily morally legitimate. Whether they are legitimate or not depends upon their relation to the collective interests of the society at a given time." The fact that a person has a certain right under the constitution does not make it morally correct to exercise that right to the fullest. Rights in China thus are not considered to be derived from human personhood. It is citizenship in the state that confers rights. As rights are granted by the state they can be changed, withdrawn and legitimately limited by acts of legislation. In liberal democracies rights, though they are codified by the state, are not considered to originate in a grant by the state but to be inherent in the dignity or personhood of the individual.

As regards the relationship between state and the individual it may be pointed out that unlike in liberal democracies where the state is seen as partly an adversary of the individual and hence the need to protect individual rights against encroachment by the state, in Chinese perception a harmony of interests obtains between state and citizen. The state is a replica of the family, a paternalistic authority. And relations between ruler and subject are analogous to those between parent and child. Just as the Confucian concept of the ideal government is an extension of the ideal family, so the prime tasks of government are the same as those of the family: to provide security, stability and national unity. For understandable reasons Chinese rulers remain hypersensitive to organised protests and criticism. The Democracy Movement in 1978-79 was initially tolerated. Problems surfaced when a bold dissident (Wei Jingshen) argued that the official programme to modernise agriculture, industry, national defense, and science and technology could not succeed without a "fifth modernisation" (democracy). We asked, "The hated political system has not changed. Are not the people justified in seizing power from the overlords?" The Chinese authorities promptly sentenced him to a 15-year prison term and introduced the four fundamental principles to establish the parameters of acceptable debate: (i) the socialist road; (ii) Marxism-Leninism-Mao Zedong Thought; (iii) the people's democratic dictatorship and (iv) the leadership of the Communist Party. Any act of organising, peaceful or unpeaceful, on a grand scale makes the leadership jittery. Consider the Tiananmen massacre in 1989. It was not the content of protest but the students' act of organising that was unpalatable to the leadership. Any threat, real or imagined, overt or covert, unnerves the leadership. The conflict between Falun Gong and communist leadership was not a struggle between theism and atheism, superstition and science, and idealism and materialism. A major reason was totalitarian paranoia. Jiang Zemin authored and circulated documents stating his belief that some political rival or "mastermind" was behind Falun Gong. Jiang equated his ability to eradicate Falun Gong with his ability to remain in power, and initiated the crackdown.

Political pluralism and competitive politics breach the Chinese norm of conformity to the central leadership. China watchers warn us against viewing the implementation of village elections as a step towards liberal democratic politics. In explaining the party's agenda Jean C.O. says, "Village elections are a pressure valve to let peasants vent their dissatisfaction, but one meant to point the responsibility for continued poverty and poor leadership in villages away from the central authorities. Elections put the burden of success and failure directly on the villagers and their popularly elected leaders." He further says that party officials who may still be the most powerful decision-makers in China's villages are not subject to popular election. Note in passing that as villagers gained greater economic initiative and autonomy thanks to agricultural decollectivization and other policies, the power of the Chinese party-state to exact compliance was enormously weakened. By the mid-1980s village leadership had seriously atrophied. Leaders were enriching themselves at the expense of the community, and villagers were resisting their efforts to implement unpopular policies. In the circumstances the central authorities hope the successful implementation of competitive elections and village representative assemblies will elicit more rather than less compliance.

Educated Soviet-style in the 1950s and 1960s and inured to the Community system of rule Hu Jintao and Wen Jiabao can hardly be an altogether different lot. True enough, they in July 2003 showed tolerance in an uncharacteristic way towards an assembly of democratic Hong Kongers which forced the Beijing-backed administration in Hong Kong to postpone national-security legislation. Such tolerance is no evidence of democratic impulse of the Chinese leadership. Any act of repression against Hong Kongers would make less attractive the "one country two systems" formula under which Beijing seeks reunification with Taipei. Jintao and Jiabao demonstrated their strategic smartness by sacking the Health Minister and the Mayor of Beijing for not taking SARS seriously. To consider SARS as China's Chernobyl is to misplace optimism. Chernobyl inspired glasnost in the Soviet Union. The Chinese leadership feels that Gorbachev made a fatal mistake by loosening up.

All things considered it can be said that one-party authoritarian rule is likely to persist in China in the foreseeable further. Jiana Zemin's theory of Three Represents transformed the social identity of the Chinese Communist Party which now is the vanguard of the Chinese people including the capitalist class. And the party does not face any imminent danger of being hijacked by capitalists. The leadership may take a fancy to a dilute form of illiberality, but a sign of any power not associated with the Centre could trigger off a tightening of centralised control.

9

The Process of Democratization in Myanmar

—ANJALI GHOSH

The world today seems to represent a testing laboratory where experimentations in the various forms of procedural democracy have been taking place. The voices of rising nationalism often become incompatible with democratic desires, and nation-states are left with the dilemma as to what would constitute the norms of an ideal political life. The present trend of globalization which aims at expanding market economy and spreading its influence into developing societies creates pressures on non-democratic regimes to conform to western democratic models. Experimentation with democracy, with procedural democracy as such, therefore has been one of the most important challenges facing developing societies. Developed societies and western discourses on globalization consider it to be a precondition of growth. The present study is concentrated on Myanmar which has been one of the most vehement examples of majoritarianism, cultural authoritarianism and a garrison-state where human rights violations have become a part of the political culture.

Burma, or Myanmar, as it is currently called has been of the most isolated countries of Southeast Asia—a hermit territory—as it has often been described. Lying off the traditional sea-faring route of the West, Burma always enjoyed an "isolationist" position not only with regard to Western intrusions, but also in its relations with the sub-continent and the surrounding regions.

There has been an absence of social, political and economic interactions with the neighbouring countries in the east and the west and barring the penetration of Buddhist values the country has remained more or less insulated from the new and secular ideas of enlightenment that had been emerging from the eighteenth and nineteenth centuries and making its impact felt in the socio-political setting of the Indian sub-continent.

Burma's own history has always spelt of authoritarianism, and her only relation was with China which also bore marks of an authoritarian tradition. This relation too was only an economic one, because traditionally there had been some overland trade with China, and Chinese immigrants came down to settle in the country and worked in the mines in the north of Burma. This however was never a factor powerful enough to affect the continuing socio-political setting in Burma.

Burmese Buddhism which has always been a stronghold of the Burmans who have tried to assimilate their culture with that of the ethnic Burmese population and have always kept the reins of political power in their own hands. So while Buddism has been a binding force within the Burman society it has acted as a divisive element and restricted the entry of the ethnic Burmese (who are non-Buddhists) into the political mainstream.

The purpose of the present essay is to analyze the process of democratization in Burma. It would be therefore relevant in this context to keep in mind that, while the cults of liberalism had been emerging in neighbouring India, Burma's socio-political background was devoid of liberal values. Though there was a limited interlude of democracy from 1948 to 1962 liberal or democratic governance is still not the order of the day, neither in the country as a whole nor within the Buddhist Burman society. The ethnic factor played a part even during the parliamentary regime.

Since 1962, political power has been usurped by the Burman military through a bloodless coup; but the country began to make its present felt in the political and strategic environment of South and South-east Asia with the beginning of the pro-democracy demonstrations since 1989. The new name—Myanmar—was officially announced in 1989 by the military regime, namely the State Law and Order Restoration Council (SLORC). The latter is the name-sake of the same military clique that has been holding power in Myanmar ever since Ne Win staged a coup in 1962. Towards the end of 1997, the SLORC was replaced by the State Peace and Development Council (SDPC) which was nothing more than "old wine in a new bottle".

The process of democratization in Myanmar has two aspects. The first one involves the aspirations of the ethnic tribes vis-à-vis the Burman authority. This may be referred to as the process of cultural democratization. The second one involves the political and economic freedom of the Burman people against military rule. This may be referred to as the process of political democratization. Any discussion on the democratization process in Myanmar must take these two aspects into consideration.

In order to understand the ongoing process of democratization in Myamnar—a process that has been going on through the cauldron of history—it is imperative to have a brief insight into Burma's recent political history. A distinction between the term 'Burmese' and 'Burman' is also to be understood.

The Burman, who originated from the Tibetans, migrated into the territory in the ninth century when they defeated the indigenous people chasing them out into the peripheral areas. The latter constituted the Shans, Mons, Karens, Kachins, Chins and the Arakanese—each with a distinct racial and cultural identity and all of them with a history of war, torture and unhappy relations with the people of Burma proper, that is, the Burmans who inhabit the rich valley on the two sides of the Irrawaddy.

The Burmans, who practice Buddhism, have held the different minorities under their sway through a system of absolute monarchy which has traditionally been a prerogative of the Burman Buddhists. Thus while the term "Burmese" denotes the entire population of Burma including the indigenous races, the term "Burman" is limited to the ethnically superior Buddhist inhabitants of Burma proper. The land barriers (that is the forest and hills) that criss-cross a large part of Burma have led to the unhappy seclusion of the minorities and there have been few efforts to assimilate them into the national mainstream.

Independence came in 1948 through a process of negotiation between the British colonial power and the Burman nationalist leadership. The dominant modern Burman culture which developed from the pre-independence days struck at the very roots of Burman/Burmese national identity and with independence it was updated with the blending of Buddhism and socialism—and presented or served to the masses under the banner of 'Burmese way to Socialism'. This blended product was imposed by the leadership in the name of Burmanization. A cultural synthesis involving the diverse groups in the country as a whole was rarely thought of and the actual policy was to impose *one* upon the *others*. The Union of Burma, to begin with, was by no means a union between equals and neither did the founding fathers intend it to be so; besides the Burmans, the indigenous races of Burma included the Arakanese Chins, Kachins, Karens, Kayahs, Mons and Shans who, because of their distinct cultural identity, were persistally clamouring for autonomy but nowhere did the constitution of 1948 provide any provision for a federal division of powers. The nature of the federal structure was defended by Aung San who had said—"We have not tried to copy anything for the sake of copying.... Anything we have tried to utilize from modern constitutions of the world, we have selected ... and thoroughly adapted to suit Burma's aspirations and the Burmese genius".[1] It has also been alleged (by rebel spokesmen) that Aung San had planned a gradual cultural absorption of the races into the mainstream through a process of Burmanization,[2] and this was kept a topmost secret national guideline for the Burmese people who would shoulder the institution as a compulsory duty. As a result a simmering sense of regional identities has always kept brewing, sometimes with volatile outbursts.

The techniques of national mobilization on the eve of the Burmese freedom movement and the promises made by the

Thakins to the aspiring ethnic peoples also had its impact on post-independence politics in Burma. In order to mobilize the entire population on a common platform prior to the country's independence, the nationalist leadership had drafted the Panglong Agreement in 1947 whereby the various ethnic groups were promised provincial autonomy ten years after independence if they so desired. The Union Government did not hesitate to fall back on its promises. Even with the pledge of a parliamentary democracy, Independence opened up the Pandora's Box for Burma. Ethnic demands for autonomy—aspirations for self-identity, or democratic aspirations of the ethnic groups have, therefore, been a major issue which the Union Govern-ment had to reckon with from the very beginning. This process of democratization is yet to take off today and modern Myanmar has failed to be a melting-pot of varying cultural and social identities.

The parliamentary government which was in power in Burma till 1962, and the autocratic military government which came into power since 1962, have acted more or less in the same manner. This shows that transcending political techniques and ideologies the majoritarian character of ethnic nationalism, represented in the Burman culture, has been the crucially dominant factor and has acted as a major impediment towards the fulfillment of the democratic aspirations or the process of democratization of the indigenous inhabitants of Burma/Myanmar. This shows a conflict in cultural nationalism. The unresolved ethnic religious tension represents a greater threat to the State than the continuing presence of the pro-democracy leader San Suu Kyi. It is not even known whether Suu Kyi has any adequate response to minority discontent, or any plans on how the minorities might fit into a new nationalism. It is also not yet clear how many ethnic members are included into the rank and file of the NLD.

The second perspective relates to the phenomenon of political nationalism or political democratization. The issue of political democratization has became a controversial issue and an object of political analysis from after the coup of 1962. As mentioned before, the process of democratization in Burma/

Myanmar has been two-fold—one involving cultural democracy and the other involving political democracy. To begin with the latter, the military coup in 1962 was not unwelcome. People had more faith in the army as a sophisticated and efficient body than on political institutions. As was evident from past instances, the former was more dynamic and disciplined while the latter was always plagued by factionalism and political bickerings.

Though there was a simmering grievance against the restricted policies of the military government in Burma led by the Revolutionary Council and the Burma Socialist Programme Party (BSPP), active protest or demonstration against the "misrule" of the military junta began with the pro-democracy movement in August 1988. It was an instinctive reaction to a quarter-century of political repression and economic underdevelopment and formed part of a truly widespread popular movement, as hundreds of people, motivated by the student demonstrations met and marched against the ruling military government in Burma, with the manifest support of the general population who cheered at them. The demand for the replacement of military rule by a democratic government became more pointed and focused with the entry of the national hero Aung San's daughter into the political scene. Aung San Suu Kyi, as she is called, took over the leadership of the movement and posed a challenge to the BSPP Government in Burma then led by General Ne Win. Though the movement was curbed with unprecedented repression by the military, killing hundreds and hundreds of pro-democracy protestors, mainly students, under government orders, no form of physical violence however was targeted against its high-profile leader, Aung San Sun Kyi. There was total repression of political forces in every form. As far as economic development was concerned, Burma had already applied for a LDC (Least developed country) status whereby creditors could reduce the nation's indebtedness or cancel it altogether. This was seen as a major blow to national pride and self-esteem. In fact, luxury items were always discouraged by the military government in order to keep the expectations of the people low. Traditionally, Burma has never had a rich elite class or a feudal landed class and while the intellectual elite of the bygone days who had led the freedom movement are partakers of the government, a vibrant middle class has hardly developed; instead in its place the military emerged as the dominant privileged class and enjoys a larger-than-life image in the socio-political setting of Burma. The prominent military leaders had also been partners during the freedom movement and had taken interest in post-independence politics, like Ne Win and others. There is, however, no such marked discrimination between the rich and poor, and the only better-off people after 1962 were in the army who also comprised the political leadership. There has been, to be precise, shared poverty; over and above, Burma was insulated from all news pouring into the country from other places. Totalitarian ideology has never been so vehemently manifested than in Ne Win's basic ideological text which castigated the egotistical nature of individuals and emphasized the need to keep their self-aggrandisement and desire of freedom within bounds in order to achieve the unity of individual and social interests.[3]

The pro-democracy movement was initially sparked off over a minor incident leading to a clash between a group of students of the Rangoon University and some young men from outside who were related to some military officers. This led to a protest from the students against the authorities. The latter reacted sternly and ultimately it snowballed into a pro-democracy movement against the military, demanding the military to step down and be replaced by a civilian government. The government responded with a heavy hand and much bloodshed and torture followed. The name of the government was changed to SLORC (State Law and Order Restoration Council) led by General Saw Maung who promised elections. Elections were ultimately held in 1990 on which the National League for Democracy (NLD) spearheaded by Aung San Suu Kyi won a landslide victory with 82 per cent of the seats. The election results were dishonoured and Sun Kyi was kept under house arrest. The SLORC's actions had called for condemnation from all the world, mainly the western powers. India had also voiced her protests against the violation of basic democratic rights—the right of political choice and freedom. The stalemate continues up to this day with the military in full control of the government. The battle between pro-democratic forces and an authoritarian political regime had been at its peak from the period of the SLORC. In November 1997, the SLORC was replaced by the nineteen-member SPDC (State Peace and Development Council) which more or less continued with the same political policies. The entire phenomenon was limited within the Burman populace and hardly affected the ethnic people. The above problem may be regarded as the second aspect of democratic violations in Myanmar, where the right to choose one's own government remained thwarted and for which the SLORC faced confrontation and sanctions from the West. This ultimately led to a change in the government's economic policies and Myanmar began to open its doors mainly towards her Asian neighbours particularly in the north. In 1989, a high-level delegation from China visited Burma/Myanmar and from then on throughout the SLORC and later the SPDC regime, Myanmar's economic and moral succour has been mainly derived from China.

While Western opinion, at large, has been critical towards Myanmar's efforts at democratization (at both the levels), Asian neighbours have been lukewarm in their response. Strategies of engagement have been negotiated by Asian governments including Thailand, Indonesia, South Korea, Hong Kong and, above all, China; in all these instances, the latter have extracted favourable economic concession from the military junta in Myanmar in lieu of their political support.

It has been argued that while Myanmar has been a persistent target by human-rights advocates for denial of basic political rights to the population, for ethnic cleansing and for harsh punishment without due process of law, efforts at imposition of democratic norms from outside or the prescription of Western democratic norms has been regarded as an imposition on Burmese social and economic values. In this context, Aung San Suu Kyi was supported as a protègè of liberal democracy outside the country, she was awarded the

Nobel Peace prize in 1991 and it was held that the return of democracy in Burma/Myanmar could come only with the transfer of political power to the National League for Democracy led by Suu Kyi. Since the latter's main support came from the capitalist countries, the military junta in Myanmar projected her as a symbol or agent of capitalistic infiltration into the country. This fitted well into the Burmese mindset which always nurtured an explicit abhorrence against foreign economic domination. From a strategic point of view, the government is apprehensive of the introduction of a Western democratic model as it would bring the genie out of the bottle and lead to outbursts of demands for ethnic autonomy. The US government's pressure to resolve the political deadlock in the mid-nineties rebounded because the US Secretary of State Madeline Albright had failed to understand the configurations and the sensitivities of the "culture of power" in Myanmar's society.[4] The situation deteriorated further when Sun Kyi called for trade and investment sanctions on Myanmar and an international boycott of the much publicized "Visit Myanmar Year 1996" campaign in conjunction with a US stand to further isolate the Myanmar government. Aung San Suu Kyi's appeal to Western nations to inflict sanctions against her own country earned her the wrath of the military junta which projected her as anti-people. In 1998, the United Nations had send a special envoy to Myanmar to resolve the political deadlock that was continuing since 1990. The envoy presented a proposal on behalf of the United Nations whereby the United Nations along with the World Bank would reward the Myanmar Government with up to US$ 1 billion in financial and humanitarian aid if the latter would enter into a meaningful dialogue with Aung San Suu Kyi. The Myanmar government regarded the proposal as an insult and its spokesman stated, "This is like offering a banana to a monkey and asking it to dance. We are not monkeys. We won't dance".[5]

The Western media's interpretation of the pro-democracy movement versus an authoritarian military regime tarnished the image of Burma. The pro-democracy movement, was being led by the emotionally charged image of a young determined woman fighting the might of the Burmese army or the country's military hegemony almost single-handedly armed with only her determination and charisma, her genealogy, and separated from her children and her husband whom she could not meet even during time of his death in order to fight this cause. She became the symbol *par excellence* of democracy, of human rights and resistance to authority, indirect ethnic autonomy feminism and, of course, the free market—Burma or Myanmar became the laboratory for these testing issues.

The ruling political authorities in Myanmar believe that there is a destructive aspect of democratization and that is decentralization. The authorities fear that it could lead to social and political anarchy. In Myanmar, given the political divisions as they are, anarchy is feared more than tyranny, an idea not supported or fathomed by Westerners where democracy is prescribed as the universal panacea for all universal evils. Professor Michael Aung-Thwin draws a very interesting analogy of the Burmese argumentative controversy with the West to the conflict of values between Ram and Vali in the epic Ramayana. The former tried to universalize his own values ignoring the cultural relativism of the latter. Universalizing of the American ideas of democracy and human rights as universal doctrines have been defined by critics as "parochial universalism", and there has been much rhetoric rationalization of this "parochial universalism".[6] The superimposition of "universal parochial" values on Asian values set in Asian socio-political, economic and cultural configurations have been compared with the argumentative rationalization of Rama's Aryan values over that of Vali's indigenous "monkey" values, where Rama kills Vali because he does not conform to the values of the former. In such cases cultural and economic relativism has no value. The imposition of the Western ideas on Asian values, or the universalizing of "parochial" values accordingly is not a new or unique American strategy, but "an established, predictable rationalization of the strong, the ideology of the superpower to validate its hegemony". Though in today's context it has taken a secular form and the goals it sets forward are "this world-oriented rather than the next, nevertheless the zeal, the righteousness, the imagery, and the voluntary zeal with which this universalism is proclaimed are uncannily evocative of earlier religious evangelisms".[7]

On May 6, 2002, Aung San Suu Kyi was released from house arrest and the SPDC government lifted a restriction on the movement of the NLD leader, stating that it was done to "mark the start of a new page for the people of Myanmar and the international community". Aung San Suu Kyi also responded by stating that the "phase of confidence-building" with the government "was over" and that the "national reconciliation" process was in the offing. She had also managed to convince the SDPC regime that she was acting on her own and not receiving instructions from any foreign party. This was important because in previous instances, Sun Kyi's publicity outside the country especially in the West, the international hype involved and the consequent pressures had made the government reticent towards the process of national reconciliation. Asian countries welcomed the process of national reconciliation in Burma. There was already a policy of engagement with the Asian countries and countries like Japan welcomed the move in Myanmar and rewarded the government by resuming developmental assistance. Behind-the-scene efforts or persuasion from Asian neighbours also helped in pushing the Burmese authorities towards a process of reconciliation with the opposition. The Chinese leadership, led by Jiang Zemin was fully aware of the fact that further tightening of sanctions on Myanmar by the West, especially the United States would be against the interests of China and therefore it began to persuade and press the military regime in Myanmar to move on with political reforms. A positive role has also been played by the Malaysian Prime Minister Mahathir Mohammed who convinced the military leadership not only to go ahead with promised political reforms but also to clean up the house and create a better business climate for foreign investment.

Suu Kyi was, however, taken into protective custody by Burmese authorities on May 20 - an act that soon grabbed the attention of the US, the EU and Japan. The US clamped tighter sanctions on Myanmar, Japan suspended all aid and EU was considering similar measures. The Malaysian Prime Minister warned that Myanmar's continued detention of democracy activist Aung San Suu Kyi might ultimately lead to the country's expulsion from the ASEAN. These countries broke away from their traditional non-interference in each other's internal affairs by calling for Suu Kyi's release. Thailand even offered a "road-map" to solution. Thai Foreign Minister Surakiart Sathirathai's main concern was that political instability in Burma could lead to a further move of illegal Burmese immigrants entering Thailand and a further spate in the smuggling of drugs across the Thai-Burmese border into Thailand. Besides, Thailand, Singapore and Malaysia along with Britain, were the top four investors in Myanmar and they had critical financial stakes in the stability and progress of the country.

In spite of the above, however, the Generals were not moved, and along with Suu Kyi's confinement, a large number of NLD supporters were still languishing in jails. According to observers, the military had no intention of giving up power and the release was a mere gesture to reinstate foreign aid rather than a commitment to political change. From Suu Kyi's point of view, the principles and guidelines laid out in the proposals of the National Constitutional Convention which provided for a major governing role for the military in the draft constitution were unacceptable. Sun Kyi was again re-detained on May 30,2003, and it seemed that the military junta was determined to stick to power rather than make efforts for a transition to democracy which would actually jeopardize the future prominence of the military. The "road map" to democracy from the part of the military government in Myamnar that calls for the drafting of a new constitution and holding of "free and fair" election has been defined by critics as a "cosmetic jugglery". The government's lack of seriousness follows from the fact that no time frame was outlined, no details were worked out, there were delays, wilful policy alterations, retracting commitments and preconditions and lack of openness in dealing with the issues. Myanmar therefore faces complex and difficult challenges in its transition to democracy and in its quest for national reconciliations.

The seven-stage road map for transition to democracy put forward by the government in 2003 and the National Convention convened in 2004 for the drafting of the new constitution had been regarded as incomplete by the Secretary-General of the United Nations. The views of the NLD and other political groups were not taken into account and, needless to say, the ethnic nationality groups were also kept outside its purview. This has only led to mounting international pressure on the Myanmar government by the international council, particularly the Western nations and the UN. This, as discussed before, has been counter-balanced by the policy of engagement pursued by the ASEAN nations. A peculiar combination of abundant natural resources - teak, minerals, gems, a long coastline for abundant fishing and a regime-imposed praetorian policy that has carefully curbed "development" has provided the ASEAN nations with an important source for raw materials for running their own business ventures. Sharing a long border with Myanmar, Thailand and Malaysia have intensive trade and investment relations with the Government at Yangon and their economic relations stand in the way of pressing the military junta to embrace reform. The Japanese government which is Myanmar's biggest donor and investor has adopted a measured approach in its call for democratization and market economy in Myanmar. The country's strongest support however, comes from her northern neighbour, China. Sino-Myanmar trade registered a phenomenal increase in 2003, with Myanmar importing 900 million dollars worth of Chinese goods and exporting 170 million dollars of goods to China. In the year 2004, Beijing signed thirty-three aid and trade agreements with Yangon and a production-sharing contract to cooperate in oil exploration in Myanmar. The military leadership declared China to be Myanmar's "most important friend" and that "Yangon will side with Beijing on all issues concerning China's interests".[8] Similarly, Beijing also pledged to continue its "friendly" policy towards Yangon. In this context, both the countries have shed the "democracy" paradigm and both the countries have common interest in holding out against full participation in the globalization project in Myanmar. Given its attractiveness to regional investors as a primary source of raw materials in the form of natural resources, it is unlikely that Myanmar would be hurt by sanctions imposed by the West, namely the United States. It will not be in the economic interests of Bangkok to surrender its economic relations with Yangon, Tokyo will not want to lose the stakes it has in Myanmar and Beijing has every interest in keeping the military junta in power and preventing the emergence of a reform that would make her neighbouring government in Myanmar tilt towards mainstream globalization and welcome American investment and influence. Precisely analyzed, China needs access into Myanmar to spread her political and economic influence in the region and therefore when the Myanmar government is faced with crises, China provides support from behind.

There is also an added factor behind the present political tension in Myanmar—namely, an elite conflict within the Burman society that lies just beneath the surface of the acrimonious rivalry that takes place between the ruling and the opposition pro-democracy forces. It is in effect the result of a conflict amongst the political elite who had begun their careers from the time of the freedom movement and amongst their heirs and representatives who want to carry on with the reins of power they deem to have inherited. Elite conflict however is not new to Asian societies. From a holistic point of view the process of democratization in Burma/Myanmar also represents a tension between the indigenous forces and the forces of modernization normally found in transitional societies. Rising ambitions and inner-tensions between the young and older generations is also a case in point that has been a common phenomenon in almost all the socio-political conflicts that has been simmering throughout the developing societies. The process also involves tensions between market and non-market forces, military and non-military, Burman and non-Burman, and the interests of the outside nation vis-à-vis the interests of the Burman nation as portrayed by her military rulers.

The struggle between the Burman and the non-Burmans has been one of the greatest impediments in the process towards democracy. The agenda of the various minority groups have never been addressed by the political authorities, whether military or non-military and no political agreement has actually taken place between both the sides, even though peace agreements have been signed between most of the rebel groups and the government. Conflict with the Karea National Union (KNU) still goes on and sporadic clashes between the KNU and governments troops are reported along the Thai-Burmese border. Because of the divided agenda, mobilization of the forces of democratization led by the country's opposition elite has not been able to muster enough strength. On the other hand, the stifling ethnic problem has boosted the flourishing narcotics trade in the Golden Triangle.

After 1997 when Myanmar gained entry into the ASEAN, economic interactions with her South-east Asian neighbours have become even more meaningful. At this stage, for the vast number of the Burmese people economic and infrastructural development seems to be more important than the exercise of political choice, and any regime providing that would become acceptable, especially with the well-being of the Buddhist order which is still held in the highest esteem and is one of the important loyalty structures within the country. Michael Aung-Thwin goes to the extreme of stating that "Democracy... is not even an issue for most of the people of Burma most of the time.[9]" This explains the efforts of the present military junta to open up its economic relations with the neighbouring countries including India.

The issue of national reconciliation has in fact become more of a preoccupation outside the country than amongst the people living within the country. According to Burma watchers, building trust and mutual confidence in a "distinctly Myanmar way" constitutes an important element in the reconciliation process between the government and the opposition rather than sanctions and pressures imposed from outside which tends to enhance mutual tensions and the government's suspicion against the opposition forces, making the former reticent in making any genuine move towards reconciliation. Like the "Burmese way to socialism" where the clarion call was to practice/implement socialism through the Burman cultural ideology, the process of democratization or national reconciliation also tends to follow the traditional national pattern, that is "Myanmar's problem should be left to Myanmar and the Myanmar people themselves, and it should be done in a traditional Myanmar way". This in effect follows the Burman pattern which includes the military's prescription of doing things. As stated in the official declaration of the SLORC, the military government within the country "was bound by no constitution and ruled by martial law";[10] it also admitted that it "had no support from the people of Burma and sought none" and its "legitimacy came from international recognition". Its main stated goal was to prevent the disintegration of the Union, protect national unity and perpetuate sovereignty. Its moral succour and ideological ammunition is derived from its Asian partners who hold high the "Asian value hypotheses". The common belief which exists is that Asian history and cultural traditions are incompatible with liberal democracy and Western concepts of human rights. The author is a strong champion for democracy, both in spirit and procedure, but has observed with skepticism that in recent instances open societies have been facing greater difficulties in countering threats to state sovereignty than non-democratic regimes. However, the main precondition for democratic development is economic growth. Myanmar's General Than Shwe's recent economic overtures seem to be a pointer in that direction.[11]

NOTES AND REFERENCES

1. For details see Josef Silverstein, *Burmese Politics: The Dilemma of National Unity,* Rutgers University Press, New Jersey, 1986, p. 186.
2. S.T. Aung, "Union of Burma and Cause of its Abortion" in *Hidden Colony: The New Outlook on Nationalism,* Arakanese Comrade Publishing, September 1985, Vol. 1, No. 1, p. 12.

3. For an excellent discussion on the issue see Robert Taylor, "Stagnation and Stalemate" and "Stifling Change: The Army remains in Command" in Robert Taylor (ed.), *Burma: Political Economy under Military Rule,* Hurst and Company, London, 2001.
4. See Maung Aung Myoe, "The National Reconciliation Process in Myanmar", *Contemporary South Asia,* Vol. 24, No. 2, August, 2002.
5. Roger Mittan, "Sending Out Feelers", *Asia Week,* January 13, 2000, p. 30.
6. Michael Aung-Thwin, "Parochial Universalism, Democracy *Jihad* and the Orientalist image of Burma: The New Evangelism", *Pacific Affairs,* Winter 2001-2002.
7. *Ibid.*
8. Dr. Michael A. Weinstein, "Myanmar's Costless Shift to a Hard-Line", *Power and Internet News Report,* October 27, 2004.
9. Michael Aung-Thwin, *op. cit.*
10. For details, see Announcement No. 1/88 of the State Law and Order Restoration Council, September 18, 1988.
11. See Anjali Ghosh, "Myanmar; Realpolitik at Work", in *India and Neighbours: Yearbook 2005,* Contemporary News and Features, New Delhi, January 2005.

10

An Ever Closer Union

National Identity and the Quest for Integration in Europe

—PURUSOTTAM BHATTACHARYA

I

Nationalism has been defined by Elie Kedourie as a "doctrine invented in Europe at the beginning of the nineteenth century…the doctrine holds that humanity is naturally divided into nations, that nationals are known by certain characteristics which can be ascertained, and that the only legitimate type of government is national self-government." (Kedourie:1960:12). This is a useful definition to begin with to understand the power of nationalism and especially the European Union of today which was created with the ostensible objective of laying to rest the awesome destructive potential of this nationalism.

The Second World War was a huge blow to Europe's status in the world. It not only left a devastated continent in terms of political, economic and social damages suffered. Most important of all was the psychological consequences which affected all major and minor states setting in motion an unprecedented crisis of confidence in Europe. It exposed in bold relief the real problems of Europe in the first half of the twentieth century—the perils of unrestrained, aggressive nationalism associated with the rise of the sovereign state the most notable form of which was the Franco-German rivalry for supremacy unleashed after the French Revolution and further strengthened by the emergence of a unified Germany in 1871.

The sovereign state was a European invention whose genesis can be traced back to the fourteenth century. The peace of Westphalia (1648) further expedited the process enabling thereby the sovereign entities to exercise power within reasonably defined territorial limits not contained, however loosely, within a wider constitutional scheme (Holy Roman Emperor or the Pope). The French Revolution and especially the Napoleonic wars provided more inputs in the development of the concept of nationhood and by the end of the nineteenth century nationalism emerged as a significant force in Europe with political consequences. Following their political unifications in 1871 the nation states of Italy and Germany were created from smaller entities while the aspirations of other national groupings such as the Poles, the Serbs, Bulgars and the Romanians threatened the existence of large multi-national empires like the Russian, Austrian and the Ottoman imperiums of which they were parts.

The First World War was a culmination of nationalist rivalries among the major European powers which led to the destruction of the continental empires—Imperial Germany, Austria-Hungary, Czarist Russia and the Ottoman—and the emergence of new nation-states such as Estonia, Latvia, Lithuania, Poland and Czechoslovakia. The withdrawal of American power from Europe at the end of the War, the economic unviability of many of the newly created nation-states which had their own national minorities who could not be provided adequate protection and finally the rise of Fascism marked the disastrous inter-war period paving the way for the Second World War.

The two world wars which started essentially as European civil wars and spread to other continents were thus the culmination of unabated and unrestrained nationalist rivalry involving the great powers of Europe. But at the end of it all it was Europe itself which lay shattered politically, economically and psychologically. It was not just a question of reconstruction nor even recovery of the lost great power status of some of its major states. The basic issue was more fundamental. The question uppermost in the minds of thinking and visionary Europeans was—are the peoples of Europe capable of drawing the necessary lessons from the ravages of the two world wars and display their readiness to reconcile nationalistic rivalries that brought so much misfortune to the continent? It is in this background that the issue of nationalism and national identity in post-war Europe and the quest for unity among the warring European states in the aftermath of the Second World War has to be understood.

The history of European integration is a story of increasing encroachments and limitations imposed on national power and authority during the course of the different phase of the unity movement. At the root of this entire exercise was the objective of the creation of a sense of common European identity which had to be achieved through a process of assimilation of and not necessarily at the expense of the national identities. The question of national sovereignty was however a sensitive issue and the decade after the Second World War witnessed a lively debate in Western Europe among the votaries of inter-governmentalism and supra-nationalism. The more conventional idea of cooperation at the regional level is termed the inter-governmental approach whereby the participants in the process initiate action themselves and decide the extent upto which they are prepared to go in adopting and abiding by the general policy endeavours emanating from the institution in question. In contrast to this supranationalism is an approach whereby member-states belonging to a supra-national organisation give its central institutions the right and the ability to take decisions independently of and even in spite of the member states in fields traditionally in their preserve. As is well-known to students of European integration differences among the major West European states regarding which of the two approaches should be adopted that best reflected the prevailing realities led to a divergence resulting in the emergence of two parallel organisations—the European Economic Community and the European Free Trade Association in the late 1950s. It took several more decades for all these states to come under the umbrella of one all Europe organisation—the European Union.

II

Institution building at the European level has essentially been a tussle between attempts to transfer more and more areas of jurisdiction from the national levels to the community level on the one hand and resistance put up by member states to such transfers. As a result the pioneers of the movement had to make a conscious distinction between the so-called relatively high politics and low politics arenas. When the European Coal and Steel Community (ECSC) and the European Economic Community (EEC) were formed in 1952 and 1957 respectively only the social and economic sectors—the so-called functional areas—were transferred to the jurisdictions of these institutions from national hands. In contrast attempt to create a similar European Defence Community (EDC), designed to handle high state defence and security issues at the European level, failed as national sensitivies were not prepared to hand over such matters of supreme national interest to supranational jurisdiction. As a result in spite of the success achieved by the leaders of the community in fashioning the Common Foreign and Security Policy (CFSP) regime recently, cooperation in the field of foreign and security policy is still largely inter-governmental.

In spite of such national roadblocks a steady impact of the community on the national identities of the member states through the promotion of a commonality of interests is noticeable over the past four decades. In the words of Paul Taylor, an eminent analyst of the European integration process, taking the mid-1950s as a starting point "a condition would be found which had existed in Western Europe, certainly for two centuries and possibility for much longer, and design and method of work of the institutions in a sense represented that condition. It was summed up in one of the great insights about Western European identity penned by Montesquieu in the eighteenth century: that it contained an inner dialectic, 'unity in diversity', or 'diversity in unity' ". (Taylor:1996:141).

In Western Europe there were certain transcendent elements in the attitudes and values, common in the various states, which were essentially inheritance of the Renaissance and the experience of the industrial revolution. "They generally formed the starting-point of thinking about society and recurred in various national contexts." (Taylor:1996:141). These common elements included "a preference for rationalist as a mode of thinking, a tendency to draw a line between the religious and secular aspects of society and to reject too close an involvement on the part of the church in civilian arrangements." (Taylor:1996:141). Additions to this list would be a concern with parliamentary democracy and a belief in a special mixture of capitalism and socialism leading to the evolution of a welfare state in Western Europe with a more pronounced tilt towards socialism than in the United States though not far enough as in the former communist states in Eastern Europe. (Taylor:1996:141).

There were also elements of separateness acquired through long periods of struggles and sacrifices. These comprised separate myths, own sense of identity and clear distinction with others. Each nation-state had its symbols, ceremonies and special histories which marked it out as a distinctive entity in its own right. Each was proud of its national identity and heritage.

Notwithstanding this diverse and contrasting mosaic the Community experience made an impact on the nations participating in the European experiment. There was a gradual strengthening of the web of unity through such measures as the introduction of the EU passport, or the gradual extension of the use of the European flag and logo. These symbols contributed to the creation of a sense of Europeanness and strengthened the perception of differences between Europeans and others. Other notable changes include gradual mutual acceptance of each others' food habits as a result of the Common Market's encouragement of wider distribution of foodstuffs which had previously been local. There is a marked similarity in the appearances—especially in terms of dress—of the younger generations of European born after the Second World War-be they British, French, German, Italian or Spanish.

There was also active encouragement and support for the promotion of the European identity by Community institutions especially the European Commission which, until the late 1960s, preferred to deal with interest groups having European level federations. Such a practice was designed "to promote the convergence of national institutions, interests and attitudes, and the development of supranational non-governmental organisations." (Taylor:1996:143).

However it has to be noted that there was no uniform strengthening of the sense of the common European identity throughout the union. It varied from state to state. The importance of and attachment to national symbols continued to hold sway especially in the major member states. Higher level of support for more powers for the Community institutions was provided by the original six founding member states—France, Federal Republic of Germany, Italy, the Netherlands, Belgium and Luxembourg. In contrast a member state like Britain has usually displayed much greater degree of skepticism and even at times hostility towards the Community ideals of supranationalism. (Purusottam Bhattacharya:1994).

Paul Taylor has shown that the development of a stronger European identity has not been a linear process. There was no simultaneous stregthening of a European loyalty and a weakening of national loyalty. Any conceptualization along such lines would be an oversimplification. In the context of the diverse, complex and often conflicting mosaic of the European experiment possibilities of development of multiple identities have to be given due considerations in such an exercise. In a framework of this kind loyalties to a particular group can coincide and be continuously reconciled with loyalties to other groups each with their associated symbols. But it is also possible for the evolution of identity to support redistribution of responsibility for performing basic tasks and fulfilling basic human needs without directly affecting sovereignty or security (Taylor:1996:146-7).

In this context what has also to be taken into account is the changing nature of nationalist loyalties in a globalising world.

Exposures to other nations and cultures through travel, communication, media and cyberspace has been an overriding feature of this globalisation leading to the existence of virtual communities, nations and states in today's world. As the capability of the nation-state to face the complex challenges of the late twentieth century dwindled regional projects such as the European Union become increasingly salient as responses to the changing world order. Exclusive national strategies are no longer enough for pursuing national economic objectives.

A degree of movement in the direction of a sense of common destiny did indeed take place in the European Community between the mid-1950s and the end of the century. But the moot point is if such a development indicates a movement in the formation of a European nation. Post-Maastricht developments—especially recent events—do not hold out any such possibilities even in the distant future.

III

The question thus arises—what is likely to be the future shape of Europe? As indicated earlier the debate, over the last half century—has been focussed around two contrasting visions. The federalist vision dreamt of a federal European state in the lines of the United States of America. The most important proponent of such an objective was Jean Monnet, widely regarded as the founding father of the European unity movement. The other approach opposed such a prospect and preferred to sustain a Europe of nation-states. Mention may be made of President Charles de Gaulle of France among the most notable votaries of such a course of action.

What has emerged however is an intermediate status which is reflected in the institutions of the Community, built and progressively reformed through four basic treaties. As it stands today the Community comprises of supranational policy-making in areas such as the single currency, agriculture, foreign trade, energy, etc. while issues such as foreign and security policy and justice and home affairs are still in the inter-governmental domain. End of the cold war and the transformations in Eastern and Central Europe gave rise to the question of the enlargement of the Community into hitherto uncharted parts of the continent. The consequent debate regarding "Deepening" (re-inforcing and further extending integration in new areas amongst the existing member states) and "Widening" (enlarging the Community into Eastern and Central Europe) added a new dimension to the question of integration with its concomitant implications for the debate on national and European identities.

The latest instance of how the issues of nationalism and nationalist loyalties are impacting on the European project is the debate surrounding the adoption of the EU constitution which is intended to replace the big and complex four basic treaties on which the Community is founded with a single, shorter, simpler document spelling out the EU's purpose and aims and stating clearly who does what. The "Convention on the Future of Europe"—a group of eminent people representing the EU institutions, the national governments and parliaments—drew up a proposal for the EU constitution in 2003 and the final text was agreed by EU leaders on 18 June, 2004. The document was signed by the EU heads of state and government at a summit in Rome on 29 October, 2004 and the new constitution is scheduled to enter into force once all member states have ratified it. The proposed constitution describes the EU's values, objectives and competences, increases the power of the European Parliament and creates the post of EU Minister of Foreign Affairs in order to increase the EU's influence on the international stage. It also includes the Charter of Fundamental Rights.

The tussle between nationalist and European loyalties was brought into sharp focus during the course of the French and Dutch referendums on the proposed EU constitution in May-June 2005. Public referendums—rather than Parliamentary approval—has been chosen as an option by several member states for ratification of the constitutional treaty. As it transpired both the French and the Dutch rejected the treaty by large margins (the French by 55 to 45 per cent and the Dutch by 63 to 37 per cent). As a result the future of the treaty—and the shape of European integration itself—has been thrown into disarray since it had been stipulated that the proposed constitution could only come into force following ratification by all the member states of the Union.

Regular observers of EU affairs are nearly unanimous that these reverses carry serious implications for the future course of integration in Europe in so far as reconciling nationalist and European loyalties are concerned. Leaders of the Community are however trying to put on a brave face by pointing out that the French-Dutch rejections of the treaty do not necessarily denote a repudiation of the European ideal and the proposed course of ratification of the treaty by the remaining member states will continue to be followed.

There is no doubt that the EU of today is a far cry from what had been envisaged in the 1950s. With 25 member states—and others waiting in the queue—the ideal of a federal Europe *a la* the United States of America is no longer a practical proposition. As already mentioned even before the present crisis regular EU watchers were pointing out emergence of an intermediate status as the most likely scenario. While such a set up will not threaten the nation-state it will bring with it the advantages of integration for its citizens in vital sectors of daily life.

It has to be borne in mind that the world and Europe of today are very different places from what they were in the 1950s and the 1960s. The generation of Europeans who had experienced the horrors of the two world wars were determined to banish the scourge of what they perceived as essentially European family conflicts. The super-structure of integration they created not only facilitated the emergence of an ambience that increasingly pushed nationalist passions into the background—especially among the founding member states—but also made the economic and social benefits of such cooperation more readily available. While the "spillover effects" in the economic and social sectors did not lead to a federal Europe, as envisaged by the neo-functionalists in the 1950s and 1960s, it certainly made public opinion more alive to the benefits of the whole project which greatly enhanced their prosperity and turned the Community into one of the richest regions of the world.

However the end of the cold war and the imperatives of integrating the Central and Eastern European states into the Union increasingly transformed the nature and dynamics of the European project though the leaders of the Community did not openly acknowledge it as such. Public opinion in the West European member states—especially within the original six countries—began to sense that decisions relating to both "deepening" and "widening" were being taken without adequate consultations with the people in these countries. Expanding areas of integration were begun to be viewed as attempts on the part of the leaders of the Community to garner more powers for themselves at the expense of the people thus contributing further to the "democratic deficit" which has been a long standing grievance against EU policy-making. The rejection of the EU constitution by French and Dutch voters has been interpreted by many analysts as not so much a refusal to accept the proposed document—complex and difficult though it is for ordinary people to comprehend—but more as a protest against the arrogance of the political establishment which drew up the treaty and is now seeking to enforce it. As one Dutch voter put it "I want the country to have its identity. That's why I am against the constitution."

In view of the increasing complexities it is becoming hazardous to predict the direction Europe will be taking over the next five to ten years in its efforts to unite. Paul Taylor's assertion, made almost a decade ago, that the EU is "a unique arrangement between states which benefits the majority of individuals without threatening national sovereignty" seems to hold true even now. (Paul Taylor:1996:6). A more pessimistic note has been struck by another British commentator recently when he says, "...the general point surely stands that Europe will evolve more as a group of independent nations, cooperating most of the times but competing quite a lot. It will not be an ever closer union: that concept is surely dead." (Hamish Mcrae: The Independent reprinted in The Statesman: 2 June, 2005).

As the debate on federalism *vs.* hard inter-governmentalism regarding the essential character of the EU continues what seems to emerge is the conception of a body-politic combining elements of federalism (community activity with a degree of self-containment) and inter-governmentalism (strong linkages with a set of national polities). Today's is a struggle for successful adaptation by the member states to its ever evolving organizational framework. It is a veritable laboratory in the experimentation of nationalism, nation-state and accommodation of vital national interests beyond traditional state boundaries. It offers a multi-layered framework facilitating treatment of specific interests within the national boundaries leaving scope for other interests to be dealt with in the European framework.

Recent developments have clearly demonstrated that nationalism in Europe is not dead and the nation-state within the European Union does indeed survive. However the level of integration achieved in the last four decades seems to indicate that the continent has left behind the bitter legacy of the recurrent cycles of bloody conflicts that engulfed the nations of Europe over the past five hundred years. Whether Europe succeeds in evolving a model where competition and co-operation co-exist within a framework essentially underpinned by harmony among the nation-states of the EU remains a critical challenge in the decades ahead.

NOTE AND REFERECNES

1. Birch, Anthony M, *Nationalism and National Integration*. (London: Unwin Hyman,1989).
2. Bulmer, Simon, and Scott, Andrew (eds.), *Economic and Political Integration in Europe: Internal Dynamics and the Global Context*. (Oxford: Basil Blackwell, 1994).
3. Butler, Sir Michael, *Europe: More than a Continent* (London: William Heinemann, 1986).
4. Bhattacharya, Purusottam, *Britain in the European Community: Implications for Domestic Politics and Foreign Relations*. (Calcutta: K.P. Bagchi & Co., 1994).

5. Archer, Clive, and Butler, Fiona, *The European Union: Structure and Process*. (Pinter: London, 1996).
6. Cini, Michelle (ed.), *European Union Politics*. (Oxford University Press: Oxford 2003).
7. Dinan, Desmond, *Ever Closer Union? An Introduction to the European Community*. (Basingstoke: MacMillan 1994).
8. Burgess, M. *Federalism and European Union: The Building of Europe, 1950-2000*. (London: Routledge 2000).
9. George, Stephen and Bache, I (eds.). *Politics in the European Union*. (Oxford: Oxford University Press 2001).
10. Milward, A.S. *The Eureopean Rescue of the Nation State* (London: Routledge and Kegan Paul 1992).
11. Shonfield, Andrew, *Europe: Journey to an Unknown Destination* (Harmondsworth: Penguin Books, 1972).
12. Taylor, Paul, *The Limits of European Integration* (London and New York: Croom Helm and Columbia University Press, 1983).
13. —, *The European Union in the 1990s*. (Oxford University Press, 1996).
14. Tsoukalis, Loukas, *The European Community: Past, Present and Future* (Oxford; Basil Backwell 1983).
15. Wallace, Helen, *Europe: The Challenge of Diversity* (London: Routledge and Regan Kaul, 1985).
16. Kedourie, Elie, *Nationalism*. (London: Hutchinson, 1960).

11

Welfare States in Europe Viewed from India

—B. VIVEKANANDAN

Europe has been the cradle of welfare states. Germany pioneered it. With a very different motivation of appeasing the organised industrial labour of Germany, and to arrest the growing influence of German socialists, Chancellor Otto von Bismarck had pioneered this concept in the closing years of the 19th century by introducing social insurance schemes to protect industrial workers. But, in course of time, the idea was adopted by others. Indeed, socialists themselves were attracted by its potential. In their hands, the welfare state idea became a dynamic concept. It became an important instrument to attack the charity approach to fight poverty and squalor and to free the recepients of welfare benefits from the humiliating means test. Indeed, there is an overarching agreement everywhere in Europe today that some sort of public welfare provisions should be there for people's social protection. Social security and social assistance have begun to be seen as a social right of everybody.

It may be noted that in Europe welfare states flowered in different countries in different times. As a result, the welfare state systems that had come up in Europe during the last one century varied from one another in their features and contents, depending upon the national context in which they were rooted. Indeed, in Europe one can see examples of all three models of welfare states which Gosta Esping-Andersen has categorised—Liberal (Britain and United States), Conservative-Corporatis (Germany—between individualism and Swedish statism), and Social Democrat (Sweden); or examples of the three models in which R.H. Titmus has classified them—the residual model (Britain), corporatist industrial achievement model (Germany), and institutional redistributive model (Scandinavia). The east European countries represent a blend of corporatist model and institutional redistributive model.

Significantly, long before the British economist J.M. Keynes developed the idea of welfare state in his seminal work the *General Theory of Employment, Interest and Money*, published in 1936, the term "welfare state" was used by Gustav Moller, the architect of the Swedish welfare state, in the 1928 Election Manifesto of the Swedish Social Democratic Party. The Swedish economist, Wigforss was also instrumental in elaborating the concept at that time. Indeed, during the inter-war period itself the Swedish Social Democrats had adopted the establishment of welfare state in Sweden as their political goal. From then onwards the welfare state concept got intertwined with the ideas of equality, solidarity, distributive justice and full employment.

In Sweden, the construction of welfare state was begun in 1930s in a systematic manner. This was facilitated by the fact that from 1932 the Swedish Social Democratic Party was in power continuously for 44 years. As a result they could build a cradle-to-the-grave welfare state system in Sweden. Universalism and non-discrimination were its cardinal features. Beyond alleviation of poverty, the programme was directed towards equality distributive justice and solidarity. As a result, welfare state concept became almost a synonym for social democracy. Other Scandinavian countries followed Sweden.

But, in many other countries of Europe, the impetus to build up welfare states came from common hardships people suffered during the second world war. And many of them, like France for example, were influenced by the Beveridgean ideas. The French followed an egalitarian welfare model based on equality, fraternity and national solidarity, and established a well developed social security system. It may be seen that the welfare state system in France is founded on a basic general insurance scheme, complemented by additional schemes managed by mutual or private insurance. Without these additional schemes, benefits drawn from the general insurance scheme would be quite inadequate. However, the key components of the system in France are composed of well developed health care, unemployment and pension schemes. Under the system anyone born or residing in France is entitled to social security benefits. The French do not accept the mercantile logic on social welfare matters, on the ground that market rules cannot meet the requirements of solidarity and social cohesion. Rocard reforms of 1992 ensured that any person who is unable to work due to his age, mental or physical status or economic situation has the right to obtain from society "decent means to live". Besides, a law enacted in July 1999 in France entitles everyone in the country to health care without any contribution prerequisite.

In Germany too, the present welfare state system is a post-war construction. A notable factor is that when the system was introduced, it was not wedded to egalitarian principle. This was mainly because the social policy institutions in Germany were established under the centre-right government of Christian Democrats. The distinct nature of German welfare state model is indicated by using the term "social state" instead of "welfare state" in the Basic Law of 1949. While the "social state" indicated a combination of freedom of individual plus market, "welfare state" indicated state provision and control.

In 1957 an important old age pension reform was introduced in Germany. But a major expansion of social policy in Germany took place after the German Social Democratic Party joined the government in 1966. It introduced a wide range of benefits and services. Cumulatively, Germany is seen as a centrist welfare state—a blend of collective and individualist values through compulsory membership and earnings related benefits. Indeed, there is a welfare mix of public and private services in Germany which is manifest in the provision of welfare services, health services and social housing. Therefore, basically, the German welfare state system is attuned largely to security than to equality.

The British welfare state was founded on the ideas of Keynes and Beveridge and was characterised by universalism. Keynes favoured increased governmental spending to generate more employment. Beveridge complemented it by charting a welfare state system, covering people's needs from cradle-to-the-grave. In his famous *Report on Social Insurance and Allied Services,* published in 1942, he underlined the imperative need to establish a minimum standard of living, below which no one should be allowed to fall. So, conceptually a citizen in the British welfare state is an employed person, insured against all eventualities in life—illness, disability, unemployment, and so on. And, all along there was a political consensus in Britain regarding the welfare state. But this consensus was broken in 1980s after Margaret Thatcher became the British Prime Minister. Under her stewardship, the neo-liberal perspective began to dominate the British welfare state reform debate. The idea was to whittle down the content of statism in the British welfare state system. As a result, many welfare state benefits got slashed down.

Tony Blair's "Third Way" has acquiesced into most of the changes already brought in by the Conservative administrations during their preceding 18-year rule. The "New Labour" tends to refashion the British welfare state as a "wage earners' welfare state". It tries to link welfare to work and tries to impel the unemployed people to return to work by increasing the economic insecurity of employees at all levels.

It is not necessary to go into the details of welfare state systems existing in various other countries of Europe. But, without exception, all of them faced a new situation. In 1980s, welfare state became the target of attack of neo-Conservatives everywhere who pressed for rolling back the role of the state. Coupled with it was the economic crisis following recession in the 1990s. As part of their cost-cutting exercise, many countries pruned their welfare benefit provisions and trimmed people's social assistance entitlements. Many of them diversified some of their public welfare provisions to private providers.

However, most of them readjusted their welfare state benefits keeping in view the fiscal constraints caused by economic crisis. But these adjustments were not on basic policies nor on core structures, but on its various distributive and allocative details. Therefore, at the end of the day, everywhere the system survived with marginal changes.

The question that needs to be asked in the present context is: what are the challenges before the welfare state systems in Europe? Certainly, the ideological challenge from the neo-Conservative Right is constantly present through its relentless attacks on the welfare state systems in the name of growing cost. It takes the form of partial privatisation of the public welfare system's responsibilities. Some European Union countries have started privatising social benefits by increasing the role of the private sector in organising and administering health care and health insurance schemes. In a significant judgment, delivered on 12 September, 2000, the European Court of Justice has conceded free competition in additional pension schemes. In fact, this runs counter to the basic European social model in which public welfare cannot be treated as a regular market. Needless to underline that introduction of competition and market approach in the social sector will undermine social solidarity. Although partial privatisation has been introduced in the public welfare sector, the European Union laws have not questioned the state monopoly of social security and basic welfare.

Apart from that I see three major challenges the European welfare state systems are faced with. They are globalisation, demographic change and the European Union.

When we look at globalisation in the context of welfare states in Europe, an important factor to be kept in mind is that the welfare state systems in Europe have grown up with the nation state as the fundamental unit of planning and organisation. But globalisation is causing erosion to the vitality of nation states by systematically undercutting their resource base (or tax base) and thereby weakening their ability to carry out public welfare responsibilities. It is forcing countries to change their policies and priorities to remain competitive in the global market. In the process, full employment policy has become a low priority in countries' economic policy. Similarly, globalisation has accelerated the mobility of capital to favourable locations, which can undercut national tax bases on which many states rely for financing their welfare benefits. It is forcing enterprises to shift to labour saving, capital intensive production technologies to reduce labour cost and to maximise profit. It undercuts the progressive taxation system, wherever it exists, and promotes inequality in society. It has created new forms of marginalisation and social exclusion and has considerably weakened the position of the nation-state as an autonomous unit of social organisation. Therefore, a closer look into globalisation will reveal that it is a threat to all national systems of social protection. The challenge is how to preserve social protection in an open, globalised market economy.

Another potential threat to European welfare state systems emanates from the European Union and the mercantile ideology it is attuned to. It goes without saying that EU follows a policy of supremacy of economy over social values. Its basic approach is driven by market ideology which is inimical to people's social rights.

Today, the European Union is composed of national welfare states. Social security provisions are organised and implemented at national level to meet the requirements of national electorates located in specific situations. Therefore, essentially, the welfare state system in the European Union is national in character, which makes supranational governance of it by the Union extremely difficult. At the same time the Union may indirectly try to harmonise these systems through erosive actions of globalised markets. But the European Union cannot do much in this regard directly, except by stipulating convergence and harmonisation policies and emaciate advanced welfare state systems to the lowest common denominator. Certainly, fiscal harmonisation, including reduction of tax rates, which the European Monetary Union entails, will be dangerous to EU states with advanced welfare state systems, like the Nordic States, which depend upon high tax rates. Therefore, there is bound to be resistance to harmonisation of fiscal and welfare policies at EU level which is not on cards. However, the European Union in its vigorous pursuit of convergence policies, market orientation and low priority for social policy may cause steady erosion of public welfare state content in Europe. This needs to be guarded against. European Union is a peace project. If it wants to be a genuine and enduring peace project, it has to be more benign to the social security systems of its member states and others.

The ongoing demographic change in Europe due to low birth rates is another potential challenge to welfare states in Europe. In concrete terms, it would mean that the number of people getting into the job market will be less than the number of people retiring. It would also mean a reduction in contributory revenue and an increase in social expenditure. It can also create problems for the social insurance programme. Since in many countries social insurance schemes are pay-as-you-go systems, rather than capital funding, these schemes are more vulnerable to the effects of the ageing of population and the consequent change in the employment pattern. This is particularly true of Germany where social benefits are financed mostly by contributions rather than by taxes. A crisis in the employment front can upset the system.

It will increase expenditure on old age pension. Some countries have already introduced pension reforms, keeping in view the context of the ageing population. For example, in 2001 Germany has reformed its old age pension insurance and made it a public-private mix, in which the private pension constitutes a larger share in it. So, Germany introduced a private provision, rather than privatisation, in the old age pension scheme. Similarly, it will increase expenditure on health insurance also. As a response, some countries, like Finland for example, have extended the retirement age so that people are encouraged to stay in service for longer period. In countries like Denmark there is now less emphasis on early retirement schemes like "golden handshakes" and Voluntary Retirement Schemes.

In 1997 France has created a "Saving Pension Funds", which is a scheme of partial privatisation of pension funds. Critics say that this would weaken social solidarity and institutionalise inequality in France. However, the effects of the ageing of population in the economies and societies of Europe have not yet been fully felt since its peak is yet to come in the late 2020s and early 2030s. As the proportion of older people in society grows, the cost of maintaining the existing social support system also would grow. That would call for new re-adjustments.

What appears clearly is that despite new challenges and weakening of political support for welfare, there is no sign of a fundamental break with the established institutional structure of welfare state. Most reforms do not aim at the establishment of new institutions or at fully privatising social services. They are reforms from within, and aimed to mobilise intermediate institutions—non-state and non-market institutions. The moves were to establish links between the public and private providers.

Europe's welfare state systems have exercised considerable influence on the societal reconstruction in many other countries in the post-war period. India has also drawn inspiration from it and tried to emulate the basic idea of welfare state and framed many policies in tune with it. There is wide recognition in India that freedom from want, fear, ignorance and disease are basic for human development. Therefore, public health, education, pensions and so on are broadly attuned to eradicate poverty and promote equality and distributive justice in society. In India, welfare programmes are pursued by states, although the Central Government also plays a role in it. As a result, there is no uniform level of welfare programmes applicable to the whole country.

In India, the social sector expenditure includes the total expenditure incurred on social services and rural development. The social service expenditure includes money spent on education, health and family welfare, water supply, and sanitation. The rural development expenditure involves mainly the anti-poverty programmes. As per statistics, in aggregate terms the Centre and the States together spend about 24 to 28 per cent of their budgets on the social sector. The ratio of social expenditure between the States and the Centre in India is 80:20. Though the Centre spends less in the social sector compared to States, the Center's role in it is very important because the Centre sets the priority and gives policy directions for the whole country.

However, like in other parts of the world, in India too liberalisation phase which began in 1980s, and became more explicit from 1991 onwards, has applied brake in the process. There were talks of rolling back of the state from the social sector. Yet, what is notable is that the Center's overall contribution in the social sector is growing, especially in the rural development sector, whereas there is a decline in the proportion of social spending by the States in the post-reform period. But, according to some analysts, the expenditure on social sector schemes has been increasing in real terms in the era of liberalisation.

To sum up, the welfare state system is a civilisational project, anchored in human solidarity. It is good economics, good politics and good sociology. It explicates how public spending on people's welfare can create general conditions for economic growth; how preventive policies can reduce potential social problems and promote the development of a healthy stress-free society; and how it can bring sea change in the ethos and psyche of people and countries. The Nordic countries exemplify it.

Today, social benefit has been recognised as a social right and not charity. In France the Rocard Reforms of 1988 and 1992, during the Presidency of the Socialist leader Francois Mitterand, have legitimized the principle that right to live entails the right to live "decently" and that the State is responsible for it. That is indeed revolutionary.

However, in Europe welfare state has expanded citizens' social rights—like social security, education, health care, employment and so on which are assured through various insurance schemes, state funding, and contributions from employers and employees. Under certain influences, some countries have shifted their economic policies from full employment, which has caused a spurt in unemployment figures, causing strain on unemployment insurance programmes. Moreover, what is being done in the job front is regressive. Job insecurity has been assiduously promoted under one pretext or another. Public sector units which provided job security has been down sized or privatised across Europe. The new job pattern is increasingly contractual and part-time, outflanking the labour unions.

In this context, I would like to emphasise that a full employment policy should form an integral part of the welfare state system. Full employment is not a programme of the past. It is also a programme beckoning the future which can prevent social unrest in any society. It means, concretely the countries should follow employment-friendly economic and technology policies. Some countries of Europe were carried away by the idea that cutting down welfare benefits or even dismantling welfare states and cutting high taxes would keep their economies competitive. That is not necessarily true. Empirical evidence proves the contrary. However, it is imperative that welfare state systems should remain attuned to solve problems of social inequality and social exclusion, and should not be driven primarily by budget concerns.

PART II

Democracy and the System of States

12

Alternative World Systems and Global Future

—JAYANTANUJA BANDYOPADHYAYA

Any system, physical, social, or political, is identified by its distinctive structural characteristics. The international system is no exception. The study of alternative international systems, therefore, implies an analysis and examination of the structural characteristics of all possible international systems, including the prevailing international system. In this keynote address we shall focus our attention on the structural characteristics of only some of the major alternative international systems, and comment on the future of the international system in an empirical as well as ethical and emancipatory perspective.

***The *structure of a system* is defined as (1) a finite set of component units into which it can be decomposed and (2) the relations among these units.

(1) Where K is the structure of a system, the finite set of its component units can be illustrated as follows:

$$K == [\ k_1 \\ k_2 \\ . \\ . \\ K_n]$$

[Based on the Keynote address delivered in the seminar on "Alternative Global Futures" in the Department of International Relations, Jadavpur University, Kolkata on March 5, 2003].

The component units of the prevailing international system are sovereign states. We ignore the non-state actors in international relations for the present purpose, because such actors, including transnational corporations, can and do act across state boundaries only with the permission of the state, sometimes as the agents of the state. The present international system has 192 component units, namely, sovereign states. Hence K_n = 192nd state.

(2) *Relations among the structural units of a system* are of two main types, namely, (a) hierarchical and (b) coplanar. If the relations among the structural units of an international system are hierarchical, the international system concerned can be called a hierarchical one. Similarly, an international system whose structural components have coplanar relations among themselves can be called a coplanar system.

The structural characteristics of a hierarchical international system can be explained with the help of the diagram at Figure 1.

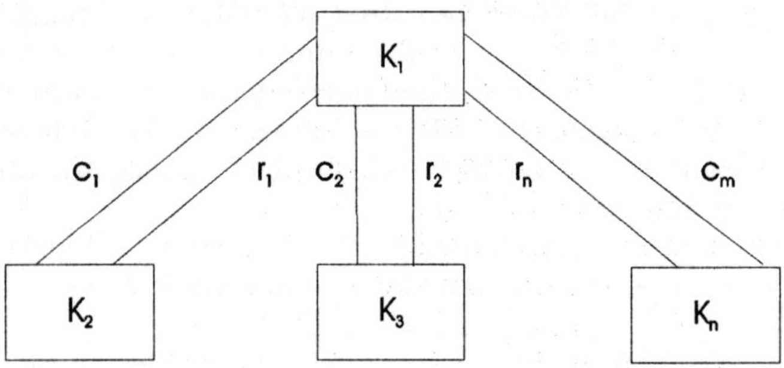

Fig. 1. A two-level hierarchical international system.

In the above diagram:

: K : structure of the international system $\{k_1, k_2, k_3 \ldots k_n\}$

C : a set of commands $\{c_1, c_2, c_3, \ldots C_m\}$

R : a set of resistances $(r_1, r_2, r_3, \ldots r_n\}$

C>R

R>0, because societal systems, unlike mechanical systems, possess:

- Cognitive capability
- Volitional capability
- Heuristic capability

In concrete terms, a hierarchical international system means that there is a command-control relationship among the states of the international system, so that some states in the international system dominate and control the others. The dominance and control, however, can never be complete, as in a mechanical system. On account of the cognitive, volitional, and heuristic capabilities of the dominated units, they always enjoy a measure of behavioural autonomy, and are able to resist the control of the dominant states to some extent.

***Coplanar international systems may be of two types, depending on the nature of the relationship among the component structural units of the system concerned. One type is the (1) stateless, anarchical international system, while the other is (2) an interstate system that is formally anarchical, in the sense of the absence of suprastate regulatory authority, but operationally oligarchic. The first type of coplanar international system is illustrated by the Gandhian model of an anarchist international system in the diagram at Figure 2, while the second type is illustrated by the model of the prevailing international system in the diagram at Figure 3.

Type 1 : Classical stateless model: coplanar and anarchical

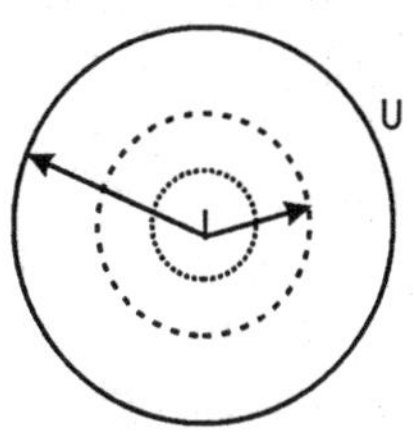

Fig 2. Stateless anarchist international system : Gandhian model.

The classical anarchist international system is a stateless one. Hence, it is both coplanar and without any political boundaries. The Gandhian model of the anarchist international system, which is illustrated by Figure 2, is an anarchist and coplanar international system of this type. In this model, the individual or small group, I, is at the centre of a series of concentric or oceanic circles. The universe U is the outermost of the circles, which can be approached by any individual or small group without being obstructed by any boundaries. This Gandhian model of an anarchical international system is composed of "oceanic circles" of villages and other social and geographical aggregates on the same plane, without any relations of command and control among them. Individuals and groups can traverse the boundaries of these oceanic circles without being obstructed by territorial sovereignty at any frontier.

Type 2 : Sovereign territorial state and interstate system : anarchical and oligarchic

The anarchical structure of the prevailing interstate system is a logical corollary of the empirical reality of the sovereign states, which are the basic structural units of this system. All the sovereign states composing the international system theoretically exist on the same plane in the sense that all of them have equal juridical status within the system. This in fact is the theoretical model of the international system that is rationalized and glorified by the Realist discourse of IR theory. But the present international system is also acutely asymmetric in terms of the distribution of power, because a few of the 192 states are much more powerful than the rest. The five permanent members of the UN Security Council enjoy much greater political and military power than the other states of the international system. In the same manner, the G-7 states enjoy much greater economic power than all the other states. Hence while the prevailing international system is formally and theoretically anarchical in structure, it functions informally like an oligarchy. The strong states, which are few, exercise *matsyanyaya,* i.e. predatory hegemony, over the weak states, which are many. Both the theoretical and the empirical situations are explained below with the help of the diagram at Figure 3.

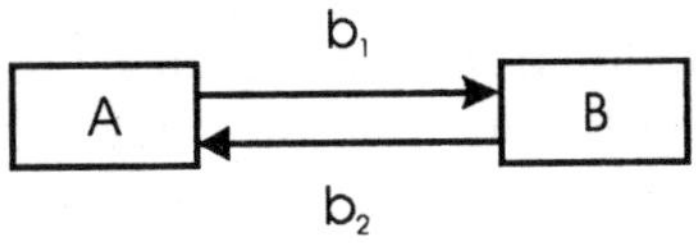

Fig 3. Anarchical international system : Realist model.

In this diagram:

b_1: A's power projection to B.
b_2: B's power projection to A.

If $b_1 > b_2$, A dominates B.
If $b_2 > b_1$, B dominates A.
If $b_1 = b_2$, there is balance of power between A and B.

But the international system being acutely asymmetric in terms of the distribution of power, in reality $b_1 >> b_2$, while $b_2 \rightarrow 0$.

The realist reply to this argument is that the asymmetry of the international system in terms of the distribution of power would be rectified by the balance of power. The weaker states would form an alliance against one or more strong states and thus safeguard their sovereignty and external security through the balance of power. The equilibrium and stability of the anarchical international system would be maintained in this manner. While the classical Realists believed that the balance of power was an inevitable and irreversible law of history, the Neorealists deny such historical inevitability of the balance of power. The latter have "refined" the balance of power to assert that the "major states" should and would consider the establishment of a balance of power system to be their own political and moral responsibility in an anarchical international system. Hence an anarchical international system would in reality be characterized by balance of power. But as numerous scholars, including the present speaker, have shown, the theory of the balance of power is semantically ambiguous, logically fallacious, empirically invalid, and leads inevitably to a hegemonic and predatory international system. Besides, there can be no real balance of power between a nuclear-weapon state and a group of non-nuclear-weapon states, or between an industrially and technologically advanced state and a group of predominantly agricultural states. Since the collapse of the Soviet Union, the increased asymmetry of the international system in terms of the distribution of power has generated the virtually unbridled imperialism of the USA, rather than a new balance of power system. Hence the balance of power theory offers no real solution to the problem of predatory hegemony that would be inevitably generated by an anarchical but asymmetric interstate system.

***Historical international systems* have been anarchical and hierarchical systems of two main types: (1) colonial or imperialist, and (2) oligarchic and hegemonic.

1. *Colonial/hierarchical and anarchical international system.* The modern international system is also an interstate system that has developed pari passu with the development of capitalism as a global economic system. The close correspondence of the historical development of global capitalism and the modern interstate system is not, moreover, spurious or accidental, but in fact represents a cause and effect relationship. The development of capitalism from the 16th century to the 20th was associated with and assisted by the global colonialism of the developing capitalist states in search of cheap labour and raw materials as well as markets for manufactured goods. The draining of the wealth of the colonies led on the one hand to the growth of economically and militarily strong states located at the center of the international capitalist-colonial system, and to the impoverishment and military as well as political weakening of the vast

colonies across the globe. During the last four centuries, therefore, the international system had a colonial or imperialist structure that was characterized by:

- Nearly total control and exploitation of colonies by metropolitan states.
- Resistance by national liberation movements through violence or non-violence.

But this predatory and acutely oligarchic interstate system was formally and juridically anarchical, because unlike a state system, there was in it no central regulatory authority. In this international system a small and closed oligarchy of a few economically and militarily strong capitalist states exercised predatory dominance over the great majority of countries and peoples of the world inhabiting the vast periphery of global capitalism.

2. *Post-colonial anarchical and hierarchical international system.* The decolonization process, which was virtually completed in approximately the third quarter of the twentieth century, led to the nominal political independence of most of the colonies. This historical process led to the emergence of a post-colonial international system that consisted of nominally and juridically sovereign states in a state of synchronic interstate anarchy. But on account of their economic impoverishment and retardation and consequent military weakness, the new states inevitably came under the economic, military and political domination of the economically and militarily strong states. In other words, the ex-colonial states came under the predatory hegemony of the ex-imperialist states. The oligarchic structure of the UN helped the few strong states to sustain and perpetuate their neo-imperialistic control over the vast majority of the countries and peoples of the world. The basic structural characteristics of this post-colonial and neo-imperialistic international

system were two kinds of relations of control and subordination between the militarily and economically strong global oligarchs on the one hand, and the weak ex-colonial states on the other:

- Military and political governance by P-5 states:

  ⇒ Through UN Security Council
  ⇒ Through international military regimes
  ⇒ Through private military intervention

- Economic and political governance by G-7 states:

  ⇒ Through unilateral or multilateral action
  ⇒ Through international regimes
  ⇒ Through globalization of markets and sources of cheap labour and raw materials.

Since the collapse of the Soviet Union the international system has virtually returned to the classical form of imperialism. Through a deliberately calculated and contrived global grand strategy, the G-7 states led by the USA have set out to establish their own imperialistic control over the natural resources, labour, and markets of the world, especially those of the less developed states, through:

- Economic globalization, mainly involving control of the natural resources, labour, and markets of the less developed states of the international system.
- Military globalization, involving private and illegal invasion of other sovereign states, and the establishment of new foreign military bases.
- Ideological globalization, involving the establishment of capitalism all over the world, and the destruction of all alternative socio-economic systems everywhere, especially all forms of socialism.

It is in this way that the prevailing interstate system, which is formally anarchical but informally oligarchic, and the theoretical model of which was presented in Figure 3, came into existence historically. The future alternatives to it are briefly as follows.

****Alternative World Order I* : **Classical anarchist future.** The classical anarchist model of the future international system, the pure Gandhain form of which was depicted in Figure 2, would, of course, be a stateless international system without any internal territorial boundaries. Needless to say, this is a purely utopian model of the future international system, in the sense that it almost completely transcends the given reality of the prevailing interstate system. In theory, all forms of imperialism or other forms of hegemony would be non-existent in such an ideal international system, which would be characterized by nearly complete liberty and equality of the nations and peoples of the world. In reality, however, it is difficult to establish how:

- The prevailing interstate system is to be abolished in the absence of an inconceivably vast and total global anarchist revolution, violent or nonviolent.
- Human society is to be organized on an international scale without any hierarchical structure.
- Conflict will be resolved in such an anarchist international society.

****Alternative World Order II* : **Quasi-anarchical pluralism within the prevailing interstate system.** This model of a future international system is being advocated and promoted, in both theory and practice, by a wide spectrum of anti-realist scholars, thinkers, and activists, including the exponents of Critical Theory, Postmodern Theory, Feminist Theory, and Green Theory. Although there is considerable difference of opinion among these different schools of IR theory, as well as within each of these schools, they have collectively and effectively challenged the prevailing interstate system, and the Realist discourse that sustains it intellectually, on epistemological, ontological, historical, and sociological grounds. They have correctly pointed out that the basic paradigms of realism, including those of state sovereignty, synchronic interstate anarchy, and state power, have been deduced from unexamined major premises, are both logically and empirically faulty, and represent the ideological rationalization of an unjust and immoral international system. The Postmodern theorists, in particular, have forcefully argued that the Realist discourse is in fact nothing but a textual interplay that seeks to construct and perpetuate the prevailing international system, and serves the interests of a few strong states. The millions of activists in Europe and America who have been periodically demonstrating against capitalism, globalization, and war, including those belonging to the Seattle Syndrome and the Global Social Forum, have also been mainly inspired by such non-conformist thinking, especially postmodern thinking.

However, the main collective weakness of this amorphous anti-realist school is that its attitude towards the sovereign state is rather uncertain and inarticulate. While emphasizing its general commitment to spontaneous mass action, localism, connectivity, and certain other elements of classical anarchism, the theorists and practitioners of this heterogeneous school of thought do not propose either to abolish the state or to restrict its sovereignty through democratic international regulation. With marginal exceptions they appear collectively to advocate the undermining of the power of the state through the empowerment of the civil society mainly in the form of quasi-anarchistic mass activism. Similarly, there is a wide spectrum of views among these diverse radical groups on the ideological question. While some of them, especially the Critical theorists, appear to advocate some form of global socialism, others seem to support some form of state-regulated capitalism. On the whole, therefore, they have collectively failed seriously and effectively to challenge the prevailing interstate system, or to make any dent in its oligarchic and predatory structure. Although they represent on the whole a positive and forward movement in the history of international relations, the theory and practice of these radical theorists lack sufficient clarity regarding:

- The role of the state in the future international system.
- Organization of international relations in a future world order.
- The consummation of democracy and justice in international relations.
- Methodology of global transformation for an alternative world order.

*****Alternative World Order III:* **Democratic world government**. Within the imperialist international system there has been a movement towards international organization since the Hague Peace Conferences of the end of the 19th century. In many ways the League of Nations and the UN represent the further development of this process of developing international organization. The structure of the international system at this time, as we have already noted, was empirically imperialistic and oligarchic, but juridically anarchical. In the 30s and 40s of the 20th century, however, there developed an intellectual as well as political movement for the establishment of a democratic world government, which was visualized as a culmination of the developing process of international organization. Numerous scholars and intellectuals, including renowned professors of the best Western universities, lawyers, and other intellectuals published serious academic works on the desirability and feasibility of establishing a democratic world government in order to ensure the collective security and development of mankind. There was also a political movement for world government led by intellectuals, legislators, and workers in Europe and America. Resolutions were also moved in several European legislatures and the US

Congress demanding the amendment of the UN Charter with a view to the establishment of a world government (For details see my *World Government for International Democracy and Justice,* Manuscript India, Howrah, 2002). By the early 1950s the movement for world government led by the liberal internationalists had gathered considerable momentum, although neither the US nor the Soviet governments had reacted favourably to this movement.

The onset of the cold war, however, seriously stymied the movement for a world government. The zero-sum game that developed between the two power blocs in an effectively bipolar world undermined the feasibility, though not the rationale, of the world government movement. The new international situation generated the school of political Realism, which sought to rationalize and legitimize the cold war, more particularly the American global strategy against the Soviet Union. The liberal internationalists who proposed a world government were called Idealists in a pejorative sense, and subjected to ridicule by the Realists. Nevertheless, the movement for world government did not altogether die down during the cold war, at least at the intellectual level. After the collapse of the Soviet Union and the consequent end of the cold war, academic works on world government have increased in number. The emergence of the USA as the only superpower of the world, and the imperialistic and predatory use of this power by it across the world have strengthened the arguments of liberal intellectuals for the establishment of a democratic world government that would replace the prevailing un-democratic and unjust international system. Moreover, the case for a world government in the post-Soviet imperialistic world order has become stronger than ever before due to the following factors:

- The virtual impossibility of ensuring international security through balance of power, international security regimes, military alliances, overseas bases, and unilateral military intervention by a superpower and its strategic allies in the age of nuclear, chemical and biological weapons.

- International terrorism, which is rooted in perceived global injustice in an imperialist world order, and cannot be eradicated without global democracy and justice.
- The threat to the global environment, caused by both anthropogenic and natural factors, which cannot be met by any single state or group of states, howsoever powerful, without the global pooling and management of resources.
- The grand strategy of economic, military and cultural globalization unleashed by the G-7 states led by the USA, which threatens to convert the rest of the world into peripheral and dependent semi-colonies of these global oligarchs.
- The essentially undemocratic, unjust, oligarchic, imperialist, and predatory structure of the UN and the prevailing international system.

The structural characteristics of the model of a democratic and just world government visualized by us would include the following:

- Federal structure with residuary powers for UN
- Abolition of veto
- Transfer of power from SC to GA
- Direct representation on the basis of population
- International judiciary.

The functions of the democratic and just world government in this future model would include the following:

- Maintenance of international security
- Resolution of international conflict
- Promotion of international development with distributive justice
- Management of the global environment and its security
- Promotion of global democracy.

This model of a democratic, just, and rational international system can be illustrated by the diagram at Figure 4.

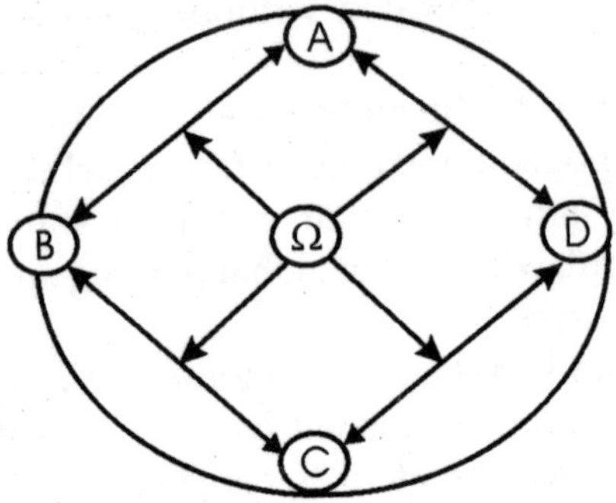

Fig 4. World Government model of the international system.

In this diagram:

A, B, C, D : states constituting the international system.
Ω: world government.

The arrows indicating the relations among A, B, C and D are all on the horizontal plane. The system is coplanar and not hierarchical, since international democracy and justice imply that all the states of the international system enjoy equal security, development and welfare. The arrows emanating from Ω, which indicate the control exercised by the democratic and just world government over the external behaviour of the constituent states, gives this international system a formally hierarchical structure, as in the case of the domestic structures of all the constituent states of the system. But just as the central authority the state in a democratic and just form of government is ultimately derived from the will of the people constituting the state, so also the regulatory authority of a democratic and just world government is ultimately derived from the will of the constituent states of the international system. In other words:

$$\Omega = F(A, B, C, D)$$

It has been argued that although the case for a democratic and just world government is indisputably rational in the present international context, the establishment of such a world government is not practicable because of the non-existence of a conflict-free international community. International conflict caused by nationalism, racism, ideological and cultural differences, the clash of civilizations, etc. is too widespread and intractable to permit the creation of a democratic and viable world government in the present context of international relations, so runs the argument of the skeptics. But as in the case of the evolution of the state in human political history, the development of a world government is necessary for the taming of conflict, rather than the celebration of the descent of a conflict-free society on earth. The major obstacle to the establishment of a democratic and just world government appears to be the adamantine and relentless opposition of the closed, small and privileged oligarchy that rules the prevailing international system to the democratization of the UN system. As indicated by the diagram at Figure 2, the command-control structure of an oligarchic international system can be transformed into a democratic one only by increasing the resistance of the structural units of the system that are the victims of predatory control. A global and protracted political struggle spearheaded by the leading Third World states therefore appears to be necessary and unavoidable for breaking down the resistance of the ruling oligarchy against the democratization of the international system. India, as the largest democracy of the world, should adopt the organization of such a global political movement for the democratization of the UN and its transformation into a democratic and just world government as the global grand strategy of its foreign policy.

13

Liberal Democracy and World Order in the New Millennium

—SHIBASHIS CHATTERJEE

This study is about the liberal paradigm in International Relations (IR) and political theory in relation to democratization of the world order. The study evolves in three sections. The first looks at liberal IR theory and its arguments linking peace, democracy and prosperity. The second section tests these liberal arguments against the contemporary reality of world politics and offers explanations for its shortcomings. The third section deals exclusively with the theory of democracy in its association with democratization of the world order. The study argues that clarification of democratic theory is an essential prerequisite for understanding the problems of global democratization, and the existing body of work unfortunately does not take us very far in this direction.

1

There are three sets of arguments that liberal International Relations theory pursues. The first of these builds on various forms of interdependence that create conditions propitious for peace through intense mutual interaction and communicative

---

This study received financial assistance from the UGC ASIHSS Program (Field Trip Grant 2004-2005) of the Department of International Relations, Jadavpur University.

reciprocity. A liberal economic order, by encouraging free exchange among states and non-state actors, creates the condition of peace. The second argument relates to the pacific effects of democratization at the global level. The central contention here is that democracies do not fight/war with each other, although they fight harder against authoritarian states. The third argument maintains that international institutions trump conflict by inducing higher transparency, sharing the cost of collective action, guarding against cheating, and formalizing targeted action against violators of rules and other arrangements. Institutions prescribe the desirable and prescribe the unacceptable. Taken together, these arguments suggest that the world is poised for a liberal and democratic future, which would bring opulence and peace to all states. In the following paragraphs, we present a summary of the liberal thesis, culminating in the ideas of Fukuyama.

The central idea underlying commercial liberalism is old and simple. It follows form the belief of the classical political economists, particularly Adam Smith, that free trade in beneficial to all participants and the resultant prosperity is conducive for world peace and cooperation between rational agents. The liberal case can be explained from two distinctive routes. The first concerns the wealth generating consequence of free trade acting as a deterrent for war. In brief, the prospect of suffering huge economic losses deters warfare amongst states.[1]

The second route concerns domestic level variables. The benefits of trade are also expected to have positive domestic consequences in terms of greater and better internal resource distribution. When people are by and large prosperous and happy, there is little scope for politicians to exploit the rhetoric of war as a parochial survival strategy or to use harmful and exploitative external linkage as a rationale for under-development.[2] Some liberals also believe that free market policies promote peace by strengthening the constituencies who have a direct stake in maintaining peaceful environment as a necessary precondition to successful commerce. Such shifts in domestic coalitions neutralize the supporters of war. When a large number of states espouse similar liberal, open market policies, and as more effects are multiplied, or norms of international cooperation become embedded, the negative effects of anarchy are mitigated to a large degree.

Perhaps the most powerful argument that the liberals employ in their defense of peace and cooperation consists of the hypothesis that liberal democracies do not fight each other. This proposition has been claimed not only as the most observed empirical relationship in international relations, but also qualifying perhaps as the only law of the discipline. An enormous amount of research has been devoted to study this relationship, and although findings are diverse, the basic relation is found to hold in an overwhelming body of work in the subject.[3] Developments in research, both quantitative and qualitative, have refined the hypothesis and qualified it in certain ways. Thus democracy is no longer understood as an undifferentiated category. Accordingly, the nature of democracy is supposed to determine the kind of behaviour expected out of it. In particular weak, new democracies, consisting of unreliable and unsafe elites and a population devoid of sufficient resources, are now thought to be rather unpredictable and dangerous in their dealings with the outside world. Again, although democracies do not combat each other, they often fight non-democracies more intensely than conflicts between authoritarian states. Further, scholars also refer to the need for a democratic culture and shared norms of understanding or identity to make democracies genuinely peaceful towards each other. Others, in contrast, point out the recorded evidence of covert action instigated by one democracy against another to refute the claim of shared norms and identity as a necessary precondition to democratic peace. Variations are thus numerous and seem to be growing by the day. Yet, the explanation(s) of the relationship are now widely acknowledged by IR scholars to be sound and the promotion and consolidation of democratic norms, institutions and practices are almost universally regarded as the best, though not the easiest, means of ushering in a peaceful, cooperative world.

The first argument of the peace-democracy brigade relates to democratic culture and norms.[4] The idea here is that democracies, unlike monarchies and autocracies, respect people's rights as equal rights. Hence in a democracy the public counts in decision-making. The consequence of this respect for people's right is to abstain from courses thought to be injurious to people's welfare. Since war leads to massive human and material destruction people do not support governments who send them to frontiers to fight costly wars. In addition, the modern international system is predicated on the principle of equal state rights. Therefore, the domestic culture of respecting people's rights flows outside and promotes the ever-widening pacification of a liberal political union. Since democracies are raised on a culture of restraint and peaceful resolution of differences, these principles automatically transcend national frontiers and bind democracies together in a union of peace. Similarly, since democracies cannot hope to be spared by autocracies or take risk with the latter's motives, they prefer conflict to accommodation whenever their interests contradict.[5]

The second argument presses on the institutional constraint button.[6] Here the emphasis is on separation of powers, checks and balances and other institutional restraints, the need for public approval, the role of free press and open debates within the democracy. Institutional separation diffuses power and cause greater moderation even in crisis decision-making. The need for public opinion introduces further circumspection and hesitancy. Debates and deliberations enjoin the need for leaders to obtain a broad base of public support behind harsh decisions like declaration of war. The role of the free press and that of political opposition are also taken as additional explanations of the success of democracies in having and sustaining peaceful mutual ties. The free press and the critique of the oppositional forces increase the transparency of the democratic set up and show to the outer world whether a country is united or divided in times of crises. If a nation is divided on a conflict, it ties the hands of the government to implement tough policies. The adversary then forces a settlement more vigorously and this deters the democratic leadership to settle the dispute by war. In contrast, if the nation is united, the adversary can see its resolve and refrain from adopting risky policies, knowing that hard policies will be responded in kind.[7]

Of all branches of liberalism, liberal institutionalism is closest to the logic of realism. Thus Robert Keohane and Lisa Martin, two of the most well known institutionalists, argue:

> "When states can jointly benefit from cooperation ... we expect governments to attempt to construct (such) institutions. Institutions can provide information, reduce transaction costs, make commitments more credible, establish focal points for coordination and in general facilitate the operation of reciprocity. By seeking to specify the conditions under which the institutions can have an impact and cooperation can occur, institutionalist theory shows under what conditions realist propositions are valid. It is in this sense that institutionalism claims to subsume realism."[8]

Liberal institutionalism thus adopts the 'realist model of rational egoism', and shows that rational egoists functioning in an anarchical international system can produce cooperation through institutional arrangements. The analytical centre-piece of liberal institutionalism is the prisoners' dilemma game, the logic of which can be summarized as follows. As states are rational egoists, they seek the fulfillment of their own selfish interest in every domain of life. However, pure individualism cannot work in life, because vital collective gains must be realized in key spheres. But can rational, selfish, egoistic agents realize collective goods? Institutionalists answer in the positive. The main problem for egoists in any collective endeavour is the fear of cheating. Thus in any game, agents seek to obtain other's cooperation but cheat on their part. The best solution for any agent in such a game is to receive the other's cooperation while cheating for him. But this would lead to a possible double cheating solution that is bad for both. Therefore, the rational agents, in order to avoid this worst pay-off, decide to satisfy themselves with the second best solution, which is double cooperation. But the real difficulty is to convince rational egoists to agree to a sub-optimal mutual collaborative solution. Institutionalists believe that institutions play a vital role in this.

Institutionalists are particularly enthusiastic about the role of regimes. Regimes have multiple benefits. They create transparency, reduce transaction costs, provide information, help punish cheating and protect victims, reward cooperative moves and encourage reputation for sustaining mutual cooperation. The institutionalists develop a handful of concepts to substantiate their optimistic predictions. The most important of these are a defense of absolute gains, the shadow of future, tit-for-tat games, etc. that explain the possibility of cooperation in an essentially anarchic set up.[9]

Of several contributions to the peace-democracy argument, the work of Francis Fukuyama stands apart from the rest. It is true that several analysts and commentators of world politics predicted the home coming of an era of unprecedented peace and global prosperity as the benefits of triumphant liberalism reached more and more states. However, the most dramatic prophecy came from Francis Fukuyama, a Japanese social scientist settled in the United States. In an unusually bold essay entitled *The End of History*, Fukuyama advanced his remarkable philosophical judgment that with the collapse of socialism, the last contender to the unsurpassable supremacy of liberal capitalist democracy was eliminated, paving the way for human history to achieve its highest teleological culmination in the celebration of the philosophy of the market. These ideas were subsequently developed even further in a comprehensive work of philosophy and sociology of daring originality that set the tone for one of the most important debates of the post-Cold War era.[10]

Fukuyama's work is singled out for two reasons. First, it represents the most optimistic variant of scholarship within the liberal paradigm as a whole, one that sought to link up issues of war and security with democracy and the market. But more importantly, Fukuyama's work is unique for its philosophical sophistication, however controversial his ideas might be and regardless of the arbitrary nature of his intellectual borrowings. Fukuyama's work therefore nicely complements that of the peace-democracy brigade, although it also shows the limitations of applying the connection in the under-developed regions of the world.

Built on imposing foundations of Hegel and Alexander Kojeve, the central thesis of Fukuyama consisted of the uncomplicated claim that humanity has completed its ideological evolution with the final victory of Western liberal democracy at the end of the twentieth century. History records the defeat of totalitarian alternatives to liberal democracy — the emphatic destruction of the barbaric doctrines of fascism and Nazism in the Second World War, and the visible collapse of communism at the end of the Cold War. With the eclipse of global contenders, there remained only the threat of local disturbances —unsettled historical residues—whose impact was limited to the historical backwaters of the Third World. Probably the most attractive part of Fukuyama's work consisted of his treatment of these distressing local residues of the past. They included the gradual emptying of nationalism of its exclusivist yet universal appeal and social distinctiveness, denial of the increasingly antiquated appeal of perverse fundamentalism barring a few isolated global pockets, and growing obsolescence of the threat of deadly weapons in the face of steadily growing dividends of surrendering to the magical powers of liberal capitalism. For Fukuyama the triumph of liberal democracy was not confined to the Euro-American theatre alone. Selected states like Japan, South Korea, Taiwan and Singapore were claimed to have been successfully liberated from the grip of history and the liberation of the rapidly industrializing economies of South-east Asia and even China was only a matter of time.

In the developed world of post-history, states would continue to direct their attention and resources towards security. But inter-state competition would be limited to economic issues as military confrontation and doctrinal hostility would have become a thing of the past. International relations of the developed world would, therefore, be conducted within innovative, collaborative frameworks based on the calculations of absolute gains. Sectarian violence and parochial sub-nationalism(s) would continue to burden history without compromising "the deep configurations of time". It is wrong to criticize Fukuyama for having predicted the end of all conflicts and mutual rivalries. Fukuyama's basic contention was that fundamental conflicts would not recur in post-history since all major rival paradigms to liberal capitalism have been defeated and consigned to the waste-bin of time forever.[11]

The fundamental philosophical heritage behind this controversial thesis that Fukuyama so boldly invoked was that of Hegelian dialectics as mediated by Alexander Kojeve.[12] Fukuyama agreed like Hegel that the march of the world spirit would eventually come to an end with the consummation of the idea of the Spirit or the *Sittlichkeit*. Drawing upon the ideas of Kojeve, Fukuyama established the essential liberal character of that redeemed ethical community. According to Kojeve, the victory of Napoleon in the battle of Jena (1806), where he defeated the conservative Prussian monarchy, marked the *fin de siecle* of human history. This was the moment of actualization of the *Sittlichkeit*, securely embodied in the immortalized triumvirate of the French Revolution—liberty, equality and fraternity. In a modern adaptation of this Kojevian reading of Hegel, Fukuyama wrote; "The state that emerges from the end of history is liberal insofar as it recognizes and protects through a system of law man's universal right to freedom, and democratic insofar as it exists only with the consent of the governed." Most crucially, Fukuyama related the political order of liberalism to the economic system of capitalism without demonstrating any causality between the two. Implicit in Fukuyama's thought was the conviction that the unbridled prosperity of capitalism could not but con-solidate the virtues and norms of a democratic way of life. But just why capitalism is a partisan for democracy Fukuyama never clarified.

Most significantly, however, Fukuyama did not seem very confident with the ability of liberal democracy to sustain world peace. The problem he sees is not external to that idea. Liberal democracy has indeed, for Fukuyama at least, vanquished its macro ideological rivals. But it was not safe from within. In a peculiar, and theoretically speaking, confused, adaptation of Plato's theory of the tripartite soul with Hegel's dialectical philosophy of change, Fukuyama mourned the incapability of modern consumerist liberalism to accommodate the thymotic stirrings of the soul, since wars were too risky and expensive games to be played out by the ruling aristocracy of the liberal order. Despite its victory as a normative political order over its rivals, Fukuyama shuddered at the prospect of the subordination of *megalothymia* (pursuit of excellence) to *isothymia* (pursuit of equality) since, if there was too much of the latter, and nothing to satisfy the claims of recognition, people may strike at the very root of the system that had brought them peace and security. Fragmentation and dispersal being natural to liberal democracy, there was bound to be tensions within them. Unless buttressed by some social bond, like the idea of trust or social capital, there was little guarantee against the atrophy of the liberal order. Fukuyama confirms this in his later work:

"Virtually all economic activity in the contemporary world is carried out not by individuals but by organizations that require a high degree of social cooperation. Property rights, contracts, and commercial law are all indispensable institutions for creating a modern market-oriented economic system, but is possible to economize substantially on transaction costs if such institutions are supplemented by social capital and trust. Trust, in turn, is the product of pre-existing communities of shared moral codes or values. These communities ...are not the product of rational choice."[13]

2

Between 1989 and 2004, the fate of the liberal democratic vision of the new world order has slipped from good promise to a disappointing collapse. At present, in the brooding shadow of 9/11, its plausibility seems seriously circumscribed. The crass perverseness of the present epoch partially explains this retreat. Yet, deeper conceptual fallacies had been no less significant as causes for its decline. The liberal paradigm falters at the inside/ outside divide. Its case for democratization and human rights predicates on that divide, espousing different standards for each sphere. Thus Western democratic states, particularly the US, while emphasizing the need for democratic transition and then consolidation of such structures, continuously sabotaged the cause of global democratization in the interest of crude geo-political needs. Hence, the US did not support the movement for complete democratization/empowerment of the United Nations, or encourage genuine multilateralism, or approve the coming into power of a host of democratic regimes in Central and Latin America, Africa and Asia, since these regimes were vocal against American foreign policy objectives. In the words of Margot Light: "Western tolerance of egregiously undemocratic practices... undermined people's belief in democracy."[14] By condoning corrupt regimes and justifying the rampant abuse of power in the name of establishing democratic structures, the liberal democratic states not only emptied their own democratic credentials, but also weakened the appeal of these features in the eyes of the struggling masses of the South.

At another level, the much-vaunted democratic transition of the non-liberal world, a la Fukuyama, did not materialize. The policy of exporting democracy did not succeed in Central and East European states or in Russia as the infrastructural prerequisites for sustaining democratic grafting were missing, and since the West betrayed little sensitivity towards the promotion of "norms, social institutions, social capital, and trust" as essential preconditions for a successful market economy. As a result, the liberal-democratic panacea to the problem of war by means of generating structural peace-effects came a cropper. In some cases, the worst fears of the critics of the liberal-democratic school came true: Conflicts intensified between settled democratic states and confused, transitional ones.

A similar paradox straddled the issue of human rights. There was no evolution of any universal discourse or language of human rights, or any evidence of a shared social contract on rights between the rich North and the relatively poorer South. As a result, human rights quickly degenerated into a dirty coinage, grist to the mill of neo-imperialism, a dangerous contrivance to legitimate the intervention of the rich states into the sovereign jurisdiction of their underdeveloped counterparts. The role of the West was once again tragic. Tied to the conservative, anti-rights social forces of the developing world by commercial needs, it found it impossible evolve a convincing dialogue to address the actual constituencies of rights, the poor and the lower middle classes. Even when its intentions were good, the Western states failed to communicate their vision to the target groups, who mostly rejected the enterprise either on the ground of compromise of sovereignty, or as a brand of imperialism. Rights failed to overcome the barrier of mistrust between the two worlds. The West failed to advance respect for human rights world-wide, primarily due to their own inability to bring their domestic policies and practices in line with the substantive essence of their international obligations, and to allow multilateral bodies to oversee their own conduct.[15] The overtly externalized connotation of human rights meant that the inside/outside divide got reinforced through the new exclusionary language of human rights.

In addition to these, the liberals never theorized the relation between the market economy and the process of democratization. The confusion between support for democratic procedures and democratization as a process was most unfortunate. As a result the liberals could never indicate the direction of causality between the two variables. While some thought that democratization would enhance market efficiency, others felt that a market economy can only be sustained by a free democratic system. No liberal theorist suggested a way out of this circularity. Liberals also took the virtues of the market economy for granted. Margot Light has rightly remarked: "The effects of the particular types of economic reform advocated by the West are a good example of the way that external factors exacerbate internal problems, making the establishment and consolidation of democracy more difficult."[16] Rampant privatization further polarized the fragile social fabric of the transitional states, encouraging ultra-radicalism on the one hand, and opening the floodgates to widespread corruption on the other. It is also very surprising that the proponents of the liberal school overlooked the hard fact that the most successful market economies in East and South-east Asia, such as Singapore, Taiwan and South Korea, Brunei, Malaysia and Thailand were either outright authoritarian regimes or quasi-democracies at best. The country that for Fukuyama was poised to leap into *post-history*, namely post-Mao China, was not a liberal democracy by any stretch of imagination during the time of its outstanding economic performance qua market reforms. During the last few years, democratization lost out to unbridled marketization the world over. As more and more concessions had to be given to the market forces, there was hardly much left for the democratic forces to cheer about.

3

If liberal democracy in close conjugation with capitalist globalization is unable to account for much of what is happening in today's world, the problem is as much conceptual as practical. By this I mean that the failure of liberal democracy would need to be addressed at two levels, first, on the conceptual terrain, and secondly at the level of practice. It is common to find engagements with the latter much more than the former. Thus weak domestic institutions, the absence of value pluralism and commitment to a culture of autonomy and tolerance, and the lack of a political culture conducive to peaceful resolution of differences through dialogue and understanding, the predominance of totalitarian forces, and chronic poverty, among others, is routinely suggested as the reasons for the dearth of working democracies the world over.[17]

To begin with, I wish to problematize the commonly held notion that democratization of the world order is a sufficient condition for international equity and justice. My argument, however, is that mere democratization of the global order would not lead to the fulfillment of justice-claims any more than democracy within states sufficiently settle the equity demands of people living within them. There are fundamental, unresolved controversies within democratic theory itself that would not be resolved by its spatial extension to the global level. Unless, a satisfactory solution to such problems come about, democratization of the world order is not going to radically alter the properties of the latter. This argument, however, is not an excuse to withhold the democratic transformation of the world order. That transformation is and remains an ethical imperative of the highest order. However, to create a politics of democratic transformation at the global level one has to clarify the meaning of the kind of democracy one supports. This is not the place to engage in a full-scale interrogation of the ethical meaning and implications of democracy. I shall therefore restrict myself to the problems of defining democracy in relation to the global order only.

David Held in his *Models of Democracy* (1987) and *Democracy and World Order* (1995) constructs a model of civic republicanism and liberal democracy that builds on the lineage of Locke, Kant and Rousseau.[18] The model is based on the universal commitment to the idea of autonomy and recognizes individual rights and the promotion of active citizenship, thereby making individual and collective self-determination coeval in an arena of value pluralism that allows individuals and collective entities to choose their conception(s) of life/good without any interference or encumbrance. A very important aspect of Held's model is his conscious separation of democracy and the nation-state. Held argues that democracy and states are not mutually constitutive, and the latter is not a constituent ingredient of the former. Democracy insinuates domestic and sub-state practices and permeates aspects of the inter-state and trans-national institutions and practices. Held tries to respond to two limits of contemporary democratic theory: the insulation of democratic practices from the world order, and the moral excesses of both triumphant liberalization of the Fukuyama brand and some of the claims of civic republicanism and of Marxist critiques of liberal democracy. In Held's words:

> "...the conditions of enactment of the principle of autonomy can be specified adequately if one (1) draws

upon aspects of republicanism, liberalism, and Marxism and (2) appreciates some of the strengths and limitations of these over-all positions." [19]

I refer to Held because his work brings into sharp focus both the positives and pitfalls of liberal democratic theory. His work is exemplary for the fact that it recognizes the significance of incorporating and synthesizing the internal and international dimensions of democracy in order to erect a comprehensive theory of democracy that is independent of space. For this reason, Held espouses the cause of a cosmopolitan model as his ideal since the various forms of constraints under which the states currently operates do not allow the restriction of the political to the state alone. Held's work also exposes the serious democratic deficit of contemporary institutions and practices as these do not stand up to the specifications demanded by Held's cosmopolitan variant.

However, Held's work is also a good example of the limits of the model of liberal democracy itself, particularly in its civic republican form. First, the model is distinctively liberal despite its eclectic leanings as it derives the model of collective self-rule entirely from the a priori notion of individual self-rule.[20] But more significantly, it denies the "we" component of collective self-determination any genuine normative weightage by neglecting the exclusionary cultural boundaries of democratic determination within such collective bodies' altogether. This silence over liberal democracy's exclusionary proclivities is explained by Held's redefinition of democratic commitments in terms of individual self-interest alone, bereft of any substantive identity.[21] The problem with Held is that he fails to recognize the conditions under which the liberal model holds, and as a consequence, to claim a selective case as universal. The cosmopolitan model would gather adherents only if they share a prior commitment to a political culture of respect for autonomy and agree that their other (cultural) differences do not come in the way of their fundamental pre-commitment to autonomy. This requires Held to undertake a detailed empirical account of identifying such a consensus across cultures, particularly in mixed settings, where people hold political views drastically opposed to liberal democracy. Most unfortunately, Held does not deliver here. As a result, his version of a democratic world order becomes in reality an extension of his variant of the liberal democratic model in global terms by excluding the other possibilities across cultures. Thus Held's cosmopolitan democracy needs to defend first why it is preferred over rival concepts and in this defence he needs to show sufficient sensibility to the fact of cultural diversity and difference that cultural settings make to the articulation and choice of democratic principles. Given Held's disconcerting silence over this issue, he fails to immunize his model against communitarian critiques that accuse him of neglecting diversity, and radicals like Mouffe, who finds his model to be too deterministic or rigid for democratic purposes.[22]

Mouffe criticizes the idea of a liberal democracy committed to universal values on the ground that liberalism is essentially a political project based on irreducibility of differences. Liberalism tames and disciplines competing, contingent and fleeting identities within a common polity. In Hutching's rendition:

> "In the end, the rationalist defence of liberalism, by searching for an argument that is beyond argumentation and by wanting to define the meaning of the universal, makes the same mistake for which it criticizes totalitarianism: it rejects democratic indeterminacy and identifies the universal with a given particular."[23]

Mouffe's radicalism takes to the other end of the spectrum. While conceding the appeal of her communitarian concerns against Held's unsubstantiated claims of universalization of the liberal model (particular), Mouffe takes her critique too far. She questions not merely the false equation of the universal and the particular, but rejects any attempt to define a democratic project as ethically unacceptable, since such a definition amounts to a rejection of indeterminacy, contingency and malleability that she associates with the meaning of democracy itself. In a strange play of words, she turns attempts to cognitively capture democracy into ploys of totalitarianism or the very death of the subject itself. Held's vision of a cosmopolitan democracy might suffer from many defects and partiality for his own normative position, but Mouffe's contention that it errs by attempting to define what should never be defined in the first place is clearly misplaced and indefensible.

The problem of making democracy compatible with cultural diversity without being imperialistic is a more serious affair. In a way, Held's position is comparable with Rawls's defence of political liberalism, the only difference being the latter's primary concern with liberalism (and democracy) within rather than at the global level.[24] Therefore, some of the criticisms that apply against Rawls are also relevant for Held. Hence, it can be fairly safely argued that Held's cosmopolitan democracy is not free standing and requires a prior grounding in liberalism to assume its form. Held's insistence that individual self-determination is the basis of collective self-determination and his belief that that the universalism of his model inheres in a generic commitment to a culture of autonomy are clearly symptomatic of his liberal preferences. Held's abstraction of the notion of the goods that binds societies, communities, states, trans-national entities and even individuals together in a common democratic commitment is thus far from being universal. While it abstracts other's idea of a democratic project, it cleverly retains its own.[25]

However, the dangers of cultural essentialism are many. Stephanie Lawson in a powerful study has urged for a distinction between pluralism and unqualified relativism in conceptualizing democracy in cultural terms. Severe universalism and rigid relativist positions on the relations between democracy and culture are equally problematic. While cultural essentialism turns democracy into purely contextual, the universalist excess decontextualizes democracy into a reified and lifeless category. The first often becomes the cognitive cover for authoritarian regimes who advertise their respective cultural brands of democracy without any meaningful demonstration of democratic practices, while the second might turn imperialistic vis-à-vis non-western cultures. There is enormous sense in Lawson's point that the best position on democracy is the one "underpinned by a pluralistic epistemological position ... [that] supports a sufficiently flexible approach to understanding democracy which is neither dogmatically relativist nor universalist".[26] A good example of this is the Asian values model of democracy, one that is defended by relativists, who are otherwise sympathetic to the democratic project, on cultural grounds, a thin cover for hierarchical leadership principles and authoritarian state practices completely bereft of the fundamental democratic norm of empowering people and their rights. The role of culture in democratic politics is significant. But to defend or critique democracy in cultural terms would not contribute to democratization unless one anchors democracy in an ethical minimalism that is independent of institutions and agency across the world.

Many scholars have found in Habermas an epistemological basis to create a democratic project that is dialogic and rational. As democracy is essentially a mechanism to find stable solutions to chronic problems marked by an intense interplay of multiple identities, a dialogic mode is easily preferred over a hieratic one. But do Habermas's tools aid the cause of democracy? A categorical judgement seems difficult to pronounce since some of the shortcomings of critical theory are quite in the line of Held's cosmopolitan version surveyed above. A brief discussion of Habermas at this point would clarify the matter.

Habermas's discourse ethics is predicated upon his distinction between strategic and communicative action.[27] Strategic action induces success-oriented behaviour of another by means of the threat of sanction or the prospect of gratification, in an attempt to perpetuate interaction in line with the more powerful actor. In communicative action, on the other hand, the key is the notion of *understanding*, where understanding connotes a process seeking to arrive at a rationally motivated argument. Discourse, according to Habermas, refers expressly to processes of argumentation designed to establish whether specific validity claims are supportable, with the force of the better argument being the only compulsion to attain a rational consensus.

This automatically raises the question of how to decide the legitimacy or otherwise of competing claims to normative validity of the dialogic modes of interaction prevailing in any democratic context. The claims to normative validity are borne essentially by norms and are only derivatively held in speech acts. However, by Habermas's own admission, the "mere existence of a norm is not sufficient to imply its worthiness to the recognized," and often norms with claims of validity do not attain recognition or approval. Habermas's solution to the problem is the principle of discourse ethics according to which "only those norms can claim to be valid that meet (or could meet) with the approval of all affected in their capacity as participants in a practical discourse."[28]

At this point it is essential to bring out the logical problems or deficiencies of the steps leading to Habermas's argument. The most crucial limitation in Habermas's agreement exists in the form of an unstated underlying assumption-one that links understanding a speech act with agreement over its content. It is, however, not clear whether it is logically compelling to agree to the validity claims involved in a particular speech act in order to understand it. Understanding can be shown to be logically independent of agreement. It automatically follows then that free understanding, unencumbered by power or any other consideration, cannot be, and is possibly not, an obvious guarantee to the attainment of an overarching and universal rational consensus.

Moreover, Habermas seems to be saying that in order that speech acts generate understanding, the participants (speakers and hearers) must share their meaning. However, continuity in communication among the participants, and the fact that this communication is possible due to certain assumptions shared by the participants regarding the life world, are inadequate as the basis for inferring the truth or value of each of these assumptions. Moreover, even though communicators or participants may sincerely aim at a rational consensus, and act with the presumption that such a consensus is, in fact, possible to attain, it still does not follow that the rational consensus would inevitably emerge. [29] The theory of communicative action and discourse ethics would apparently work where all the participants share the assumptions of the eventual possibility of obtaining an overarching rational consensus by means of open dialogue, where only the force of better arguments prevail. It would not explain situations where the participants fail to agree to the possibility of a rational consensus through open communication and/or where such rational consensus could not be reached in spite of all the background factors and conditions operating favourably to the process.[30] This reinforces the fear that in contexts either by a gross asymmetry of power or habituated by groups whose cultural diversity cannot be fairly represented because of their numerical weakness, even formal use of discourse ethics and communicative action would not provide just, democratic solutions. The neutrality of Habermas's theory in multi-cultural contexts therefore cannot be taken for granted.

Most seriously perhaps, the theoretical treatment advanced thus far is quite removed from the existential reality of a majority of Third World states, which lack formal democratic structures, no matter how flawed formal democracy can be.[31] This raises two questions. First, how to build democracy in states where the experiment has failed for most part of their past. There are a number of critical issues that bear on this, the most significant in my opinion being the relation between development and democracy in an era of global capitalism. The relation is complex to say the least. On the one hand it involves an ethical exercise regarding normative desirability of the two values as ends, individually and in mutual relationship. Scholars like Amarya Sen have prioritized democracy as an ethical norm, showing that there is no structural contradiction or incompatibility between the two ends. Sen goes to the extent of arguing that genuine participatory development is impossible without democratization of the polity.[32] Although there is hardly any opposition to the idea of democracy at present, there is wide divergence on what it entails, its genesis, variants and effects. The debate is particularly germane on agency. If globalization is an unalterable context or externality of all societal structures, then its chosen agency is invariably the market, whose inegalitarian, and hence anti-developmental, consequences are not supports but threats to a democratic order. The claims of democratic consolidation therefore might come in the way of the demand of the market, according to the supporters of welfare democracy, a contradiction that is evident in the rapidly accumulating literature on corporate governance. In simple words, the preferred agency of democratization (polity) in many Third World states, where democracy is inherently weak, might conflict over the chosen agency of development (market), generating a series of complex theoretical as well as practical difficulties.

The second problem is whether democratization of the world order may proceed without full democratization within states. If the answer is a categorical no, then the project of global democracy is stillborn. One has to wait till the second aspect (internal democratization) assumes sufficient maturity to engender the first (global democracy). But is the relation so obvious? I suspect the direct relationship and offer the following illustration to explain the problem.[33] Suppose we assume that there are two levels of democracy, one at the international level and the other applying to the domestic regulation of states. By democracy we mean the power of self-determination over a range of choices. Within states, the subjects of such self-determination (or self-determining agents) are individuals. At the international level, the national collective, or the state, is the subject of such self-determination (or self-determining agent). At the domestic level, a state is democratic to the extent it allows the individuals to realize their constitutionally guaranteed rights. At the international level, the states are recognized as having a personality of their own, a sense of distinct identity, that cordons off a particular territorial sphere within which the states are particularly sovereign. Now let us further assume that a state refuses to obey the rights of a minority on grounds of security, confines members of such a group without fair opportunity of self-defence, tortures and even kills political activists who resist such imposition and disability. At the international level, the state would defend its right to self-determination and thus resist any attempt by the international community to intrude into its sovereign space. How does one settle a case like this? What does the right to democratic self-determination entails here? Does it sanction humanitarian intervention (priority to individual self-determination)? Or shall the sacrosanct character of the norm of non-intervention into domestic affairs of states, which is based on the idea of sovereign equality of states, a vital component of democratic theory itself (equality of subjects capable of exercising the right to self-determination), must prevail? Even if all states became democratic, and the international order gets democratized as a matter of fact, the tension between the normative claims and counter-claims of the two levels will not *ipso facto* end. The contradiction between the identity claims of individuals as people and as citizens would affect democracy since these identities themselves are not open to democratic determination as of now.

Conclusion

This essay has sought to discuss three things. First, it analyzed the different arguments liberals make within the disciplinary bounds of IR, particularly the celebrated liberal thesis on the linkage between liberal democracy and peace. It scrutinized three variants of liberal arguments based on trade/commerce, democratization and institutionalization/regime-building to explain how the liberal paradigm builds it case. I gave particular importance to the ideas of Francis Fukuyama, since his work appears to be a philosophical defence of liberal capitalism. The general consensus of the paradigm seems to be an unbridled optimism regarding the capacity of liberal democracy and market capitalism to usher in an unprecedented epoch of material prosperity and peace. Although the developed West and the more successful capitalist states of East Asia and South-east Asia were to be the initial beneficiaries of the liberal opulence, the Third World was also not supposed to lag behind indefinitely, if their leaders had the wisdom to cultivate market institutions and build democratic structures.

The second part of the article went on to test the liberal case in the contemporary world and found rather poor correspondence between liberal optimism in theory and actual trends of world politics in practice. The failings of the liberal project are both conceptual and practical, and the study has endeavoured to explain them separately. The study questions the presumed linkage between democracy and market reforms, and finds enough contrary evidence that drills holes into the paradigm itself. There are more examples of economically successful but authoritarian states than sustained democratic structures amidst poverty and hunger. The idea of exporting democracy to create conditions of peace and stability is equally problematic for its silence on the nature of domestic variables and the quality of the baggage that gets imported in most cases.

The Third section of the study has been entirely theoretical. It dealt with the idea of democracy and the global order and grapples with some of the enduring fallacies associated with this project. The study found wide variation in our ideas of democracy and shows how our normative underpinnings condition us to look at democracy through specific lenses. Even if we grant the ethical desirability of a cosmopolitan model of democracy, as I do, true cosmopolitanism demands dense negotiation with the issues of diversity, difference and multiculturalism before a model can be erected that faces the charge of being insufficiently sensitive to the notion of particularity in a theoretically self-conscious manner as against the banality of convenient evasion. Additionally, the study found no necessary corroboration between the successful completion of democratization of all states (itself a gargantuan task) on the one hand and the consummation of a project of global democracy on the other.

Despite a lot being written on democratic theory and world orders and their connections, much needs to be done to clarify our understanding of what a democratized world order means, before contemplative reflections on pragmatic measures to fulfill this vision can be taken as something more than naïve, wishful thinking.

NOTES AND REFERENCES

1. Jack S. Levy, War & Peace", in Walter Carlsnaes, Thomas Risse and Beth A. Simmons (eds.), *Handbook of International Relations*, Sage Publications, London, 2002, p. 306.
2. *Ibid.*
3. The literature on the subject is extensive. For a standard compilation of some of the more important contributions, see Michael E. Brown, Jean M. Lynn-Jones and Steven E. Miller (eds.), *Debating the Democratic Peace (An International Security Reader*), The MIT Press, Cambridge, Massachusetts, 1996.
4. Bruce Russet and John R. Oneal, *Triangulating Peace: Democracy, Interdependence, and International Organization*, W. W. Norton, New York; Bruce Russet and Harvey Starr, "From the Democratic Peace to Kantian Peace: Democracy and Conflict in the International System", in Manus I. Midlarsky (ed.), *Handbook of War*, Studies II, University of Michigan Press, Ann Arbor, 2000, pp. 93-128.
5. Levy, *n. 1*, p. 359.
6. Clifton T. Morgan and Sally H. Campbell, "Domestic Structure, Decisional Constraints, and War: So Why Can't Democracies Fight", *Journal of Conflict Resolution*, Vol. 35, No. 2, pp. 187-211; Randolph M. Siverson, "Democracies and War Participation: In defence or the Institutional Constraint Argument", *European Journal of International Relations*, Vol. 1, No. 4, 1995, pp. 487-89.
7. Jack Levy, n. 1, pp. 359-60.
8. Robert Keohane are Lisa Martin, "The Promise of Institutionalist Theory", in Michael E. Brown, Owen R. Cote, Jr. Sean M. Lynn-James and Steven E. Miller, eds., *Theories of War and Peace. An International Security Reader*, The MIT Press, Cambridge, Massachusetts, 1998, p. 387.
9. For an excellent survey of these themes, see the various article in David Baldwin(ed.), *Neorealism and Neoliberalism: The Contemporary Debate*, Columbia University Press, New York, 1990.
10. The initial essay by Francis Fukuyama was carried by the conservative journal *The National Interest*, (Washington D.C.), Summer 1989, pp. 3-18. The book appeared in 1992. For details, see Francis Fukuyama, The End of History and the Last Man, Free Press, New York, 1992.
11. Perry Anderson, "The Ends of History", in Perry Anderson, *A Zone of Engagement*, Verso, London, pp. 281-85, pp. 331-41.
12. *Ibid.*, pp. 282-83, pp. 315-24.
13. Francis Fukuyama, *Trust: The Social Virtues and the Creation of Prosperity*, Hamish Hamilton, London, 1995, pp. 335-36.

14. Margot Light, "Exporting democracy", in Karen E. Smith and Margot Light (eds.), *Ethics and Foreign Policy*, Cambridge University Press, Cambridge, 2001, p. 89.
15. Margo Picken, "Ethical foreign policies and human rights: dilemmas for non-governmental organizations", *n. 14*, and pp. 103-04.
16. Margot Light, *n. 14*, p. 88.
17. This is corroborated in the writings of Lipset, Linz and Diamond, Vanhanen, Przeworsky, and Huntington. See, Adam Przeworsky, "Some Problems in the Study of Transition to Democracies", in G. O'Donnell et.al.(eds.), *Transition from Authoritarian Rule. Comparative Perspectives*, John Hopkins Press, Baltimore, 1986, pp. 47-63; S. M. Lipset, *Political Man*, Heinemann Educational Books, London, 1960; S.M. Lipset, "Social Requisites of Democracy Revisited", *American Sociological Review*, Vol. 59, 1994, pp. 1-22; L.Diamond, J.L. Linz and S.M. Lipset (eds.), *Democracy in Asia*, Vistar Publications, New Delhi, 1989; Tatu Vanhanen, *Prospects of Democracy. A Study of 172 Countries*, Routledge, London and New York, 1997; Samuel P. Huntington, *The Third Wave: Democratization in the Late Twentieth Century*, University of Oklahoma Press, Norman, 1991; Samuel P. Huntington, "How Countries Democratize", *Political Science Quarterly*, Vol. 106, No. 4, pp. 579-616; David Potter, David Goldblatt, Margaret Kiol and Paul Lewis, eds., *Democratization*, Polity Press, Cambridge, 1997.
18. David Held, *Models of Democracy*, Polity Press, Cambridge, 1987; *Democracy and World Order: From the Modern State to Cosmopolitan Governance*, Blackwell, Oxford, 1995.
19. Held, Models of Democracy, *n. 18*, p. 305.
20. Kimberly Hutchings, Modelling Democracy, in Hazel Smith, ed., *Democracy and International Relations: Critical Theories/Problematic Practices*, London, Macmillan Press Limited, 2000, p. 45.
21. *Ibid*.
22. For a very good treatment, see Bhikhu Parekh, "Cultural Diversity and Liberal Democracy", in David Beetham, *Defining and Measuring Democracy*, Sage, London, 1995.
23. Chantal Mouffe, *The Return of the Political*, Verso, London, 1993, p. 147-149. Cited in Kimberly Hutchings, *n. 19*, p. 47.
24. Rawls's political liberalism claims to solve the problem of how citizens with very different comprehensive conceptions of the good can nevertheless create and sustain a stable and just society that is hospitable to the idea of diversity. Rawls admits that even a democratic public culture might not guarantee stability and help realize the political conception of justice unless it carries with it other broad-based comprehensive doctrines, something he designates as an "overlapping consensus". But Rawls does not proceed to examine the pathologies of other comprehensive doctrines to find out how

this "overlapping consensus" can be created in polyglot societies. He does not take up this exercise for two reasons. First, he assumes that most citizens of advanced Western liberal democracies would not hold comprehensive doctrines contrary to liberal public/political culture. Second, he seems sufficiently confident that those comprehensive doctrines that are incompatible with the overlapping consensus can be shown to be unreasonable and hence altogether eliminated from the purview of consideration. See, John Rawls, *Political Liberalism*, Columbia Press, New York, 1993.

25. This criticism follows Bhikhu Parekh's crique of Rawls. See, Bhikhu Parekh, *Rethinking Multiculturalism: Cultural Diversity and Political Theory*, Palgrave, New York, 2000, pp. 80-113.
26. Stephanie Lawson, "Democracy and the Problem of Cultural Relativism: Normative Issues for International Politics, in Hazel Smith (eds.), *Democracy and International Relations: Critical Theories/ Problematic Practices*, Macmillan Press, London, 2000, p. 83.
27. For Habermas's analysis of the concepts of discourse, discourse ethics, communicative action and the ideal speech situation, see Jurgen Habermas, *Knowledge and Human Interests*, Polity Press, Cambridge, 1987 (first published in 1968); *Communication and Evolution of Society*, Heinemann Educational Books, London, 1979; *The Theory of Communicative Action*, Volume-I: *The Critique of Functionalist Reason*, Polity Press, Cambridge, 1987; *The Theory of Communicative Action*, Volume-II: *Reason and Rationalisation of Society*, Polity Press, Cambridge, 1991; *Moral Consciousness and Communicative Action*, Polity Press, Cambridge, 1990. For a good introduction to Habermas's works, see Stephen K. White (ed.), *The Cambridge Companion to Habermas*, Cambridge University Press, UK and USA, 1995.
28. Jurgen Habermas, *Moral Consciousness and Communicative Action*, Polity Press, Cambridge, 1990, pp. 60-61.
29. Brian Fay, *Critical Social Science: Liberation and its Limits*, Cornell University Press, Ithaca, New York, 1987, p. 189.
30. It is doubtful, nevertheless, whether this criticism is logically inexorable to the theory of discourse ethics, for it is still possible to reasonably argue and demonstrate cases where the favourable operation of discourse ethics actually lead to rational consensus, i.e. a solution agreeable to all the participants in the dialogue. The utility of the criticism, nevertheless, is in exposing practical possibilities where discourse ethics and communicative action might not supply the desired outcome. Therefore, if nothing, at least the universal validity of Habermas's conceptual tools becomes somewhat suspect.
31. For extensive treatment, see Jayantanuja Bandyopadhyaya, *World Government. For International Democracy and Justice*, Manuscript India, Kolkata, 2002.

32. Amartya Sen has developed his thesis in a number of publications. Among others, see Amartya Sen, *Poverty and Famines,* Clarendon Press, Oxford, 1981; *Choice, Welfare and Measurement,* Blackwell Publishers, Oxford, 1982; *Inequality Re-examined,* Clarendon Press, Oxford, 1992. For a succinct summary, see Jean Dreze and Amartya Sen, India: *Economic Development and Social Opportunity,* Oxford University Press, New Delhi, 1995, pp. 9-26.
33. The argument advanced here is a response to the view expressed by Mervyn Frost. Frost argues for a strong humanitarian principle that would not falter due to statist rejection on the basis of sovereign entitlement. Although *prima facie* well-intentioned, this is a dangerous argument to follow, particularly when it comes to the vast majority of Third World states. For details, see Mervyn Frost, "The Ethics of Humanitarian Intervention: Protecting Civilians to Make Democratic Citizenship Possible", in Karen E. Smith and Margot Light (eds.), Ethics and Foreign Policy, Cambridge University Press, 2001, pp. 33-54.

14

Communication and the (Un) Making of Global Order

The Struggle from within

—DIPANKAR SINHA

INTRODUCTION

In this paper, at the very outset, we make Samir Amin, a distinguished Marxist social scientist and one of the founders of the World Forum for Alternatives, a point of reference. We do it because in an interview in January, 2003, held during the Asian Social Forum (ASF) in Hyderabad, Amin, made the following observation which is supportive of the basic contentions of the paper itself.

> "*We have to look at what is new in a different way.* How can the popular forces reorganise to reduce the damage associated with global capital expansion? What can they do to impose their own agenda...to create the conditions for alternative?"[1] {Italics mine]

This statement by Amin is perfectly compatible with our two basic contentions. First, that critiquing and subverting the prevalent global order are to be carried on *from within*. Second, that the need is to contest and challenge the discriminatory and inequitable global order, not in terms of a pre-fixed, readymade, close-ended alternative order, but in terms of the exploration of such alternatives in a space marked by resistance and protest against the prevalent form of globalization. We would also argue that both the tasks—that of critiquing and subverting the prevalent global order, and the exploration of alternatives to it—are intimately related to communication. We would explain why it is so in the next section. But for the time being let us refer back to the implications of Amin's remarks.

The two questions raised by Amin are of fundamental significance for us because the construction of alternatives (we would subsequently explain why we put it in plural form) to the prevalent inequitable, discriminatory world order is not an easy struggle pregnant with instantaneous results. That the struggle for *alternative global futures*[2] is an extremely difficult one has been proved again and again, most recently by the Iraq War which has displayed how the *one and only superpower* can take it unilaterally upon itself the task of teaching the "rogue state" a lesson, that too by neglecting popular opinion and articulation from different parts of the world, including its own. Even Amin's own case is interesting and instructive. Once the chief proponent of the "delinking thesis" through which he had once aggressively advocated the detachment of the Third World economy from the global economy controlled by the developed Western states, he now visualises a much more pragmatic step—of changing the world by being in it and waging the struggle from within. Second, even if Amin still prefers socialism as the "best possible alternative" he has become more cautious in his approach. As he explains, "(Socialism) has the same name...(b)ut the way we imagine socialism will not be the same as our fathers imagined it to be."[3] Here he hints, even within the paradigm of socialism, of change-orientation, not subscribing to any particular "manual" as containing the sacrosanct guidelines. In a significant development the well-known journal *The Socialist Register 2000* dwells with the theme "Necessary and Unnecessary Utopias"[4], indicating a broad canvas of alternative futures.

Then again, the evident shift in Amin's stance is symptomatic of the changing realty and spirit of the times. One can justifiably argue that even though there were a number of protests organized against the working of the now-prevalent global order[5], particularly since the Seattle protest (1999), against the functioning of the World Trade Organization (WTO) it has become more and more evident that we are moving from the days of dark pessimism condensed in the dictum *There is No Alternative* (TINA) to various optimistic explorations and articulations of alternatives on the basis of construction of a better and more humane world order. However, the observation must be qualified by the point that there is no quick way to achieving alternatives. As hinted earlier, the struggle demands a lot of "spadework" in order to develop decisive challenge to the dominant form of globalization and the associated world order. In hindsight, one can argue that several "alternatives" that were posed against the liberal-capitalist world order in the past have either failed to pose any challenge at all or have, as in the case of the socialist alternative, ultimately failed to sustain themselves, despite being able to pose challenge for some time. These cases of failure of "alternatives" lead us to yet another important question of *alterity* of alternatives. We shall deal with the question subsequently.

Communication Matters

As noted earlier, we relate the twin questions of making and unmaking the prevalent global order to communication. Information and communication—the most powerful "factors of production" in contemporary global politics, finance, economy and culture—are shaping the ideas, orientations, perspectives and worldviews of more and more people, overcoming the barriers of time and space. The spectacular rise of the information and communication technologies and their ever-growing application has only intensified the impact. Yet there lies a great discrepancy as far as the access to and utilization of information and communication are concerned. The Digital Divide results in the Communication Divide which, in turn, goes hand in hand with the Development Divide. Most obviously, the post-colonial societies are at the receiving end of it. The negative effect of such Divide is bound to affect exploration of alternative global scenarios because those who have the leverage in deciding the character of information and communication that are to have global circulation, would construct and seek to perpetuate the dominant-mainstream form of the order of things. It necessarily follows that any meaningful and effective exploration of the possible and plausible alternatives to the prevalent inequitable global order needs a simultaneous focus on the role of communication *both as a facilitator of status quo and as a means of change*. As a power-laden process of meaning generation and meaning circulation, through which the "reality" is constantly produced, maintained, transferred and transformed, communication, on the one hand, facilitates production and reinforcement of the dominant order; on the other hand, it also lights up what we would prefer to call the *zones of exclusion*—both material and symbolic—of the prevalent global order to provide clues to possible routes of transformation.

Let us at this stage refer to the question of *alterity* of alternatives. In most studies on alternative (global) modes the alterity question is not addressed directly, with the result that in these studies there is some kind of taken-for-grantedness about the specific kind of alternative being advocated. Alterity here connotes *difference from particular others*[6]. To explain further, did the alternatives that were being regarded as so, have sufficient alterity in the sense of having completely different constitutive rationale and order? Or were they basically trying to advocate a supposedly alternative order on the basis of the same constitutive logic, say of development? If, for instance, the erstwhile socialist countries wanted to constitute an "alternative social order" by following the capitalism-friendly logic of industrialism and technologism, could that ever ensure alterity of the much-publicised alternative? A detailed discussion of this predicament of the received socialist paradigm which has been analysed elsewhere[7] is beyond the scope of the paper but we needed to refer to it to present a it as a sort of background to the subsequent discussion.

Form the post-colonial vantage point, communication

assumes great significance for exploring and evaluating the *alterity of alternatives*. It is because it not only helps to expose the epistemic colonization and the subsequent performance failure of the so-called alternatives but also to rescind the process. These twin tasks are of paramount importance in any search for alternative global futures because the inequitous globalization *project*[8], through the (neo)liberal-capitalist epistemology is not only colonizing our present but is also patenting our future. The colonization process is marked by varying symbolic calls— "the end of history", "the end of geography", "the death of utopia", "the death of distance" and so forth— all of which share the same animosity and antagonism towards the imagination and construction of alternatives.

The significance of the process of colonization, being mentioned here, is not limited to the colonization of the political, economic and commercial institutions; it has, perhaps with more disastrous long-term implications for the struggle for alternatives, engulfed a lot of our aesthetic expressions as well. The developed states and the regimes that rule them, the non-governmental organizations, transnational institutions and multinational corporations, which decide the rules of the global political economy, are ruling out any kind of alternative arrangement which does not cater to their interests as unfashionable or illegitimate. The "dominant communication" to this effect comes in various forms: from the terms and conditionalities vis-à-vis liberalization and privatisation to the embargo against Cuba to the war against Afghanistan and Iraq to the violent suppression of protest movements in the streets of Seattle, Buenos Aires and Genoa. The leading analysts[9] of political economy of communication have shown how the states combined with the non-state actors in devising specific systems of telecommunications, broadcasting and information dissemination to create a world communication order appropriate for perpetuating a partial and discriminatory world order. It is generally estimated that communication facilitates the operation of about sixty thousand transnational corporations in the year 2000. The same year also witnessed the rise of transnational advertising to the tune of US$ 235.5 billion through the operations of transnational communication corporations (TCC).

But what is perhaps more dangerous than these evident and concrete forms of communication is the more subtle and subjective form, which induces us to subscribe to the idea that it is neither practicable nor possible to resist what is being imposed on us. It is dangerous because it breeds apathy, inaction and pessimism. The TINA logic, mentioned earlier, is itself an instance of how the communicative acts of the predominant form of globalization can impair vision and space for alternatives. We have to remember that TINA has become part and parcel of the discourse, not just of the sponsors of the globalization *project*; it is part of the discourse of the Third World policy-makers as well. The only difference between the two may be that while the former use it authoritatively, the latter do it somewhat apologetically.

If the successive protest movements against the current show of globalization raises the possibility of a "new dawn" in the struggle for alternatives it remains overwhelmingly a struggle not only by communication but in communication. If communication is the *infratsructural backbone* of the discriminatory global order it would remain so for progressing towards any viable alternative global order as well. The fundamental distinction between the two cases would be that in the prevalent inequitable form of global order rests largely on centralised communication order, but the path towards more equitable global order lies through creating and nurturing of diffused communication channels and communication orderings which pose and question global issues in their own way and within their own space.

The diffused communication channels and orderings being referred to here could operate at various levels: interpersonal, inter-group, intra-group, institutional-organizational and society-wide. The germination of the alternative modes can be found in as different situations as, say, a group of people articulating discontent against the prevailing global order or members of the society doing the same in a much larger span and strength. But the fundamental trait that these orderings need to have is that they must simultaneously inhabit and critique and subvert what they are part of. By which we do not mean that they would become sort of "internal critique" because this particular genre of critique is not radical enough. The status of these orderings distinguishes them from the earlier attempts to counter the (then) prevalent communication order with a proposed "mega-order" like the New World Information and Communication Order (NWICO) and national-level National Information Policy[10]. It is interesting to note that even one of the most eminent advocates of the NWICO, Oliver Boyd Barrett, today advocates "global communication orders"[11] in stead of a single, ubiquitous alternative order. A word of caution: when we stress on the diffusion of communication *orderings* we are not providing them the status of "fragments". The description is inappropriate because despite being spontaneous and scattered in most cases and even "unattached" in many cases these orderings are supposed to be related to the notion of a "whole" which in this case might be any or all of the following: alternative mode of communication, alternative globalization and alternative global futures. Let us now explore the instances of protest and resistance against the dominant-mainstream form of global order in terms of their communicative dimensions and ramifications.

The Challenging Context

The happenings in the contemporary global order are increasingly making it evident that it is quite impossible to fit it in to a pre-conceived "alternative". It is an era which is marked by events that are often unpredictable, events which are products of sharp twists and turns which in many cases are not comprehensible. While the communicative mode of the prevalent global order has been able to ensure some degree of visibility and predictability in terms of its measures and actions the situation is extremely fluid for the possible alternatives. If one examines various events relating to the struggle against the prevailing global order one could be impressed by their increasing number, spread and most important, diverse character. As Jose Seoane and Emilio Taddei rightly remark[12]:

> "...the boundaries of the anti-neoliberal globalization movement greatly transcend those of the labour movement, extending (and even further finding its most dynamic participants in) a multitude of movements...and a diversity of associations and networks of struggle against corporate power and commercial and financial deregulation. The breadth and heterogeneity of the social alliance can be appreciated...in associations which signed the 'Call of Porto Alegre'".

But a deeper look would reveal their disparate character. There are, for instance, many protests against the triad of World Bank—International Monetary Fund—World Trade Organization—widely considered to be the mainstay of the current global order. But many of them might just be "spontaneous" protests, motivated primarily by an immediate reaction against retrenchment or wage cut or cut in subsidy. Do these kind of protests have a broader alternative agenda which is supposed to replace as ubiquitous an order as the mainstream global order? Do these protests have long-term character? Or do they fizzle out, say, after a particular summit/meet of the G-8 countries or the World Trade Organization or the World Bank is over?

There is little doubt that the simultaneous waves of liberalization, privatisation and corporatisation have hit the common (wo)man hard all over the world. This has been a result of what is going on in the name of competition. As political economist Amiya K. Bagchi explains[13], competition in economic life fragments and then produces new aggregations of labour, capital and sectoral interests, just as the fragments of a nation or political entity can provide new opportunities for mobilization and aggregation. Such aggregation, Bagchi notes, is usually in the interest of the "dominant property—holding classes". But in recent times such mobilization and aggregation, in favour of the deprived classes, are on the rise. With their survival at stake it cannot but be so.

But how does one articulate the frustration, anger and sense of deprivation? Even more important in this context is the question of articulation of these sentiments and emotions towards construction of alternative(s). It is especially so because, as mentioned earlier, there is the absence of overarching alternative in the world today. One might contest this point by pointing out that in many of these protests a major slogan has been "Socialism is the Alternative" (SITA). But as Amin's remark, quoted at the very outset of this discussion reveals, even those who believe in it do not think that socialism needs change-orientation. One major avenue of change, it could be presumed, is to refrain from mechanistic implantation of socialism and to impart it an *organic* character. However, such organic character would by itself necessitate multiple forms of socialism, suited to the specific soil. The problem is compounded by the fact that there are as many protest movements which deny socialism the status of alternative, despite sharing many ideas about the dehumanising consequences of the prevailing pattern of globalization with the socialists.

Yet another source of "flexible reality" is the divergence in attitude towards the globalization process itself. Is globalization an evil by itself, to be discarded without hesitation? Or is it a desirable process for the populace of the world to develop closer bonds, which is, however, becoming discriminatory and oppressive by making it, as we have noted earlier, a "project" for domination by few over many? The question assumes much significance in view of the split that one finds in the protest movements in terms of those who want to discard globalization log, stock and barrel, and those who wish to replace the oppressive globalization "project" with "creative and humane" globalization process. One of the most illustrated example in this case is that of Naomi Klein, a foremost scholar-activist in the contemporary protest movements against the "brutalising global order". In her book on

Fences and Windows: Dispatches from the Front Lines of the Globalization Debate, she clarifies[14] her stance:

> "The irony of the media-imposed label "anti-globalization" is that we in this movement have been turning globalization into a lived reality....(G)lobalization is not restricted to a narrow series of trade and tourism transactions. *It is, instead, an intricate process of thousands of people trying their destinies together simply by sharing ideas...*" [Emphasis and brackets mine.]

In a letter to the Belgian Prime Minister and the European Union President, Guy Verhofstadt, Klein argues[15] that branding the protest movements as "anti-globalization" is a deliberate strategy of false depiction, adopted by the proponents of the prevalent mode of globalization. She writes:

> "...I strongly object to your term "anti-globalization". The way I see it, I am part of a network of movements that is fighting not against globalization but for deeper and more responsive democracies.... *The network is as global as capitalism itself. And no that's not a "paradox"...*" [Emphasis mine.]

In view of this there could be no single-track 'reading' of the slogans, posters and graffiti, such as, "Down with World Bank", "WTO is the end of democracy", "Resist Corporate Tyranny", "Smash Capitalism", "Wipe Out World Economic Forum", "The G-8 is CRAP" and so forth. They cannot be explained only in terms of "resist globalization" stance; they are simultaneously the favourite battle- cry of the likes of Klein.

The leadership question in the protest movements constitutes yet another source of the shifting context and flexible reality. The correlation between leadership and success of struggles, which constitutes a perennial issue in academic explorations, cannot be discussed in detail in the context of this paper. But history reveals that pre-fixed alternative required pre-fixed leadership. In contrary, most of the current protest movements lack conventional forms of leadership in which a few people with organizing ability, "gift of grace" (a la Max Weber) and power, residing at the top of the hierarchy, would guide the followers to political battlefields. In a way it is a refreshing sign that most of these movements are led from the front by the ordinary people themselves, who could be workers, artisans, peasants, discriminated women, unemployed youth and so forth. Even in more organized and more pluralistic meets like World Social Forum (WSF)— held at Porto Alegre (2001) and at Mumbai (2004)— or the ASF there was little visibility of "central" leadership. It is quite expected because be they street-corner protests or meets the events are basically aggregations of struggles of trade unions, peasant organizations, women's organizations, youth organizations, indigenous people's organizations, non-government organizations, voluntary agencies—all coming together even without any compulsive desire for codification of the discourses on dissent. As the following remark[16] on the WSF reveals: "(it) has served as a platform for the articulation of a breathtaking range of views. But in hosting these discourses of global dissent...the WSF remains...an oral tradition yet to be codified in written texts...(t)he intervals between successive gatherings are spent in exchanges in small communities and groups, spreading outwards in concentric circles".

But this development has its share of problems. While the emphasis in street-based congregations seems to be on "protest by all, from the front" in the organized meets like WSF, ESF (European Social Forum) and ASF it is on free flow of interactions, discussions, deliberations, debates and construction of alternative discourses and models, based on participation of all. Lack of leadership "from above" may help the events of resistances and protests to remain more "democratic" but lack of leadership of any kind might at the same time come in the way of these sporadic protests graduating to *movements* with some kind of alternative vision. It could, on the one hand, make the protests temporary phenomena—mainly concerned with immediate relief, which could be brought about by cosmetic solutions without going through any radical process of restructuring. It could, on the other hand, run into the danger of being infiltrated and subverted by *agent provocateurs,* sponsored by the state and/or market forces, who would wreck the resistance from within without being identified as such.

Counter-communication

Does the common target, which in this case is the oppressive global order, necessarily promote common goal and common means of achieving the goal? It is evident from the course of events that even if that would have been an ideal way to wage the struggle for alternative global order it does not happen that way. What then is the appropriate counter-communication mode for this pluridimensional search for an alternative order? The appropriate mode of counter-communication would be the articulation of subaltern, subjugated, popular, discordant, frenzied, disruptive and even frantic voices which utilise the reach of the mainstream communication order to develop and disseminate critical messages of its *political scheme.* As Amartya Sen so emphatically argues[17] while indicating the importance of such protests in "questioning and disputing" our complacency and contentment:

> "The global protests of activists across the world can indeed play an importantly constructive role. However, in order for that to happen, we have to assess these movements and challenges in terms of the global questions they pose.... Indeed, the...protests are themselves part of the general process of globalization, from which there is no escape and no great reason to seek escape."

Such mode needs to occupy both *physical* and *virtual* space, simultaneously and in a complementary manner. Let us elaborate the observation.

In terms of occupying the physical space such communication would have its sources in ground-level street-corner demonstrations, marches and processions, slogan mongering, industrial strikes by labourers, burning of seeds by farmers, and even street-corner drama. The physical struggle is waged against the oppressive "conditionalities" associated with the Structural Adjustment Programme; it is also waged against the highly discriminatory Intellectual Property Regime; it is also targeted against violent events such as the Iraq War. Interestingly, a welcome feature of the struggle is that it does not call for a separate "autonomous" economic order detached from the mainstream economic order; it calls for a radical restructuring of the mainstream order itself *from within*. One major reason for this might be that such struggle in the contemporary world is being waged by those who are directly hurt by the discrimination and oppression of the neo-liberal global order. The struggle is initiated by those who wear the proverbial shoes and feel the pinches. The articulation of messages in this struggle varies from violent forms to silent protests. This physical struggle has also developed a different kind of "symbolic" communication, the most publicised instance of it being the "first martyr of the resistance movement"— Carlos Giuliani. Giuliani, who was brutally murdered on 20 July, 2001 in a Genoa street by the security forces while he was demonstrating against the G-8 summit, became a symbol of protest in different parts of the world.

In terms of generating such discordant communication in the virtual space the possible avenues could be as diverse as ethical hacking (in which the websites of the International Monetary Fund, the World Bank and the World Trade Organization among others are defaced with messages of the protestors), culture jam (jamming of websites of the G-8 states and multinational corporations with messages of protestors), the introduction of counter-websites with oppositional messages and not the least, virtual interaction with likeminded organizations and groups through extensive use of e-mail and other mechanisms of the Global Information Order (GIO). Incidentally, one of the earliest and successful attempts at what has become known as the *electronic civil disobedience*—now well publicised in media and academics[18]— is the meticulous effort by the Zapatista National Liberation Army to use simultaneously the physical and the virtual space (particularly, the Internet) for espousing the cause of their struggle against the "oppressive", "dictatorial" Mexican government cutting across the national frontiers.

The three main objectives of the struggle were: (i) to ensuring "unified global action" against the Mexican government; (ii) isolation of the Mexican government in the international community and (iii) virtual destruction of the US corporate presence in Mexico. The Digital Zapatismo model, which has become a sort of inspiration for the advocates of alternative communication orders and alternative global orders, significantly has the motto "Our Word is Our Weapon". The tactics of the InfoWar, based on the assertion that "we have the technical capacity to bring the Mexican government to its knees", targeted all information flows and continuous tracking of the backbone routes, to bring down specific zones of resistance covering the following: commercial communication systems, broadcasting network, financial data systems, transportation systems, digital network, Internet Server network and military and intelligence network. The Zapatista model is also important because it has made us aware of one of the most important developments in the GIO. It has revealed its reflexive character in the sense that it has proved that despite the best efforts at surveillance and control by the highly sophisticated New Technology, there are space and scope for unintended consequences and unpredictable developments. In Manuel Castells' view, this is being made possible by the very nature of informationalism in the "network society". As he writes[19]:

> "Networks are open structures, able to expand without limits, integrating new nodes...Networks are appropriate instruments...based on innovation, globalization and decentralised concentration...based on flexibility and adaptability; for a culture of endless deconstruction and reconstruction; for a polity towards the endless processing of...public moods..."

This may be called the great paradox of the New Technology. The great paradox itself comes as a boon for the advocates of alternative communication, who are supposed to wage the struggle from being a part of the very system they want to subvert and replace. In other words, the great paradox itself should be a strong incentive to desist them from waging the struggle from outside the GIO itself. To reiterate, the struggle for alternative global order must use both the physical and virtual spaces simultaneously and in a complementary manner, and must not treat the two realms separately. If this happens, the happenings in the physical space and the messages can be instantaneously disseminated through the Internet which, despite the best efforts to the contrary by the powers that be, remains reasonably successful in escaping surveillance and censorship. The instantaneous manner in which the pictures and messages of the successive protests are being "globalised" since the Seattle days substantiate the point. One must, however, be careful about the technophiliacs who tend to glorify the power of the virtual struggle at the cost of the physical struggle. But at the same time one must understand that the physical struggle acquires immense strength if it is complemented by the power of the New Technology and New Media.

Concluding Observations

There is no doubt that people have an inherent tendency to rely on an overarching ideology or strategy when it comes to waging the struggle for an alternative order. It makes them feel secure that they have a world to win by virtue of the ideological claim that it can homogenise disparate elements to provide common guidance and leadership. On the other hand, the lack of an overarching ideology or strategy breeds uncertainty and insecurity among people. The current events of protest against the prevailing global order also come under criticism for the reason that being "chaotic, decentralised, multi-headed webs" they do not yet produce any spectacular alternative in sight. To this kind of critique our response, informed by the prevailing reality, is that let such instances of mainly "disruptive" and "reactive" protests and resistances prevail and gather strength and sustainability for the time being to acquire "constructive" character. This in turn would increase the possibility of establishing a linkage on the basis of some sort of *common minimum programme* in future. Any haste in defining an alternative at this stage would put the multipolar struggles against the dominant oppressive and inequitable order many steps backward. To sum up, let us visualise *from within* "another world" and nurture multiple voices to convince ourselves that *we shall overcome*.

NOTES AND REFERENCES

1. "For Struggles, Global and National: Interview with Samir Amin", *Frontline*, 31 January, 2003, p. 14.
2. In this paper "alternative global futures" is used in a broad and general sense, by dissociating it from both the dominant methodology of Futures Research and Planning and Forecasting and the political project, sponsored by the Central Intelligence Agency of the USA. The project seeks to identify major trends and regional variations in demography, science and technology, global economy, governance, social and cultural identities and conflict among others, in order to construct a plausible, policy-relevant scenario of how the future might evolve in the year 2015. However, the very project reinstates our claim that even visualization and construction of alternatives are being "colonized".
3. Amin, p. 14.
4. Leo Pantich and Colin Leys eds. *The Socialist Register 2000*, The Merlin Press, Suffolk, 1999.
5. Even before the Seattle protest one could find germination of discontent and anger against the current mode of globalization in workers' protests, mainly in the form of strikes—in Nigeria, Indonesia, Paraguay, Taiwan, India in 1994, in Bolivia, Canada and France in 1995, in Brazil, Argentina, Greece, Italy, South Korea, Spain and Venezuela in 1996, in Belgium, Columbia, Haiti, Ecuador and South Korea in 1997 and in different parts of the developing world in 1998. Many of these protests were sporadic, spontaneous and even without the glare of the media they can still be regarded as a sort of background to the well-publicised Seattle protest.

6. Kenneth J. Gergen, *An Invitation to Social Construction*, Sage, London, 1999, p. 148.
7. For critical perspectives on the deficiency of the Soviet-type alternative, analysed by (former) Soviet scholars themselves, A.N. Yakovlev et al. *Soviet Society: Philosophy of Development*, Progress Publishers, Moscow, 1988.
8. Here we distinguish between the globalization *process* which we regard as accessible, inclusionary, democratic and conducive to development of marginalised states, and the *project* which is largely inaccessible, exclusionary, undemocratic and favouring the hegemony of the developed states. It is because of this distinction that the paper would not advocate rejection of globalization as such.
9. It perhaps started with Dallas W. Smythe's study on *The Structure and Policy of Electronic Communications* (University of Illinois Press, Urbana, 1957) and developed further by Herbert Schiller's works, such as, *Mass Communication and American Empire* (Beacon Press, Boston, 1969) and *Culture Inc.*(Oxford University Press, New York, 1989), and Nicholas Garnham's *Capitalism and Communication* (Sage, London, 1990). The cited works have a representative status but they are only a fraction of the research output.
10. The struggle for NWICO was waged in the seventies by the developing states simultaneously on through the Non-Aligned Movement (NAM) and the UNESCO. It was meant to replace the discriminatory communication order based on the so-called free flow of information with a new order in which there would be balanced flow. For details of what went wrong with the NWICO movement, Dipankar Sinha, *Communicating Development in the New World Order*, Kanishka, Delhi, 1999. Chapter on "The NWICO and the NIEO in the Seventies", pp. 22-82. The idea of National Information Policy was based on the idea that the developing states should dissociate themselves from the prevalent information and communication order and construct their own information policy, based on their own requirements. For details, Cees J. Hamelink, *Cultural Autonomy in Global Communications: Planning for National Information Policy*, Longman, New York, 1983, pp. 87-124.
11. Oliver Boyd Barrett, "Global Communication Orders" in William N. Gudykunst and Bella Mody eds., *Handbook of International and Intercultural Communication*, Sage, Thousand Oaks, 2002, pp. 325-42.
12. Jose Seoane and Emilio Taddei, "From Seattle to Porto Alegre: The Anti-Neoliberal Globalization Movement", *Current Sociology*, Vol. 50, No.1, January, 2002, p. 118.
13. Amiya Kumar Bagchi, "Procedural and Substantive Democracy: Can they be Reconciled in a Market Society, and especially in an era of Globalization?" in Bernard Founou-Tchuigoua et al. Eds. *Critical*

Social Thought for the XXI Century, The Third World Forum, Dakar, 2003, pp. 425-41.
14. Naomi Klein, *Fences and Windows: Dispatches from the Front Lines of the Globalization Debate*, Leftword, New Delhi, 2002, p. xv.
15. Klein, p. 77.
16. Sukumar Muralidharan, "Globalised Struggle", *Frontline*, 13 February, 2004, p. 9.
17. Amartya K. Sen, "It is Right to Rebel", website: www.yaleglobal.yale.edu/display.article?id=444 Accessed on 20 February, 2003.
18. Critical Art Ensemble, *Electronic Civil Disobedience and Other Unpopular Ideas*, Autonomedia, Brooklyn, NY, 1996. Also, Harry Cleaver, "Zapatistas in Cyberspace: An Accion Zapatista Report,", 1998 Website: http://www.eco.utexas.edu/faculty/Cleaver/zapsincyber.html
19. Manuel Castells, *The Rise of the Network Society*, Basil Blackwell, Malden, MA and Oxford, 1996, pp. 470-71.

15

Emerging Threats in South-east Asia in the Post-Cold War Era

Towards an Alternative Discourse

—TRIDIB CHAKRABORTI

Since the end of the Second World War, the region of South-east Asia has undergone tremendous changes, the most fundamental being the establishment of politically independent nation states. Except Thailand, the severance from European colonial rule for some of the territories was really dramatic and bloody, while others accomplished their freedom through grave but peaceful means. Subsequently, each nation-state got engaged in a journey of its own, encountering and struggling with a myriad of influences, constructive or venomous, from within and from without.

After more than four decades of nation-building, each of the nations of South-east Asia could look back with pride at their manifold achievements. While many of these nations faced set backs and disappointments, some of them were mired in protracted armed struggle, political upheavals, bloody military coups and separatist struggles, while others enjoyed unprecedented economic growth and development, wealth and affluence. In spite of these ups and downs, the nation-states of South-east Asia endeavoured to maintain peace and sustained security through organizations like the Association of South-east Asian Nations (ASEAN) and the concept of a Zone of Peace, Freedom and Neutrality (ZOPFAN). However, the end of the

Cold War failed to resolve some outstanding post-colonial issues of the nation-states of South-east Asia, such as subterranean tensions among states, power politics, military coup d'etats and separatist revolts, civil-military power struggles, centre-periphery relations, and insurgency and low-intensity conflicts. While many of these issues remain unresolved, the nation-states of South-east Asia got engulfed in several new major issues in the post-cold war era. Among these — human rights and the strong state debate, environment, ethnic unrest, gender issue, impact of globalization, Asian values syndrome and the state, rising Islamic fundamentalism, new terrorism etc. remain most important. The purpose of this paper is to analyse some of the emerging threats in detail and to find out the existence or possibility of an alternative discourse (if any) for the countries of South-east Asia and region as a whole, in the context of New World Order.

Globalization and South-east Asia

By globalization, we mean unbound flows of information, goods, services, capital, technology, cultures and values at the global level, including social problems like AIDs and pollution. It means transcendence of national barriers and emergence of a "borderless world". It is no doubt a new phenomenon with a number of characteristics:

(i) Unprecedented economic interdependence, driven by cross-border capital movements, rapid technology transfer, and "real time" communication and information flows;

(ii) Emergence of new actors which challenge state authority, particularly non-governmental organizations (NGO's) and civic groups, verily global firms and production networks, and even financial markets;

(iii) The emergence of an increasingly western-dominated international culture, a trend which has gleamed concern about the erosion of national identity and traditional values in many South-east Asian countries;

(iv) Growing pressure on nation-states to conform to new international standards of governance, particularly in the areas of transparency, accountability and the rule of law;

(v) The growth of severe transnational problems — such as energy and environmental problems, large-scale migration flows, ethnic unrest and organized crime networks — which require multilateral cooperation to resolve.

Thus, the forces of globalization have largely produced a new set of challenges and opportunities for the policy-makers of the nation-states of South-east Asia. One far reaching impact of globalization on local societies of South-east Asia has been the expansion of Western values and cultures. In most of the countries of South-east Asia, teaching of English has appeared more and more popular in the lower grades and efforts at training English teachers are being intensified. The popularization of English is caused by the greater influence of Western higher education. As a result, international study programmes have become increasingly very popular at many universities in the region.

Another impact of globalization on the nation-states of South-east Asia is the weakening of nationalism. These influences can be seen in the following ways. First, economic nationalism has lost its rationale. The anti-Japanese movement in Thailand criticizing "Japan's economic domination", for example, has lost its base. Secondly, it is becoming more difficult to impose a national identity on "minorities". More and more, minority peoples are less willing to accept such imposed "national identities". They have criticized past national identity campaigns that humiliated their own identity and their individual dignity. East Timor case is a clear example of this problem. Finally, the role of the state in the overall national economic management has been on the decline, and the multi-national corporations, especially in the field of telecommunications and computers, which practically controls the global market and influence.[1]

The final impact of globalization is the dilution of local identity and the worsening of the plight of the rural population. Gradually, some villagers have initiated to leave their indigenous identity behind and are more attracted towards their national culture and customs to reach for a global identity. This has happened due to rapid development of information technology, which has closely linked villages with the outside world. Thus, globalization brought more investors, traders, machinery and capital into the village and narrowed the distance between the village and the city. This kind of information revolution, due to globalization on local market, culture and economy has signalled a major alarm to the critics of globalization.

Repartee to Globalization: Regionalism

Globalization has no doubt challenged the existence structure of the nation-states of South-east Asia. How to overcome these challenges by these countries remains a major subject of study in international politics. The difficulty lies in the fact that this is not simply a western challenge. There are multiple centres of globalization and each nation-state manages globalization by its own mechanism. However, it has been observed that there are three levels of responses regarding globalization, and they are: regional, national and communal. The end of cold war has largely created a favourable environment for regionalism and ASEAN has utilized it in its entirety. First, in the context of new globalized world, the ASEAN has quickly expanded its membership. Vietnam became the seventh member of ASEAN in 1995. In 1997, Laos and Myanmar and in 1999, Cambodia joined in ASEAN. Thus, with the inclusion of these countries under the ASEAN platform, the likelihood of power rivalry and hegemonic outlook in the region have declined very sharply and ASEAN has emerged as a larger regional body than EU and NAFTA, containing a market of 480 million population.

Secondly, establishment of the ASEAN Free Trade Area (AFTA), which was decided in the Singapore Summit of 1992, in order to boost ASEAN's intra-regional economic cooperation, was no doubt a major response to globalization by the South-east Asian Countries. The main design of AFTA was to stimulate intra-regional trade by lowering the tariff rate to not more than 5 per cent within 15 years since 1994.

Thirdly, establishment of ASEAN Regional Forum (ARF) as a regional security dialogue platform was another response of ASEAN members against globalization. ARF was established in 1994 and presently consists of 21 members. The main objective of the ARF has been to promote confidence by encouraging frank discussions on security issues and build up under-standing of the different points of view and concerns. The ARF is a cooperative security arrangement, not a collective security or defence arrangement. The idea of a cooperative framework, has over time, evolved certain principles and codes of conduct and established international rules and norms to be adhered by all. The ARF has created three working groups: on Confidence-Building Measures, Preventive Diplomacy and Elaboration of Approaches to conflict. It also promotes input from academics and other non-governmental organizations, which is formally known as "second-track" diplomacy. In a nutshell, the real meaning of the ARF is to involve its members in dialogue and maintain self-restraint, without resorting to arms in setting their disputes, and to advance the cause of cooperative security.

Fourthly, the emergence of globalization and liberalization process and the formation of a new global economic order clearly opened the eyes of the ASEAN members to strengthen its economic bonds more with other developed and developing regional organizations. While realizing the depth of the impact of globalization the ASEAN members made serious efforts to strengthen its role through the meeting with the European Union, known as Asia-Europe Meeting (ASEM). Launched in Bangkok in 1996 between the 15 member countries of the European Union (EW), the European Commission and 10 Asian Countries (Brunei, China, Indonesia, Japan, Malaysia, the Philippines, Singapore, South Korea, Thailand and Vietnam), the ASEM process has developed a global agenda and a new dynamism between two strategic partners, Asia and Europe. ASEM generally covers all issues of common interest to Europe and Asia, and is not a formal organization, but rather an ongoing dialogue process. Its primary characteristics are informality, multi-dimensionality, openness and evolutionary nature, and equality between partners. It generally deals with the full spectrum of relations between the two regions and attempts to ensure a good balance between politics, economics and social/cultural/and intellectual aspects. ASEM is not a substitute for other bilateral or multilateral fora between Asia and Europe, and it can best work to facilitate and stimulate progress in other fora. Thus, the ASEM forum could be seen as ASEAN's efforts to deal with and make full use of globalization.

Fifthly, like the ASEM, the ASEAN countries in early 1990s' decided to develop a more cooperative bond with other regional groupings in the economic field. The ASEAN-MERCOSUR and ASEAN-SAARC cooperations have no doubt a major initiative of ASEAN in the context of globalization. Likewise, while reflecting its forward looking tendencies, ASEAN has also taken the lead in establishing institutional links with the countries of North-east Asia and South-east Asia through the ASEAN + 3 and ASEAN + 1 process. The realization of such entities would no doubt create a profound impact on the geopolitics of the region and international order.

Sixthly, the ASEAN members at its Bangkok Summit, held in December 1995, agreed to cooperate in the field of social development also. The central focus of this social development policy are — human resource, technological development and social cohesiveness.[2] At the ASEAN Standing Committee Meeting, held on 31 May - 1 June, 1996, a slogan for ASEAN's sectoral cooperation was accepted and the slogan was "shared prosperity through human development technological competitiveness and social cohesiveness."

Finally, apart from these agendas the ASEAN has taken a number of other specific initiatives in the field of culture and information. At the 31st Meeting of ASEAN Committee on Culture and Information in Bali during July 1-5, 1996, four important initiatives were accepted and they were — (1)

ASEANWEB; (2) an ASEAN Satellite Channel; (3) an ASEAN Arts Festival and (4) an ASEAN Youth Friendship Programme. Further, free flow of information, in the context of cyberspace, which has been dominated by Western media, was severely demanded by the countries of ASEAN.

Repartee to Globalization: Nationalism

Aside from the regional outlook, the countries of South-east Asia have their own policy and programmes in handling with free flow of information, goods-services-capital-technology, entertainment goods and values cultures. Each individual member try to adopt their own policy according to their own propriety. Some members of ASEAN keep the gate wide open to goods-services-capital technology, but totally close the door to the kind of values and cultures which might contaminate and one deemed incongruous with their societies. For example some countries are deeply sensitive to films and music from Hollywood, while the others are not. Chinese films are welcomed in Thailand, but not in Malaysia. Like wise, the cultural aspect of globalization, namely entertainment goods and values-cultures, remains quite debatable. Except in Singapore, various attempts have been made with reference to policies and programemes to reactivate national culture and identity with reference to globalization. Sensible efforts have been initiated to strengthen national symbols and identity such as Buddhism, Islam, Confucian values, national flags, monarchy, armed forces, socialist ideology, meritocracy, etc.

Asian Values Debate

The effects of economic globalization and interdependencies, advances in communications and transnational forces can be multiple. Some have argued that there has been a revival of traditional values as a result of the uncertainties of social change and as cultures rub up against each other. Whilst education, democracy and development may reflect a superficial Westernization, they can lead to a rediscovery of indigenous values, even a "cultural backlash."[4] The more popular liberal view is that this process results in a dilution of cultural differences and the breakdown of traditional values and institutions as the volume of shared experiences and behaviour increases sharply. As a generalized consequence of "modernization-industrialization, urbanization, education, democratization — this is undeniable. East Asian leaders have sought to exploit the opportunities of this environment whilst resisting the globalizing culture which accompanies this process. This resulted in the debates on Asian values. The debate on this concept has been originated after Samuel P. Huntington's book titled *The Clash of Civilizations*. In the early 1990s, the concept of Asian values has been advanced by various Asian political leaders, most notably Lee Kuan Yew and Mahathir Mohammed, who argued that certain Asian cultural values were the root of Asia's remarkable post-war success. These leaders maintained that in the political sphere, "Asian Values" supported the paternalistic brand of authoritarian government that they both practiced, while in the economic sphere these values supported a work ethic, savings, education and other practices conducive to economic growth. The Asian value are a kind of defence against Western way of life. It covers five ethics are humanity, righteousness, propriety, wisdom and faithfulness. These values are said to include work, good education, family centeredness and gratitude or comprise culture, tradition, moral, order, religion and way of the thoughts. Also "Asian Values" believe in duties, rather than rights. They also viewed that the Western model is not easily exportable and not necessarily desirable. They pointed out that drugs, gangs, guns, endemic violent crime, unsafe streets and increased divorce rates have clearly made a sharp decline in family values in the Western world. However, some have interpreted the "Asian Values" as a philosophical and cultural alternative to Western approaches to questions of government, civil liberties, economic management and human rights. The idea in a brief account is that there is an Asian way of doing things. By definition, the "Asian Values" differs from the Western way and denies the West any monopoly on the one right approach to the important issues.

Many in the West have been severely reluctant to accept the notion of a different but equally valid set of values. At the extreme, they have seen no basis for an alternative viewpoint to Western thinking on the important questions of what constitutes good governance and how best to protect human rights. They have considered these issues as universal; they have argued the solutions must also be universal. Thus, they have sought to promote Western liberal democracy and the protection of human rights through binding law as the goal to which countries, societies and peoples should universally aspire. It is therefore around these two issues that the Asian Values *vs*. Western Values debate has been most intense. For many in Asian countries, the West's approach is arrogant, provocative and basically another form of colonialism. Many in the West worry that Asian Values are a cover for oppressive Governments. The situation has been aggravated by public and sometimes acrimonious exchanges between governments. The result has been undesirable friction between the countries involved. This has made it difficult for them to work together to address the perceived differences with both sides believing that they have nothing to learn from the other. For example, take the human rights issue. Human rights are universal, but cultural values differ. There is no one single approach to good governance or the protection of human liberties. This might come as a surprise to many from the West, who often take for granted that Western style democracy is what everyone should aspire to and that political, social and economic progress is measured in those terms. But others are not ready to see things in that manner. Just as Western commentators and politicians also expressed worry about human rights loopholes in Asian or other countries, so too from an Asian perspective there can be doubts about whether Western countries always deliver on good governance and social and economic freedom for their people in theory, but not in practice. Besides this, some Western scholars argues that the "Asian Values" remained the key factor of the 1997 Financial Crisis. They argue that Asian value created improper characters of economic and political patterns. They also argued that "Asian Values" hindered independent thinking and creativity and fostered authoritarian regime – e.g. dictatorial governments in places such as China, Vietnam and Myanmar. Thus, we see that the debate on Asian Values have clearly emerged in the context of globalization. However, Asian Values in all their diversity, have played a role in shaping the economic and political institutions in Asia, and given Asian societies a very separate degree of social order than the developed countries of the West.

Effects and Criticism of Globalization

In South-east Asia, globalization has resulted in the reality of unsustainable development, overconsumption of life sustaining resources, adverse impacts on environment, ecology, and on the lives of indigenous communities, and a sharper contrast between the rich and the poor. It also resulted in growing foreign debts of poor countries, the financial crises of 1997 in East Asia and South-east Asia, growing inequality within and among countries, unemployment, underemployment and poverty. These uncertainties are largely responsible for social unrest, drugs, growth of the culture of violence, trafficking of people and might ultimately give rise to the mushrooming of global cross-border terrorism, secessionist movements in multi-ethnic societies, and attempts towards the balkanization of states. Malaysian Prime Minister Mahathir Mohammed was a well-known critic of globalization. He believed that globalization is a concept devised by and made use of by powerful and rich countries to open up the economies of weaker countries. He sketched an alternative approach to economic recovery of Malaysia as well as other countries of South-east Asia for the trauma of an unexpected financial and economic crisis caused primarily by the forces of financial globalization, he described globalization as the brainchild of absolute capitalism and said:

> "Its objective is to enlarge the sphere of capitalist activities to the whole world. The capitalists had always resented their confinement to their own countries. They resented the independence of nations with their own systems and

policies which prevent their full economic exploitation by those with the capital and the know-how. If the borders of these independent countries could be brought down and a single policy and system for the whole world adopted then capital could move freely and be fully employed to make even more capital. With huge amounts of capital at their disposal they could develop even bigger ambitions. So the world is presented with the great idea of a global nation, of globalization. But this globalization is to be confined to the free flow of capital across borders."[5]

Mahathir further said that "the major players in the system have devised unfair rules of the game for their own benefit, keeping developing countries out of the benefits and causing them to lose out"[6], and suggested critically that globalisation "must be planned and planned carefully. The planning must involve everyone from every part of the globe. It must be for the good of every one and it must be proven to be good for everyone. It must be implemented slowly, with the biggest effort directed at the least developed parts of the world."[7] Finally, he questioned whether "Globalisation at the service of Mankind or Mankind at the service of Globalisation?"

Another criticism of globalisation was that it links social issues to trade. For example, the issue of human rights. Most of the Western countries always linked trade with the human rights situation in South-east Asia. They conditioned that the improvement of human rights situation will automatically improve the trade ties. Further, the use of airwaves to globalize democracy — another feature of globalisation initiated by the United States (known as Radio Free Asia, later renamed as Asia-Pacific Network) was vehemently rejected by the countries of South-east Asia who demanded that globalisation should not have an exploitative character, and must not result in loss of economic, political and social independence.

The Ethnic Strife in South-east Asia

The second issue which disturbed the countries of South-east in the post-cold war years, has been the ethnic unrest, and the emergence of secessionist movements. Following the separation of East Timor from Indonesia, there has been a growing demand in other regions to separate or to have a more autonomous status. Some of these regions are the provinces of Aceh, Irian Jaya (Papua), Riamand, East Kalimantan, and these ethnic conflicts are mainly termed as either centre-periphery problem, or conflict between military rulers and indigenous people relating to mining companies, or a problem between two religious communities. The centrifugal forces are threatening the national identity of Indonesia, and could, in turn, determine the future status of the unitary state of Indonesia. The interests and demands of regions to have greater sovereignty could lead to more violent conflict with the Central Government as struggles develop into insurgency movements.[8] In the case of the Philippines, although many indigenous groups have been involved in armed struggle against the Central Government, it is the Moro movement in the south that has come to the forefront in recent times. The Moro Islamic Liberation Front (MILF) and the Abu Sayyaf Group (ASC) remain locked in a bitter religious separatist struggle with the Central Philippines government, which ultimately turned into violence between Christians and Muslims. In Vietnam, the ethnic minorities of the central highlands who protested against transplanted northerners from the Kinh majority and other ethnic minorities from the low lands, who had encroached on the central highlands, undermining their cultures and taking their lands, created serious ethnic unrest in February 2001.[9] The protestors, who were Protestants, categorically demanded the right to practice their faith and insisted on the return of ancestral lands confiscated for coffee plantations and also demanded political autonomy. The Vietnamese authorities unfortunately cracked down this ethnic agitation with the help of soldiers and riot police. This ethnic unrest in central highlands has been essentially a struggle between North and South Vietnam. In Cambodia, old ethnic hatred between Khmer Rouge and the Vietnamese, and in Laos, between the Pathet Lao and Hmong Community, occasionally created deep ethnic unrest. In Laos and Cambodia, ethnic minorities have been regularly pressured into assimilation with the "culturally superior" ethnic cores, by being officially classified as Lau Theung (Upland Lao) and Lau Sung (highland Lao) in Laos, or as Khmer Loeu (Upland Khmer) and Khmer Islam in Cambodia.

In Myanmar, one of the dominant issues of contemporary politics is that of ethnic rebellions against the central state, and the domination of that state by ethnic Myanmarese. There has been a long history of military power and legal force being used to control and dominate the various indigenous communities. This inflamed the struggle for increased autonomy from the centre, with each of the indigenous group, like the Shan, Rakhin and Karens, having their own insurgent movement. Since the early eighties, the central leadership of Myanmar seemed to have carried out all kinds of strategies that caused severe resentment and deep discontent among the indigenous people. Among these were: to arrogate political, economic and social power of the indigenous people; to forcefully regroup them into fenced "strategic hamlets", and to carry out policies or programmes that practically brought out internal colonisation and ethnocide. The indigenous people of Myanmar, in order to speed up their struggle against the government, established a front known as the National Democratic Front (NDF) in 1976. In this front, the major political organizations were the Arakan (ALP), Chin (CNF), Karen (KNU), Kachin (KIO), Kayan (KNLP), Lahu (LNO), Mon (NMSP) and Wu (WNO). These various indigenous groups, dissatisfied with the functions and ruthlessness of the military regime, were forced to resort armed struggle,[10] and are still prevalent in various parts of Myanmar.

In Thailand, the ethno-religious conflict between Malay Muslim and Thai government resulted in the emergence of secessionist guerilla movements. Islamic fundamentalist violence in Thailand centres on the separatist activities of the Malaya Muslim population in the southern provinces of Pattani, Satun, Yala and Norathiwat. Muslims account for 80 per cent of the population of these four provinces and their opposition to the Central Government has been the result of neglect, discrimination and maltreatment. This dissatisfaction resulted in repeated outbreaks of unrest and civil disturbances associated with the secessionist struggle. Nonsensical and sometimes inhuman government responses occasionally stimulated intensified resistance and serious acts of violence.[11]

Finally, domination of majority community of minorities has remained a major reason behind ethnic unrest and internal security problem of South-east Asia. In Malaysia, there has been tension between the Malays and the Chinese and between Malays and Indians. This tension repeatedly focuses upon the issue of the relative economic positions of the different ethnic groups. This issue of ethnic economic rivalry has generated a flourishing literature on class, ethnicity and the state, so that a clarification of the relationship between the class character of the state and the structure of ethnic politics offers a potentially illuminating approach to the study of internal conflict of Malaysia.[12] The economic upliftment of the Bumiputera (i.e. son of the soil) through special privileges (Article 153 of the 1957 Constitution) and the New Economic Policy largely marginalized the Indian community of Malaysia as well as the Chinese. This domination of the Malays, sometimes led to social unrest and political conflict between the two groups. Thus in Malaysia, the dominant class is able to promote a 'divide and rule' ethnic policy so as to achieve a responsive impact on ethnicity and hence to maintain UMNO and Barisan rule.[13] Therefore, ethnic minority communities of Malaysia (i.e. Chinese and Indians) have perceived their lower status as deriving from discrimination by a state seen as the agent of the ethnic core, and have been pushed to accept low status as "second class citizens."

In South-east Asia, ethnic strife and state intervention into ethnic minority homeland regions in many cases involved the disruption of traditional authority structures, since ethnic minority elites were replaced by governmental officials recruited from the ethnic cores; and as social cohesion was disrupted by the progressive impositions of new fiscal, administrative and educational structure as well as by migrations of labour. Such attempts to expand state control over peripheral ethnic minority regions have frequently had a reactive impact, provoking some amongst the dislocated elites and disrupted communities into ethnic rebellion. These have been occurred, for example, among the Patani Malays in Thailand; the Mindanoo Moros in the Philippines; the Karen Shan, Kachin, Chin and others in Myanmar, the Papuans and Acehnese in Indonesia, and the Hmong in Laos. In many occasions these rebellions could trace their roots both to pre-colonial disputes and to unrest in the colonial period directed against the expanding influence of the modern state. Thus ethnic strife in South-east Asian region can be termed as a struggle between the righteous "Us" and the demonized "Other".[14]

Sub-Terranean Tensions among ASEAN Members

Thirdly, sub-terranean tensions among the South-east Asian countries have remained a major threat in the post-cold war years. Thirty-eight years of interaction within ASEAN have fed a strong norm against the use of force to resolve conflicts among ASEAN states. So, as a whole the ASEAN members have never experienced an intra-ASEAN armed conflict since its formation in 1967, but only minor local infighting in the South China Sea region and the Cambodia[15] conflict. However, the East Asian Financial Crisis has largely weakened the ASEAN consensus and intraregional tensions regarding long standing antagonisms — never far below the surface — temporarily resurfaced and fuel international conflicts. Malaysia's relations with both Singapore and Indonesia have been strained over refugee, immigration, island, water and other economic issues. In insular South-east Asia, the principal source of friction is the historical animosity between Malaysia and Singapore. Singapore has been portrayed as "a Chinese nut in a Malay nutcracker"[16], but this metaphor belies the actual situation. Since Malaysia is a maritime nation, its sea boundaries with Thailand, Singapore, Indonesia, Vietnam, Brunei and the Philippines are all in dispute. Malaysia's claims in the South China Sea (which it called "Subah Sea") and

Singapore's claim in tiny Batu Putih Island — located about 35 km. east of Singapore — in June 1992, has created serious tension between the two countries. Singapore's claim has been contested by Malaysia and it views this demand as an attempt by the island Republic to push out its maritime frontier. Malaysia has submitted papers supporting its claim of the island, where a lighthouse has been presently maintained and administered by Singapore. Malaysia justifies its claim on Singapore's inability to prove that the island was ceded to it by the Sultan of Johore in the early 19th century. However, Singapore argues that it has always had administrative jurisdiction over the island, and till date the problem has not yet resolved and occasional irritation cropped up between these two countries.

Sabah, an east Malaysian state, constitutes another problem between Malaysia and the Philippines. Over the years, the Philippines government has refused to drop its claim to the resource rich Malaysian state of Sabah. This claim has been further intensified because the Philippines government firmly believes that Malaysia was tolerating secessionist Moro training camp in Sabah and acting as a supply base. The Philippines has claimed sovereignty and ownership of Sabah as the Sultan of Sulu's successor. In 1963, Sabah joined the Federation of Malaya, but the issue continued to rankle with the adoption of the Baseline Act as an appendix to the Marcos Constitution in 1972 which publicly claimed Sabah as part of the Philippine territory.[17] The Philippines under President Marcos, had also attempted to pursue its claim by promoting a training camp for an intended Sabah separatist rebellion in 1968. However, a mutiny by the trainees at the camp fully exposed the operation. Meanwhile the Philippines government alleged that certain Islamic groups in Malaysia were involved in aiding the Moros, and it does appear that the Malaysian government did not actively prevent them from doing so, in recognition of the potentially serious domestic political fall out from its local Muslim constituency. The unofficial Malaysian support for the Moros has been the main obstacle to the Philippines dropping its claim to Sabah, which could use the claim to put pressure on Malaysia to prevent the activities of its Moro sympathisers.[18] On the other side, the Malaysia government firmly believes that the Philippines had been assisting the Catholic Kadazans, such as cooperating with the then Kadazan State Government to import Filipino Christians to Sabah in the early 1990s to counter balance the presence of Muslim refugees.[19] The huge influx of illegal aliens from Southern Philippines to Sabah regularly, created deep rooted sub-terranean tensions between Kuala Lumpur and Manila. The problem came into international limelight, after the 11 September, 2001 incident, and aggravated further following the illegal migration to Malaysia.

Further, in the South China Sea region because of the contrasting claims relating to the law of the sea, Indonesia and Vietnam are in dispute over the potentially oil-rich continental shelves surrounding the Indonesian owned Natuna islands, which are close to James School, lie in the Southern part of the Spratly islands. Indonesia and Malaysia are also in dispute over two small islands in the Sulawesi Straint between Sabah and the Indonesian province of Kalimantan (i.e. in Ligitan and Sipadan islands). Indonesia is not out to claim any of the Spratly islands but it has long standing disputes with Vietnam and Malaysia in areas surrounding the South China Sea. In any way Indonesia, being a widely scattered archipelago in which several important straits are located, has legitimate strategic concerns over access to the sea lanes of communication in the South China Sea. It has already an air base on Natuna Besar, from which it conducts regular aerial surveillance of the South China Sea.[20] Besides this, friction between Thailand and Myanmar over political and border issues involving cross border smuggling and drug trafficking remain a cause for major sub-terranean tension between these two countries. It is said that some of the indigenous armed groups who have refused to come to terms with the Myanmar government have benefited from alleged safe havens on the Thai side, occasionally generated bilateral excitements. Thus, cross border crimes and insurgent problems by various ethnic and religious groups, island and water land disputes etc. often create sub-terranean tensions in the countries of South-east Asia and naturally place a big question mark about the ASEAN's principle of "non-interference".

Transnational Threats of South-east Asian Countries

Fourthly, transnational security threats, such as crime, narcotics, maritime piracy, human smuggling etc. are some of the growing security challenges of the South-east Asian region. This trend has been accentuated by the region's economic crisis that cropped up in mid-1997. Percolable borders, corruption, mass employment and economic malaise – particularly in countries such as Indonesia and Philippines – are significant contributing factors. New forms of crimes, such as computer or 'cyber' crime, are also challenging governments within the region. Piracy has been on the increase, particularly in waters around Indonesia and the Philippines. Narcotics trafficking has also been an endemic problem, particularly in mainland South-east Asia, but of late it has taken on some new dimensions. The Thais consider the smuggling of methamphetamines from Myanmar a major security concern. Illegal migration and "people smuggling" have been another major transnational challenges of South-east Asian countries. This region has emerged as a key transit region for human smuggling from Iraq and Afghanistan to Australia and elsewhere. The transit smuggling of migrants via Indonesia to Australia has emerged as a major irritant in Australia – Indonesia relations. Indonesia and Malaysia have also experienced mutual tensions over this issue. As unemployment rises in Indonesia this drives thousands to try their luck in Malaysia. Alarmingly, human smuggling is likely to grow alongside growing disparities in economic growth and income levels throughout the region. Further, since 1970s, ASEAN countries have experienced a huge influx of people. The causes of displacement were civil and ideological war, repression and military invasion. In particular, the "boat people" from Vietnam and "monk people" from Cambodia created serious challenges for ASEAN countries. In Myanmar, continued political repression has become the major reason behind the source of displaced persons. Continued military operations against guerrilla movements in several states (Kachin, Karen, Shan, etc.) has created much misery and thousands of people have left their homes, many of them crossing the border to Thailand, and some particular Muslim Rohingya, to Eastern Bangladesh. In the Philippines, the continued violence in South Mindanao has also prompted the movement of people.[21]

In Indonesia, the scorched-earth policy of pro-Jakarta militias sparked violence across East Timor, North Maluku/Ambon, Aceh and many people fled the region out of terror and insecurity. The Indonesian government lacks the budget or the commitment to deal with them. Thus, the problem of human displacement in South-east Asia continues to pose a major transnational threat in South-east Asia.

Growth of Islamic Fundamentalism in South-east Asia

Fifthly, the emergence of Islamic fundamentalism has been treated as a major threat to the countries of South-east Asia. The Islam that has been practiced in South-east Asia is unlike its Middle Eastern counterpart. Islam is said to have first arrived in the region in the 14th century by way of India. By the time it was introduced in areas of the region presently known as Indonesia, Malaysia and Thailand. Islam got infused with elements of Indian Sufi mysticism. The result was that Islam had to adapt itself to the entrenched Hindu Buddhist traditions already in the region. It is not only the geographic distance of South-east Asia to the rest of the Islamic world that accounts for the moderate Islam practiced in the region. Among the countries where Islam is politically significant are Indonesia, Malaysia, the Philippines and Singapore. However, in recent years the growth of Islamic fundamentalism or radicalism and its connection with various terrorist groups has emerged as a major political factor in South-east Asia and invited external intervention like in the Philippines where the US started its operation against the Abu Sayyaf group. Leaders of Malaysia and Indonesia have already started to seriously ponder over the issue. It would be wise for them to rein in disruptive forces by restoring liberalism and tolerance, which were the hallmark of their societies. Islamic fundamentalism is not new in South-east Asia. There have been instances earlier. An example is the Padri Movement of Indonesia. Islamic fundamentalism also appeared in Kelantan, North Malaysia and Southern Thailand. Today, the entire northern states are under the political control of Islamic fundamentalist parties. Its appearance in Indonesia has been only in the recent past and especially after President Suharto's fall.[22] The Jemaah Islamiyah of Indonesia, which is the most important Islamic terrorist organization in South-east Asia, has links with the Al Qaeda but also has very important indigenous roots, which can be traced back to the Darul Islam of the 1940s. Similarly, Islamic fundamentalism has been too prominent in the Christian state of the Philippines, where Western tourists are being held hostages, by the extremist separatist, Abu Sayyaf, a splinter group of the Moro Islamic Liberation Front (MILF). This Abu Sayyaf group is believed to have received millions of pesos in ransom, which they have used to buy weapons, and have linked up with the Al Qaeda. In the wake of September 11, thousands of Philippines troops and hundreds of American soldiers were deployed in the Southern island of Basilan, where the separatists were holding hostages. After several months of training and assistance, the Americans withdrew. However, the Abu Sayyaf continue to plague the South. The group was responsible for bomb attacks in the MILF and against the government which took place in February 15, 2003. Two hundred, mostly rebel forces, died in the firefight, in which the military overran the rebel's stronghold in the Southern Philippine province of Cotabato.

However, the moot question is why Islamic communities in South-east Asia, long known for tolerance and liberalism, fell pray to the West Asian brand of Islamic fundamentalism? There is no doubt that Saudi and Gulf State's money have largely accelerated their fundamentalist activities. But regional economic disparities within the states remain an important reason behind their upsurge. It is from these economically backward regions that there has been a large outflow of young people to theological seminaries in Pakistan and Saudi Arabia in the last 10-15 years. It has largely flourished because it became a tool in electoral politics in many countries of South-east Asia.[23] Therefore, the growth of transnational radical Islam and Islamic resurgence in South-east Asia have converted Islam into a force of radical and violent revisionism and has greatly changed the image of Islam in South-east Asia as a moderate and constructive force, as well as created political instability and regional chaos.

The Struggle between Democracy and Authoritarian Rule

Sixthly, the struggle between democracy and authoritarian rule in South-east Asia has emerged as a major threat in the region. The political structure being followed by most of the South-east Asian countries are either military rule, or quasi-democratic system or party dictatorship. Since the mid-1980's, the process of democratization has to appeared be a major political force in South-east Asia. The arguments that were made by the authoritarian regimes in this region have been that there was a connection between their high speed economic growth and their authoritarian political systems. The establishment of quasi-democratic structures in place of military rule, never altered the entire structure of the political system be it transparency, accountability and the rule of law. It also failed to protect minority rights within its so-called democratic structure. The outbreak of racial violence in March 2001 at Petaling Jaya Selantan squatter settlement between Indians and Malays had sent severe shock waves in Malaysia and had put a big question mark about the hitherto pluralist structure of the Malaysian society. In the Philippines the struggle between Catholics and Muslims, which refueled perceptions of local alienation and deprivation by majority on minority, in Singapore the domination of People's Action Party in its so-called democratic institutions (e.g. a strong central bureaucracy and management of the political affairs through tricky means of conciliation and consensus-building, efficient manipulation of judiciary, the press etc.), clearly exhibited the absence of common democratic norms that are deeply prevalent in the Western democratic model. In Myanmar, the domination of ethnic Myanmarese on various ethnic indigenous communities through autocratic means, clearly and forcefully legitimize the existence of autocratic military junta. The Burmese military, though physically in control, has been morally bankrupt and fighting for survival, and thus unlikely to take the initiative in democratization. Although history is not always a reliable guide, the political system transformations in Burma and Indonesia, in the past, and presently in Cambodia, Laos, and again in Indonesia (after the fall of Suharto in 1996) have been abrupt and severely violent. In Cambodia, after the peace keeping operation in 1993, democracy becomes an on-going "war", rather than producing a national consensus on the path ahead. There may not be regular violent clashes, as they were previously. But unless there is more reconciliation between victors, runners-up and indeed the opposition, society and polity remain overall divided and this clearly obstructs national development of consensus and the process of democratization. In Thailand, after its long history of military rule, in 1992, the May events resulted in the fall of the Suchinda military dictatorship and start of the process which has since "seen two powerful handovers of power from one parliamentary coalition to another."

The process of globalization, which accelerated since early 1990s, clearly generated the new wave of democratization and amply signalled many weaknesses of the authoritarian state. Among them — the absence of democratic norms and institutions and reliance on economic performance to sustain political legitimacy — are most important reasons. Although the importance of authoritarian ideology lost its momentum in the context of new global order, in its place the democratic revolution also unfortunately lost its stream in the last few years. In most of the South-east Asian, the novelty of free elections, party competition, and separation of powers has worn off, to reveal several sources of discontent associated with the model of democracy after which insurgent elites patterned their systems of governance after ejecting authoritarian rule. Further, in South-east Asian region, there is doubt whether the protection of the interests of minorities, be it ethnic, racial or religious, can be safeguarded under democracy, which by definition is the rule of the majority. It is not at all clear, for instance, if democratic rule has been an advance over authoritarian rule for the Muslims in Thailand, where a Thai majority holds sway. It is amply clear that 11 years of democracy has not resulted in significant political and economic gains for the Muslim in the Southern Philippines. So, the authoritarian regimes in South-east Asia did not have a much worse record in terms of assuring minority rights than the democratic government. The debate between democracy and authoritarian rule and the debate within democracies of the South-east Asian countries have been convulsive in the regional politics of Southeast Asia. Besides this, with respect to other member states, the impact of the Financial crisis of 1997 in Indonesia is of great consequence to other ASEAN members and to the nature of the association itself. The political reform in Indonesia as the "positive" impact of the economic crisis had given new expectation for Indonesia as a democratic state. Furthermore, it is a fact that no universal values of democracy should be applied to all countries, and it seems that some ASEAN countries have become more democratic than others. Consequently, this may cause tensions between ASEAN members.

Uneven Economic Status among the ASEAN Members

Finally, the development gap in the level of human resources among the countries of the ASEAN could be a cause of major threat before the countries of South-east Asia. Unequal economic development due to poverty and existence of wide regional disparities in terms of living standards in countries like Laos, Cambodia, Vietnam and Myanmar one the one hand, and Singapore, Malaysia, Indonesia, Thailand, Brunei and the Philippines on the other, remain another contentious problem in South-east Asia. The major reasons behind poverty among the new members of ASEAN (e.g. Vietnam, Cambodia, Laos and Myanmar) are manifold. Among these, lack of entrepreneurs, relatively closed economy, high military spending, forced relocation of people, corruption, lack of access to basic social services, lack of food security, environment degradation, high illiteracy rate, lack of human capital, transition from command to market economy, high population density, exclusion of indigenous groups etc. are mainly responsible for the economic vulnerability of these states. The governments of these countries have introduced various poverty alleviation programmes through National Plans in order to combat poverty. But these initiatives so far failed to remove poverty, due to the following reasons:

1. In the planning stage, key stakeholders have missed or are excluded from this poverty reduction programme.
2. Lack of resources, inter-agency coordination, collaboration with private sector and civil society groups are absent in the implementation stage.
3. Corruption and weak governance and sustained anti-poverty campaigns are virtually limited in these countries.
4. The process of democratic decentralization (via local governments) for the implementation of poverty reduction programmes is still limited.
5. Lack of effective monitoring and evaluation systems are practically absent in these countries.

These weaknesses were further amplified by the negative impact of liberalization as well as the 1997 East Asian Financial Crisis, which brought back poverty in these countries, as various economies succumbed to the volatility of financial market. It has been argued by the critics that globalization has increased inequality worldwide and has not reduced poverty in most of the developing countries. Geographically, it has benefited more the developed rather than developing countries. This seems to hold for the South-east Asian states as a whole.

From 1995 to 1999, ASEAN membership has increased from six to ten, and the new members are Vietnam (1995), Laos and Myanmar (1997) and Cambodia (1999). These four new members are also the four poorest members of ASEAN. And if "integration" is to have any meaning, ASEAN must bring these four new nations up from the heap of poor countries. According to World Bank statistics, the average Singaporean makes more than 60 times the average Vietnamese, nearly 80 times more than the average Laotian and nearly 92 times the average Cambodian. Statistics from Myanmar are not available, but the World Bank estimates its average yearly income to be in the "very low" category. Similarly, the level of development index among the ASEAN members, according to United Nations Development Pro-gramme (UNDP), could be a cause of major concern. The survey report of the UNDP clearly ranked Singapore the best, coming in 25th in the "developed" country group, followed by oil rich Brunei. Malaysia was placed highest in the "developing" category, ahead of Thailand, the Philippines, Indonesia, Vietnam, Myanmar and Cambodia. Laos was the only member to fall within "the less-developed" group, coming in 143rd of the 190 nations. Bridging this development gap, enabling the four new members to catch up with the rest and join them in advancing the ASEAN into a more prosperous economic community would be one of the hardest jobs of the rich ASEAN members. So, as integration with the world economy increases, ASEAN finds itself facing important opportunities and challenges including the need to better integrate the new members into the regional and global economy. So, a truly sustainable or enduring ASEAN Economic Community can only be realised, if it is considered just and legitimate by the ASEAN members beyond state and commercial interest. Nevertheless, the new ASEAN members face a more daunting set of challenges compared to the original members, given their transition status and weaker institutional capacities for national economic governance. To reduce the intra-ASEAN disparities and thereby facilitate regional economic integration, the ASEAN leaders have agreed to develop a Road map for Integration of ASEAN (RIA) in order to provide a framework for more coherent implementation of the regional programme. It visualized a stable, prosperous and highly competitive ASEAN Economic Region, in which there is a free flow of goods, services and investments, a freer flow of capital, equitable economic development and reduced poverty and socio-economic disparities.

Among ASEAN's greatest challenges in the new millennium is the one if faces within: the integration of market diversity and the transitional economies of its new members countries. To reduce intra-ASEAN disparities, the ASEAN members initiated to launch four major initiatives and they are: the Initiative for ASEAN Integration (IAI), Mekong Basin Development Cooperation, the Joint ASEAN—World Bank Initiative on Mainstreaming Social Development and the ASEAN—UNDP Partnership Facility. In November 2000, the ASEAN leaders agreed to launch an IAI programme, which gives direction to sharpen the focus of collective efforts in ASEAN to narrow the development gap between ASEAN's older and newer members. To realise the objective, the ASEAN leaders, at their Summit Meeting in Phnom Penh in November 2002, endorsed a Work Plan (with 48 projects) that will ensure dynamic and sustained growth of the sub-region and prosperity of the peoples. Although the IAI does not specifically point to the development divide between new members and the original set, nevertheless, its work programme in the four priority areas — infrastructure, human resources development, information and communications technology and capacity building for regional economic integration — all are directed mainly at the new members. Besides the Cambodia, Laos, Myanmar and Vietnam (CLMV) countries, there are also pockets of under development in the ASEAN-6 countries.[24] The ASEAN as a comprehensive regional organization, have given due importance for the economic development assistance to the weak economic countries of ASEAN-6. In fact, the IAI to bridge the development gaps in the ASEAN Action Programme (VAP) has been broadened to include development efforts not only for the CLMV but also the poorer sub-regions in the ASEAN-6 countries, in order to make their economies more competitive in facing the new realities in the global economy, as well as for the speedier integration of ASEAN.

Besides the IAI programme, the Mekong Basin Development Cooperation engages in a wider range of activities than the IAI, but for similar purposes, namely the development of the new members of ASEAN and to create a favourable environment of economic linkages between them and the old members.[25] Both these programmes deeply involve external funding, while ASEAN contributes in kind through a range of technical assistance programmes and other non-financial contributions.

While these two programmes are essentially practical mechanisms to attain key economic development goals, the Mainstreaming Social Development (MSD) Initiative is especially interesting. Since it attempts to alter at a normative level the core goals on which national and regional economic governance should be based.[26] Its main function is to highlight that growth alone is insufficient. Instead, growth must be integrated at the planning level with a social development agenda, which would naturally include poverty alleviation and social protection, employment, labour and health issues. The MSD Initiative, together with technical and advisory services offered under the ASEAN-UNDP Partnership facility[27], are attempts to extend regional understanding and practices of development to include that of social and economic development. All these programmes are vital as attempts to embed regional economic integration within a single framework, namely one that takes socio-economic governance as seriously as market integration. All these efforts and realization of the benefits of these various ASEAN initiatives will take time to produce a positive outcome. However, ASEAN's commitment, priority and responses to changing circumstances for the development needs of all underdeveloped economics of new ASEAN members remain vital to ASEAN's integration process. Here, one of the major problems could be how far the domestic economic resilience of every member state can create togetherness and cooperation in order to achieve regional economic strength and power in the global arena.

The ASEAN's Way Out

The countries of South-east Asia in the coming years will still struggle to face some of the challenges mentioned above. Although, there are sharp differences on many issues among these countries, but these countries always took serious initiatives to resolve their problems – sometimes locally, regionally and globally. The most significant strength of the South-east Asian countries are their solidarity and cohesiveness among themselves. There is no doubt that every leader of each country of South-east Asia always tries to keep their commitment to strengthen solidarity and cohesiveness of ASEAN. However, they also realise that there are many weaknesses and challenges, both domestically and regionally, that should be handled seriously. Issues like poverty eradication, human rights, ethnic unrests, haze crisis, terrorism and transnational crime, financial crisis, South China Sea, Cambodian crisis etc., are important in this connection. Regarding these problems, the ASEAN members have become more enthusiastic and dynamic, in order to develop their capability in all aspects of life, particularly the economic, which is the most important driver for the future of ASEAN. However, this "positive" initiative has not always been enough to resolve the conflicts among the ASEAN members within the region, although it has definitely covered the intensity of differences. This has been possible due to ASEAN's principle of non-intervention. In South-east Asia, the founding members of the ASEAN namely Indonesia, Malaysia, Singapore, Thailand and the Philippines, signed the Treaty of Amity and Cooperation (TAC) in February 1976 at Bali. This treaty aimed at promoting perpetual peace, everlasting amity and cooperation among their people, which would contribute to their strength, solidarity and closer relationship. Article 2 of the TAC clearly emphasised the principle of "mutual respect for the independence, sovereignty, equality, territorial integrity and national identity of all nations." It also highlighted "the right of every state to lead its national existence free from external interference, subversion or coercion." Most prominently, the TAC enshrined the principle of non-interference in the internal affairs of one another.[28] However, important changes in certain areas of international relations require a re-assessment of such a principle, especially when the domestic problem of one state have far-reaching effects pervading the borders of neighbouring states. On many occasions, these domestic problems sometimes pose a serious threat to the peace and stability of the region. In mid-1990s', Thailand's devaluation of the Baht, Myanmar's military repression, Cambodia's coup d'etat and the sacking of Malaysian Deputy Prime Minister Anwar Ibrahim have all generated acute critical comments on government policy from political leaders in the neighbouring countries,[29] and raised a big question mark about ASEAN's principles of non-interference and non-confrontation. Besides this, the South-east Asian region also witnessed many domestic problems that have obvious transnational dimensions, adversely affecting neighbouring countries as well as the region. Issues like financial crisis, transmigration and influx of refugees, drug trafficking, criminal syndicates and terrorism are some of these intra and inter-state problems.[30]

These issues led Thailand's Foreign Minister Surin Pitsuwan, to challenge ASEAN's "principle of non-intervention", and called for suitable changes in the ASEAN's Foreign Ministers meeting held in June 1998 at Manila. He demanded that the ASEAN members be allowed to openly discuss each other's domestic affairs, if these have an impact outside their borders. He dubbed his proposal as "constructive intervention", and a month later, at the ASEAN Ministerial Meeting in Singapore, to remove the impression that he was suggesting a modification of the principle of "non-intervention", renamed the idea "flexible engagement". In the Singapore meeting, he made it clear that ASEAN must adhere to the principle of non-intervention, but at the same time find a way to deal with new problems and challenge which damage ASEAN's credibility if left unaddressed: "The principle of non-intervention is not the real issue.... the real issue is how we can work together in dealing with the new challenges of a new millennium."[31] This proposal of Surin Pitsuwan received the support of the Philippines. Unfortunately, the Thai Foreign Minister's proposal was strongly opposed by the rest of ASEAN members who advocated "constructive interventions" on certain regional issues. However, the Singapore meeting decided, as a compromise, to have "enhanced interaction" in the future. "Enhanced interaction" was not clearly spelt out, but presumably it meant more frank and frequent exchanges of views in private. In the next Ministerial Meeting, held in July 1999 in Singapore, all members regarded the retention of the principle of non-intervention as essential. What is at issue is the need for some adjustments to take account on the changed circumstances. Above all, the need to rethink non-interference should be seen not as an abstract moral concern associated with human rights protection, but as a matter of a "practical" necessity without which ASEAN cannot stay relevant and address real world changes and challenges.[32] Therefore, the principle of non-intervention have made ASEAN, a successful regional organization in global politics, in the past and will continue to do so in the future. Discarding them will not make ASEAN stronger. On the contrary, to do so may weaken ASEAN's past effectiveness and adversely affect its future functioning. Thus, after 38 years, ASEAN has not only survived but has developed into an important force internationally, being held up as a model of regional unity worthy of emulation.

Alternative Discourses of South-east Asia

The countries of South-east Asia and especially the ASEAN members have faced diverse challenges since its establishment in 1967. From the time of its inception to the end of the cold war, ASEAN's main preoccupation has been with challenges to its security in terms of military threats. With the end of the cold war, as the military confrontation subsided, the challenges appear to come from other fronts, notably in the aspects of economic growth and cooperation. The East Asian Financial crisis was probably one of the greatest challenges faced by South-east Asian countries. With the financial crisis, confidence in the Asian economic miracle has been severely shaken. Serious doubts have since cropped up in the region about the "benefits" of rapid globalisation and economic inter-dependence. Globalization, which had been a significant phenomenon in this region, has been blamed for exacerbating the contagious spread of the financial crisis from one country to the entire region.

The effects of globalization are multifarious. The economic, political and security environment of South-east Asian region has been shaped by globalization, so much so that it has become the framework on which business, the economy and government relations operate. Besides its nominal positive effects, globalization has also exhibited negative effects, as reflected in the contagion effect of the financial crisis. Therefore, the question now arises, whether any alternative model against existing world order would be possible. The New World Order's (NWO) ideological and economic agendas are globalized laissez-faire capitalism, under the rhetoric of "free-trade" and "increased competitiveness". The so-called free trade treaties are not about trade, but about opening up the world's economic resources and labour pools to unregulated exploitation by the multi-nationals. The NWO's political and economic agendas are the removal of the state's importance in society and democracy. The main vehicle of the propaganda branch of the NWO is the global mass media with ownership increasingly centralized in a small number of corporate agencies. These news pool, entertainment and propaganda vendors provide a highly biased and selective interpretation of world events, aligned with interests and agendas of the NWO. However, the countries of South-east Asia firmly believe that this NWO is

(i) Inherently socially amoral. Its only imperatives are the expansion of corporate power, the accumulation of poor's wealth and the establishment of a global political system that expedites those objectives;
(ii) It is expansionist in character and cancerous in motion;
(iii) It is inherently anti-democratic in nature;
(iv) It flatly opposes national sovereignty and clearly promotes unaccountable internationalism.

As against this New World Order, the leaders of South-east Asian countries in February 2000, at the United Nations Conference on Trade and Development held in Bangkok, categorically demanded a "New Global Order". In this meeting, Singapore Prime Minister Goh Chok Tong, demanded that UNCTAD should produce a programme to shape more equitable trade and development policies at a time, when free trade and liberalization has been suffering a backlash from countries and groups left out of its benefits. Like Goh Chok Tong, the Malaysian Prime Minister, Mahathir Mohammed firmly demanded that developing countries should be allowed to participate in the global decision-making process in order to manage the pace and direction of liberalization and globalization.

In August 1996, at Manila, the countries of South-east Asia in a meeting titled "South-east Asia Beyond the year 2000: A Statement of Vision," firmly pronounced the region's future path and endorsed certain principles as an alternative discourse in the context of New World Order. It emphasized need for a "community building" mindset, which is a process of creating a new state of mind. It prescribed "a human agenda", which should be elevated to the top in the regional governments, individual and collective priorities and that successful implementation of "a human agenda" should be considered the principle of achievements on the road to building a South-east Asian Community in the 21st century. These countries prescribed certain principles and they are:

(i) Peace at all levels – international, regional and domestic;

(ii) Physical and material well being – which means open market mechanism as an instrument of efficiency and distribution, without state intervention except where it is necessary to ensure fair play and to protect those who can't protect themselves. To achieve these agendas, it requires freedom of movement of goods and services, capital and labour, information and technology across the political boundaries within and outside the region;

(iii) Need to protect the family institution;
(iv) Need to safeguard and to enhance the dignity of the human person by the rule of law, traditional values, education and employment;
(v) Need for strengthening the spirit of local community;
(vi) Need for more just, equal, tolerant and caring societies;
(vii) To promote greater social equity;
(viii) Need to create harmony between man and nature;
(ix) Imperative for generating "cultural synergy";
(x) Need for an open mind.

Although, these concepts look rather utopian in nature, these are representative of the general outlook of the South-east Asian in the context of New World Order.

The countries of South-east Asia in the last four decades, through its regional organization i.e. ASEAN, have not only survived but have developed into an important force internationally. The existence of ASEAN has no doubt played a crucial role in strengthening regional peace and security in South-east Asia. ASEAN realises that there are some differences between its members and in many aspects of life. However, these differences should not restrict the willingness of all ASEAN members to cooperate to achieve common goals based on the ASEAN fundamental principles. Working through practical dialogue and confidence building, no tension has escalated into armed confrontation among ASEAN members since its establishment more than thirty nine years ago. The ASEAN, in retrospect, did suffer the 1997 crises, but ultimately prevailed on it. Thus, the 1997 economic crisis has in fact reduced tensions among members by forcing a reduction in their defence budgets. Moreover, their common difficulties and struggles have strengthened cooperation, solidarity and cohesiveness. The expansion of the ASEAN membership has increased its political bargaining power in the region.

Furthermore, the greatest success of ASEAN has been the peace that has prevailed between member states for the past thirty nine years. This is no doubt a major achievement considering that at one time South-east Asia was viewed as the Balkan of Asia. This happened because it had served as the umbrella for the promotion of cooperation amongst its member nations and helped to manage conflicting and divergent interests. This has been possible since all members of ASEAN, strictly adhered to the principle of non-interference in the internal affairs of any member country. Besides this, the countries of South-east Asia through ASEAN, have been successful in creating and entrenching a habit of regional cooperation among themselves. The members among themselves have always consulted each other prior to any meeting with its dialogue partners. In various areas, regional cooperation has always been evident, such as environment, health, education, trade and industry, prevention of transnational crime, terrorism etc. It has also become the regular practice among the member states of ASEAN to lend support for each other's candidatures in various international organizations.

In the context of new global order, the ASEAN members have responded by striving ever harder to remain attractive to foreign investors, by adopting the ASEAN Free Trade Area (AFTA), which aims to almost eliminate intra-ASEAN trade barriers of 2011. The main rationale for ASEAN has long been to collectively negotiate better terms of trade with the United States and Europe. Adoption of the AFTA in the early 1990s directly responded to the formation of the European Union and the North American Free Trade Agreement (NAFTA). Essentially, the South-east Asian countries realized that they could not maintain attractiveness to foreign investment and trade competitiveness without lowering regional trade barriers. Upto now, these trends can be seen as positive, in the context of expanding positive sum response to globalization. Besides this, the countries of South-east Asia through the ASEAN have recognized early on the growing world of interdependence. To this end, it set out to create linkages with other countries and regions, in both the developed and developing world. ASEAN had thus far established linkages with Australia, Canada, China, Japan, North Korea, the EU, New Zealand,

Russia, India and the United States. In addition, ASEAN member countries were active members of APEC and were instrumental in establishing linkages with Europe and Latin America through the Asia-Europe Meeting (ASEM) and the Forum for East Asia-Latin America Cooperation (FEALAC) respectively.

Further, reflecting its forward looking tendencies, ASEAN has taken the lead in establishing institutional links with the countries of East Asia through the ASEAN + 3 process and with India through the ASEAN + 1 process. Inspired by Malaysian Prime Minister Dr. Mahathir Mohammed's vision of a East Asian Caucus, the countries of the region are slowly moving towards an East Asian Community. The First East Asian Summit meeting, held on 14 December, 2005 among all the economic power houses in East, South-east and South Asia (i.e. ASEAN + 3 + India) besides Australia and New Zealand, was a historic event of regionalism in the context of new global order, for it did not include the EU, Canada and the US, and most of the non-ASEAN members of ARF. Therefore, the East Asian Summit can be viewed as an attempt on the part of ASEAN countries to evolve an alternative path to the US-styled globalization model. These countries have clearly recognized that stronger regionalism remains the only way to brace countries against the powerful winds of globalization. In other words, ASEAN's response to global challenges has come not through national assertiveness, as countries might normally have reacted in the past, but by initiating greater regional integration and cooperation. In the context of globalization which gave rise to the emergence of new regional economic blocks that compete for power and influence, whether this new form of regionalism qualifies as a distinct paradigm apart from the dominant Western (US led) model on the one hand, and different from traditional South — South Cooperation, on the other, remains to be seen.

Conclusion

In this new global order, the countries of South-east Asia, have been, in economic terms, the most dynamic region. Over the past thirty nine years, there have been various bilateral differences and conflicts between ASEAN members, including territorial ones, but those differences and conflicts have been peacefully contained and except for Vietnam and Cambodia, there has been no war in the region. Today, it is difficult to think of military conflicts between ASEAN states. The "ASEAN spirit" or "ASEAN Fundamental Principles" emerged from the manifold meetings among political leaders over the years. Its main principles emphasize personal relationships rather than formal legalistic structures, an informal rather than formal approach to problem-solving and consensus-building. These principles have served the ASEAN well during its turbulent period and explain its successful existence in this complex global order.

Although, the impact of globalization has created a negative response among the members of ASEAN, but its irreversible character in the context of new global order has not been missed altogether. Knowing fully well the dark side of the globalization, as ASEAN progresses with phenomenal economic growth, in this age of technology, it has embraced globalization as a means of conducting its political and economic activities. Although globalization was branded as a cause of the spread of the financial crisis in 1997, but ASEAN, through its comprehensive regional policy achieved economic normalcy to a large extent in the region. It is therefore not difficult to envisage ASEAN holding on to the same principles of consensus that has held the members of ASEAN together since its beginning. This past experience of ASEAN's political will and economic astuteness, is expected to be exerted in the coming days too in response to its emerging threats as well as to establish itself as an alternative model in this rapidly changing global order.

NOTES AND REFERENCES

1. Prasert Chittiwatanapong, "Challenge of the Response to Globalization: The Case of South-east Asia," *www.iuj.ac.ip/research/wpap002.cfm* (2 November, 2005).

2. *Press Release,* Department of Information, Ministry of Foreign Affairs of Thailand, Bangkok, No. 427/2539, pp.1-2.
3. *ASEAN News,* ASEAN Affairs Department, Ministry of Foreign Affairs of Thailand, Bangkok, No. 6, June 1996, p. 2.
4. Samuel P. Huntington, "The West: Unique, Not Universal", Foreign Affairs, November-December, 1996, pp.37—38.
5. *Globalization and the New Realities,* Selected Speeches of Dr. Mahathir Mohammed, Pelanduk Publications (M) Sdn. Bhd, Selangor, Malaysia, 2002, pp. 101–02.
6. *Ibid.,* p. 9.
7. *Ibid.,* p. 99.
8. Riefqi Muna, "Reasons for Regional Instability: Internal Fractures and Crises", *http://216.239.33.104/search?q=cache:ZqmDnupco—IC: www. fesspore.org/pdf/15Muna.pdf.*
9. Tridib Chakraborti, "Terrorism and the ASEAN States: A Classificatory and Prescriptive Analysis," in Omprakash Mishra and Sucheta Ghosh (eds.), *Terrorism and low Intensity Conflict in South Asian Region,* Manak Publications Pvt. Ltd., New Delhi, 2003, p. 330.
10. *Ibid.,* p. 328.
11. *Ibid.,* p. 335.
12. David Brown, *The State and Ethnic Politics in South-east Asia,* Routledge, London, 1994, p. 30.
13. Tridib Chakraborti, n.9, p. 331.
14. See *wwwarc.murdoch.edu.au/wp/wp117.pdf.*
15. In January 1979, Vietnam intervened in Cambodia. During this year, Cambodia was not a member of ASEAN. Cambodia became a permanent member of ASEAN in 1999.
16. Tim Huxley, "Singapore and Malaysia: A Precarious Balance," *Pacific Review,* Vol. 4, No. 3, 1991, p. 210.
17. *The Straits Times,* 4 March, 1986.
18. Tridib Chakraborti, n. 9, p. 337.
19. Paridah Abdul Samad, "Internal Variables of Regional Conflicts in ASEAN's International Relations", *The Indonesian Quarterly,* Vol. 18, No. 2, Second Quarter, 1990, p. 174.
20. Tridib Chakraborti, "The Territorial Claims in South China Sea: Probing Persistent Uncertainties", in Arun Kumar Banerji and Purusottam Bhattacharya (eds.), *Peoples Republic of China At Fifty: Politics, Economy and Foreign Relations,* Lancer's Books, New Delhi, 2001, pp. 192-93.
21. Riefqi Muna, n. 8.
22. Tridib Chakraborti, n.9, pp. 333-34.
23. *Ibid.,* p. 334.
24. The ASEAN-6 countries are Indonesia, Malaysia, Singapore, Thailand, Brunei and the Philippines.

25. For details see *www.aseansec.org*.
26. See the Joint—ASEAN—World Bank Initiative on Mainstreaming Social Development, *www.aseansec.org*.
27. For details see the *ASEAN Secretariat Press Release*, "ASEAN and UNDP team upto promote regional development and integration", 18 June, 2001.
28. *ASEAN: An Overview*, ASEAN Secretariat, Jakarta, 1995, p. 56.
29. Nayan Chanda and Shada Islam, "In the Bunker", *Far Eastern Economic Review*, 6 August, 1998, p. 24.
30. Tridib Chakraborti, n. 9, p. 339.
31. Daljit Singh, "South-east Asian in 1999: A False Dawn?", *South-east Asian Affairs: 2000*, Institute of South-east Asian Studies, Singapore, 2000, p. 6.
32. Tridib Chakraborti, n. 9, p. 340.

16

Reflections on Issues of Post-coloniality and International Relations in Africa

MURINDWA RUTANGA

Introduction

Historiographical traditions have a way of going into hibernation, shedding their aged and hideous scales, and beginning life anew, ready to spit the same old poison. That is what seems to have happened to imperialist historiography, dealt crushing blows in the 1960s and 1970s by nationalist and Marxist historians. The partial, but powerful, images that dominated the world's media in the 1980s and early 1990s, of a continent wracked by coups, chaos, and carnage, of people dying from drought and disease, and countries collapsing under the weight of state corruption and coercion, provided a fertile ground for the resurgence of crude, rabidly racist perceptions of Africa. And like vultures smelling death, supply-side bankers, with IMF or World Bank attaché cases, sanctimonious western politicians, award-seeking journalists, self-appointed 'aid' missionaries, and even publicity-starved "pop stars", descended on the continent for their pound of flesh. In this atmosphere, imperialist historiography and neo-classical developmentalism flourished. [Tiyambe, Paul Zeleza (1997) Manufacturing African Studies and Crises. Dakar: CODESRIA]

Africa's integration into the western capitalist project began with the Europeans' travelling to a land that they soon named

America, killed the indigenous owners of the land and took over the land and other resources. It was soon after that Africa was drawn and integrated into the service of western capitalism: first when it was transformed into a source of profitable human cargo to America, then as a producer of raw materials for Europe and lastly as a producer of products for all the imperialists in the World. The centrality of this globalising agenda goes beyond the colonial compulsions of production and export of raw materials such as cotton, cocoa, coffee, timber and tobacco, uranium, tantalite, diamond and gold to modern slave labour by the willing economic refugees through brain drain which they labelled brain gain while locally it is known as the *Nkabakyeyos*. These range from child and adult female sex slavery to intellectuals.

Any reflections on issues of post-coloniality and International Relations in Africa *ipso facto* require one to begin by reflecting historically, materialistically, dialectically and philosophically on the *locus* and importance of Africa within the imperialist agenda since Columbus' accidental landing on the lands that the Europeans had the audacity to relegate to themselves powers to rename it America. This therefore, calls for an epistemological navigation back to the 15th century. It is such a historicisation that will enable this study to grasp the reasons that underlay western imperialism in invading Africa, globalising* it and integrating it into the western capitalist project. All this was achieved by first transforming Africa into a depository of profitable human cargo for selling to America to service capitalist interests in America and Europe.

Without going into the debates regarding the primitivity, barbarism and positivities of this five-century old slave trade, we need to recognise though in passing the fact that this trade brought enormous profits to the slave merchants and their

* Here, we use the concept globalisation not in its current usage of "global lies" about global village "global pillage", with imperialism masquerading as a "partner in development" with its victim. We instead use it in its etymological, non-ideologised and racialised sense to mean the process through which Africa was opened up for international capitalist exploitation.

home countries; it enriched the slave economies with robust labour. This labour from Africa was highly skilled and experienced in, *inter alia*, agriculture, mining and smithing. It thus possessed what capitalism desperately needed for its extractive purposes: resources for export to the then highly developed capitalistic Europe. It is this historical approach that will unravel the new inter-imperialist contradictions, which came to maturation in America's declaration of independence in 1776, and the subsequent war of liberation. It is this approach that will unravel how all these developments gave rise to new dynamics that compelled Europe to search for other reliable, alternative sources of cheap raw materials; and how this search brought Africa once again into a firm imperialist grip (Beaud, Michael, 1984). The inherent contradictions characterising capitalism, and those between capitalism and labour, and the new challenges of the newly formed European nations combined to expose the genesis and materiality of imperialism in form of colonialism.

Britain, by then the leading industrial power in the world— dubbed the workshop of Europe — was setting the pace for imperialism. It took initiatives to block any more capturing and trading in slaves. This had been a very lucrative trade, which Britain had up to then held so dear and from where most of British capital had been raised. It had now turned round and designed a new capitalist exploitative project, which entailed enslaving the Africans onto their own lands to serve its interests. This was a very profitable venture with minimal costs. Why? The Africans would provide their own resources, tools, supervision, accommodation, food, etc. to produce the required raw materials. It is this approach that will help this study to understand the imperialist exploitative and oppressive roles and the people's anti-imperialist struggles up to independence. It is also this approach which will enable this study to understand the new dynamics of imperialism in post-coloniality, the reasons why Africa has not managed to reclaim its independent positionality, push for its interests internationally, influence and regulate international relations, interrogate and rupture the existing paradigms and espouse new discourses that would be based on local conditions and praxes.

As a point of reminder to the readership, this study is neither oblivious of Africa's enormous contributions to the world, given that Africa is the origin of human beings. It follows logically therefore that it is the origin of human civilization and development, socio-political, epistemological, religious, superstitious, magical, philosophical and dialectical constructions and advancements. Nor is it blind to the factuality regarding Africa's invasion of Europe in 711 AD and the establishment of the Moorish Empire, which lasted up to 1492 (John Jackson, 1970; Patrick Tabaaro, 2004; Anta Cheikh Diop, 1991). Given the shortage of time and space in this paper, the focus of this study will be restricted to post-coloniality or neo–coloniality — a period of the reign of multilateral imperialism. Kwame Nkrumah had defined it as the last stage of imperialism.

For purposes of this study, we shall begin with a short historical review of imperialist military invasion of Africa, which helped to expose Africa to the vicious exploitation of western capitalism — a western globalising agendum. It will historicise the ravages of imperialism up to the contemporary epoch, which the west in its totalising and universalising approach has branded globalisation.

Initial European Globalisation of Africa through Slave Trade

The first question to reflect on is about the relationship between Africa and the capitalist west. In terms of factuality, Africa was transformed into an overflowing granary or depository of resources for the capitalist west. Given their differing modes of production, and Africa's innumerable problems — most of which stemmed from the inhuman slave trade — Europe bombarded it into submission to serve its higher order (Jean Suret-Canale, 1988; Walter Rodney, 1972). This needs historicizing.

The first major external assault and massive plunder of resources from Africa came in the cruellest mercantilist capitalism of slave trade. While not blind to the Trans-Saharan slave trade that predominated from around the seventh century and the subsequent Eastern African slave trade from around the twelfth century, the indiscriminate capitalist Trans-Atlantic slave trade from 1490s to 1880s wrecked persistent havoc all over the continent. Credit goes to the Africanist scholars – mainly of the dependency discourse for their epistemological commitment and invaluable intellectual contributions in unearthing archival materials on this man-made horrendous catastrophe for Africa. Among these was Walter Rodney (1972) who brought out shocking data of the millions of Africans who were shipped as human cargo to America and those that died in this whole chaos. The reader should not lose sight of the fact that these merchants also made these slaves carriers of other merchandise from Africa. Examples included ivory and skins, vegetation resources and minerals. This marked double exploitation in which human cargo carried other merchandise for the slave merchants. Needless to say, this trade had untold adverse and tragic consequences on the whole continent (Walter Rodney, 1972, 1978; Basil Davidson, 1992; Diop, 1973). They killed through raids; others were attacked and killed or injured by ferocious animals while fleeing the slave raiders or hiding in forests; many others died of diseases occasioned by those insecurity-situations, lack of shelter, food, medicines, etc. Famines became permanent occurrences. All these went on unchecked until the late 1880s.

Transforming Africa from Being Sources of Human Cargo to Producers of Raw Materials

The inter-capitalist contradictions between the emerging American capitalism and the hegemonised exploitative European capitalism, together with the dynamics in industrial Europe combined to give rise to European colonisation of Africa. Colonialism in Africa was a form of European imperialism that lasted until the 1960s. This excludes many settler colonies. Examples included the Portuguese colonies of Mozambique, Angola, Namibia, Guinea Bissau and Cape Verde, and the British Settler colonies of Zimbabwe and South

Africa. The Colonised Africans in these colonies had to wage arduous militant wars until when they won their independence, the last being South Africa just over a decade ago, in 1994.

The political economy of colonialism involved a people of a higher level of production invading a people occupying a lower level of production and development, fighting, and defeating them, disorganizing and reorganizing them to serve alien material interest. In other words, colonial imperialism implies people occupying a higher position subordinating those of a lower order to serve their material, economic, political and social interests. It is this, which explains the vicious, virulent and cruel character of European colonisation in Africa (Frantz Fanon,1966).

What needs to be clarified is that to achieve capitalist material interests at that historical material time required occupation of physical space. The main imperialist requirement at the 1884/85 Berlin Conference was for the occupation of territoriality by the capitalist powers before making any territorial claims. Colonisation entailed struggles over territoriality or physical space, political spaces, economic spaces, medicinal spaces, and other spheres — whether of sociality, or religiosity, epistemological, conceptual, magical, superstitious or philosophical, zoological, botanical, etc. In other words, the materiality of colonial imperialism involves not only occupation and domination and controlling the material aspects of the conquered peoples but also other aspects of their lives: ontological, metaphysical, philosophical, nutritional, inspirational, etc. (Mahmood Mamdani,1976, 1984, 1994, 1996: Basil Davidson, 1992; Murindwa-Rutanga, 1991, 1994, 1999; Jean Suret-Canale, 1988; Partha Chatterjee. 1993; H. Jaffe, 1985; John Iliffe, 1969).

These works explain in detail the forceful and merciless colonial occupation of the physical, territorial, political, economic, spiritual and epistemological aspects of the colonized peoples. Partha Chatterjee brings a contrary dialectical scenario between colonialism and nationalism within the economic, socio-cultural, religious and intellectual domains in colonial India. It is this dialectical relationship between the colonialists and the nationalists, and the Hindu leadership that kept off imperialism from much of the Indians' social and cultural domains. Regarding Africa, Mamdani (1996) unravels the imperialist mechanics in their colonial project, the political explanation for adopting of indirect rule following the Indian Mutiny of 1857 and the despotic character of this form of governmentality. He exposes the despotic character of this colonial project, which he terms "decentralized despotism". Here, one of the most memorable, dreaded examples in Uganda is Bigwera, a petty colonial chief who ruled some parishes in southern Kigezi. Though a petty chief, he extracted maximum benefits from whoever was under his jurisdiction. Though long time dead, he is still feared. Old women still living do not wish to be reminded of him. Men dreadfully talk about him with seething anger. Women were forced to compose obscene songs, sing in chorus and dance in praise of Bigwera's masculinity in bed with them. All women would have to stop whatever they were doing whenever Bigwera's entourage passed, carrying him in *engozi,* (a carrier woven like a stretcher to carry chiefs, brides, or the sick). His despotic activities and compulsions can only be understood through the Fanonian explication of how colonial imperialism inflicted psychological violence on the minds of the colonized peoples. To accomplish this, colonialism applied a multi-barrelled approach. This included balkanization of territories and societies, and combining incongruent peoples and societies under the same rule. To demonstrate this, while the minute Belgium could curve out, claim and exploit the whole of the Congo — by then including Congo Kinshasa, Congo Brazzaville and other territories as its colony; Germany's imperial claims over Rwanda left out certain peoples formerly of Rwandese origin and relationship in Congo, Burundi, Tanzania and Uganda.

Another aspect was the imperialist re-organization of the newly created economies into import-export economies. Through this process, imperialism integrated them into what the dependency discourse termed the metropolitan capitalist systems. With time, this colonial distortion transformed these countries into permanent producers of what they did not consume and consumers of what they did not produce. The negativities of colonial rule, its dislocation of the colonies, the colonized peoples' knowledge systems, industrialization, commerce and trade, intellectuals and professionals, artisans and other skilled peoples, etc. impaired and blocked Africa's possibilities of influencing international relations. As Frantz Fanon demonstrated, this colonial system was violence and it had to be maintained by violence. The explanation for this was that the colonized peoples were contesting it bitterly, using a multiplicity of struggles. (Mahmood Mamdani, 1996; Murindwa-Rutanga, 1991, 1992, 1999)

All these so far demonstrate how Africa was not the subject or the main actor in this imperialist relationship. Africa was drawn in as a victim and it could at best influence the events and their course only through resistance. Whether the Nyabingi Movement, (Karen E.F. 1985, Murindwa-Rutanga, 1991), the Watch Tower Movement (David, Lan 1985), the Mau Mau Movement (Carothers 1954, Throup, W. David 1988, Gakaara wa Wanjau 1988, Karogo, T. 1987), the Algerian War of Independence (Ian Clegg, 1971) or the guerrilla wars in Guinea Bissau and Cape Verde (Cabral, Amilcar, 1969), Zimbabwe (T. Ranger 1985), or the latest forms of anti-colonial struggles as in South Africa up to 1994 (Davies, R. 1984), they could inform the new courses of history and change them but they could not determine the nature of international relations in those colonies. To demonstrate this, despite the strong workers' voice for independence in the Congress of South African Trade Unions (COSATU) and other workers' organizations in South Africa, together with the African National Congress mass membership and the revolutionary voice of Pan African Congress and other parties, still, they were the white minorities who determined the nature and course of international relations. We need not forget that up to independence in 1994, the Anglo-American multi-national corporations were controlling over 84 per cent of the investments in South Africa. One would wonder as to how much has changed since then and in whose favour.

The Price of Sliding from Coloniality to Post-coloniality

The dynamics and conclusion of the Second World War transformed the colonial powers into vulnerable objects of attack. Inside the colonies emerged anti-colonial militant struggles. Then, there were pushes by the unkind US for open door policy. In addition was the Soviet Union's diplomatic pushes especially at the UN. These compelled the colonial powers to grant independence to the colonised peoples. However, the practice proved that the new independent states were no different from the colonial states. The change was in running the system. Local faces replaced the Europeans though most of those in the civil service were retained through a new ploy under the rubric of Africanisation process that followed. The new leadership still lacked initiative, independent decisions, vision, ideological clarity and cognitive praxis. It is this which largely explains why there was no radical break with imperialism when African countries got independence. It is this, which explains why the former colonial powers were the first countries to establish diplomatic relations with these newly independent countries and were the first to open up embassies there. The reality was that this was a legitimate way of opening headquarters for intelligence network and spying in these newly independent states. They would also use these headquarters to plot mischief and sabotage against these new states.

To demonstrate this, it was Britain, the former colonial power over Uganda, which opened the first diplomatic relations with Uganda at independence. This is evidenced by the registration of the Diplomatic cars. The registration of British cars in independent Uganda starts with CD 01. Any wonder that this vehicle numbering is followed by the US imperialist power, whose vehicle registration starts with CD 02. Then the other European imperialist powers followed. These car numbers demonstrate very clearly two things. First is that the former colonial powers did not leave their former colonies. They instead disguised themselves under the cloak of diplomacy. It is through such changing of colours like chameleons rather than their roles and *modus operandi* that Belgium played a central role in the liquidating of Patrice Lumumba, the first democratically elected Prime Minister of the Congo, and ousted his government. Secondly, the other imperialist powers rushed to these newly independent countries with exploitative purpose. This was a new phase of multilateral imperialism, where the former colonies, which had been retained as personal properties of the individual colonial powers, were now opened up for all forms of imperialist exploitation. This was simplified by the fact that the physical presence of the imperialist powers in form of colonialism was neither welcome nor tenable. Rather, the World Bank settled in their stead, supported by the UN and its numerous arms. This however, would lead to a new complex crisis of imperialist exploitation without accountability.

Unlike countries like USA and Norway, both of which got independent economically and politically, the USA in 1776 and Norway in 1905, the independence which was granted to the African peoples was in form of political power without economic power. This *nouveau* rush by so many imperialist powers to get their share in these newly independent countries created a problem for the latter regarding consolidation of their independence. Given their lack of a coherent national bourgeoisie in control of the economy and their national politics, the post-independence leadership inherited the anti-people colonial state machinery without any critical positive modification. Worse still, they inherited the import-export economy without any critical reflections on how to redirect or revolutionize it to serve the national interests. In other words, there was absence of a nationalist project and a nationalist programme. The crisis for these countries stemmed from the lack of strong foundations. Imperialism had weeded out or sidelined any leadership that had demonstrated any nationalist foresight, preaching or leanings towards nationalism. The list of those that this vicious imperialism weeded out is long and painful as virtually every colony paid the price. On top of the list are Patrice Lumumba and Kwame Nkrumah, the two democratically elected leaders. These two were committed to the total liberation of Africans and were working tirelessly towards a free United States of Africa. The list, which includes Stephen Biko, Mondlane, Machel and Karekyezi, is unending. Those who, though sidelined, had been struggling to liberate their countries returned from the bushes to experience a multitude of new frustrations. They were sidelined right from the beginning constitutionally as well as through power distribution arrangements. They found power being handed over to the petty bourgeoisie, a class that had been sewing imperialism. It had also harboured dreams of sitting in the places of the colonizers and take over whatever the Bazungu owned. This class had no plans of handing over land to the masses, creating jobs for them, let alone effecting any social transformation for the vast majority. Most of these returnees ended in jail and others returned to the forests. Many of them lost hope and lived miserable lives till death. Ignatius Musaazi from Uganda remained a good example. He started his anti-colonial struggles in the 1920s, organized farmers in the 1930s, organized workers in Tanzania and engineered the strikes of 1940s. He founded the UNC in 1952 and opened with others UNC offices in Cairo. He was marginalized in the politics of independence and died a miserable death in late 1980s. The only memorable act was to bury him in the heroes' corner at Kololo Independence ground.

Contrary to these negative developments, independence had held enormous promises for the decolonising Africans. These included increased freedom, increased material well-being and development without toil. Their utopia included a time of bliss without colonial, foreign or domestic domination, forced labour, taxation, without public executions, public Kibooko floggings and other forms of state instituted brutalities, oppression and exploitation. They envisioned a society of progress, where their children would go to good schools and study up to the highest levels; where they would control their land and determine the nature of production, without repressive laws and punitive measures — whether relating to production of export crops, processing or marketing.

Crisis of Post-coloniality

Post-coloniality was marked by a serious absence of committed organic intellectuals to plan and effect social transformation. The new leadership that assumed power had been groomed in the colonial schools, missionary teachings and bureaucracies. They constituted a *nouveau* cadreship that had been longing for western lifestyles, thinking and practices. Many of them had been to Europe, on guided tours, or studied there; others had read the corrupting western literature that was ideologically riddled or had watched ideologically packaged western films that were depicting European modernity. Still others had read the wonderful stories about its modernity. Programmed theories were being obeyed all over the continent. Among these was the US constructed modernization theorization, which preached how to move societies from situations of lack to stages of high mass consumption à la Rostowian theorisation. (W.W. Rostow, 1960; S.P. Huntington, 1961; Goran Hyden, 1980, 1980; Bates, 1981). These western intellectualizations and constructions were meant to provide the modular of the societies these new rulers were supposed to construct. All this ideological exposition had a great bearing on the new leadership. They became more inclined towards development of their societies along the European paths. This was consolidated by the modernization discourse, which was being imported wholesale from the US and was implemented uncritically. It was the purveyance of a glorious and fascinating future that largely explained why the newly independent African countries embraced the modernization discourse. Needles to say, this discourse constituted a very highly ideologised, utopianised and romanticized theorization and political programme. It had within it empty trappings and rhetoric of rapid modernity and development without toil. It provided romantic solutions without risks and or hard work. Strange as it may sound, resources and other ingredients for modernity and development were supposed to flow in from without while the population sat back and enjoyed the benefits. In other words, it was a developmentalist project without the people. Aid, loans, grants and capital would come in and do miracles in the classical, biblical sense.

Unfortunately for Africa, the new African leadership and intelligentsia embraced this project without subjecting it to criticality. As if very late for something very important, no one ever questioned its ideological import, let alone its political, economic and imperialistic mission. This whole process had the negative effect of depriving Africa of any initiatives — political, economic, epistemological, philosophical or ideological. It instead helped the west to maintain and consolidate its monopoly of production and dissemination of epistemes, ideas, information, medicine, policies, etc. It helped the west to retain its unquestionable epistemic domains, which provided stability to its citadels of knowledge and epistemologies instead of destabilization that could have resulted in paradigmatic interrogations, instabilities and shifts. This detained African intellectualization in marginality and invisibility within the periphery. In the process, it continued to deny African intellectuals a central locus within the continent. All these denials had negative consequences of dwarfing African intellectualisation. It also denied the African intelligentsia class and practitioners a platform for effective participation in international relations, and in generating knowledges and theories about it. The Africans had rare opportunities only at the UN and its related institutions such as the GATT. Internally, they constructed others such as the Organisation of African Unity (OAU), the East African Community (EAC) and Economic Commission of West African States (ECOWAS).

The Betrayals of Independence and their Negation

It needs to be noted at this stage that the continuous uncritical wholesale implementation of the modernization theory led African countries into heavy indebtedness. Coupled with this was the widespread irresponsible, non-accountable corrupt leadership, and all these made the African countries lose credibility. These gradually became crucial interstices for the imperialist west to make giant steps and begin dictating over these countries. Added to this was the US intervention and spreading of the cold war. This provided a justification and an occasion for the US to begin propping up and grooming dictatorships in Africa. These were a *sine qua non* for the longevity of its imperialist oppression as these dictatorships began to depoliticise, traumatize the population in a bid to containerize them, keep them meek, docile and submissive without raising questions or trying to shift loyalty to the Soviet Union. Topical among these were Presidents Idi Amin Dada of Uganda, Mobutu of the then Zaire — now the Democratic Republic of Congo, Macias Nguema of Equatorial Guinea, Bokassa of Central Africa, Saidi Barre of Somalia, Houphouët-Boigny of Côte D'Ivoire and Kamuzu H. Banda of Malawi. Most of these were military elites, a category which one strand of the modernization discourse had identified as the modernizers. This was premised on the ground that they controlled the coercive machinery to enforce law and order.

Contrary to this discourse's promises, these military elites suppressed the masses and unleashed state terror upon the population. They exhibited extreme hostilities towards their people, negated their concerns, became insensitive to their wishes and demands. Their actions led to the hijacking of the states. They became synonymous or surrogates of the state. In Mobutu's words, he was the state. As President Idi Amin declared himself life President of Uganda and Conqueror of the British Empire, President Mobutu declared himself the State, and President Bokassa crowned himself emperor. Macius Nguema reached extremes by massacring hundreds of school children for refusing to wear uniforms bearing his portrait. This category of dictators became insensitive to the sufferings of the subalterns. Whether stemming from military background or emerging through democratic elections, the attention of this leadership was on rapid primitive accu-mulation of wealth from above. They used state power for their capital accumulation drives. To achieve this required them to deny people their democratic rights. Whatever they wanted could be achieved by force. Anybody who questioned their actions was a saboteur, sabotaging the nationalist project. The imperialist west was more than willing to facilitate them with whatever they desired — materially, economically, technologically, diplomatically, militarily or in terms of espionage, intelligence equipment and skills, etc. Given the raging cold war, the external environment was favourable to them. It is a combination of these negativities that largely explain the continued conspicuous absence of coherent movements in these countries during the Cold War (Jean François Bayart, 1993, 1999; Mamdani, 1983, 1996, 2001; Nzongola — Ntalaja, 1999, 2001; Claude Ake, 2000) etc. It would not be farfetched and false to opine that it is this containerizing the discontented and aggrieved societies for so long under the dictatorial machinery of the neo-colonial states and the imperialists that led some individuals to emerge as war lords after the waning of the cold war and wreck anarchical insurgencies in their societies. The politics of oppression, neglect and exclusionism ended up creating grounds for dissension.

What needs to be explained here is the new dynamics in post US — SU inter-imperialist rivalry. The collapse of the Soviet Union had brought with it the collapse of the Eastern Bloc. This was depicted through the breaking down of the Berlin Wall. This development had four important consequences. First, it temporarily shifted the world order from a bipolar order to a unipolar order, where the US temporarily became the only major actor. This temporality became an occasion for it to begin bullying and threatening the whole world. However, it also became an occasion for other capitalist economies including China to increase their chances of taking over the Soviet Union's place. Second, it effaced the usefulness of the imperialist support for dictators in the third world. In the process, the west shifted its focus from the developing countries to Eastern Europe. With no communist threat to overrun the world, Africa no longer mattered to the capitalist world. This then had the effect of obliterating any possibilities of maneuverability, which the developing countries had previously maximized between the US and the SU. Lastly, it ushered in profound changes in international relations.

Crisis of Militarized Conflicts in Africa

Africa in post-coloniality has been a terrain characterized by murderous anarchical conflicts. Every region of Africa has had its share in this. Right from RENAMO in Mozambique to UNITA in Angola, Gibeny's Movement in the Congo, Charles Tailor in Liberia to Foday Sankoh in Sierra Leone, and Said Barre in Somalia, plus the secession struggles in Ethiopia and Sudan, and the genocide in Rwanda. In the Great Lakes Region, it had to take the Tanzanian state and Ugandan guerrillas to fight and defeat the military dictatorship under Idi Amin Dada in Uganda. Not long after, a guerrilla Movement – the National Resistance Movement (NRM) had to be launched and it used Maoist guerrilla tactics to fight and defeat the fascist dictatorships that succeeded the Amin dictatorship. Thereafter, it had to take a faction of the NRM to form a guerrilla force – the Rwanda Patriotic Front (RPF) – and invade Rwanda in October 1990 to oust the Havyarimana dictatorial regime. The RPF was a struggle, which at the inception was expected to be a walkover to Kigali, 85 miles from the border where they launched their invasion. Contrary to the invaders' expectations, those within the RPF leadership who survived death had to change from conventional tactics to guerrilla tactics, after experiencing enumerable human losses. This was a war that claimed not only over one million lives of Africans but also of many European soldiers. It was a war characterized by enormous losses in form of human beings through a horrendous genocide, (Mamdani, 2001) resources and military equipment. What needs to be noted here is that this war constituted a prelude to a major military adventure against the Mobutu regime in the Congo. Having defeated and thrown out the Havyarimana's government, the Rwanda Patriotic Army (RPA) combined with the National Resistance Army (NRA) and invaded the Congo. Their purported object was to remove the Mobutu dictatorship from power. They travelled thousands of kilometers from the eastern Congolese border and toppled Mobutu's dictatorial regime. The question is why they could defeat the Zaïrean forces so easily.

We need to face the reality that the Congolese Defence Forces were ill equipped and ill-prepared for war. They depicted a sorry state which was a clear reflection of the leadership's betrayal of Africa. The leadership had neglected them. It failed to remunerate them properly in the face of the hyperinflation, which had eroded the salaries and wages and ruined the national economy. Though Mobutu had the elite guard to protect him and his family, he left the business of the war and national defence in the hands of the mercenaries. True to Niccolò Machiavelli's advice, the mercenaries whom Mobutu had hired fled whenever they heard that the invading forces were approaching their positions. This reflected the level to which Africa had stooped — people who were struggling against whites the other day now hiring white mercenaries to defend them. The overthrow of Mobutu's military dictatorship became grounds for new conflicts. Kabira's installation to power created new contradictions with the joint Rwanda-Uganda forces. He immediately sought military assistance from Zimbabwe, Angola and Namibia to chase away these "external forces" from Congo in 1998. This move created new grounds for the rise of a bitter war between the joint Rwanda-Ugandan forces against the Congo government forces. This war was launched from the eastern border of Congo. The invading allied forces could not have a second walkover to Kinshasa. They still encountered resistance from the Congolese forces supported by allied forces from Zimbabwe, Angola and Namibia. This impasse gradually created sharp differences amongst the allied forces. Each of them began to set up new movements in Congo. Among these was the Rally for Congolese Democracy, which gradually became the leading opposition organisation in Congo. (Sunday Vision, June, 2005). What came to pass was the fulfillment of the African proverbial endless war that leads to the humiliation of the invincible and courageous warriors. In this particular war, it did not take long before the allied Rwandese forces and the Ugandan forces fought amongst themselves three times in Kisangani. It is alleged that the first round in 1999 left over 200 soldiers dead on both sides, while the second clash the following year left 70 soldiers dead.

(Sunday Vision of June 5, 2005). It was these clashes in Kisangani that exposed the souring relations between Rwanda and Uganda and created an enormous rift in the Uganda-Rwanda relations. Some pessimists have depicted all these negative developments in Africa right from the 1970s to the present as Africa's lost decades. The view of this study is that though they constitute negativities, without major signs of progressive movements, they still reflected signs of internal capacities to resist negative forces. They also reflected the capacity of the African peoples to survive in cruel circumstances. They however deprived the continent of the capacities, time, resources and attention to focus on international relations and shape them, whether at the local level of theory, discipline and/or practice. They have continued to threaten and project Africa as a disintegrating continent, full of wars, famines, crises, poverty and hopelessness instead of an integrating one. The west has been at the forefront of these false and baseless depictions.

****

They are these internal weaknesses which to some extent explain why the African nation-states have not developed internal, regional and/or continental mechanisms for resolving their various contradictions. Their common approach is to appeal to imperialist powers led by the US and the global financial institutions to intervene wherever they are confronted by problems — socio-political, economic or epistemological. The Uganda-Rwanda conflict in Kisangani demonstrates this very clearly. Contrary to expectations, Uganda and Rwanda had to appeal to Britain for intervention to resolve their Kisangani conflictual relations. A conflict between neo-colonies had to be settled by an imperialist power, which was their historical enemy. In this spirit, the Presidents of Uganda and Rwanda had to fly to Britain to present their defence and await the verdict and Britain's subsequent intervention. This left out all the other African states. This is reflective of Africa's international relations in post-coloniaty. However, these conflicts in the post-cold war period are building a strong case for Africa's active participation in international relations. There have been enormous opportunities extended beyond the militarized politics to the political, diplomatic and epistemological arenas. However, these opportunities seem to have been lost. The conflicts in Liberia and Sierra Leone seem to provide a better example (Ibrahim Abdullah 2004). This is where the West African States organized, under Economic Community of West African States Ceasefire Monitoring Group (ECOMOG) to intervene in these conflicts. They are such local, regional, continental initiatives that are crucial, sometimes with external support. This approach should be applied to try and halt the tragic bloodletting in Darfur, Sudan where African states have so far failed to provide prompt and appropriate intervention to save lives of people and property. In other words, Africa has to move from incompetence, inaction, lack of initiatives to a new proactive approach aimed at active participation in local, regional, continental and global matters.

The Cost of Debt Bondage

One of the main markers of the transition from coloniality to post-coloniality was the *nouveau* entanglement of the newly independent states into the debt trap designed by imperialists. That is why all African countries in post-coloniality have become victims of the trap, which was set by the modernization paradigm. While duping and misadvising the decolonising countries that the solution to all the problems that they were facing and any future ones lay in acquiring external loans, aid and grants for modernity, this theory never revealed to them the innumerable dangers which were lurking underneath. In other words, it preached the sweetness of honey in a beehive while deliberately hiding from the inexperienced audience crucial information regarding the killing stings of bees poised to kill whoever ventured to *okuhakuura* — to harvest honey from beehives.

Thus, Africa's crises were compounded by the debt traps set by the imperialist west — mainly through the World Bank, the International Monetary Fund (IMF), USAID etc. Worse still, most of the externally borrowed money was not put to use as originally planned. Given the coldwar context and its usefulness to the US, there was no one in Africa who would raise a finger when the politicians of the day salted away money for their own use. Mobutu and S. Abacha's externalization of the accumulated wealth in billions of dollars bears sufficient credence. This corrupt and corrupting situation opened the floodgates for all forms of malpractices. It is not surprising therefore, that these countries began to experience persistent economic, political and epistemological crises. The situation has ever since been worsening to the extent that many national budgets are largely foreign funded. For instance, 48 per cent of Uganda's recurrent expenditure is covered by money from donors. Contrary to expectations of decreasing the debts, they are on alarming increase. There is heavy foreign funding for unnecessary, non-productive ventures such as civic education for elections and for electoral and other political and non-political activities. No wonder therefore that a small country like Uganda owes the international community over five billion dollars.

All this heavy indebtedness and dependence on external sources put into question the issue of freedom of African countries to take actions that were independent of the western donors. At the epistemological and informational levels, it is an intellectual shock that epistemes are being imported wholesale from without, mainly from the west, without any inputs and initiatives from Africa. African intellectuals and practitioners are placed in incapacitating *loci*, just waiting for the imported finished products, packaged either in book or journal form, internet, films, or reports. There seems to be a conspiracy to continue keeping away the local intellectuals and researchers from organic and professional intellectualisation and cognitive praxis. The ploys include the heavily funded though useless consultancies and short-term research projects that are already defined and answered by the funders themselves. There are concerted efforts to transform African universities into consultancy bureaus to gather valueless or common knowledge information and data that in most cases are irrelevant to the societal needs and even to the funders. A lot of money is being flooded all over the continent to lure and derail committed professors, intellectuals and researchers from serious, organic, relevant intellectual work and researches to energy and time consuming, useless though well-paid pseudo-researches. The most crippling aspect is that the hired researchers find the research projects already defined, problematized and answered by the funders. Even most of the research results are provided in the proposal before the research is undertaken. What they are praying for so heavily is for the researcher to endorse and authenticate them. Worse still, most of the research findings end up being piled up without any reading or follow-up. (Micere Githae Mugo, 2005).

Another harmful development is that a lot of external money is pumped into government departments and ministries. This money is then availed to junior staff and/or fresh graduates and other amateurs to conduct surveys or rural rapid appraisals. These junior researchers and technical staff then bring back whatever information they come across. Their funders then use these findings as the authentic and credible data to confront and fight, discredit and dismiss research findings and conclusions drawn from long-term researches by local professors, intellectuals and senior researchers. In explaining this new phenomenon, Rutabajuuka, the Executive Director of the Centre for Basic Research showed that money had become an opium that detracted ongoing basic researches. This is in line with what Mamdani had underlined in the early 1990s when he dismissed the donors' intentions to transform research institutes in developing countries into surrogates for universities. By then still Executive Director of the Centre for Basic Research, he had explained to those donors that research institutes could not be substitutes for universities whether in research, teaching and/or dissemination of researched knowledge.

Unfortunate as it may be, the same donor thinking is crippling local intellectual efforts. Donor money is flooding the leading universities in Africa albeit not to augment the resilient though very poorly funded research efforts but to derail them and any other intellectual and epistemological projects by committed local scholars, intellectuals and practitioners. Another method being used to push African intellectuals and universities from knowledge production is being spearheaded by the World Bank, IMF, intellectuals and journalists. They have mounted a crusade to force African universities to abandon their duty of knowledge production and teaching students how to think and start on a new one of teaching skills for the local needs. Fascinating as it may sound, it remains shallow and dangerous. On the whole, all these have enormous long- erm crippling effects not only on research and knowledge production but also on the country, its unity, its nationalist project and even on the research institutions themselves.

Other problems continent-wide include the uncritical implementation of neo-liberal theories and policies which were espoused and dictated by the World Bank, the IMF etc. In the name of its "New World Order", the West is pushing the post-colonial states into oblivion through its ahistorical and anti-dialectical dictates of "rolling back the state." This project is not aimed at fulfilling the Marxian prediction of the withering away of the state and bureaucracy to give way to communism but this theorization seems to be guided by malice and racism. It seems to be following the law of displacement, whose object is to take over all the spaces earlier controlled by the states and all their organs. This marks a major shift from the Benthamite utilitarianism to the Lockean profit maximization project. The invention and deployment of NGOs in all domains all over the continent constitutes another imperialist agenda and machination aimed at weakening and effacing the African states. Although the inventors and beneficiaries of this subversive category of NGOs treasure them as *magic bullets*, peoples in Africa have concluded that they are *Nothing Going On*. Their object is to dominate and take control of Africa and its resources. Their object is to try and replace the African states, which had been discredited before the people when dictatorships in Africa received imperialist acclamation, support and resources to negate people's concerns, suppress democratic struggles and demands. Given the exposure of the direct role of imperialism during the dictatorships, the imperialist west found it imperative to hide behind NGOs. What needs to be noted is that most of these NGOs get their funding from western states and related organs. As such, they are averse to Africa's rights, well-being and development, indeed negative and hostile to its independence and sovereignty.

Another problem stems from the subversive and direct interference of the western powers in any situation where Africans try to generate independent solutions and successes. Examples include Algeria, Angola, Zimbabwe and Mozambique where western imperialism played very destabilizing and crippling roles. This is well brought out by Amilcar Cabral (1969).

Another problem stems from the gradual shift of the *loci* of power from Africa to the donor countries. Increasing external indebtedness has *inter alia* resulted in a crisis of self-negation. Africans are losing confidence in themselves. This is leading to their vulnerability. It creates a tendency of impatience and intolerance amongst the politicians and rulers to internal criticisms or dissension. As Thomas Y. Clive (1984) shows, this breeds authoritarianism. State repression and suppression become rife and the situation degenerates to dictatorship. The states feel that they are besieged; they begin to externalize search for friendship, alliances or support and end up in a destructive embrace with imperialism. This interstice enables the latter to increase its leverage over them. It increases its subversion of their political and economic decisions. These include budgetary, monetary, fiscal and other policy aspects. It is common knowledge that annual national budgets of many of these countries are now made in Washington and then flown into these countries on the budget day for reading to parliaments and subsequent implementation. This is normally achieved through the collaboration of some highly-placed blue-eyed boys and girls of IMF and World Bank in the critical sectors of national Finance and Treasury in these countries. The monolithic, neo-liberal structural adjustment problems — initially introduced as programmes but ended creating problems and themselves becoming problems – and their implementation in all the developing countries demonstrate this very clearly. What is most heartbreaking is that African states seem not to be ready to challenge or shift from the current fallacious, destructive path of the current traumatizing imperialist world disorder.

Following the striking at the deepest heart of the US on September 11, the US set it upon itself to decide for the whole world how they were going to relate with it. This was clearly put by the US President Bush that whoever was not with the US was against it. This in turn left the world with minimal options in determining their international relations. It was the US giant that took it upon itself to dictate how the world would behave without dissension. The US has taken it so far as to dictate to all the airlines to submit lists of their clients booked for travel on their planes long before the flights. Failure to adhere to this would invoke punitive reprisals.

The restrictions of the World Trade Organisation regime, trade related intellectual property rights (TRIPS) and other barriers have created serious problems for the externalized African States. Some openings and avenues to trade and interventions that GATT had been providing have been effaced. It is shocking to find that the only way out is for the outsiders to feel so sympathetic and demonstrate against western imperialism on behalf of these peoples. The most memorable ones include the demonstrations which took place in Seattle followed by others in Europe, etc. All these demonstrate the numerous complications and frustrations which inhibit and preclude Africa from taking an active part in international relations and contributing in a big way theoretically and practically.

Conclusion

What we have done in this article is to show at the level of generality some of the numerous forces and activities that have been eroding and/or effacing grounds for Africa's independent participation locally, nationally, regionally, continentally and globally. They echo Ojinga Odinga's famous work: *Not Yet Uhuru* (Not Yet Independence) and Kwame Nkrumah's warning against neo-colonialism which he exposed as the last state of imperialism. As this article showed, imperialism in form of neo-colonialism has continued to determine, define and shape Africa's international relations. The most unfortunate thing is that all these negative trends have continued to worsen without any visible signs of reversal. Collective initiatives, whether under Non-aligned Nations, OAU, SADEC, COMESA, EAC, etc. ended up being sabotaged, eroded and undermined or hijacked and harnessed by imperialism and its local allies. The same fate befell all individualized efforts by groups or nation-states. Topical among these in Africa were Marxism, Socialism, African Socialism, African Humanism, etc. This assertion is verified by US's generous gift of millions of land mines planted in Angola to maim and wipe out the Africans under the disguise of fighting the SU and Marxist Government in Angola. Hand in hand with these was RENAMO's malignant, ferocious and atrocious counter-revolution in Mozambique and its horrendous heinous mass murders, maiming and other untold crimes that it committed onto humanity. The 1994 genocide in Rwanda by the *Nterahamwe* (genocediare militias in Rwanda) together with Rwanda's armed forces is one of the latest testimonies in Africa. Cynic racists do not hesitate to applaud Africa for its contributing to international relations by implementing and extending practically the frontiers of Malthusian theory on population control. This however cannot detain us from looking into the struggles within the continent for positivities and solutions.

All these demonstrate how international relations in post-colonial Africa cannot be understood outside imperialism. One needs to break the ideologically constructed pack of lies by imperialism that Africa's problem stem from the fact that Africa is besieged by ethnicized and tribalised politics and conflicts, religious and linguistic divisions. Rather, there is need to understand the panopticonic loci of imperialism. One needs to see whether civil societies in Africa have worked together with the state and NGOs to reverse these trends and processes.

Imperialism is increasing its vices of hiring and deploying a multiplicity of individuals, groups and professions into its services. These include *inter alia,* intellectuals, academicians, lawyers, civil servants, politicians, and other social groups in society.

This article brought out a grim scenario where states are recruited in the service of imperialism. This is complicated by the fact that most NGOs are externally funded by the imperialist powers and multi-national corporations. As such, their orientation and outlook are exteriorized. As the saying goes, who pays the piper calls the tune. The work showed how NGOs are increasingly becoming pervasive, anti-democratic, dichotomizing, atomizing, divisive and anti-nationalistic. Above all, given their satellite character, they lack any independence existence, sustainability and continuity. As such, there are no possibilities for them to work together for the good of Africa since they are in the service of imperialism. While we may take pride in the general acclamation that it is only Africa which was free of pollution since it is unindustrialized, and free of nuclear and other toxic waste, the new President of World Bank, Mr. Slowotz's latest definition of Africa's international relations is most worrying. The new solution is for the west to dump part of the pollution, nuclear waste and other toxic wastes in Africa so as to make it have a share of the world pollution burden. In this new definition of Africa's international relations lies total destruction for Africa.

BIBLIOGRAPHY

Abdullah, Ibrahim (2004) *Between Democracy and Terror: The Sierra Leone Civil War.* Dakar: CODESRIA.

Anyang' Nyong'o, Peter (Ed.) (1987) *Popular Struggles for Democracy in Africa.* London: Zed Books Ltd.

Barya, John Jean & Oloka Onyango, J. (1994) *Popular Justice and Resistance Committee Courts in Uganda.* Kampala: FES.

Bates, Robert (1981) *Markets and States in Tropical Africa.* University of California Press.

Bayart, Jean François (1993) *The State in Africa: The Politics of the Belly.* London and New York: Longman.

Bayart, Jean François et al. (1999) *African Issues: The Criminalisation of the State in Africa.*

Beaud, Michael (1984) *A History of Capitalism 1500-1980.* London: The Macmillan Press Ltd.

Bernal, Martin (1987) *Black Athena: The Afroasiatic Roots of Classical Civilisation.* London: Free Association Press. Volume I.

— — (1991) *Black Athena: The Afroasiatic Roots of Classical Civilization.* New Jersey: Rutgers University Press. Volume II.

Bernstein, Henry et al. (1992) (Eds.) *Rural Livelihood: Crises and Responses.* Oxford: Oxford University Press.

Cabral, Amilcar (1969) *Revolution in Guinea: An African People's Struggle.* Kent: Whitstable Litha Ltd.

Campbell, Horace (1987) *Rasta and Resistance.* Trenton: Africa World Press Inc.

Carothers, J.C. (1954) "The Psychology of The Mau Mau." Nairobi: The Government Printer.

Chatterjee, Partha (1986) *Nationalist Thought and the Colonial World: A Derivative Discourse?* Delhi: Oxford University Press.

Chatterjee, Partha (1993) *The Nation and its Fragments: Colonial and Post-colonial Histories.* New Delhi: Oxford University Press.

Clayton, A. (1976) "The General Strike in Zanzibar, 1948," *Journal of African History.* Vol. XVII, No. 3.

Clegg, Ian (1971) *Workers' Self-Management in Algeria.* New York: Monthly Review Press.

Clive, Y. Thomas (1984) *The Rise of the Authoritarian State in Peripheral Societies.* New York: Monthly Review Press.

Cohen, D. & Daniel J. (Eds.) (1981) *Political Economy of Africa: Selected Readings.* London: Longman.

Cooper, Fredrick (1983) (Ed.) *Struggles for the City: Migrant Labour, Capital, and the State in Urban Africa.* London: Sage Publications.

Crummey, D. (1986) (Ed.) *Banditry Rebellion and Social Protest in Africa.* London: Heinemann.

Davidson, Basil (1992) *The Black Man's Burden: Africa and the Curse of the Nation State.* London: James Currey.

Davies, R. (1984) *The Struggle for South Africa.* London: Zed. 2 Vols.

de Lacger, L. (1959) *Premiere Partie Le Rwanda Ancien.* Kabgayi: Imprimatur.

Ddungu E. (1989) "Popular Forms and the Question of Democracy: The Case of Resistance Councils in Uganda." Kampala: CBR Working Paper No. 4.

Ddungu, Expedit (1989) "The Crisis of Democracy in Africa: A Case of Resistance Councils in Uganda." MA Thesis: University of Dar es Salaam.

Diop, Anta Cheikh (1978) *Black Africa: The Economic and Cultural Basis for Federated State.* Chicago: Lawrence Hill Books.

— — (1991) *Civilization or Barbarism: An Authentic Anthropology.* Chicago: Lawrence Hill Books.

Edel, May (1957) *The Chiga of South Western Uganda.* New York: Oxford University Press.

Ellis, D. (1976) "The Nandi Protest in 1923, in the Context of African Resistance to Colonial Rule in Kenya." *Journal of African History.* Vol. XVIII, No. 4.

Fanon, Frantz (1966) *The Wretched of the Earth.* London: Penguin.

Freund, Bill (1984) *The Making of Contemporary Africa: The Development of African Society Since 1800.* London: The Macmillan Press.

Gakaara wa Wanjau (1988) *Mau Mau Author in Detention.* Nairobi: Heinemann.

Gebre-Medhin, J. (1989) *Peasants and Nationalism in Eritrea.* Trenton: The Red Sea Press Inc.

Goodman, D. & Redcliff, M. (1981) *From Peasant to Proletarian, Capitalist Development and Agrarian Transition.* Oxford: Basil Blackwell.

Guha, Ranajit (1983) *Elementary Aspects of Peasant Insurgency in Colonial India.* New Delhi: Oxford University Press.

Gutkind P.C.W. and Wallerstein I. (1985) (Eds.) *Political Economy of Contemporary Africa;* California: Sage Publications.

Gutto, B.O. Shadrack (1993) *Human and Peoples' Rights for the Oppressed: Critical Essays on Theory and Practice from Sociology of Law Perspective.* Lund: Lund University Press.

Harriss John ed. (1982) *Rural Development Theories of Peasant Economy and Agrarian Change.* London: Hutchinson University Library.

Huntington S.P. (1968) *Political Order in Changing Societies.* New Haven: Yale University Press.

Hyden, Göran (1980) *Beyond Ujamaa in Tanzania: Under-development and an Uncaptured Peasantry.* London: Heinemann.

Hyden, Göran (1983) *No Shortcuts to Progress: African Development Management in Perspective.* Heinemann: London.

Iliffe John (1969) *Tanganyika Under German Rule 1905-1912.* London: Cambridge University Press.

Jackson, G. John (1970) *Introduction to African Civilisation.* New York: Carol Publishing Group.

Jaffe, H. (1985) *A History of Africa.* London: Zed Books Ltd.

Kabwegyere, B.T. (1974) *The Politics of State Formation.* Nairobi.: East African Literature Bureau.

Karen, E.F. (1985) *Revival, Rebellion in Colonial Central Africa.* Princeton University Press.

Karogo, T. (1987) *Squatters and the Roots of Mau Mau.* Nairobi: Heinemann Ltd.

Karugire, R.S. (1980) *A Political History of Uganda*. Nairobi: Heinemann.

Karugire, R.S. (1988) *The Roots of Instability in Uganda*. Kampala: Fountain Publishers.

Klein, A.M. (1980) (Ed.) *Peasants in Africa, Historical & Contemporary Perspectives*. London: Sage Publications.

Lenin, V.I. (1982) *Imperialism: The Highest Stage of Capitalism*. Moscow: Progressive Publishers.

Lindblade, Kim *et. al.* (1996) *More People, More Fallow: Environmentally Favourable Land-use Changes in South-Western Uganda*. Rockerfeller Foundation.

Lofchie, M.F. (1971) (Ed.) *The State of the Nations: Constraints on Development in Independent Africa*. Berkeley: University of California Press.

Mamdani M. (1996) *Citizen and Subject: Contemporary Africa and the Legacy of Colonialism*. Princeton: Princeton University Press.

Mamdani, M. (1976) *Politics and Class Formation in Uganda*. London: Heinemann Educational Books.

— — (2001) *When Victims Become Killers*. Princeton: Princeton University Press.

Mamdani, M., Mkandawire T. & Wamba dia Wamba (1988) "Social Movements, Social Transformation and the Struggle for Democracy in Africa." Dakar: CODESRIA Working Paper.

Michael, John (1986) *Africa's Refugee Crisis*. London: Zed Books.

Mudimbe, V.Y. (1988) *The Invention of Africa: Gnosis, Philosophy, and the Order of Knowledge*. London: James Currey.

Murindwa-Rutanga and Mukama, Ruth (2004, 2005). *Confronting Twenty-first Century Challenges: Analysis and Re-dedication by National and International Scholars*. Vol. I-III. Kampala: Faculty of Social Sciences.

Murindwa-Rutanga (1991) *Nyabingi Movement: People's Anti-colonial Struggles in Kigezi 1910-1930*. CBR Working Paper No. 18.

Murindwa-Rutanga (1994) "People's Anti-colonial Struggles in Kigezi Under the Nyabingi Movement, 1910-1930," in Mamdani M. & Oloka Onyango J. (Eds.) *Uganda: Social Movements: Studies in Living Conditions, Popular Movements and Constitutionalism*. Kampala: Centre for Basic Research & JEP. pp. 299-71.

Murindwa-Rutanga (1996) "A Historical Analysis of the Labour Question in Kigezi District," in M. Mamdani (Ed.) *Uganda: Studies in Labour*. Dakar: CODESRIA. pp. 53-135.

Murindwa-Rutanga (1999) "Struggles for Rights in the Great Lakes Region: The Case of Women and Children in South Western Uganda." In *Human Rights: Theory and Practice*; edited by Debi Chatterjee et al. New Delhi: South Asian Publishers.

Museveni, Y. Kaguta (1997) *Sowing the Mustard Seed: The Struggle for Freedom and Democracy in Uganda*. London: Macmillan.

Nabudere, D. (1980) *Imperialism Revolution in Uganda*. Dar es Salaam: Tanzania Publishing House.

Nkrumah, Kwame (1974) *Neo-colonialism: The Last Stage of Imperialism*. London: Panaf.

Nzula, A.T. (1979) *Forced Labour in Colonial Africa*. London: Zed.

Ramkrishna, Mukherjee, (1984) *Uganda: An Historical Accident? Class, Nation, State Formation*. Trenton: Africa World Press.

Ranger, T. (1985) *Peasant Consciousness and Guerrilla War in Zimbabwe*. London: James Currey.

Rodney, Walter (1972) *How Europe Under-developed Africa*. Nairobi, Kampala, Dar es Salaam: East African Educational Publishers.

Ronald, H. Chilcote & Dale, J.L. (1983) *Theories of Development*. London: Sage Publications Ltd.

Roscoe J. (1922) *The Soul of Central Africa*. London: Cassell & Co. Ltd.

Rostow, W.W. (1960) *The Stages of Economic Growth: A Non-Communist Manifesto*. Cambridge: Cambridge University Press.

Samir, Amin (1974) *Accumulation on the World Scale*. New York: Monthly Review Press.

Samir, Amin (1975) *Unequal Development*. New York: Monthly Review Press.

Seers, Dudley (1981) (Ed.) *Dependency Theory: A Critical Reassessment*. London: Frances Pinter Publishers Ltd.

Sen, Amartya (1981) *Poverty and Famines*. New Delhi: Oxford University Press.

Shivji, G. Issa (1985) (Ed.) *The State and the Working Class People in Tanzania*. Dakar: CODESRIA.

Subaltern Studies. New Delhi: Oxford University Press. All Volumes.

Suret-Canale, Jean (1988) *Essays on African History: From the Slave Trade to Neo-colonialism*. Trenton: Africa World Press Inc.

Tabaaro, Patrick (2004) "Rediscovering Africa in the Contemporary Globalisation Epoch"; paper presented to the 3rd International Cultural Studies in Uganda, Held at Makerere University, Kampala, August 9th-11th, 2004. Forthcoming as a CBR Publication.

Throup, W. David (1988) *Economic and Social Origins of Mau Mau 1945-53*. London: Heinemann.

Wamba dia Wamba (1996) "Experience of Struggles for Democracy in Africa: The Case of the People's Republic of Congo." *Eastern Africa Social Science Research Review*. Vol. II, No. 1.

Wertheim, F.W. (1992) "The State and the Dialectics of Emancipation," *Development and Change*. Vol. 23, No. 3.

World Bank: (1993) *A World Bank Country Study: Uganda Agriculture*. Washington DC. The World Bank.

Zeleza, Tiyambe Paul (1997) *Manufacturing African Studies and Crises*. Dakar: CODESRIA.

In Theory: Post-colonialism, International Relations and World Futures

—AMARTYA MUKHOPADHYAY

Writing about the relevance of Post-colonial Theory (PCT) and criticism in International Relations (IR) is essentially risky business. This is so initially because the approach has not only sprouted in theoretically distant and dissimilar grounds of literary and cultural studies, but shuns grand-or- meta-or-master narratives to such an intractable extent that it becomes difficult to accommodate it in a field that in spite of its recent origins petulantly insists on calling old Thucydides father. Still on closer thought it may seem that in a world that is still reeling under the effects of colonialism and its aftermath, neo-colonialism and neo-imperialism, a body of theory that explores the relations of the colonizer and the colonized, as also their Manichaean co-existence, cannot but be immensely germane. Besides, in the present post-Cold War world of contrary tendencies, like globalization with its homogenization, migration, multi-culturalism and the consequent demand for recognition of difference, ethnic turmoil and other activities of identity-seeking groups, etc., an approach that puts such a high premium on heterogeneity, difference and otherness cannot be put away for long. Further, in the backdrop of the post-positivist ferment in the domain of IR theorizing, caused by the leaven provided by such thoroughgoing critiques of the Enlightenment Project as the Critical Theory, Post-modernism, Post-stucturalism etc., PCT may not altogether have to break new ground all by itself. For, to a large extent, it extends the post-colonialist critique of Enlightenment rationality to the colonial periphery.[1]

It should however be informed at the very outset that the present scholar is no specialist in the field of PCT, abreast of all its manifold tendencies and developments. I am rather pursuing the question of payoffs from PCT in the IR theory field in the spirit of the famous Princeton University physics graduate, who wrote a dissertation on how to manufacture a nuclear bomb from the unclassified pieces of information in nuclear physics journals in a motor garage, and got a Ph.D for it. The payoffs are intended to be used to offer a few insights into the current and future states of the world that the current tendencies of international politics are etching out.

But Why PCT may not Readily Apply in IR

Spatiality vs. *Discursiveness*

However, the propitious factors mentioned above notwithstanding, the problems of applying post-colonial theoretic insights to the complexities of pre-war, post-war, and post-Cold War international politics are not at all negligible. The problems do not merely have to do with the temporal and epistemological confusions regarding the prefix "post" in "post-colonial".[2] Nor are the problems exhausted by the extreme diversity of ways of thinking of post-colonial writers, though diversity among them is truly enormous. For example, Edward Said, whose trilogy, *Orientalism, The Question of Palestine* and *Covering Islam*[3] truly pioneered post-colonial thinking, at least as it was understood up to the turn of the last century, approached the subject of post-coloniality in a way that is not done these days. Steering clear of a perceived Marxist misreading of colonialism as a subplot of capitalism, casting anchor firmly in post-modernist discourse analysis, and combining Gramscian and Foucauldian insights to break through the maze of liberal (specially Auerbachian) and

Marxist versions of universalistic humanism,[4] Said gives an interpretation of Orientalism that is not fully shared by many later key exponents of post-colonial theory and criticism itself. For Said Orientalism, or the formal study of the Orient (really the present day Middle East), buttressed as it was by key literary and cultural texts, solidified certain ways of thinking and seeing that served as cognitive aids to Europe's imperial forays into the hypothetical East. These texts acquired "the authority of academics, institutions and governments." They not only created knowledge, but even more importantly created the very reality they appeared to be describing. In time this knowledge generated a tradition, or a *discourse* in a Foucauldian sense, that became synonymous with the distinctively "Western style for dominating, restructuring and having authority over the Orient." According to Said, portrayal of the Orient in European literary texts, travelogues and other writings not only led to the crystallization of the dichotomy between Europe and its "others", and helped European culture to maintain its hegemony over other lands, but perpetuated the difference between the "familiar" Europe and "strange" Orient or the East. It was so because "[w]hen one uses categories like the Oriental and the Western as both the starting and end points of analysis, research, policy, ... the result is usually to polarize the distinction — the Oriental becomes more Oriental, the Westerner more Western — and *limit the human encounter between different cultures, traditions and societies*." [Italics mine] [5]

Of course the same method of colonial discourse analysis and the same conclusions do not inform the writings of other post-colonial theorists. For example, at thematic, programmatic and methodological levels, Gayatri Chakrabarty Spivak, another key post-colonial theoretician, treads a different ground from Said. As one eminent commentator puts it, "[b]roadly speaking, Spivak reverses the emphasis in early Said... on colonial discourse as the principal object of attention. Despite some brilliant examples of colonial discourse analysis like 'The Rani of Sirmur'(1985), 'Three Women's Texts and a Critique of Imperialism'(1985), and 'Imperialism and Sexual

Difference'(1986), Spivak instead more characteristically focuses on various manifestations of counter-discourse... this broad range of interests is consistent with Spivak's demand that post-colonial analysis should embody above all else a 'persistent recognition of heterogeneity' in respect of all the cultures of (post) colonialism." Besides, Spivak does not, according to him, see the effects of imperialism as merely destructive, as Said does. She refers sometimes to its positive effects too, through such paradoxes as "enabling violence" or "enabling violation".[6] For Spivak, PCT is primarily an "otherness machine" in a Derridian deconstructive mode.[7]

Again, Homi Bhabha, perhaps the most contentious figure in PCT, differs from both Said and Spivak in important ways. As Moore-Gilbert so graphically points out, in contradistinction to early Said, who concentrates almost entirely on the colonizer, and later Fanon, who remained nearly exhaustively focused on the colonized, Bhabha seeks to highlight the mutualities and negotiations across the colonial divide. He wants to show that the relationship between the colonizer and the colonized is far more complex, nuanced and politically loaded than Said or Fanon understood it to be. This is so because the circulation of contradictory patterns of psychic affect in colonial relations, like ambivalent love-hate attitudes towards the Other, explode the myth that the identities and positionings of the colonizer and the colonized reside in fixed, unitary and perennially conflictual relationships with each other. Rather Bhabha, according to the commentator, implies that the colonial relationship is structured on either side by "forms of multiple and contradictory belief." In spite of Bhabha's decision to shun "general theory" in his article "DissemiNation", this last implication is the leit motif of most of Bhabha's later writings.[8] Actually Bhabha criticizes Said roundly for offering and developing a static model of colonial relations where "colonial power and discourse is possessed entirely by the colonizer", leaving little or no room for negotiation or change.[9]

The diversity of approaches of post-colonial theorists to the subject of colonialism/imperialism and its political cultural effects can of course be circumvented by any statement of the approach that steers clear of individual angularities, quirks, or idiosyncrasies of the exponents, and focuses on the commonalities instead. But the problems of application of PCT to IR may remain even when such a common ground is found and stated. In the course of considering Gayatri Spivak's momentous question "can the subaltern speak?"[10] Such a rounded statement of the major premises of PCT has been offered by one commentator through his efforts to answer a related question: can the Third world write its own history? [11] While arguing about the novelty and originality of the post-colonial approach Prakash admits that it would be wrong to say that till the emergence of this approach colonialism and its legacies remained unquestioned, as nationalism and Marxism did pose powerful challenges to colonialism. "But", Prakash reminds with great circumspection, "both of these operated with master-narratives that put Europe at its centre. Thus when nationalism, reversing Orientalist thought attributed agency and history to the subjected nation, it also staked a claim to the order of Reason and Progress instituted by colonialism; and when Marxists pilloried colonialism, their criticism was framed by a universalist mode-of-production narrative. Recent post-colonial criticism, on the other hand, seeks to undo the Eurocentrism produced by the institution of the West's trajectory, and its appropriation of the other as History. It does so, however, with the acute realization that post-coloniality is not born and nurtured in a panoptic distance from history. The post-colonial exists as an aftermath, as an after—after being worked over by colonialism. Criticism formed in the process of the enunciation of the discourses of domination produces a *space that is neither inside nor outside* the history of Western domination but in a tangential relation to it. This is what Homi Bhabha calls an *in-between*, hybrid practice and negotiation, or what Gayatri Chakravarty Spivak terms catachresis, 'reversing, displacing, and seizing the apparatus of value-coding'." (Italics ours).[12]

Even if we start out with this lowest common denominator of PCT, presenting, as it does, the barest fundamentals of agreement between so discordant voices as of Said, Spivak,

Bhabha, Prakash and Lata Mani,[13] and take the spatial location of post-colonial critics as something "neither inside nor outside" but rather "in-between" at face value, the very nature of IR as a theory field presents some obstacles to introducing PCT in its realm.

This is because while the social sciences are by and large constituted on the basis of "analytic categories",[14] around some principal conceptual units, according to some scholars the subject of IR is not easily amenable to such a conceptualization. It rather falls towards the concrete end of an analytic-concrete-category-continuum. This point is not as abstract and arcane as it may first appear. For it may go to explain the belated entry of approaches already firmly established in other social sciences into the charmed island of IR, to the utter dismay of more theoretically minded scholars,[15] and may help in explaining the blurring of the distinctions between post-positivistic approaches, once they entered this continent of Circe.[16] Can it be that in a field long dominated by power-thinking around the billiard-ball type nation-states, from the time of Morgenthau to Mearsheimer, that continually draws empirical validation from their behaviour, spatiality is so overwhelmingly foregrounded[17] that analytic or discursive approaches can find space here only up to a degree?

But this alone would not suffice to establish any possible mismatch between PCT and current IR. At least some fault-lines of PCT itself may have to share part of the blame. For this let us briefly revisit some of the problems of the words "post-colonial" and "post-coloniality" and their implications for the one schema which has been unavoidable for long in IR theorizing, viz. the three worlds theory.

Post-colonial/Post-coloniality: Semantic Confusions and Epistemological Dead-ends

The question was posed by one with exemplary directness: "When exactly... the 'post-colonial' begins?" The inquirer's doubts had sound reasons behind them. Since the "post" in "post-colonial" also means "after", it raises important ambiguities in "spatio-temporality". Starting from India and entering Anglo-American academic contexts, "post-colonial" includes Third World countries which gained independence after World War II. But it could similarly include places like America, Australia, New Zealand, South Africa, etc., i.e. "lands of original settlement", because colonialism has had its sway for more than three centuries. The history of the decolonization of the former two groups and of Angola, Mozambique, Rhodesia, Malta, Namibia etc. may be readily called in support of this statement.[18] Again three other adherents of this approach reserve the term "post-colonial" for literary productions for societies transformed by colonialism. Though they have prefaced the word "post-colonial" by the announcement that they use the term to cover all the cultures affected by the "imperial process" to the present day, to take in the continuity of pre-occupations throughout the historical process initiated by European imperial aggression to the present day, this instance is good for bringing out the extensive connotation of the term. According to Ashcroft, Griffiths and Tiffin countries as diverse as African ones, Australia, Bangladesh, Canada, Caribbean countries, India, Malaysia, Malta, New Zealand, Pakistan, Singapore, South Pacific island countries, Sri Lanka, even the USA as also their literatures become "post-colonial" in the same sense, just because of the transforming nature of their relationships with the metropolitan centre.[19]

In Shoat's view, and possibly rightly so, this unorthodox and contentious formulation of the term "post-colonial" is truly confusing. It "collapses very different national-racial formulations...as equally post-colonial." The coinage is problematic according to her in many senses. First, it glosses not only over center-periphery relations, but also differences in the nature of the peripherals. "Positioning India and Australia in relation to an imperial center, simply because they were both colonies, equates the relationship of the colonized white settlers with the Europeans at the 'center' with that of the colonized indigenous populations with the same Europeans. It also assumes that white settler colonies and emerging Third World nations broke away from the 'center' in the same way." Besides, looking internally into the white settler countries, Shoat finds it extremely messy to place white Australians and Aboriginal Australians in the same "periphery", thereby blotting out at one stroke of the pen long and painful stories of genocidal oppression and ethnic cleansing targeted against the latter.

Secondly, in Shoat's view, even the seemingly innocuous term "post- colonial society" does not solve the problem of uncertainty regarding referents. This is because the "disorienting space of the 'post-colonial' generates odd couplings of the 'post' and particular geographies, blurring the assignment of perspectives." The potential scholar out to use this conceptual framework would have to decide for her/him if the prefix "post" indicates the perspective and location of the ex-colonized, the ex-colonizer, the ex-colonial settler, or the displaced hybrid in First World metropolises.

Thirdly, the confusions of spatiality are confounded by those of temporality. This is because the lack of historical specificity in the "post" leads to deeper problems than of collapsing of diverse chronologies. Aside from raising the question of what time-frame to choose for contemporary anti-colonial, anti-racist struggles waged under the banner of national and colonial oppression, the term incommodes "forceful articulations of neo-coloniality" in countries like Egypt, India, Latin-American republics etc., that were striving to go beyond formal decolonization to end continuance of imperialistic interests.

Fourthly, Shoat incisively points out that the term unfortunately conveys the impression that colonialism belongs to the — even if immediate — past. It "*inadvertently* glosses over the fact that the global hegemony, even in the post-Cold War era, persists in forms other than colonial rule" (italics ours). Here Shoat speaks of things that would be immensely relevant for any student of the post-Cold War theory of IR. I quote her in some length below:

> "As a signifier of a new historical epoch, the term 'post-colonial', when compared with neo-colonialism, comes

> equipped with little evocation of contemporary power-relations; it lacks a political content which can account for the eighties and nineties-style U.S. military interventions in Granada, Panama, and Kuwait-Iraq, and for the symbolic links between U.S. political and economic interests and those of local elites. In certain contexts furthermore, racial and national oppressions reflect clear colonial patterns, for example the oppression of blacks by Anglo-Dutch Europeans in South Africa, and the Americas, the oppression of Palestinians and Middle Eastern Jews by Euro-Israel. The 'post-colonial' leaves no space, finally, for the struggles of the aboriginals in Australia and indigenous peoples throughout the Americas, in other words of Fourth World peoples dominated by both First World multinational corporations and by Third World nation-states."

While Shoat is obviously right in positing that hegemonic structures and conceptual frameworks built up over the last five hundred years cannot be conjured away merely by swishing a magical word like the "post-colonial", her critique of the term, together with its parlance and terminology[20] would fail to satisfy many other critics of the term and of the underlying approach because of its many "silences"[21] and prevarications.

For example, one Marxist critic of PCT condemns it for more serious charges: (a) for making a "fetish" of the West; (b) for giving a very diluted reading of Marxism; (c) for substituting (as in Dipesh Chakravarti's writings) "Europe" or "European" for "capital" or "bourgeois"; (d) for pursuing, after Samuel P. Huntington and Theodore von Laue, a "civilizational" and cultural mode of analysis that sweeps under the carpet any talk about the "world revolution of capitalism"; and (e) for replacing a concrete ideological specification encapsulated by words like "bourgeois", "capitalist" etc. with a pseudo-geographical one like "Europe", "the West" etc., elevated to the status of a methodological principle.[22] In this schema, "[n]ot only has the specter of capitalism been exorcized: there is no mention of any material principle whatsoever." In the commentator's view the sole motivating factor of the disavowal of Marx and Engels is "the need to demonstrate that there are no resources within the conceptual universe of modernity adequate to the task of unthinking Eurocentrism."[23]

Still another Marxist critique of PCT starts by critiquing it for soft-pedaling many of the examples in Marx's theoretical practice, that display his sensitivity to heterogeneous and disparate motions of diverse collectivities. Had he taken on Shoat his charge would have been mostly directed against Shoat's language. He pillories post-colonialism for its reticence about the problematic of uneven development. But to him post-colonialism's failure to address this problematic is rooted in its particular provenance. "In essence, the most blatant flaw of post-colonial orthodoxy (establishment post-colonialism employing a post-structuralist organon) lies in its refusal to grasp the category of capitalist modernity in all its global ramifications, both the regulated and the disarticulated aspects." As a result a mechanical formula takes the place of a dialectic analysis of historiography. And in the wide-ranging critique of the Enlightenment ideals by post-colonial critics, the antithesis of capitalism — proletarian revolution and socialist internationalism in their first formulation by Marx and Engels — is submerged in the miasmal logic of the global system of capital without further discrimination. The monomaniac desire to decimate everything connected with totality, foundations, universals, and systemic analysis leads, in his view, to a mechanical reification of ideas and terminology, as well as the demarcation of the experience they refer to. The end results are a general relativism, skepticism and nominalism— even nihilism — that finally play the deuce with the post-colonial claim to truth, plausibility or moral high ground.[24]

Some Marxist-minded thinkers are of the view that the blindness of post-colonial theory to the worldwide doings of capitalism is itself a resultant of its consistent repudiations of several related master-narratives. The game begins with the most powerful of master-narratives, "a post-Enlightenment European constitution of history", to then flow into its multiple derivatives. Among the numerous components of the Eurocentric master-narrative the first is of modernization, in both its Marxist and bourgeois incantations. This is because in PCT Marxism is also seen to be complicitous with the Western conception of modernization, due mainly to its distinctive, revisionist reading of colonialism. The next to come for repudiation is "Orientalism's constitution of the colony as Europe's Other, that is an essence without history." By implication nationalism and its procedures of representation also come under attack. This is because while challenging Orientalism they have allegedly perpetuated the essentialism of it through discovering a national essence in history.

Moreover, repudiation of master-narratives is itself premised upon resistance to "all spatial homogenization and temporal teleology," which in its turn necessitates another series of repudiations, starting with that of foundational history writing. But repudiation of foundational historiography leads as a corollary to rejection of capitalism as a foundational category. According to Dirlik once capitalism and structure are successfully "unthought" there need not be any allusion to a capitalistic structuring of the world.[25] As in a hilarious Scottish play, reconstruction of the broken iconic statue is allowed to go on even when its genitalia are missing.[26]

Now some over-conscientious readers may at this point be tempted to think that all this talk about semantic uncertainties, silences and avoidances is a little too peripheral for the hard concerns of IR theories and practices. This complacency may however be rudely shaken if we pause to consider the fate of the category of the Third World in the rarified atmosphere of post-colonial cogitations.

Reification of the Third World and PCT

A much maligned term for its conceptual cumbrousness, the concept of the Third World has been the proverbial bee in the bonnet of many IR scholars both in the North and the South ever since the Cold War started in the arena of East-West one-upmanship. Even the détente-time duumvirate of the superpowers could do little to diminish the utility and the appeal of the concept, not only for analytical purposes, but as a call to action. There is no shred of doubt that in PCT the word "post-colonial" is not just viewed as synonymous with the Third World, but is regarded as a better successor term. It allegedly resolves the crisis that gradually wove around the concept of the Third World. It did not, according to Shoat, emerge merely to fill an empty space in the language of political- cultural analysis. On the contrary, its wide acceptance in the late nineteen eighties was due to the eclipse and desuetude of the older paradigm of the Third World as a signifier of non-First World reality. The "terminological shift" was not occasioned merely by the need for novelty. It was rather a pointer to the heightened "professional prestige" and "theoretical aura" the issues of post-coloniality have recently attracted, to the detriment of the "activist aura" once associated with the Third World within progressive academic circles. Another reason for substitution of the older term was according to her the "terminological crisis" of the term, attributable directly to the problems of the three-worlds theory. Drawing examples, somewhat inappropriately for practitioners of IR, from literary – cultural studies of national allegory, cinema, feminism, etc. in Afro-Asian countries, Shoat makes her not too original point that the historical processes of the last three decades offered a number of very complex and politically ambiguous developments that militated against the theoretical solidness and applicability of the concept.

According to Shoat these momentous developments are: the collapse of the Soviet communist model, the discomfiture of the hoped for tri-continental revolution dreamt around the Ho Chi Minh – Franz Fanon – Che Guevara ideological triumvirate, lack of unanimity among the proletarians of the less developed countries (LDCs), some capitulation of the socialist regimes to transnational capitalism under the pressures of international geopolitics and of the global economic system, intra-Third World conflicts and internal wars within Third World nations, and the constantly changing relations between dominant and subaltern groups, settlers and indigenous populations typified by post-independence immigrations to First World and to more affluent Third World countries.

In Shoat's view, apart from the crisis in "Third World" thinking induced by these developments, the semantic potentials of the word "post-colonial" also hastened the process of the replacement of the former by the latter. For, just by dropping the suffix "ism" from "post-colonialism", the residual adjective could not only be made applicable to a "space" or "condition" (in contradistinction to "Third World", circumscribed to "nations", "countries" and "peoples"), but the word is also transformable into a noun, in both the singular and the plural, that could be used for designating the subjects of the post-colonial condition.[27]

Of course, not everyone would agree with Shoat's enthusiasm for the new word. As Aijaz Ahmad wryly points out, the term post-coloniality which resurfaced during the 1980s, "this time in literary and cultural theories, and in deconstructive history-writing," lost all memory of how the term had come into being in the first, employed different periodizations in the writings of different critics, and became the locus of "mutual citations and cross referencing" among a number of self-referential writers.[28]

But the presumed superiority of the term "post-colonial" over the term "Third World" for encapsulating the reality outside the First World and the LDCs falls flat on its face once we analyze what post-colonial theorists have made of the word Third World. Seeking to concentrate on the contrast between the two words Dirlik agrees with the post-colonial theorists that the term Third World was quite vague for encapsulating within one uniform category "vastly heterogeneous historical circumstances", and for "locking in fixed positions, structurally if not geographically, societies and populations that shifted with changing global relationships." But his basic point is that this "fixing of societal locations" at least permitted identification of Third Word intellectuals with the "concreteness of places of origin", even if erroneously. This is something that is impossible within the contours of the "post-colonial". After being released from the determinacy of Third World locations, post-coloniality turned the identification of the "post-colonial" into something that was not structural but discursive. Considered in this light post-coloniality merely signifies "an attempt to regroup intellectuals of uncertain location under the banner of post-colonial discourse. Intellectuals in the flesh may produce the themes that constitute post-colonial discourse, but it is participation in the discourse that defines them as post-colonial intellectuals. Hence it is necessary to delineate the discourse so as to identify post-colonial intellectuals themselves."[29]

Dirlik's words, quoted at some length, have greater implications for IR theory that at first glance appear. If the new word starts meaning intellectuals engaged or ready to be engaged in colonial discourses, then they are no better than a type of what in some brands of regime theory are called "epistemic communities".[30] But if Third World becomes nothing more than discursively oriented intellectuals of "uncertain location", then the spatially inclined subject of IR cannot but suffer. The problems and anxieties of geophysical areas of the earth, sharing certain political and economic characteristics, have to be left in the hands of a group of individuals, "ironist liberals" "secular intellectuals" or "academic tricksters" in Rorty's sense.[31] Their trustworthiness or otherwise is also not beyond question. Consider these cutting remarks of a scholar about post-colonialism in the African context:

> "Post-coloniality is the condition of what we might ungenerously call a comprador intelligentsia: a relatively small, western—trained group of writers and thinkers who mediate the trade in cultural commodities of world capitalism at the periphery. In the West they are known through the Africa they offer. Their compatriots know them both through the West they present to Africa and through an Africa they have invented for the world, for each other, and for Africa."[32]

If this is a sad commentary Bhabha's celebrated in-betweenness, in a way these intellectuals may be compared with the pilgrim Creole nationalists described in Anderson's modern classic, making journeys between "times, statuses and places" and constructing a consciousness of connectedness through trying to solve the riddle of "why is this man doing what I am doing, uttering the same words that I am uttering, even though we cannot talk to one another?"[33] This might show that the difference between them consist in the fact that while the former can represent their compatriots the latter cannot. This is because they are by Appiah's description "post-nationalists" and post-nativists.[34] Their refined dialogue can never substitute for the raucous, robust, if confused protests by earlier third worldists against the palpable vivisection and "triage"[35] arranged for their lands and people by the present masters of the world.

Why does PCT seek to further obfuscate the already unclear concept of the Third World? Some argue plain failure because of its conceptual blinkers, while others smell something more sinister. Both types of arguments have been adduced with commendable clarity by San Juan Jr. He begins by claiming that "post-colonial paradigms of hybridity and ambivalence" fail to provide "frames of intelligibility that can analyze and critique the internal contradictions embedded in the neo-liberal reality and ideology of the "free market". And he blames the lack of general theory in PCT for this failure. He says by way of clarification that the "pragmatic empiricism" of post-colonial criticism stands in the way of providing a "cognitive mapping" of all these historical trends that marked the breakdown of developmentalism, modernization theory, and other theoretical solutions to the crisis of monopoly capitalism since the onset of the October Revolution in Russia in 1917 up to the scrapping of the Bretton Woods Agreement and a unified monetary system.

But instead of stopping at PCT's epistemological infirmities and blindness San Juan hints at something far more serious. He points out that in the opinion of many "the logic and rhetoric of post-colonialism coincide suspiciously with the anarchic "free market" and the vicissitudes of finance capital on a global scale. Bound by its problematic, the post-colonial critic cannot even entertain the question that Samir Amin so graphically poses: "how can we develop the productive forces without letting commodity relations gain ground?"[36]

In a similar vein Dirlik also thinks PCT to be complicitous with, and its respectability to be dependent upon, those transformations within the capitalist world economy marked by "the emergence of what has been described variously as global capitalism, flexible production, late capitalism and so on, terms that have disorganized earlier conceptualizations of global relations, especially relations comprehended earlier by such binaries as colonizer/colonized, First World/Third World, and the West and the Rest, in all of which the nation-state was taken for granted as the global unit of political organization."[37] In the next section we are going to spell out how, in spite of the malaise at the heart of its genealogy, PCT can, in our opinion, be applied to more advantage in IR, what are the potential niches of applicability, and which the best strategies for it.

Niches of Applicability

Trade-talks, Othering and New Orientalisms

A thoroughly creative application of PCT in IR has been attempted by a scholar[38] that not only mitigates to some extent the culturological bias of this branch of study, but provides a new way of looking at trade discourses that highlights future new domains of textual strategies. He uses an Asia-Pacific case study of trade-competitiveness discourses in the post-Cold War era between the USA, Japan and the East Asian newly – industrializing countries (NICs) and the meanderings of them to point to the fuzziness of the binaries of "East-West", "Occident-Orient" (West-rest), "insider-outsider", "order-threat" etc, employed by some first generation scholars of critical international relations. Supposedly the contents of these discourses indicate that the range of "others" to be examined is to be broadened, so that the various types of discourses deployed to construct difference and otherness can be understood better. As per his contention this will bring into sharper relief not only "different types of others on the outside", but 'different types of others on the inside' too, and tease out different types of Orientalisms on the basis of their inter-actions.

Beginning with differentiating two main types of others as "outsiders" and "internal others", Sum further sub-divides them through the criteria of equality and inequality. This gives us a repertoire of four groups of "equal outsiders", "unequal outsiders", "equal internal others", and "unequal internal others". The whole game is, or sought to be, controlled by a hegemon who characterizes lesser nations on the basis of their trade behaviour. This and the reaction of the latter cause different types of Orientalism to come into play. "Equal outsiders" are considered close to the hegemon's time/space and are not marked off in inferior-superior terms, as in US-EU trade relations discourses, and is not generative of any new or old Orientalism. But where the discourses happen between the hegemon and "unequal outsiders" and the latter are sought to be otherized by the hegemon through evaluative "superior-inferior" "fair-unfair" labels, the first type of "new Orientalism" is born. Sum sees this in America's "neo-liberal" trade discourse with Japan in the post-Cold War era. The simple equation is rendered complex by "internal others". Among them some are labeled "equal" because they allegedly belong to the social formation where the "hegemonic discourses" are prevailing and occupy the same time/space as the hegemon, their difference being seen in relatively non-antagonistic terms. They resort to the same "discursive repertoire" as the hegemonic centre but interpret similar issues in an alternative way by inverting the otherizing cultural categories and interpretations foregrounded by the hegemon. By contrast "unequal internal others" are manifest or manifest themselves within the "self-defined time/space of the (Eastern) hegemon. Their inequality is stamped on them through the use of labels employing vocabulary of superiority/inferiority. After typologizing discursive contestants in this fashion, Sum makes the important methodological point that the existence of the "otherized" as real subjects incite or tempt social forces to reposition themselves in a way that helps them to turn such "otherization" to their advantage. This generates the second and third types of "new Orientalism", and is exemplified in the assertion of economic nationalism by the US's "equal internal others", and in countermoves by Japan's "unequal internal others".

From this innovative angle Sum shows how since the 1980s "neo-liberal" trade discourses were employed and used by the US as a "technology of power" for "otherizing Japan and labeling it as a deviant from the "universal free trade" model. The first kind of "new Orientalism" was helped by "a set of economic narratives centred around the prevailing values/ norms, governmentalities, and time/space of the US hegemon", and in its turn helped dub the economic and political institutions and practices of Japan as not only different from those of the US but pernicious to its interests. Worse, in the mid-1980s a group of "revisionist" internal others in the US tried to construct an "American self/Japanese other" binary out of these differences through evaluative propositions like "Japan is not Western" and Japan is a "threat", to plead for an American economic nationalism and even a "techno-nationalism". Sum showed how in the writings of four economists in the Wall Street Journal (1990) this stance betokened a second kind of "new Orientalism". This took advantage of "heterodox economic-cultural discourses centred around the values/norms, procedural and substantive rationalities, and time/space of the West's equal "internal others" which are deployed to interpret relevant "external others" (e.g. Japan) not only as different but also as threatening the values, interests and superiority of the hegemon on its own ground."

But even as Japan integrated parts of these heterodox economic discourses into its own self-understanding to create a new literature that started counteracting the critique of Japanese trade practices, and to plot the Johnsonian "developmental state" narrative onto Japanese time/space through a kind of "re-invented Orientalism, other social forces paved the way for the third kind of "new Orientalism". At about the time when Japan was being constructed as a threat by the US, the engineered revaluation of Yen by G5 finance ministers grievously weakened Japanese price competitiveness in export markets, and compelled it to reposition itself in East Asia. Japan embarked on the path of a Pacific integration that promised to deliver some East Asian NICs into the realm of sustained industrial success. In a way this led to the emerg-ence of the third kind of "new Orientalism" that consisted in "a development discourse centred on the prevailing values/norms, governmentalities, and time/ space of Japan that assigns a follower identity to the East's unequal 'international others' (e.g. NICs) — claiming that their interests are best realized by entering the Japan-led framework as its junior partners." This reactive, Asia- bound gaze of Japan created a host of Eastern "unequal others", and highlighted a cultural otherization of East Asian economies in a manner highly redolent of Western Orientalism.[39]

Sum's creative application of Orientalism smacks strongly of "game theory" in analyzing the initial gambits of trading hegemons and counteractive postures of subordinate powers, as also of "linkage politics", in highlighting how domestic kibitzers in all of them disturb the simple processes of the former making the latter kowtow to them. Besides, the brass tacks of trade talks have been transformed in such a subtle way by the use of the post-modernist parlance of PCT that the verbal strategies of globalization, making false heroes and undeserved villains, are laid bare as never before. While the otherization of Japan ever since the early 1980s linked Japan closely to the very economic identity of the USA and its need to readjust itself in the new global economy, the statist reading of Japan's uniqueness could be used by America to reinforce its sense of superiority based on a liberal self-identity, to pressurize Japan in America's difficult times.[40]

Unmasking of the Colonial Parading as International

This could be PCT's theoretical high ground. If we remember that for the last three centuries extra-European international relations was to a large extent the tale of colonialism, and that PCT has widely known pretensions to special expertise in theorizing about it, we cannot afford to be surprised if it claims to offer the best bait to the forces that seek to block systemic change in North —South relations. A perceptive scholar has to this end attempted to reorient PCT towards the pursuit of the political, not, however, putting behind itself "the interrogation of representations and the role of the discursive" as was suggested by a famous post-colonial theorist.[41] Claiming that these techniques did not necessarily amount to the "deferral of the political", he points out that the redeeming task is rather to utilize with their help the "new problem-space", to search "where the colonial takes on different guises and goes in another name — the international". In his view the decolonization of the international was far from complete, thanks to habits of mind regarding the workings of the international system, the nature of power, and how the North and the South were constructed, all of which strongly smack of a "structural Eurocentrism". The end result not only strengthens the authority of the centre but confuses the field of action for those who want to challenge the established order.[42]

It is from this viewpoint that Darby, in contradistinction to Scott, debunks Bandung Conference for its failure to allow a full-throated criticism of the current imperialist policies, and for laying to rest the possibility of race ever challenging the hegemonic international order. He suggests that the debate on the real gains from or the significance of Bandung as the birth-moment of post-coloniality is yet to be engaged in. It would never be fully revealing unless the post-Bandung episodes of the rise of the non-alignment movement and the Group of 77, the conflicts over Third World resources and reparations for colonial possessions, and the "quasi- parliamentary" diplomacy for a fairer international economic order are analyzed from the vantage point of "the Third World discursive" against the "dominant First World narrative of Power in interstate relations". The payoff from this engagement is supposedly first showing that post-colonial discourse might connect more directly with the politics of anti-colonialism than has been heretofore understood; and secondly that it would confirm that "IR has been complicit in shoring- up an (sic) hegemonic world order by naturalizing the terms of reference."

While the afore-mentioned benefits of applying a politicized PCT to IR hardly promises anything more than Critical Theory, or even a critical IR theory,[43] the things which Darby proposes to analyze from this perspective seem incontrovertibly relevant. For example the first is the "contemporary conceptions of global order" as manifest in their "oneness", and the smoothness with which particular doctrines, "each with its constituency and lineage", have served as building blocks of a larger neo-liberal discourse. These are "democratization and good governance, civil society, the role of the third sector and the internationalization of philanthropy, social development and the conditionalities of aid, humanitarian intervention in complex emergencies" etc. Addition of "social capital" would have nearly completed the list. Anyway Darby quite aptly points out that this humanized blueprint of an interlinked "one world" startlingly echoes an earlier project, the British- imperial that is equally gospel-like. For, it too threw up "the marvel of the market economy, the 'Great Commercial Republic of the World' as a zone of order as well as prosperity, missionary impulse, military aid in support of civil power, and above all optimism about progress." The resemblance is so striking that contrary to some scholars[44] Darby refuses to make any distinction between Empire (or the contemporary hegemonic order) and the earlier imperial project. In my opinion, however, even Darby does not get the full force of this resemblance. We may here ponder over a typical Englishman's proprietary feeling about the world, as it was so graphically pointed out by the elder brother of Lord Alfred Tennyson, onetime Poet Laureate of England, even if it constitutes a slight literary digression:

Letty's Globe
When Letty had scarce pass'd her third glad year
And her young artless words began to flow,

One day we gave the child a colour'd sphere
Of the wide earth that she might mark and know,
By tint and outline, all its sea and land.
She patted the entire world; old empires peep'd
Between her fingers; her soft hand
Was welcome at all frontiers. How she leap'd
And laugh'd, and prattled in her wide-world bliss;
But when we turned her sweet unlearned eye
On our isle, she raised a joyous cry,
"Oh! yes I see it Letty's home is there!"
And, while she hid all England with a kiss,
Bright over Europe fell her golden hair.[45] (Italics mine).

This digression, of sheer imperialism masquerading as intolerable childish innocence, would, however, strengthen tenfold Darby's contention that the resemblance between the previous British imperialist vision and the present Empire not only foregrounds the vital role that discursive criticism can play in unraveling "the power relations embedded in knowledge and discourse", but highlights the special relevance of its post-colonial version.[46]

In order to show how PCT may uncover the workings of the contemporary international system, Darby first recounts the chain of events that followed the 9/11terrorist attack to the overshadowing of the politics of Iraq by the interests of outside states, and then shows how the story can be retold a la post-colonialism. The trajectory of modern-day one worldism was, according to him, first getting the idea of the strong Third World state mauled by First World governments, scholars and the media because of the challenge mounted to the established international economic and political order by leaders such as Ben Bella, Nasser, Sukarno, Manley, Nkrumah and others. After the strong Third World state was thus compelled to genuflect, the diagnosis of the "failed state" was quickly inserted, through a selective use of history and its predilections. Then once the structural adjustments programmes of the 1980s and 1990s arrived on the scene they operated like a bull in a china shop, streamlining state structures at the behest of Western states,

IFIs and other IGOs, to bring into being the "compliant state"- the political unit that has not only made the entry of foreign capital smooth sailing but more recently has been ready to "re-jig its security system to mesh with the new global strategic paradigms." Then, secondly, he highlights the real roots of the problems of the world's asylum seekers and refugees through focusing on the iniquities of Westphalian spatiality. While on one side the Third World is used and exploited as a free site for "resource utilization, cheap labour (including outsourcing), and adventure and sex tourism", there are huge and enormous "regulatory" regimes that serve to 'lock the great bulk of the world's people in place".

There are many other areas, big and small, where according to Darby there can be really attractive purchase from PCT in IR theorizing. It could for example look into the metanarrative of the most dominant "endist" argument of today which traveled from Bell's "end of ideology, thesis to Fukuyama's end of history thesis, and question why thinking in the West soft-pedaled the Galbraith interlude where not only the "culture of contentment" at the heart of the Western triumphalism was condemned but the liberal polity was also roundly criticized.[47] This would not only have assisted us to deal better with "difference", but would have provided greater legitimacy to the post-colonial argument that politics operates very differently in non-Western societies even when it retains the signatures of universality. It could also help us in showing that the "family of doctrines that currently set the relationship between the political and the economic spheres is fast becoming international orthodoxy", and that in the current set-up the conception of democracy on offer is not only steeped in narrow neo-liberal precepts, but is closely tied to the interests of the lone superpower and of its allies. According to Darby it is PCT which would help us understand that "if politics was once regarded as the sphere of the unsettled, in the developed world in recent years it has come to connote that which is settled", and that his why working from Euro-American development perspectives may beckon us Third World people up false paths.[48]

Is Occidentalism Another Window?

At first sight roping in Occidentalism in a paper on Orientalism/ PCT may appear to be allowing arbitrary intrusion of the worst kind. But we may here remind the reader that as Darby so aptly pointed out, it is the in contexts of 9/11, the ensuing increasing resort to coercion, a narrow conception of democracy and its engineered spread, and the diminution of the political that a "new form of Orientalism" arose. We may also point his or her attention to Darby's belief that even if we take into account the obstacles created by the structure of international politics, the greatest "barrier to any substantive engagement with the North/South divide lies ...within the culture of the West", and that it is the diminution of the politics that has spawned a "new" form of orientalism.[49] This would definitely allow us to offer Occidentalism, in a different sense, as a new perspective on an emancipatory paradigm for IR theory.

The term Occidentalism has been coined in this distinctive sense by two perceptive commentators, who use it as the "dehumanizing picture of the West painted by its enemies", not reducible to any "Middle Eastern sickness" or to "a specifically Japanese disease fifty years ago". Like capitalism, Marxism and other "isms" it was born in Europe, as one of the venomous anti-dotes to Enlightenment and its secular, liberal Weltanschuung.[50] In a sense it is the reverse of Orientalism that goes one over most of the other critiques of it. This is because, as Buruma and Margalit so graphically point out, while colonialism has to do much expiation, and the revolt of the global against the local is perfectly legitimate in many senses, the view of the West in Occidentalism emulates the worst aspects of its counterpart if it does not outdo it. Many of the Orientalist discourses and practices strip the human targets of the East of much of their humanity, treat them as less than fully adult human beings, possessing minds of children.[51] But "Occidentalism is at least as reductive; its bigotry simply turns the Orientalist view upside down." By way of exploration of its genealogy Buruma and Margalit look back to all of Occidentalism's "links and overlaps, from the counter-

Reformation to the Counter-Enlightenment in Europe, to the many varieties of fascism and National Socialism in East and West, to anti-capitalism and anti-globalization, and finally to the religious extremism that rages in so many places today." But rather than pursuing this comprehensive and spatial route of the evolution of Occidentalism the two scholars take a different discursive path of deciphering traces of Occidentalism wherever and whenever they were discernible. Their polestar was a resultant chain of hostility—"to the city with its image of rootless, arrogant, greedy, decadent, frivolous cosmopolitanism; to the mind of the West, manifested in science and reason; and to the infidel, who must be crushed to make way for a world of pure faith."

The theoretical pay-off of this approach has been nothing short of revolutionary. For example to the uncomprehending and incredulous victims of the West the destruction of the twin towers and the mindset of people like Mohammad Atta and his mentor Osama Bin Laden can be rendered more accessible through this approach. For it places the whole thing in a far broader context. These are, for example, the diatribes in not only Islam but in Christianity as well against Hubris, empire building, secularism, individualism and attraction of money-all characteristic and constituent of the Sinful City of Man (or Tower of Babel); and myths of its destruction has been shown to run through The Bible and the Koran. Buruma and Margalit so insightfully show how the soullessness of the city as a consequence of metropolitan Hubris is visible even in the poetry of William Blake and T. S. Eliot, in Richard Wagner's sentiments about Paris, in Frederick Engels' feelings about "something repulsive" in the city crowds of Manchester and London, in Nazi propaganda against "Westoxification", and in Sayyid Qutb's revulsion against the "seductive atmosphere" in New York etc.[52] Again Buruma and Margalit have revealed how Occidentalism in the sense of hatred against capitalist trading go to explain the anti-Jewish sentiments found in so disparate areas as the thought of Hans Blueher; Nazi distaste for Bolshevists to the East and the "Jewified" democracies the West of Europe and in North America; the reservations of

Johann Gottfried von Herder and other German Romantic thinkers about the "cold European world" steeped in and frozen by French philosophy and its pretensions to universal reason.

Still another reason why Occidentalism, as the obverse of PCT, is relevant for IR is that it unfolds better than other traditions the dilemmas of radical modernizers regarding how to transport their countries to modernity without becoming a clone of the West, apart from explaining why an alternative route to modernity was tried and failed in Iran, Iraq, North Korea, Ethiopia, Cuba, China, and Vietnam. It also shows much better than other "isms" how "the most violent forms of Occidentalism, of nativistic yearnings for purity and destructive loathing for the west were born from this failure, or as was the case in China was a part of it."[53]

While we are ignoring, for reasons of space and focus of compass, other strands of Occidentalist hostilities, what we want to emphasize at this point is that without a proper understanding of the anti-American, anti-metropolitan mentality it would be impossible to explain not only why the twin towers in New York were targeted in the first place, but also why so many people in the world rejoiced in its destruction; and why the recent attacks by militant outfits funded and financed by the Al Quaida target tourist resorts at Bali, Shat-il-Arab etc., that hardly represent seats of Western power, but are symptomatic of frivolous enjoyment. Essentially then these are attacks against the whorishness of the city. "The image of the metropolis as a whore is not just a reflection of female sexuality...but also a comment on a society that revolves around trade."[54]

In today's terrorist politics around the world the mindset of the jihadi is something of an enigma. As various nation-states are struggling to deal with suicide bombers, human-bombs etc., they are invariably conceived as inscrutable Orientals. But Occidentalism can better explain this phenomenon inasmuch as it seeks for the roots of the cult of pure death epitomized in the jihadi in the mass sacrifice by the German youth in the Battle of Langemark against the British installations in Flanders in 1914; in the "pleasure of death" extolled by German mathematician Thomas Abt after the Seven Years' War; in Werner Sombart's tirade against the "merchant Weltanschauung" and its premium on "komfortismus"; and in the message of Ernest Junger that death might be an escape from komfortismus towards pure pleasure. Junger's "subjunctive"[55] book Über die Linnie was translated by Iranian intellectual Al-e-Ahmed in the 1960s, and it was Ahmed who coined the term "Westoxification". Since liberal democracy was the most congenial political system for the merchant peoples and their happiness meaning komfortismus, it has been denigrated by such disparate lovers of Third World revolutionary causes as French lawyer Jacques Verges, by Friedrich Georg Junger, Ernest Junger's brother and author of famous book Krieg and Krieger (War and Warriors), by the father of kamikaze tactics Vice Admiral Onishi Takijiro, and by Osama Bin Laden, whose language and belief can be traced back to a millenarian Shi'ite sect of the 11th and 13th centuries, called Assasins.[56]

The point of this exegesis is not to lend support to Occidentalism, but to drive home the point that the belief system of Occidentalism can go a long way to interpret in the mode of Hermeneutics much of the behaviour patterns of many adversaries of Western universalism. Occidentalism reveals that "the mind of the West in the eyes of the Occidentalists is a truncated mind, good for finding the best way to achieve a given goal, but utterly useless in finding the right way.[62] We learn that the oppositional views to this primacy of "instrumental" as opposed to "substantive" rationality was first discernible in German Romanticism, especially in the early "high" Romanticism of the period 1797-1815, and also that it was in Russia that they took the shape of Occidentalism.[57]

So, if we now understand Orientalism "as the expression of the bitter resentment toward an offensive display of superiority by the West, based on the alleged superiority of reason", [58] and if we further understand that much of the staple of religious Occidentalism, as manifest in the thought and writings of Iranian thinker and activist Sayyid Muhammad

Talequin (1910-1990), Sayyid Qutb and his mentor Pakistani ideologue Abu-l-A' la Maududi was targeted against a godless and materialist West[59] then the whole syndrome of anti-Western feeling of MacWorld *vs.* Jihad manifest in so many Third World Islamic and non-Islamic states becomes far more comprehensible than it would have been through portmanteau ideas like Huntington's "clash of civilizations".

Prognosis: Theory Reality Interaction

In the last few paragraphs we have first shown how PCT suffers from some conceptual limitations which queer its pitch as a repository of transformative logic. We have also shown that there are niches of applicability where in spite of its congenital blinkers and myopia this approach may shore up certain important insights. But to realize its full potential PCT has to be broadened beyond its present culturological focus, include economistic categories, stop its inexplicable averseness to many Marxist and neo-Marxist findings about the nexus between colonialism and capitalism, and in so many other ways cease to be its present constricted self, that does nothing but serve the purposes of a bilingual parvenu in the Anglo-American academia. This metempsychosis is important in an era where imperialism is steadily being transformed into Empire, an order that is far more ossified and suffocating than any one before, but where emancipation-oriented approaches are getting more and more bogged down, and wrapped in the "miasmal mist" of their distinctive concepts and ideas. What is the need of the day is compressed knowledge gleaned from multiple sources, creative syntheses, not discrete theories that in a puerile love for nominalism rename and rechristen old, weather-beaten concepts on the plea of tenuous differences. In an era where not only Third World states but Third World intellectuals too are suffering from a "post-colonial anxiety"[60] about how much of the values/norms of the hegemon is to be internalized to prevent "otherizing" at home, in the near periphery and abroad true IR theories have to serve as beacons. They have to come forward to prevent the world from irretrievably sliding into the Manichaean binary of one-worldism and violent, Occidentalist dissent. In this endeavour integrating PCT into the radical tradition of IR is a better alternative than to allow it to enjoy its distinctiveness.

NOTES AND REFERENCES

1. Jacques Derrida and Michel Foucault, in spite of their comprehensive critique of the rationality claims of Western culture and epistemology from within the West, did not really address the problem of colonialism directly, except in two very minor essays. These are Foucault's "George Canguilhelm: Philosopher of Error (1980)", and Derrida's "White Mythology: Metaphor in the Text of Philosophy" (1974). See Leela Gandhi, *Post-colonial Theory* (hereafter *PT*) (Delhi: Oxford University Press, 1999), pp. 26-7.
2. For some of these problems see Ella Shoat, "Notes on the Post-colonial", *Social Text* 31/32 (1992): 99-113 (hereinafter *NPC*), also excerpted in (ed.) Padmini Mongia, *Contemporary Postcolonial Theory* (hereafter *CPT*) (Delhi: Oxford University Press, 1997), pp. 320-34; Kwame Anthony Appiah, "Is the Post- in Postmodernism the Post- in Postcolonial?" in Mongia, *CPT*, pp. 55-71.
3. Edward Said, *Orientalism: Western Conceptions of the Orient* (1978), 3rd edn., (Harmondsworth: Penguin, 1991); Said, *The Question of Palestine* (New York: Times Books, 1979); Said, *Covering Islam: How the Media and Experts Determine How We See the Rest of the World* (London: Routledge and Kegan Paul, 1981).
4. For these roots of PCT see Gandhi, PT, pp. 23-41, 70-76.
5. Said, *Orientalism*, pp. 3, 4(1978/91), 45-46, 94, 195-96.
6. See for the quotations from Spivak (culled from Spivak, "Subaltern Studies: Deconstructing Historiography" (London: Routledge, 1987), and those culled from Spivak, "Bonding Difference: Interview with Alfred Arteaga", in the *Spivak Reader*, eds. Donna Landry, and Gerald Maclean (London: Routledge, 1996) and the comments Bart Moore-Gilbert, *Post-colonial Theory* (*PCT*), pp. 75-77.
7. For a very minute analysis of Spivak's multiple uses of "other" and "otherness" see Moore-Gilbert, PCT, pp. 84, 101, 103, 104, 109, and 117.
8. Moore-Gilbert, *PCT*, pp. 116-17.
9. Homi Bhabha, "Difference, Discrimination and the Discourse of Colonialism", in (eds.) F. Barker, P. Hulme, M. Iversen and D. Loxley, *The Politics of Theory* (Colchester: University of Essex Press, 1983).

10. Spivak," Can the Subaltern Speak? (1985)", in (eds.) Carry Nelson and L. Grossberg, *Marxism and Interpretations of Culture* (Bassingstoke, Macmillan Education, 1988), pp. 271-313.
11. Gyan Prakash, "Post-colonial Criticism and Indian Historiography" in *Social Text*, 31/32 (1992).
12. *Ibid*, p. 813.
13. Lata Mani mostly links post-coloniality and gender in her writings. See e.g., Mani, "Contentious Traditions: The Debate on Sati in Colonial India", in (eds.) K. Sangari and S. Vaid, *Recasting Women* (New Delhi: Kali for Women, 1989), pp. 88-126.
14. Dividing social sciences on the basis of "analytic categories" might mean organizing their identities on the basis of central organizing ideas (COI) and main conceptual units, like "power" and "state" for political science, "scarcity" and "market" for economics, "location" and 'space' for geography etc. The concrete categories on the other hand would be spatial, like individual, group, organization, national society, international society, etc. in an ascending hierarchical order. While political science, organized on the basis of the COI of "power" could fill anyone of these spaces, IR could be relevant for only the concrete slot of international society. For the concept of "analytic" and "concrete" categories see Marion J. Levy Jr., The Structure of Society (Princeton: Princeton University Press, 1952).
15. For example Fred Halliday wondered in 1994 why over the last two and half decades the silence of IR on the women question was so deafening. See Halliday, *Rethinking International Relations* (London: Macmillan, 1994), pp. 147-148. Sixteen years ago Richard Little similarly wondered why behaviouralism and systems thinking took so long to reach the precincts of IR. See Little," A Systems Approach", in (ed.) Trevor Taylor, *Approaches and Theory in International Relations* (London: Longman, 1994), pp. 182-83.
16. As for instance Richard K. Ashley uses postmodernism in IR as synonymous to post-structuralism, through the theorists of these two schools would shudder at the slapdash mixture; and Rengger and Hoffman's use of critical theory as a generic term which clearly includes post-modern approaches would have Habermas and Foucault turning in their graves. See Ashley, "Living on Borderlines: Man, Post-structuralism and War", in (eds.) J. Der Derrian and M. Shapiro, *International/Intertextual Relations: Post-modern Readings in World Politics* (Lexington: Lexington Books, 1989), pp. 259-321; and (eds.) N.J. Rengger and Mark Hoffman, *Beyond the Inter-Paradigm Debate: Critical Theory and International Relations* (Hempel Hempstead: Harvester Wheatsheaf, forthcoming in 1994), both cited in (eds.) A.J.R. Groom and Margot Light, *Contemporary International Relations: A Guide to Theory* (London: Pinter,1994), p. 56.

17. In a sense Hans J. Morgenthau's spatially informed neo-classical utterance of Realism in his *Politics among Nations: The Struggle for Power and Peace,* Sixth ed. (New York: Knopf, 1985) has after many modifications — through Kenneth N. Waltz's Neo-Realism, as first stated in *Theory of International Politics* (New York: McGraw Hill, 1979), Thomas Schelling's strategic Realism, as enunciated in *The Strategy of Conflict* (Boston: Harvard University Press, 1980), in none of which spatiality was given the go by, has come full circle in John Mearsheimer's spatially dominated neo-realist stability theory, as best stated in his article "back to the Future: Instability in Europe After the Cold War", in (ed.) S. Lynn-Jones, *The Cold War and After: Prospects for Peace* (Cambridge, Mass.: MIT Press, 1991), pp. 141-92. Mearsheimer, while regarding the stability attained under the Cold war bipolar system as more durable than the post-Cold War dispensation, thought consistently in terms of the East and the West, entirely unconcerned about the complexities of spatiality.
18. Shoat, NPC, p. 325.
19. Bill Ashcroft, Gareth Griffiths and Helen Tiffin, *The Empire Writes Back: Theory and Practice in Post-colonial Literatures*. Reprint ed. (London: Routledge, 1999), p. 2.
20. Shoat, "Notes", pp. 323-27.
21. For the concept of "silence" and its importance in understanding the focus of a thinker, or of a line of reasoning, especially Marxism, see Louis Althusser and Etienne Balibar, *Reading Capital* (Thetford, Norfolk: Verso 1979), third impression 1986, pp. 88-90, 143-44. In the field of IR one resounding even "deafening" silence has been pointed by Zygmunt Bauman in the context of the Holocaust. See Bauman, *Modernity and the Holocaust* (Cambridge: Polity Press, 1989).
22. Dipesh Chakraborty, "Post-coloniality and the Artifice of History", in Chakraborty, *Provincialising Europe: Post-colonial Thought and Historical Difference* (Princeton: Princeton University Press, 2000); Samuel P. Huntington, *The Clash of Civilizations and the Remaking of World Order* (London: Touchstone, 1998); Theodore Von Laue, *The World Revolution of Westernization: the Twentieth Century in Global Perspective* (Oxford: Oxford University Press); all cited in the present context in Neil Lazarus, "The Fetish of 'the West' in Post-colonial Theory", in (eds.) Crystal Bartolovich and Neil Lazarus, *Marxism, Modernity and Post-colonial Studies* (Cambridge: Cambridge University Press, 2002), pp. 45-49, 61-63.
23. Lazarus, "The Fetish", pp. 43-63.
24. E. San Juan Jr., "Post-colonialism and the Problematic of Uneven Development" in (eds.) Bartolovich and Lazarus, *Marxism, Modernity and Postcolonial Studies*, p. 222.

25. Arif Dirlik, "The Postcolonial Aura: Third World Criticism in the Age of Global Capitalism", in Mongia, *CPT*, pp. 298-99.
26. The Reference is to Joe Norton, *What the Butler Saw*, in *Joe Norton: The Complete Plays*, ed. with an introduction by John Lahr (London: Eyre Methuen, 1976). In the play while Churchill's statue was being reconstituted after its fragmentation, his organ was found missing. Intertextually speaking, the allusion in the play is possibly to Isis' efforts at reconstruction and restoration of Osiris' body after Typhon rent it into fourteen pieces and scattered them in many places. Not finding the genital member of the body, Isis made an image of it instead. See Sir James Frazer, *The Golden Bough: A Study in Magic and Religion* (Ware, Hertfordshire: Wordsworth Reference, 1993), pp. 362-66.
27. Shoat, "Notes" pp. 322-23.
28. Aijaz Ahmad, "The Politics of Literary Postcoloniality", in Mongia, *CPT*, pp. 276-93, especially p. 281.
29. Dirlik, "The Post-colonial Aura", pp. 296-97.
30. See Peter M. Hass, "Do Regimes Matter: Epistemic Communities and Mediterranean Pollution Control", in (eds.) George T. Crane and Abla Amawi, *The Theoretical Evolution of International Political Economy: A Reader* (Oxford: Oxford University Press, 1997), pp. 284-298. The Foucauldian nature of "epistemic communities" comes out in Crane and Amawi's apparently innocent statement "the notion of epistemic communities opens regime analysis to a consideration of knowledge as power in IPE.". Crane and Malawi, *IPE: A Reader*, pp. 24-25.
31. In Rorty's sense "ironist liberals", as different from "ironist theorists" are "anti-foundational". An ironist "cannot get along without the final vocabularies she inherited and the one she is trying to create for herself. Ironists have to have something to have doubts about, something from which to be alienated." See Richard Rorty, *Contingency, Irony and Solidarity* (Cambridge: Cambridge University Press, 1989), pp. 87-88, cited in Honi Fern Haber, *Beyond Post-modern Politics: Lyotard, Rorty, Foucault* (New York: Routledge, 1994), pp. 56-59. Likewise, the "secular intellectuals", characteristic of what Rorty calls the "post-philosophic culture" are philosophers who have "abandoned the pretensions to philosophy". They are "all-purpose intellectuals who were ready to offer a view on pretty much anything". They are expected by Rorty to be "polypragmatic", "informed dilettantes", completely unlike nineteenth century savants and custodians of liberal humanism, they are to negotiate blurred boundaries, plural meanings, and endless difference. See Richard Rorty, *Consequences of Pragmatism* (Minneapolis: University of Minnesota Press, 1982), pp. xvii-xl.

32. Appiah, "Is the Post- in Post-modernism the Post- in Post-colonial?" pp. 62-63.
33. See Benedict Anderson, *Imagined Communities: Reflections on the Origin and Spread of Nationalism* (London: Verso, 1983), pp. 50-56, especially p. 54.
34. Appiah, "Is the Post-", pp. 66-67.
35. The concepts of "vivisection" and "triage" have been used by Shiv Viswanathan to show how the West has used the Third World and sought to discard it thereafter. For Viswanathan "triage" combines the related "concepts of rational experiment ...obsolescence.... and of vivisection — whereby a society, a sub-culture or a species is labeled as obsolete and condemned to death because rational experiment has deemed it incurable." See Shiv Viswanathan, "On the Annals of the Laboratory State", in (ed.) Ashis Nandy, *Science, Hegemony and Violence: A Requiem for Modernity* (Delhi: Oxford University Press, 1990), p. 259.
36. San Juan, "Post-colonialism and Uneven Development." p. 229.
37. Dirlik, "The Postcolonial Aura", p. 295.
38. Ngai-Ling Sum, "New Orientalism, Global Capitalism and the Politics of Synergetic Differences: Discursive Constructions of Trade Relations between the USA, Japan and the East Asian NICS", in (eds.) Avtar Brah, Marry J. Hickman and Mairtin Mac an Ghaill, *Global Futures, Migration, Environment and Globalization* (London: Macmillan, 1999), pp. 99-121.
39. *Ibid*, pp. 100-04.
40. Sum, "New Orientalism", pp. 105-09.
41. David Scott, *Refashioning Futures: Criticism After Post-coloniality*, Princeton Studies in Culture/Power/History (Princeton, NJ: Princeton University Press, 1999), p.14, cited in Phillip Darby, "Pursuing the Political: A Postcolonial Rethinking of Relations International" *Millennium Journal of International Studies* 33:1(2004): 5.
42. Darby, "Pursuing the Political", p. 6.
43. We are making here a distinction between thinkers like Robert Cox, Mark Hoffman and Andrew Linklater, who specifically project an application of Habermasian ideas in IR, and thinkers like Charles R. Beitz, Henry Shue and Nicholas Greenwood Onuf, who also espouse a cosmopolitan ethics no less critical of the existing order than the Critical theorists with capital 'c'. For its source see "Chris Brown, Critical Theory and Post-modernism in International Relations", in (eds.) A.J.R. Groom and Margot Light, *Contemporary International Relations: A Guide to Theory* (1994) (London: Pinter,1999), p. 59.
44. Michael Hardt and Antonio Negri, *Empire* (Cambridge, MA and London: Harvard University Press, 2000).
45. See Charles Tennyson, "Letty's Globe" (1860), in (ed.), Christopher Ricks, *New Oxford Book of Victorian Verse* (1987), pp. 407-08.

46. Darby, "Pursuing the Political", pp. 6-9.
47. See Daniel Bell, *The End of Ideology* (New York: Collier Books, 1962); Francis Fukuyama, *The End of History and the Last Man* (New York: The Free Press,1992); John Kenneth Galbraith, *The Culture of Contentment* (Boston: Houghton Mifflin Coy,1992). Discussed in Darby, "Pursuing the Political", 11-21.
48. *Ibid*, p. 21.
49. *Ibid*, p. 16.
50. See Ian Buruma and Avishai Margalit, *Occidentalism: The West in the Eyes of its Enemies* (New Delhi: Penguin Books India, 2004), p. 6.
51. *Ibid*, p. 10.
52. *Ibid*, pp. 10-32.
53. *Ibid*, pp. 32-40.
54. *Ibid*, p. 18.
55. The distinction between "indicative" and "subjunctive" texts was made by Raymond Williams. While the former simply depict and record what is happening in the world around us, the latter points out the way out of it, by removing pressures and pushing back limits and constraints. See Williams, "Forms of Fiction in 1948", in (eds.) Francis Barker et al., *Literature, Politics and Theory* (London: Methuen, 1986), p.16, cited in Leela Gandhi, PT, and p. 68.
56. Buruma and Margalit, *Occidentalism*, pp. 49-69.
57. *Ibid*, pp. 77-85.
58. *Ibid*, p. 95.
59. *Ibid*, pp. 114-22.
60. Sankaran Krishna, "Introduction", Post-colonial Insecurities: India, Sri Lanka, and the Question of Nationhood (Minneapolis: University of Minnesota Press,1999), pp. i-v.

PART III

Foreign Policy: The Diplomat's Perspective

18

Alternative Global Perspective

—ERHERD ZANDER

Dear Dr. Basu,
Ladies and Gentlemen,

Alternative Global Futures is a subject with a wide range of topics. Let me try to explain the German position with the focus on Germany as part of the European Union.

The basis for Germany's success in the second half of the last century was its complete integration into the Western community. That is, above all, its membership in the European community, and — this sounds a little bit strange under the present conditions — its solid anchoring in the Atlantic Alliance with the United States.

Only in this way could Germany, or even Europe, withstand the cold war and lay the foundations for the triumph of democracy, freedom and the market economy. The fall of the Berlin wall proved that clearly.

How did we get there? It was always a mistake to think of 1945 as 0 hour, but what was new after World War II was that the Federal Republic of Germany began to see itself fundamentally as part of the West. It began to perceive its integration into the Western community as part of its own reason of being, to use our Chancellor Schroeder's words, and articulated its interests in multilateral terms. Today, every German takes these principles for granted.

A brief history. The first German Reich began in the 10th century and lasted 850 years until Napoleon conquered Europe in 1806. The Second German Reich was founded by the German Federated States, leaving out Austria, after the Franco Prussian war of 1871. It lasted until the abdication of our last Emperor William II in 1918 as a result of World War I.

Adolf Hitler, who became Chancellor in 1933, designated National Socialist Germany the 3rd Reich. The 3rd Reich ended when Germany capitulated on May 8th 1945, ending World War II for Germany. After Germany's defeat, the four powers divided Germany and also the capital Berlin into four military occupation zones. Germany was divided into two separate States: The German Democratic Republic (GDR) was created in the Soviet Zone and the Federal Republic of Germany developed out of the US, British and French Zones. The division became official with the creation of the two separate German States in 1949 and was cemented by the construction of the Berlin wall in 1961.

The German Democratic Republic claimed East Berlin as its capital while the capital of the Federal Republic of Germany was located in Bonn. In November 1989 thousands of East Germans fled via Hungary and Austria to West Germany, mass demonstrations happened in a number of East German cities. This led to the opening of the Berlin wall and the collapse of the communist regime in Eastern Germany. In 1999 a treaty was signed in which the five East German States joined the Federal Republic of Germany with effect of October 3rd 1990. This is our national day now. The capital moved back from Bonn to Berlin at the end of 1999.

Present day Germany was founded in 1949. The Western powers supervising and of course agreeing to it, made sure that this new Germany would not have any military attack capabilities. So there was no army, and even more imported coal and steel production, the backbone of any defence industry, was put under European control. This European commission for coal and steel also administered coal and steel production of our European neighbours. Within this framework, no country under this regime would be able to conduct any large scale war alone.

As a result of the communist threat and cold war Nato, the North Atlantic Treaty Organisation, was founded in 1949. Because of this threat of communist countries in Europe, and probably also the Korean war, Germany was permitted to rearm and join Nato in 1955. Joining Nato meant that all German troops were in effect under Nato command and not under the command of a German General Staff. 1956 is the birth date of the European Union. It started as a European economic community with only six member states, Germany, Italy, France, Luxembourg, Belgium and Netherlands. Today it comprises most of continental Europe and England with the exception of Switzerland and Norway. Eastern Europe will join soon. This economic co-operation agreement slowly transformed into a true union. The members of the European Union now have a common economic and trade policy, and try to have a common foreign and security policy which as it shows now on the Iraq question, is very difficult to achieve.

The US has always urged Europe to play a bigger role, to shoulder more of the burden of safeguarding peace and security. That is why the European Union will in the future be able to conduct international crises response operations when Nato as a whole is not engaged. Let me be clear on this. We want neither to act outside of Nato nor to duplicate Nato's structures. We do not want to delink Europe from the United States. What we want is to resume our responsibility to take on problems at our doorstep. That is what European security and defence identity is all about.

> The European Union has made other important strides in recent past. It introduced the common currency — theEURO-in 2002.

Ladies and Gentlemen, as Germans and as Europeans, we are convinced multilateralists. Only that, which has been jointly agreed, can serve as a sustainable basis for European action. At the same time, we are convinced the major problems of the future, population explosion, under-development, environmental disasters, climate change, proliferation of weapons of mass destruction, drug trade and terrorism — all these global challenges call for global solutions. The future of the world will be multipolar, and its challenges can only be solved multilaterally. We must therefore support multilateral institutions and above all the United Nations.

What is the future of the European Union now. Let me-quote Hubert Vèdrine, the former French foreign minister.

"Over the next two years the European Union will grow from 15 nations to 25, and will push forward with work on a new constitution likely to create the first European head of state, titular leader of 485 million citizens of a former continent turned — What? This will be a new kind of state in a world of nations. Whatever sort of power it chooses to be, or to wield, it is likely to be something fairly different from the United States. But if Europe becomes the other 'World nation', which is now conceivable, will the United States at last accept a real partnership with Europe?

The European economy, as shaped by incessant negotiations and hair-splitting among 25 member states, will most likely be less financially creative than the American but substantively more productive. It ought to be less wasteful of energy, less predatory toward the environment, more concerned with social cohesion and with the safety net of society, less hard on its people.

Looking beyond its borders, the European Union's actions in the world will depend on a series of less predictable choices. It's probable that under the influence of larger countries the partisans of Europe as a 'European power' will gain ground little by little even in the area of defense. But when it comes to the use of force, this Europe will be more restrained and legalistic than the United States. It will manage to establish a dialogue with the modernizers of the Arab and Muslim world. After many trials and errors it will agree on the necessary balance in immigration policy between freedom, reception, integration and security. Slowly but surely, Europeans will manage, as in the Balkans, to make their diplomatic positions converge. In the face of globalization, the European Union will evolve, after difficult internal compromises, toward a rather more 'regulatory' line than the United States. To contain U.S. unilateralism and militarism, it will try to channel American energy into legitimate multilateral mechanisms, but it will do that more as an interlocutor than an antagonist.

The critical moment will be the constitutional treaty, which is likely to yield a federation in the economic domain, a looser confederation in others and a more visible executive. The possibility for some state members to form an avant-garde moving more quickly to unification will be affirmed. Once that groundwork is established, ratification could be obtained in 2004, even where national referendums are required. To accomplish that, political elites will have to give up their paternalistic language and speak frankly to a wary public about the real stakes of Europe. Solutions will be found by the governments because there's really no other option; Europeans need unity to stand up to the other world nations. They are Utopian realists. And Americans will come to work with Europe to shape better rules of the game for globalization, because they are realists, too."

So far Hubert Vèdrine. I think China and India will be Global Players too, and as such Partners of the European Union.

Thank you.

19

The Challenge of Foreign Policy in a Globalised World

The United Kingdom's View

—ANDREW HALL

Introduction

Delighted to be asked to take part in this Seminar. As a diplomat I want to approach the theme of the Seminar by looking at the implications for foreign policy of global politics in the 21st century. Since this session is devoted to The European Experience I will try and put forward the United Kingdom's view of developments.

I am sorry to disappoint those of you who may be expecting a theoretical or analytical paper. As a practitioner, rather than an international relations expert, my perspective will be on the practical consequences for foreign policy of the changing world we find ourselves in.

I want to develop two main propositions for you: firstly, that as the world becomes more inter-dependent, the boundary between "foreign" and "domestic" policy is increasingly blurred. Foreign affairs are no longer very foreign. And that means that they matter more, perhaps, than ever before.

My second argument will be that we need to strengthen the international system so that it is fully adapted to today's international challenges.

New Challenges

The defeat of communism and the end of the Cold War brought liberty and democracy to millions. But it also made the world more complex, and in a sense more disordered than in the days of a global stand-off between two rival superpowers. That posed new challenges to our stability and security. In Europe, the breakdown of the Yugoslav federation unleashed conflicts the aftermath of which we are still having to deal with today. In Africa, the end of the Cold War brought the downfall of many former superpower client regimes, leading to a multiplication of conflicts and to the breakdown of state authority. Many policy decisions can no longer be seen simply as the internal affairs of a sovereign nation-state, because they affect us all.

Conflicts in the Balkans and Africa were important in themselves because of the devastating humanitarian effects on those immediately involved; but they were also important because of the threat they posed to global security. Conflict and chaos can easily spread, and their effects are felt around the world. 11 September, 2001 brought into sharp relief the impact this could have, as the extremist repression of Afghanistan mutated into catastrophic violence against innocent civilians thousands of miles away.

So when states are weak or are catastrophically failing their citizens, the international community needs to work to make them stronger and more just. In the aftermath of conflict, that challenge is particularly important. In the Balkans, Afghanistan and Iraq, the UK is devoting as much effort to reconstruction and to building durable institutions as we did to the military conflicts which came before.

To build lasting and sustainable stability we need to promote institutions which are not simply effective, but also just. That means they must be based on human rights, the rule of law and representative government. So it is necessary to work for the spread of those values around the world because in doing so we are promoting the conditions which underpin peace and prosperity.

Terrorism is not the only threat we face. Chronic poverty, disease, environmental degradation and the widespread denial of justice, all typically underpinned by corruption, the lack of decent democracy and of the rule of law, are all factors behind insecurity and conflict. And all are linked to each other. Conflict and tension in far-away countries have direct repercussions on our own security and prosperity, and allow threats such as organised crime to flourish.

Much of what we want to achieve in Britain is dependent, to at least some extent, on being active abroad. If we want to keep drugs off British streets, we must tackle poppy cultivation in Afghanistan; we must fund judicial reform projects in South America and the Balkans so that drug barons cannot escape the courts; and we must get European Union police forces to work more closely together against drug gangs. In the face of terrorist or criminal networks who operate globally we must maintain a foreign policy which is closely integrated with our domestic agenda.

Britain's safety and prosperity depend more than ever on working for a safe, just and prosperous world. To protect the UK from threats such as terrorism, the proliferation of weapons of mass destruction, and international crime, and to promote our economic interests, we must be active and engaged in the world. Our aim is to build lasting safety and prosperity underpinned by justice — by sustainable development especially for the poorest and most vulnerable, and by democracy, good governance and human rights.

This is an integrated agenda, with justice as its pivot. There is no longer, if there ever was, a distinction between "hard" and "soft" foreign policy, between pursuing your interests on the one hand and pursuing your convictions on the other. We cannot pursue lasting safety and prosperity if we do not also promote justice.

Global Partnerships

Britain can achieve none of its priorities on its own. The challenges are global, and they require a global response. Our membership of the European Union and our relationship with the United States are central to almost everything we do internationally.

The European Union stands on the verge of a historic development, the admission of ten new members on 1 May. That enlargement is a hugely important event, not just for the countries concerned, but for the whole of Europe. It is going to create the biggest single economic market in the world. The stability and prosperity of Europe stand to gain enormously.

There is no doubt that the European Union is and will remain an organisation of sovereign Member States. The draft Constitutional Treaty currently under discussion contains a clear statement that the Union only has the powers which the nations give it. The Union only acts when objectives cannot be achieved by individual countries acting alone. There will be new powers for national parliaments to be involved in EU legislation. It will be for the Union's national leaders, in the European Council, to set the strategy of the European Union and there will be a full-time chair of the European Council to drive forward that work. The European Commission will have all its necessary independent authority within that system.

France and Germany and the United Kingdom have put forward proposals on the future of European defence, which is limited of course to peacekeeping and humanitarian issues. The new articles tabled by Britain, France and Germany make clear for the first time in an EU Treaty that NATO is the basis for the collective defence of the allies, and ensure that structured defence cooperation is handled inclusively. It makes sense that Europe has the capacity to sort out problems on its own doorstep, such as peacekeeping in the Balkans, without always having to rely on the US. Cutting across NATO would weaken our defences, but better European capabilities — for which the US have long argued — will strengthen our defence.

Europe now has for the first time a security strategy which will enable the EU to deal better with the threats and global challenges we face. Initial work will include effective multilateralism with the UN at its core, the fight against terrorism, a strategy towards the Middle East and a comprehensive policy towards Bosnia-Herzegovina. A further crucial element is the strategy against the proliferation of weapons of mass destruction.

It is also of paramount importance to our future prosperity and security that the relationship between Europe and the US continues to be strong. That transatlantic partnership is deeply rooted in shared values, economic interdependence and common interests, and is essential to pursuing progressive change and global order. But we will need to keep working in order to maintain its strength. That will mean building a shared agenda, with Europe pursuing more effectively our shared security interests, and the US working with Europe and others on the wider economic development and environmental priorities that are so closely linked to our security.

Britain also has a historic opportunity to develop strategic relationships with emerging powers such as China and India as they play a greater and changing role in the international system. Russia and Japan will also continue to be key global powers and central to achieving our international priorities.

Changing role of the International System

The backbone of all our relationships internationally is the multilateral system, with the United Nations at its heart. As a permanent member of the UN Security Council, the UK has a fundamental interest in keeping that multilateral system strong and effective.

But the challenge for us now is to help strengthen the international system so that it is fully adapted to today's international challenges. International rules, embodied in the UN Charter, have provided the framework for world order since the end of the second World War. But the world today is very different from that of 1945 when the UN Charter was signed. We need today to be able to act together, through the United Nations, to prevent the breakdown of order in states around the world, because it directly affects our own security. Decisions by states which fifty years ago would have been considered a matter of domestic policy — for example on developing certain kinds of weapons – are today of urgent interest for the whole world.

We manage our interdependence through common rules; but to be truly effective we also need to be prepared to enforce them with all the tools at our disposal, including military force as a last resort.

The big question left unanswered by those who disagreed with military intervention in Iraq, is this: how do you protect global security from a regime which threatens regional or international stability, and places itself defiantly beyond the reach of the international system on which our security depends? These are questions we and our partners must now grapple with, co-operatively and creatively. We cannot ignore them. The modern world is too dangerous for that.

Take for example the global threat from the proliferation of WMD. This threat is now being taken as seriously as it must be by the international community – as demonstrated for example by the European Security Strategy. We now have a chance to reinforce our common action against it, for example through agreeing a UN resolution setting up a mechanism similar to the Counter-Terrorism Committee established by Resolution 1373.

Common action gets results. Iran has chosen to work with the IAEA and with Britain, France and Germany supported by the EU to resolve the outstanding issues surrounding its nuclear programme. Libya has chosen to engage with the UK and the US, and now with the IAEA and other appropriate bodies to disarm itself of WMD – a courageous step forward which will bring greater security to the whole region. North Korea remains a difficult case, but is engaged with China and others in the six-party talks, which we hope to see resume in the near future.

Terrorism

Institutions like the UN, conceived essentially to prevent combat between states, are having to adapt to the fact that the threats to world peace and security today are as likely to come from non-state groups such as terrorists and criminal networks.

Britain is committed to negotiating a comprehensive UN convention against terrorism including a universal definition of terrorism, because that would send a clear political signal of our shared commitment to fighting this common threat. Consensus on the exact wording of a universal definition of terrorism is proving hard to achieve. But meanwhile, through the twelve existing UN conventions and through Security Council Resolution 1373, as well as in a range of other international and regional fora, we can continue to work together.

Engaging with the Islamic World

We also need to discuss another key strategic challenge for the next decade: how we engage with the Arab and wider Islamic world. We need better to understand the forces that give rise to the hostility that some feel so deeply towards the West. And we need to show that we will help those who recognise the need for political, economic and social reform to deal with rising unemployment, low growth, low levels of human development and increased discontent.

Reform must come from and be shaped by the region itself, not be imposed from outside. But Europe, working with the US and in other groupings, must demonstrate how it can assist. We must all recognise that the structural problems confronting many countries in the Middle East are not just their problems, but ours.

We are showing that the international system is capable of discussing these new threats and the action we can take to deal with them. But we still have some way to go towards a common understanding of how best it can adapt to today's challenges.

International institutions need to work more closely together, so that for example in post-conflict situations the work of many agencies and governments can be better-co-ordinated.

It is healthy that we are beginning to debate the future of the international framework. No less than domestic law, international law has to be a living, evolving law, or it withers and dies. So we do have to come to a common understanding of the new threats we all face and of how we deal with them. Already the international community has shown a willingness to intervene in new situations and new ways, for example in Kosovo or Afghanistan. We need to build on that evolving jurisprudence and the recognition it embodies that problems far-away affect us all. Every country has a stake in that.

Conclusion

The post-Cold War world is complex and uncertain and presents new risks and opportunities. We have not yet reached a global understanding on what those risks and opportunities are, or how we should deal with them. But we are at a pivotal time for international policy. The European Security Strategy, or the formation of a High-Level Panel by the UN Secretary General, are examples of increasing efforts to develop an effective common response to today's complex challenges.

Everyone in society has a stake in its safety, justice and tolerance. States such as the UK have centuries-old traditions of the rule of law with which people identify and which form the bedrock of all civilised life. The challenge for international diplomacy in the 21st century will be to build an international order in which states and people feel something of the same stake in working for a safe, just and prosperous world as they do in their own societies.

Index